When M. I. T. Was "Boston Tech"

When M.I.T. was "Boston Tech" 1861-1916

SAMUEL C. PRESCOTT

The Technology Press, Cambridge, 1954

Copyright 1954

THE MASSACHUSETTS INSTITUTE OF TECHNOLOGY

THE WILLIAM BYRD PRESS, INC.
RICHMOND, VIRGINIA

DEDICATED to the thousands of Alumni of the Massachusetts Institute of Technology, whose service to science and industry has enhanced the reputation of their Alma Mater, and who have honorably carried its name to all parts of the civilized world.

Foreword

THIS book, happily, is more than formal history. It is a personal report, an essay in interpretation and remembrance which is important both for what it tells about M.I.T.'s first half-century and for what it tells about what Dean Prescott finds important and interesting in that half-century.

Dean Prescott has been associated with the Institute for nearly two thirds of a century. He has known all of its presidents save Rogers, the founder. He has known the Institute from the vantage points of student, teacher, department head, dean, alumnus, and parent. He has had a formative influence on its policy-making and he has been an articulate protagonist of the Institute's program and policies. It is important that a man with this long and various experience at the Institute should write interpretively of its history.

He views M.I.T.'s formative years not only with an expert's understanding but out of a deep sense of loyalty and devotion. This book is a testament of faith in an institution, an earnest of the author's abiding belief in the staff, students, and alumni he has known. Those who have had the privilege of knowing Dean Prescott and working with him will understand why this is true and will cherish this book as another example of his generosity of spirit and his deep commitment to his Alma Mater. Having had the benefit of his friendship and counsel for thirty years, I have particular reason to welcome this book.

I hope that this volume is but the first of a series of historical studies of the Institute. Dean Prescott's account concludes with the Institute's establishment in Cambridge in 1916. Great events have taken place since then and warrant another volume covering the period through 1949. In addition there should be a comprehensive historical work relating the growth of M.I.T. and similar institutions to the development of our industrial society during the past one hundred years. No one has yet adequately appraised this kind of educational institution and charted its influence on our economic and cultural life. With the fine precedent of this volume before us, we can look forward with assurance to these further studies.

J. R. KILLIAN, JR.

March 22, 1954

Preface

CARVED in the stone frieze above the principal entrance to the great gray building now fronting on Massachusetts Avenue near the Charles River in Cambridge is the inscription:

> THE MASSACHUSETTS
> INSTITUTE OF TECHNOLOGY
> WILLIAM BARTON ROGERS,
> FOUNDER

Probably few who daily pass through these portals lift their eyes to read the words in enduring stone above, and relatively few among the thousands who, as alumni, have previously gone forth from the lecture halls and laboratories of this institution since it has been located in Cambridge are cognizant of the full meaning of these words, nor of the events surrounding the Institute's birth and early years. Young men naturally look forward rather than backward, and hence today but a few of the fifty thousand alumni know intimately of the devotion, the character, and the sacrifices of many men who contributed to M. I. T.'s establishment, its growth, and its far-reaching reputation. For it is now recognized that this school, founded to carry on a new educational ideal of usefulness to the industrial and social life of the country, has attained an enviable position internationally on the roster of the world's institutions of higher learning. The fame thus acquired has come not through age nor size of enrollment, but rather from a continuous and well-recognized leadership in the training of young men in engineering, science, and architecture during its nearly ninety years of history.

For more than half a century, up to the autumn of 1916, the activities of M. I. T. were concentrated in the vicinity of Copley Square, Boston—hence the well-known sobriquet "Boston Tech." With the hope that a history of this period of M. I. T.'s life, presented in a generally chronological but not too detailed fashion, might make alive again memories of some of the truly great and inspiring figures who gave so much to the service of "Boston Tech," this volume has been undertaken. Its preparation has been a labor of love and loyalty, and a partial acknowledgment of the debt of gratitude *one* alumnus owes to M. I. T.

Somewhat as the ties of memory and family loyalty that bind a son to his early home and ever inspire in him respect and love for his parents, one may visualize the ideal relationship of an alumnus to his *alma mater*. Such a relationship depends not solely upon the mere fact of having entered its doors and attended its courses of instruction, nor on the records of its athletic prowess or other extracurricular achievements in his own day or since, nor even on the school's standing in the educational world. Instead, as time goes on, his regard for it comes progressively to rest upon something deeper in his emotions, something intangible yet vital, something best denoted as a spiritual value from which there springs an abiding concern for the continued well-being of his *alma mater*. In this way there comes the realization that an educational institution is in essence a living, continuing organism, evolving throughout the years. Of such a living body he has been a part, however insignificant.

Four vital groups—the Corporation and administrative staff, the faculty and instructing staff, the ever-growing body of alumni, and the student body itself—constitute the M. I. T. quaternary. All are bound together functionally as component parts of a living whole activated and unified by the institution's aims and high ideals, its splendid traditions, and rich memories and aspirations, which carry on from the past into the living present and the expected future. With such a concept, knowledge of the past may bring deep understanding and satisfaction to any student or alumnus, strengthen his allegiance, and guide him in his responsibilities toward M. I. T.

Regardless of his appreciation of the four-fold concept of M. I. T.'s organization, the inner feelings of an alumnus toward the Institute derive more directly from memories of outstanding personalities—whether officials, teachers, or fellow students, who specially impressed him and influenced his actions and thinking during undergraduate days and long afterward—memories which loom larger to him as years advance. To him these various individuals stand out clearly in retrospect among his many teachers and fellow-students; they are what make him realize that M. I. T. is a complex of activities, memories, and traditions involving many personalities who have played effective parts in making it a strong institution of high repute. The student of bygone years naturally thinks of the Institute as it was in his day in a brief but distinct era in its history. He may have forgotten what had preceded and be unmindful of later events. It may have been for him a strenuous and exacting place, and possibly one with fewer joys than sorrows scholastically. But few have passed this way, even for a brief period, without finding something in the way of reward through personal struggle, the inspiration of helpful teachers, and especially the lasting friendships formed in their undergraduate years.

It is a far cry from my own early days when the faculty was a group of hardly more than a score and each member, with his particular virtues and foibles, was known by sight, or at least by repute, to every student. With the passage of years and the rapid expansion of the school, and the concurrent increase in its faculty, staff, and student body, this situation has necessarily changed, and so really distinguished men of an earlier era tend to become progressively mere names without special force or significance. Thus something of real value is lost unless effort is made to recall and record appreciation for the men of leadership who have built character into the institution throughout its whole existence. Hence, it seems desirable in sketching the history of "Boston Tech," to do so more in terms of men than of eras and statistics, and thus to try to revivify some of its earlier great characters, and to recapture some of the qualities of a few of the many who have marked the Institute with a priceless stamp of their own influence and service.

Samuel C. Prescott

Cambridge, May, 1953

Acknowledgments

For generous and invaluable assistance I am deeply grateful:

To Miss Julia M. Comstock for constant help arising from her long and devoted service to the Institute and her intimate knowledge of its history.

To Dr. James R. Killian, Jr., President of the Institute, for the interest in this endeavor which is felicitously expressed in his preface.

To Harold E. Lobdell '17, Executive Vice-President of the Alumni Association, who suggested the intriguing title for this volume.

To Professor Lynwood S. Bryant for his friendly criticism and meticulous help in preparing the final revision of the manuscript.

To Mrs. William Stanley Parker for the interesting and especially valued group picture of William Barton Rogers and the Savage family.

To Dean Frederick G. Fassett, Jr., Director of the Technology Press, for many suggestions, and for his careful attention to the many details of publication.

To Miss Ethel S. Downer and Miss Anita Frey for excellent service in typing the original manuscript.

To Walter Humphreys '97, Secretary of the Corporation, for access to Corporation records, and for suggestions.

To many members of the alumni body, especially those in my own class of '94 and Henry W. Ballou '97, for their constantly maintained interest and encouragement during the years since the work was begun.

SAMUEL C. PRESCOTT

Table of Contents

		PAGE
Foreword		vii
Preface		ix
Acknowledgments		xiii

CHAPTER

I	Introducing the Rogers Family	3
II	A Great Plan Becomes a Reality	21
III	The Early Years	45
IV	A Declaration of Independence	69
V	Lean Years	89
VI	A General Takes Command	107
VII	An Era of Development	129
VIII	The Crafts Administration	151
IX	At the Turn of the Century	167
X	Growing Pains	191
XI	The Noyes Administration	215
XII	Richard Cockburn Maclaurin—Sixth President	229
XIII	The New Technology	247
XIV	The Last Years in Boston	273
XV	Dedication of the New Technology	299

Epilogue		325
Notes		327
Appendix	"A Plan for a Polytechnic School in Boston"	331
Index		337

List of Illustrations

Plans of the Rogers Building   54 et seq.
Growth of Staff and Student Body under Presidents Rogers,
    Runkle, and Walker 1865-1897   130

BETWEEN PAGES 190 AND 191

James Savage, Sr., and his family, photographed in the library of his home on Temple Place in Boston.

The first page of the basic document from which the Massachusetts Institute of Technology was to take its origin.

Formal acceptance by the "Government" of the newly formed Institute of the Charter granted by Act of the General Court on April 10, 1861.

The Boston Mercantile Library building on Summer Street, as depicted in a contemporary print.

The Rogers Building, the Institute's center for sixty years.

William Barton Rogers
    President 1862-1870, 1878-1881

John Daniel Runkle
    Acting President 1868-1870
    President 1870-1878

Francis Amasa Walker
    President 1881-1897

James Mason Crafts
    President 1897-1900

Henry Smith Pritchett
    President 1900-1907

Arthur Amos Noyes
    Acting President 1907-1909

LIST OF ILLUSTRATIONS

Richard Cockburn Maclaurin
    President 1900-1920

President Maclaurin at his desk in the Rogers Building.

Dr. William J. Walker of Newport, R. I.

Ralph Huntington of Boston.

T. Coleman du Pont, '84.

George Eastman.

The opening and the final paragraphs of Dr. William J. Walker's deed of gift of April 2, 1863.

The opening and the final paragraphs of President Rogers' reply.

The Rogers Building in 1872.

The Great Court in Cambridge in its earliest days.

In 1916, the first plantings in the Great Court.

The Tech's office in Room 30 of the Rogers Building in April, 1893.

The Rogers Building lunch room in March, 1893.

When M. I. T. Was "Boston Tech"

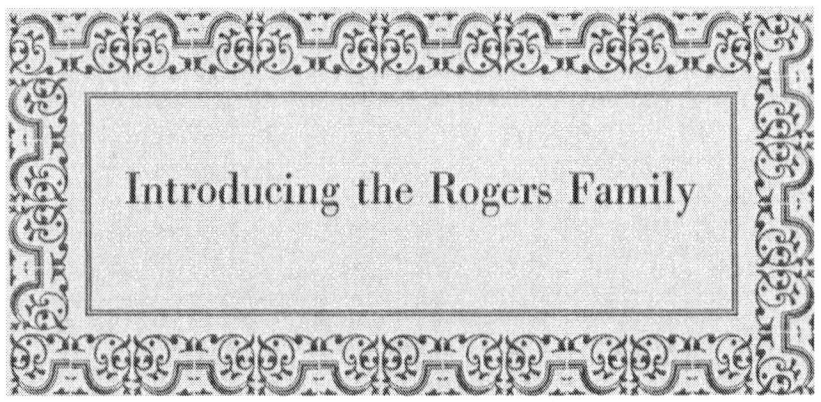

Introducing the Rogers Family

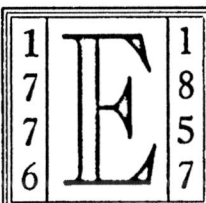

EVERY STUDENT at the Massachusetts Institute of Technology since instruction began on February 20, 1865, has many times seen or heard the name of William Barton Rogers, its founder. There is today, in the central lobby under the great dome of the Cambridge buildings, a bust that shows him as a typical gentleman of the old school, serious yet kindly in demeanor, looking toward the future with hope and faith. Portraits of him adorn several Institute rooms, notably the president's office and one room in Walker Memorial. On the north wall of the lobby in the present Rogers Building a bronze tablet, given by the classes of '82, '83, '84, '85, and '86, depicts his striking profile with its almost aquiline expression, and memorializes him as the founder of this great school.

Although these memorials of the great founder have been daily visible to hundreds, probably few of the busy students of the past four decades have even a casual knowledge of his early life, and still fewer know the impressive story of his family. A glimpse into his father's career, and some account of the family's aspirations and struggles through the first half of the last century will help explain the vision that culminated in the founding of M. I. T.

A hundred years ago William Barton Rogers was one of a notable group of four brothers, all of them distinguished scientists and educators. Like the three Compton brothers a century later who showed such a striking combination of scientific and administrative ability, each of the "Brothers Rogers," as they were known in their day, made his name distinguished in some branch of science and held some prominent academic post. They were in touch with the scientific work and the intellectual currents of Europe and America, and they worked together or corresponded intimately throughout their lives.

Patrick Rogers, the father of the Rogers brothers, was himself a man of outstanding character. He was born in 1776 in Tyrone County in Northern Ireland, of Irish, Scotch, and English ancestry. He was the eldest of the twelve children of Robert Rogers, a congenial, liberal Irish gentleman. Patrick's first school was a thatched, clay-walled little schoolhouse on his father's estate about forty miles from Londonderry. Later he was tutored, especially in the classics, by one of his two Presbyterian clergyman uncles. Patrick was keen of mind, thoughtful, and decisive in character. When it was time to decide on his future he rejected the career in the church that his family proposed, and instead entered a counting-house in Dublin. Shortly afterward, in May, 1798, the Irish Rebellion broke out, and Patrick contributed to Dublin newspapers some articles hostile to the government, which his friends thought almost certain to cause his arrest. Thereupon, assisted financially by a kinsman, Alexander Rogers, he fled to Londonderry and thence to America. In August, 1798, after a voyage of eighty-four days, he arrived in Philadelphia.

The refugee soon secured a position as tutor in the University of Pennsylvania, and in the winter of 1799 was admitted to study medicine at the Pennsylvania Hospital under the eminent Doctors Barton and Rush, and in the university under Doctors Shippen and Wistar, all men still well remembered in the annals of medicine. At the same time he also assiduously attended lectures in chemistry by Dr. James Woodhouse at the university and became thoroughly grounded in this science.

While still a medical student, in January, 1801, he married Hannah Blythe, of Scotch-English parentage and good family, who

Introducing the Rogers Family

had also come from Londonderry, and on February 11, 1802, James Blythe Rogers, the first of the four famous sons, was born. In May of that year Patrick received his medical degree, dedicating his graduation thesis to Dr. Barton, and at once started a medical practice, several thousand dollars in debt.

Patrick's father died in 1803, and as the eldest son, Patrick felt it necessary to go to Ireland to assist in adjusting family affairs and to obtain his share of the estate. A year later he returned to Philadelphia, bringing with him two younger brothers. After he had paid his debts from his small inheritance Dr. Rogers found himself "with neither money or an establishment" as he expressed it, and with a family to support. In his absence his practice had disappeared, and the outlook was not bright. Spurred by need, and sensing an opportunity to take advantage of the public curiosity about science, he energetically prepared a series of popular lectures on chemistry, with experimental demonstrations, probably the first to be given in this country. In 1810 he published "A Syllabus of a Course of Lectures on Natural Philosophy and Chemistry with the Application of the Latter to Several of the Arts." Eventually these lectures became well known, but they were not remunerative. For eight years after his return from Ireland, Patrick was constantly stalked by poverty and debt, and the family eked out a poor living in Philadelphia.

Early in this distressing period, the second son, William Barton Rogers, named in honor of the friendly Professor Barton, was born on December 7, 1804. A third son, Henry Darwin, was born August 1, 1808. Two daughters were born during this period also, but both died in infancy. Hoping for better things, the family moved to Baltimore in 1812, and there the fourth of the brilliant sons, Robert, was born on March 29, 1813.

Life in Baltimore, where the family lived for the next seven years, proved somewhat better, but continued to be a struggle with poverty. Dr. Rogers, by combining an apothecary's shop with medical practice, and by continuing his public lectures, was able to support his family and pay the debts he had incurred. He eventually acquired some distinction in the medical profession, was elected physician of the Hibernian Society in 1816, and "orator" of the Medico-Chirurgical Society in 1819. He also gained public reputation as a scientist.

Despite the difficulties, there was a happy home life. Patrick Rogers had made it a practice to give a part of each day to the scientific and practical instruction of his young sons rather than leave their education entirely to the schools of the city. Of a part of this program, William once wrote: ". . . With the exception of a short period when James and myself walked about two miles to Baltimore College [the Public High School] to receive instruction in Latin, we never spent any of our afternoon hours in school. . . . It thus happened that our education was conducted in great part at home, and by the daily personal attention of our kind and judicious father; and to this cause I may justly ascribe the thoroughness of our knowledge on all the subjects which we studied. . . ."

While this regimen undoubtedly developed in the sons an early love of science and a maturity of thought and a facility of expression far in advance of ordinary boys in their teens, it largely deprived them of the companionship of other boys and of participation in the simple sports of the period. The Rogers brothers were not athletic or sport-loving, but they enjoyed excursions into the fields and hills, and were keen observers. Music was one form of family relaxation, with Dr. Rogers and Henry playing the violin and William the flute. But for the most part the boys were steeped in serious things, and under the father's influence keen to study the unfolding sciences.

In 1819, the University of Virginia was incorporated, with Thomas Jefferson as the founder. On May 21 of that year Dr. Patrick Rogers applied to Mr. Jefferson for a professorship in natural philosophy and chemistry in the newly established university. Mr. Jefferson replied in kindly vein, stating that no funds were available for teaching, that the proposed professorship had already been assigned, and that the opening of the university was to be postponed until 1821. The ability of Patrick Rogers did not remain long unrecognized, however, for he was soon after elected Professor of Natural Philosophy and Chemistry in the ancient College of William and Mary, founded in 1693, and second in age only to Harvard among American colleges. The Rogers family moved to Williamsburg and settled in Brafferton House on the campus in the autumn of 1819.

Life at Williamsburg began auspiciously and ran smoothly. The

Introducing the Rogers Family

two elder sons, James and William, matriculated in the college. Patrick Rogers entered on his new work with zest. He loved teaching, and his lectures were brilliant and popular. He made all the apparatus required in his experiments, aided by his sons, who under his tutelage acquired unusual facility in the use of tools.

In the summer following the first year Mrs. Rogers died of the dreaded malarial fever. (At the time, the region of Williamsburg was so notorious for the prevalence of malarial fevers during the summer seasons, that it was seriously proposed to move the College of William and Mary to Richmond). The death of the mother was a stunning blow to the family. It brought the father into still closer relations with the four boys, and strengthened the intense devotion to each other that the boys showed throughout their lives.

After a second year at William and Mary, James, the eldest son, entered the Medical School at the University of Maryland, took his M.D. degree in one year, and began medical practice at the age of twenty in Baltimore. William, whose health had always been far from robust, completed his college course, and then spent the next few winters in Williamsburg, immersed in the study of physics and mathematics, and working as an assistant to his father. In 1822, at the age of seventeen, he demonstrated his remarkable rhetorical gifts at the third "Virginiad" celebrating the settlement of Jamestown in an oration that was highly praised by the press of the day. Before he was twenty he had translated an important French work on differential calculus.

In 1825 William and his brother Henry, who had just finished college, went to Baltimore to seek their fortunes. In the autumn of 1826 they opened a school at Windsor, Maryland, to which their brother Robert came as a student, but it was never large or prosperous enough to provide a suitable living for the two men. Fortunately, William soon managed to get a temporary appointment as a lecturer at the Maryland Institute, one of the earliest of the "institutes" common in that era that sponsored courses on scientific subjects as well as popular lectures and exhibitions. In the autumn of 1827 he was given a permanent appointment as lecturer, but an expected professorship did not materialize. At the request of the managers of the Institute, early in 1828 William drew up a plan for a school emphasizing in its upper years instruction in mathematics, elementary surveying, natural philosophy, chemistry, and other practical subjects, in fact, a technical high school, to be established as a part of the Maryland Institute. When the trustees accepted his proposal William and Henry abandoned the school at Windsor, and both began their careers in technical education in the new school.

For three years the Rogers brothers were all together around Baltimore, struggling to support themselves and considering the various careers open to men interested in science. Robert, at first a student in the school at Windsor, later transferred to the Maryland Institute. James, who had not been successful in medical practice, worked for a time as an industrial chemist, and then joined his brothers as a lecturer at the Maryland Institute.

In August, 1828, Patrick Rogers died of malarial fever, and on October 13 William was chosen as his successor to the chair of Natural Philosophy and Chemistry at William and Mary. For the next seven years William devoted his splendid mental energies to teaching and experimental work at Williamsburg, in which he was remarkably successful despite the climate and the competition from the new University of Virginia at Charlottesville which had opened in 1825. Later when the professorship in mathematics suddenly became vacant, he temporarily assumed this additional task, so successfully that the students petitioned the Board of Visitors to make no new appointment in the subject for the rest of the year.

As the first of the brothers to establish himself, William also assumed his father's role as head of the family. Robert returned to Williamsburg to complete his college work, and to him William gave an almost paternal protection. To the other brothers he was a constant helper, ready with substantial aid and wise counsel when it was sought.

Things did not go well without William at the Maryland Institute, and after a short time James and Henry left to seek more secure academic posts. James, after an unhappy period teaching chemistry in a struggling, second-rate medical school in Baltimore, finally received a much better appointment as professor in a medical school in Cincinnati, where in addition to medical teaching he wrote a textbook in chemistry. Henry was elected to the chair of Natural Philosophy at Dickinson College in Carlisle, Pennsylvania, but found the experience disillusioning and unsatisfactory because of the narrow religious and social views that permeated the college. His scientific ability was recognized, however, and for a year he edited a journal that published reviews of scientific matters.

Although the brothers were dispersed during this period they maintained the deepest family feeling and the closest association in their general scientific interest, so that they were in a sense an organized scientific team, exchanging ideas in a stream of letters, and contributing to each other's work. Each brother had his own interests and aptitudes, but the brothers were united by an absorbing interest in chemistry and in natural philosophy, which included mechanics and electricity. They also shared a deep interest in the new science of geology, which was then receiving much attention, especially in England.

In the spring of 1831, Henry, feeling that his future at Dickinson was insecure, resigned and went to Philadelphia. During the summer he accompanied William and Robert to New York, in the hope of securing work for Robert with a Captain McNeil, who was locating some new railway lines in New England. Robert joined the surveying party as a volunteer, and found as one of his associates a Mr. E. S. Chesbrough, later one of the founders of the American Society of Civil Engineers. Some weeks later, Henry sought and obtained employment on these field surveys, and thus it came about that in the summer of 1831 again Henry and Robert were working together in New England.

In this work they paid special attention to the geology as well as to the surface features of the regions between Boston and Providence and between Boston and Taunton. All this they reported in letters to William at Williamsburg, who was keenly interested. The region had appealed especially to Henry, who in September, 1831, wrote to William:

> I often make some observations on natural history, especially the nature of the trees and rocks. Griswold has mentioned my habit to the Captain, reporting, I presume, something in praise of my geological information: the Captain requested me to-day to record a series of geological observations throughout our route, stating that such things will

be beneficial to my prospects. So much for a little science!!! I should not omit to state that, though volunteers, we receive the full recompense usually given persons who do our duty, each of us now getting $1.25 a day. This of course will not continue after we quit the field, but for the present it more than defrays our expenditures.

Henry and Robert spent the winter in New York after their surveying season ended, and Robert returned the following spring to continue in the survey. These two seasons with surveying parties on railroad location work were the first experience of the Rogers brothers with practical engineering work. Apparently it did not attract them as a profession. Robert, at the age of twenty, wrote to William: "Engineering holds out but very few inducements, for only those who have been educated at West Point stand in the way of promotion, and can look forward to certainty of success; they alone are sure of constant occupation in the profession." The civil engineers of that and earlier days were not the product of technical schools in the now-accepted sense, since none were in existence. To be sure, West Point, founded in 1802, taught *military* engineering to men who were to become officers in the U.S. Army, and who often resigned early to use their training in more profitable civilian work. As in England, the term *civil* engineer was beginning to be used to describe men skilled in surveying, in the construction of dams, bridges, canals, and docks, or in the layout and construction of highways and railways. Aside from the Army engineers, most Americans engaged in this sort of work were ingenious and versatile self-made men, without much background in science and mathematics, other than that gained by their own efforts. In any case Robert, seeing no future for him in engineering, entered the Medical School of the University of Pennsylvania; and Henry, after a brief fling at social reform, turned to the more congenial field of geology.

In Baltimore a few years earlier, Henry Rogers had met and been strongly influenced by the brilliant but visionary Miss Frances Wright, of extremely liberal opinions, who was crusading against the accepted theological and social views of the day. Like other freethinking utopians of the time, she was interested in educational schemes, especially the establishment of "halls of science" to make

Introducing the Rogers Family

new scientific knowledge available to the people. During the winter of 1831-32, in New York, Henry met Robert Dale Owen, the leader of this movement, and his interest was renewed. As a result he developed a desire to visit England to follow up these theories and to observe social conditions in London and elsewhere. With the reluctant consent of his family he left for England in May, 1832, intending to return in the autumn. At sea on his homeward passage a series of severe storms disabled and almost wrecked the ship, and Henry was obliged to return to London for the winter. This accident was a turning point in the lives of the Rogers brothers, for it brought them into contact with the great scientists of Europe, and launched Henry, and indirectly William, on their careers as geologists.

A Geological Society had been founded in London in 1807, and one in France in 1830. Interest in geology was also well developed in America—a society was formed in the Wyoming valley of Pennsylvania in 1832—and the Rogers brothers had all taken a deep interest in this new and important science. During his enforced stay in England, Henry found opportunity to attend many meetings of the Royal Society and to make the acquaintance and gain the friendship of many of the most eminent scientific men of the period, including Faraday; Dalton, the chemist; Tully, one of the inventors of the achromatic objective; and perhaps most important of all, Lyell. Lyell was the outstanding geologist in all Europe. Henry's already strong interest in geology was tremendously stimulated, and his knowledge greatly increased, especially through a concentrated study of fossils and all the materials available in the museums in London. So eager was his pursuit of the science that he became recognized as a leader in the subject, and before his return to America he was elected a Fellow of the Geological Society of London, the most authoritative body in this field, and the oldest of the geological societies in the world. Young Henry Rogers, about twenty-five at this time, was now assured of the course his own life would take. Geology must be his professional field. He had shared his new knowledge by letters to his brother William, and on his return to America in September, 1833, they, with Robert, spent some weeks in discussing the new developments in this branch of science.

Two important results came from these discussions. Henry prepared a series of public lectures on geology, splendidly illustrated by fine models of crystals skillfully prepared by his brother Robert. These lectures were given to overflowing audiences at the Franklin Institute in Philadelphia during the following months and stirred much interest in the subject. In January, 1835, Henry was elected Professor of Geology at the University of Pennsylvania, and began an illustrious career as teacher, director of surveys, and consultant.

A not less important result was the effect on William's career, for he had already given serious attention to geology and had made careful observations in Virginia. The stimulus derived from Henry's English visit intensified William's zeal in research in the field, and had as a product the notable reports on the marls and greensands of Virginia which brought him increased reputation and wide correspondence with some of the foremost men of science in the country. He and Henry published jointly one important article in *Silliman's Journal* in 1834, the first of numerous papers by the two brothers.[1]

One outcome of William's work was an attempt to induce the legislature of Virginia to undertake a geological survey of the state like those already instituted in Massachusetts, Maryland, and Tennessee. The proposal was favorably acted on in March, 1835, and soon thereafter William was appointed chief of the Geological Survey. By a happy coincidence, Henry began a similar survey of the state of New Jersey in May of the same year. The combination of teaching and academic research with the supervision of practical field work that his position as head of the Geological Survey demanded must have led William gradually to observe the interrelations of science with industry and productive enterprises, the field later called applied science or technology.

In August, 1835, after seven years' distinguished service at William and Mary, William Barton Rogers was elected to the chair of Natural Philosophy at the University of Virginia. The change from the malaria-ridden district of Williamsburg to the higher, cooler hill country of Charlottesville was a happy one. Moreover, the University of Virginia had unlimited advantages in its form of organization, breadth of outlook, and support by State funds, as compared with the much older, already famous, but exceedingly restricted College of William and Mary. At Charlottesville, William's health greatly improved, and he was able to conduct geological explorations in the state, and also to take the positions in national scientific bodies to which his great ability and reputation entitled him.

William's main occupation was as a professor at the University, yet the other duty as director of the survey could not be neglected, and he needed competent assistance. His own brothers were, in fact, the men best adapted by knowledge and experience to serve in this important capacity, but none of them was immediately available. His first summer was spent in a personal reconnaissance in the field, from the notes of which he was able to prepare a profile map of the state during the arduous winter months that followed. This map with some descriptive material constituted his first report. He had help and much advice from his brother Henry, who was himself about to be engaged in a similar survey of New Jersey, and their exchanges of information and experience were mutually helpful. Henry was also practically engaged to make an extended survey of Pennsylvania on completion of his New Jersey work. Henry's immediate services were not fully available, although he found time to give some help to his brother in the Virginia work, and was even appointed as an assistant on the Virginia Survey for a brief period. But with the opening of the Pennsylvania Survey Henry could no longer hold the Virginia position and resigned. Such other field assistants as William had were not well enough trained to replace Henry; and the situation was so critical that William even thought of resigning his professorship in order to give full time to the geological survey which he had begun so enthusiastically.

It was fortunate that all the brothers, as a result of their previous close association, had developed an interest in the work in geology. Even the two who had been medically trained, James and Robert, had often been called on for chemical analyses of mineral substances and had acquired great facility in this work, Robert being especially competent. Just at this time, in 1836, when he had finished his medical course with the highest standing and looked forward to establishing himself in practice, a family conference decided that if possible he should postpone his plans and come to the assistance of William. Although this suggestion was somewhat disappointing to Robert, who had already been offered an appointment as physician in one of the state institutions, he cheerfully responded to what seemed to be a family duty, and, much to William's satisfaction, became for some months the chief assistant on the survey. Later he went to Philadelphia to assist his brother Henry in a similar capacity on the Pennsylvania Survey. Robert's place on the Virginia work was taken by James, who had resigned from his professorship at the medical school in Cincinnati. Thus it came about that all four of the now famous Brothers Rogers had a part in this important Virginia Survey, which had become well known far beyond the boundaries of the state.

Life at the university, although it had begun so auspiciously, became more complicated and at times burdensome to William as the years passed. A main source of distress was a long series of outbreaks by disorderly and undisciplined students. Violence was not uncommon. Riots, in one of which the Chairman of the Faculty was killed in his own dooryard, continued sporadically over several years, greatly injured the morale and the reputation of the university, and made life in Charlottesville unhappy for professors and citizens. William was deeply disturbed by them.

To make matters worse, even the survey, to which he gave so much care, began to be opposed in the legislature in 1839, and was under fire in 1841 on grounds of delay and expense. It was only by long and patient work and a brilliant defense of the value of the survey that Rogers eventually managed to get an appropriation from the legislature. But if there was criticism at home, there was praise and a growing reputation outside Virginia.

During these strenuous years William maintained his deep interest in science, especially geology, and somehow, in spite of frequent illness, he found time to do original work of much importance, such as the discovery of infusorial earth in Virginia. His reputation as a scientist grew steadily in America and abroad. He became one of the earliest members of the National Institution for the Promotion of Science, founded in 1840, and of the Society of Geologists and Naturalists, a more exclusive group also established in 1840, which became in 1847 the American Association for the Advancement of Science. In collaboration with his brother Henry, he presented an outstanding paper before the Philosophical Society of Philadelphia in December, 1841. The following year they joined in the presentation of an extremely important contribution "On the Structure of the Appalachian Chain as Exemplifying the Laws which have Regulated the Elevation of Great Mountain Chains Generally." This epoch-making paper was read before the meeting of the Association of American Geologists and Naturalists at the third annual meeting in Boston in 1842. Nathan Appleton, a leading merchant and promotor of New England industries, himself an amateur geologist, financed the publication of the proceedings. Charles Lyell, the great English geologist, was a participant in the conference, and was so impressed by this contribution of the Rogers brothers that he induced them to send a long abstract of it to the British Association.

To be honored by the leading geologists of the English-speaking world at these brilliant meetings at the Boston Society of Natural History must have given the Rogers brothers intense satisfaction. On this, his first visit to Boston, William was also undoubtedly impressed with the intellectual activity and industrial development of the Boston area. Rich in historic buildings and libraries, deeply interested in the budding sciences, distinctly in its commercial glory, and with its leading business men exceedingly active with new and great industrial development in textile and other lines of manufacturing in New England, Boston was a city of commanding interest. He returned to the city several times over the next decade, and with each visit the conviction grew that Boston was an ideal location for an institution devoted to the new kind of technical education that he and his brothers had been turning over in their minds since 1828.

In the wake of these triumphs there were disturbing and discordant notes. On his return to Charlottesville, William found that the criticism of the survey had not ceased, but funds were eventually voted for its completion. A more distressing attack on the university itself soon followed. In December, 1844, the legislative Committee on Schools and Colleges was instructed to investigate "the past history and present condition and influences of the University of Virginia, with a view of forming their opinion upon the question of repealing the Act of Assembly granting an annuity of $15,000 to that Institution." This came as a great blow to William Barton Rogers, who had just been elected Chairman of the Faculty, the chief administrative officer of the university, and to Robert, who had been elected Professor of Chemistry and Materia Medica in the university in 1842.

It devolved on the Chairman of the Faculty to prepare a memorial to the legislature in defense of the university. The document that Rogers prepared was unquestionably the ablest discussion of the function of the American college and its methods of instruction that had been prepared up to that time, and for breadth of view and thoughtful elaboration of the significance of scientific and literary education in the general culture of the country it is still notable reading a hundred years afterward.[2]

How deeply this long and carefully prepared memorial may have affected the legislature is not clear, but it was apparently successful. If so, its effect must have been considerably neutralized by a fresh outburst of student riots, which had to be suppressed by the civil authorities. Peace was eventually restored, and seventy of the ringleaders were dismissed from the university, but by then these unhappy events had so disturbed Professor Rogers that he began to consider finding a more tranquil place to live and work.

Much in need of rest following the arduous year as Chairman of the Faculty, in the summer of 1845 William visited his brother Henry in Philadelphia, and then joined him in a journey through the White Mountains, a visit to Boston, and later a trip to the shores of Lake Superior, where Henry had been commissioned by Boston men to explore the region for copper ores.

On their travels in New Hampshire, the Rogers brothers met the family of Mr. James Savage of Boston, a man of ample means and notable character, who was the first treasurer of the Provident Institution for Savings, one of the two oldest savings banks in the United States, and later the author of *The Genealogical Dictionary of the First Settlers of New England*. The Savages quickly became friendly with William and Henry, and through their hospitality in Boston made it possible for them to meet many influential people. The eldest daughter, Miss Emma Savage, a vivacious and charming young lady, was most kind to the serious-minded professor from Virginia twenty years her senior, and later became his wife.

During this summer William and Henry had time to discuss the ideas William had expressed in his memorial to the Virginia legislature, and to consider more carefully the extension of education into technological fields which were not then receiving attention in American colleges. In Boston during this summer, and also in the following two summers when William also spent his holidays in New England, they acquired new friends, widened their professional associations, and strengthened their conviction that the time was ripe and that Boston was the place for a new venture in technical education. The industrial development of New England and the energy of Boston capitalists in finding new outlets for their enterprise had created a need for well trained engineers. Various schemes for technical education to meet this demand were in the air at the time, and by 1847 both Harvard and Yale had established scientific schools.

William's experience in New England reinforced the educational principles he had conceived in his earlier thinking, and on his return to Charlottesville in the fall of 1845 he gave these matters serious consideration, stimulated by letters from Henry. Henry had resigned from the University of Pennsylvania and had already made a name for himself in Boston by courses of lectures in 1843 and 1844, had now settled there, and was a candidate for the vacant Rumford Professorship at Harvard. Early in 1846, as an alternative to the Harvard professorship, he conceived the plan of setting up a technical school such as he and William had discussed, to be attached to the Lowell Institute in Boston, and appealed to William to help him draw up a plan to submit to Mr. John A. Lowell, trustee of the Lowell Institute.

The result was two handwritten letters from William dated March 13, 1846, and called "A Plan for a Polytechnic School in Boston." Under the provisions of the Lowell will, Mr. Lowell could not accept this proposal, but it was the embryo of the Massachusetts Institute of Technology. The story of the long struggle to make this plan a reality will be told in the next chapter.

During the months immediately following the transmission of the letters with the now-famous plan, William found himself somewhat discontented at Charlottesville. Constant thought as to how the plan could be transformed into reality absorbed much of his working hours and his energy, but teaching and research, lectures and correspondence also demanded his attention. His interests were manifold, and his opinions much in demand. In the summer of 1846 he made a geological survey of parts of New England. The next year he helped to promote the establishment of the National Bureau of Hydrography at Washington that had been urged by Lt. Matthew Fontaine Maury.

After spending the summer of 1847 in Boston, William began to think seriously of resigning from the university, and of joining his brother Henry, who was then a free-lance lecturer and geological expert in Boston. On March 14, 1848, he sent a letter to the rector of the Board of Visitors announcing his intention to resign at the end of the spring session. When it became known, this decision created such a furore that he felt impelled to withdraw his resignation, out of loyalty to his colleagues and to the university.

Through his brother Henry, who had again gone abroad for a few months, he was kept in close contact with the rapid development of the sciences in Europe, especially in the British Isles, and was gratified to know how extensively and appreciatively the work of the Rogers brothers was recognized. In August, 1848, Hampden-Sydney College in Virginia conferred on him the degree of LL.D., and the spring of 1849 brought an invitation to give a course of lectures at the Smithsonian Institution in Washington.

In June, 1849, he married Miss Emma Savage of Boston, whose family had been especially friendly since the days of the memorable visit to the White Mountains several years before. Immediately after their marriage, Dr. and Mrs. Rogers embarked for England on the Cunard steamship *Europa*. It was William's first visit to foreign countries, although he knew many European scientists, and a wonderful summer was before them. With improving health, and with the many contacts he had with the leading scientists of the day, some of whom, like Lyell, he had already met in America, it was a triumphant period, culminating in the great meeting of the British Association at Birmingham, where he was not only welcomed warmly, but specially invited to be a guest speaker. At the great banquet of the Association, in response to a toast to his brother, he made an eloquent speech which was reported by a listener as the outstanding event of this occasion.

In the autumn he returned with his bride to Charlottesville and spent the next four years busily and happily in teaching, in lecturing, and in fruitful research both in geology and physics. Then, in 1853, in his fiftieth year, having the insistent desire to be in close contact with his brother and friends in Boston, and the ever-present ambition to forward his plans for a new school, he finally resigned his professorship. A break of this kind could not be made without many and intense regrets. It took courage and faith to leave his many friends, the scene of his greatest scientific achievement, the sure if small income, and the facilities for scientific work built up by his own efforts, for an uncertain future in Boston. But the desire to press on to the fulfillment of his great educational plan in association with his brother Henry was strong, and he made the break.

In June, 1853, William and Emma Rogers moved to Boston, and for many years made their home in the Savage residence in Temple Place, opposite the present location of the Provident Institution for Savings. A plaque placed by the Institute now marks the place where this house stood in the days when Temple Place was wholly a residential street. Years later, with the filling in and settlement of the Back Bay lands, they moved to Berkeley Street, and later to 117 Marlborough Street.

Since the final report of the Geological Survey of Virginia had never been published, a visit to Richmond to secure an appropriation for this purpose took Dr. and Mrs. Rogers back to Virginia early in January 1854, and resulted in another disappointment, which involved him in financial loss, and demonstrated the not unusual ingratitude of governments for outstanding public service. But he was not disheartened and turned his energies into other channels. He revamped the constitution of the American Association for the Advancement of Science, which was now becoming an important body. In August 1855, he addressed the Lyceum of Natural History of Williams College. The address was a notable exposition of the interdependence of the sciences that still makes good reading nearly a hundred years after its delivery.[3] Then followed lectures before large audiences in Boston under the auspices of the Mercantile Library Association, an imposing series of scientific papers, and, in the spring of 1857, a course of lectures at the Lowell Institute on the elementary laws of physics.

Believing that an ocean voyage would be beneficial, in the summer of 1857 Dr. Rogers again visited England, and had the pleasure of accompanying his brother Henry to many scientific meetings and on historic and scientific excursions. These opportunities were naturally most gratifying, especially as they came at the time Henry received the announcement of his appointment to a professorship at the University of Glasgow. Thereafter the brothers visited Ireland together, and when Henry had to return to England, William continued his travels alone. On his return to England he had a peculiar and serious accident on a railway train. A stone thrown into the car struck him on the cheek and fractured both jaws. After only a fortnight's inactivity, however, he went to Edinburgh for a fortnight and then to London, where he made many contacts with noted men of science. In mid-December he returned to Boston and soon became engaged in physical experiments resulting in a series of articles of note, and in preparation of a new course of lectures at the Lowell Institute.

Of the four brothers who had shared the struggles of early life, who had constantly supported each other in their efforts to follow the scientific life, each had attained eminence in his own field. James had become Professor of Chemistry at the University of Pennsylvania, but had died in 1852, and Robert, after a brilliant career at the University of Virginia, was prevailed upon to succeed him. Henry, always most closely associated with William, had achieved great prominence as a geologist and lecturer in Boston and also in Europe. In 1857 he became Regius Professor of Natural History and Geology at the University of Glasgow, but before leaving America had aided greatly in the promotion of the "Polytechnic School" that the brothers hoped to establish in Boston. Of the four able sons of Patrick, the far-seeing refugee, each played a notable part in the development of science and education in America.

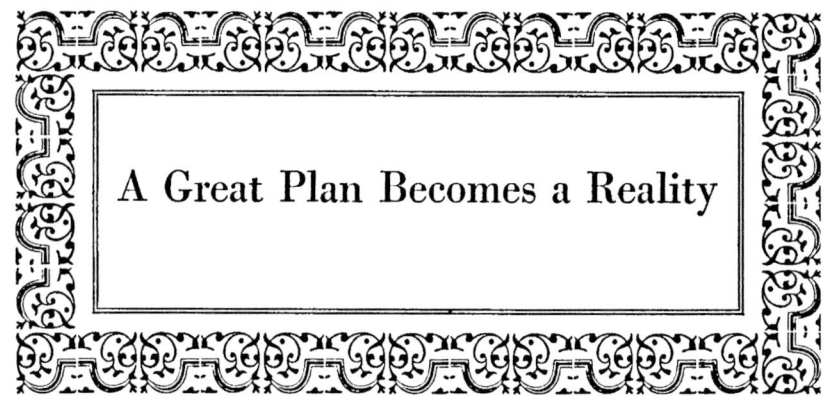

A Great Plan Becomes a Reality

THE CAREER of the Rogers brothers coincided with the rapid development of science, technology, and industry in the United States in the first half of the nineteenth century. In their early manhood while teaching in Baltimore they had shared the popular excitement over the projected canal and railway. They had participated in the geological surveys that supplied the basic information for mines and railways throughout the East, and they had witnessed the beginnings of large-scale industry in New England. With their interest in science and in education, it was natural that they should sense the need for a new kind of education to serve as the basis for the great industrial and technological development that they foresaw. It was also natural that they should choose Boston as the most promising location for an institute of technology.

When William Barton Rogers first saw the city in 1842, Boston was a small peninsula, with the spread-out waters of the Charles River at high tide covering a large area from Charles Street westward and southward to Roxbury and Brookline. This was the Back Bay area that began to be filled in during the next decade, and that later provided a site for M. I. T.

Boston at this time had a population of 100,000—largely of

British extraction. It was the leading literary center in America, dominated by Harvard College. Emerson, Whittier, Hawthorne, Longfellow, Bancroft, and Prescott were in their prime, and a distinguished younger group including Lowell, Motley, Holmes, and Thoreau were beginning to acquire fame. Men and women of searching mind, high ideals, and broad outlook, New England born or bred, dominated the life of the community.

New England, with Boston as its metropolis, was also a center of industrial development, and a source of capital, business enterprise, and technical talent for the expanding industrial and transportation network of the country. The China trade and foreign commerce in general had brought wealth to Boston and Salem and many smaller towns, and the coast of New England was dotted with small shipyards. Until the middle of the century, American sailing vessels were on all the seas of the globe. At the end of this golden age the Yankee Clippers, made famous by the skill of Donald Mac-Kay, outsailed all their competitors. Yankee ingenuity and savings had built small mills wherever streams could supply water power. Tanning and the leather industry, and especially the manufacture of boots and shoes were important, and many metal industries and plants for the manufacture of machinery developed here earlier than elsewhere in America. Large-scale industry began in textiles. During the War of 1812, Francis Cabot Lowell, son of the first John Lowell, with his brother-in-law Patrick Tracy Jackson devised a power loom and carried out successful experiments at Waltham in the conversion of raw cotton into cloth in one building. This was the first complete factory in America. The machines and processes developed here were the basis for the great industrial cities of New England that rose in the next generation. In 1822 Jackson and his associates established the Merrimack Manufacturing Company, which still survives—the oldest industrial corporation in America—in a new city named Lowell in 1826 in honor of Francis Cabot Lowell. In 1831 came the great Amoskeag Mills at Manchester, and beginning in 1846 the city of Lawrence, named for another great industrialist who also gave his name to the Lawrence Scientific School, developed quickly into another great manufacturing center. By 1850, Boston capital, founded in commerce and multiplied by industry, was largely instrumental in developing the railroads to the great West, and the mines of the Lake Superior district. Nowhere else in America was there such active and diversified industry.

It is therefore not surprising that the region around Boston, where many types of industries or processes had first developed, and which Dr. Holmes later called "the Hub of the Universe," made a strong appeal to William and Henry Rogers as they were formulating their plans in the 1840's for a new type of education that would provide directive power to utilize the new knowledge of science and supply the higher technical skill and the leadership for this new industrial society. For a hundred years prior to this time there had been architects, masons, and skilled wood workers, and mechanics such as the millwrights and dam builders who had utilized small waterpowers for saw and grist mills. Now as a result of the great Industrial Revolution that was sweeping Europe and America the Rogers brothers saw the future in a much broader way. Thus they expressed the first clear conception of engineering and applied science in the true sense.

The earliest American engineers were largely self-taught or perhaps had served a short apprenticeship to some one of the few men in America with more extended knowledge of mathematics and mechanics, a man such as Loammi Baldwin, who had been a colonel in the Revolutionary War and who later built the Middlesex canal and other public works, or his son Loammi, who designed a tunnel canal through the Berkshires at the point where the Hoosac Tunnel now serves the railroad. They and other noted early engineers were not *institutionally* trained. West Point, founded in 1802, offered the first formal training in military engineering in this country, and by 1830 its graduates had such standing in this and in general engineering lines that, as we have seen, young Robert Rogers decided that he could not enter this profession without the West Point prestige. But new schools offering some training in *civil* engineering as well had been started and grew slowly. In 1819 Alden Partridge established a school at Norwich, Vermont, known as the American Literary, Scientific and Military Academy. Here apparently could be had some instruction in mathematics, natural science, and land and highway surveying. This school was later removed to Northfield, Vermont, and in 1834 was incorporated as Norwich University. Its claim to be the oldest engineering college in the country seems to be a sound one. In 1824 the Rensselaer School was founded at Troy, N. Y., and was opened January 3, 1825. Founded to train young students "in the application of science to the common purposes of life," it was designed to give the sons and daughters of farmers and mechanics a combination of experimental and didactic instruction. The work expanded and the name of the school was changed to Rensselaer Institute in 1832. About this time emphasis was given to the teaching of civil engineering, and the first degree in civil engineering given in America was conferred there in 1835.[4a] The school was reorganized in 1849-50, and the name was changed to Rensselaer Polytechnic Institute in 1851. This change of name was ratified by an act of the State Legislature in 1861, the year the Massachusetts Institute of Technology was incorporated.

In the 1840's these schools were inadequate to meet the country's needs for trained engineers. Expansion to the Pacific and the accelerating development of industry and transportation had sharply increased the demand for technical talent. Furthermore the kind of training offered by existing schools was too narrow and vocational to suit the Rogers brothers, who were convinced that it was possible to give young men a sound foundation for a professional career in engineering and at the same time a broad education that would be more suitable for many students than the traditional college could offer. Without means of their own, their only hope of realizing their educational ideals was to persuade some established institution to sponsor a school based on the principles they had formulated.

In 1846 Henry Rogers hoped that he had found such an institution in the Lowell Institute of Boston. John Lowell, Jr., a Boston merchant of distinction and public spirit, son of Francis Cabot Lowell, had died in Bombay in 1836 and by his will established the Lowell Institute with a handsome endowment of $250,000 to support free public lectures. Henry Rogers made the first contact with the Lowell Institute in 1844 when John Amory Lowell, the sole trustee of the Institute and the dominant member of the Harvard Corporation, invited him to deliver a course of lectures before the Institute.

A Great Plan Becomes a Reality

Early in 1846 Henry again made contact with Mr. Lowell. Various schemes for scientific and technical education were in the air at the time, and Henry was hoping for a professorship at Harvard. In reply to a letter from William regarding aspects of the situation at Cambridge, Henry replied on March 8, 1846, in some detail, and then added the following long paragraph:

... But I have to speak of another interesting matter. Mr. Lowell, with whom I have been talking, after mentioning the features of the Lowell will which enjoins the creation of classes in the Institute to receive exact instruction in useful knowledge, requested me to give him, in writing, the views I had just been unfolding of the value of a School of Arts as a branch to the Lowell Institute. My communication to the corporation has, I am sure, made an impression on him, and it is possible he has seen, by what is there stated, the importance of teaching science in its applied forms in this community. He is a very cautious man, desires never to make a mis-move, fears to expand his Instiute too fast, and has doubts of the practicability of attaching this sort of practical College to the Institute, lest it might be too large an affair to build; but he sees its value, and now is a fine occasion to inspire him with the zeal which he is quite capable of feeling in its behalf. His plan would be to teach the operative classes of society,—builders, engineers, practical chemists, manufacturers, etc.; to admit in the first year only in limited numbers, and to teach them regularly; to have, perhaps, two permanent and salaried professors at the head of it, and to make up the rest of the instruction by assistants and by teachers, who would give courses of instruction occasionally on special branches. How much I want you near me at this time to aid me in digesting and submitting my views on this important scheme to Mr. Lowell! If you and myself could be at the head of this Polytechnic School of the Useful Arts, it would be pleasanter for us than any college professorship, for there would be less discipline, indeed, no more than with medical students. At no distant day, if not indeed soon, Mr. Lowell will, I hope, organize such a branch in his Institute; and if he does not, you and I can surely get one founded here by going about it in the right way. Let us give this matter our earnest and sober thoughts, remembering that if I get the professorship in Harvard, it will rather promote the plan than mar it. Can you send me a copy of our memorial on behalf of the Franklin Institute for a School of Arts? I have none by me, and shall write to-morrow to Philadelphia for a copy; perhaps you have one, but what is better yet, give me your ideas in a letter, however hastily expressed, as soon as conveniently practicable. ...

William's reply to this letter expressed his firm belief that of all places in the world Boston was most certain to derive the highest benefits from a polytechnic institution, and he then proceeded to write out in full a document later called "A Plan for a Polytechnic Institution in Boston," the first page of which is reproduced among the illustrations at page 190.

This document,[5] which turned out to be M. I. T.'s Magna Carta, opened with these words:

A school of practical science completely organized should, I conceive, embrace full courses of instruction in all the principles of physical truth having direct relation to the art of constructing machinery, the application of motive power, manufactures, mechanical and chemical, the art of engraving with electrotype and photography, mineral exploration and mining, chemical analysis, engineering, locomotion, and agriculture.

In his exposition, Rogers then proceeded to elaborate his proposals by many specific examples in these fields and others not so definitely designated, and by a far-seeing vision of future developments until practically all aspects of applied science had been touched upon.

One significant statement in the plan was that ". . . We may safely affirm that there is no branch of practical industry, whether in the arts of construction, manufactures or agriculture, which is not capable of being better practised, and even of being improved in its processes, through the knowledge of its connections with physical truth and laws, and therefore we would add that there is no class of operatives to whom the teaching of science may not become of direct and substantial utility and material usefulness." This demonstrated his belief that instruction for artisans and men of the foreman type was also most desirable.

The word "research" did not appear in the plan, but the extension of knowledge as one function of the proposed school is constantly implied in the exposition, as might be expected in a program of education proposed by one who was himself so eminent an exponent of the research spirit. The inference throughout was so clear that perhaps it did not seem necessary to labor this idea. Clearly Rogers had also in mind the more practical needs of the present, as well as

A Great Plan Becomes a Reality

of the future, for the report ended as follows: "A polytechnic school, therefore, duly organized, has in view an object of the utmost practical value, and one which in such a community as that of Boston could not fail of being realized in the amplest degree."

The hope that the trustee of the Lowell Institute might adopt the plan faded when it became clear that the provisions of Mr. Lowell's will made it impossible to use the funds for a school of this kind. Furthermore at about this time special departments or schools of applied science or engineering were beginning to appear in the already established colleges and universities. The following year the Lawrence Scientific School was opened on a foundation of $50,000 given by Abbott Lawrence, and at Yale the scientific or "philosophical" department of the college, later to be known as the Sheffield Scientific School, was organized. In the course of the next twenty years a number of universities established or reorganized scientific departments.

William Barton Rogers, who had become a resident of Boston in 1853, noted these events with deep interest. The opinion that technical training should be supplied only by a branch of a university did not appeal to his judgment. He still held firmly to the view that he had forcibly expressed, and was convinced that if a school were to play the part it ought to play in American education it should be free and independent. Since his brother Henry had been invited to become Regius Professor at Glasgow University and was in Europe after 1855, William was alone in the plans for development of the new school, and was constantly active in this and in his many scientific fields.

So for thirteen years the plan was apparently dormant, but in 1859 events took a turn which eventually made possible the fulfillment of the Rogers dream. As Boston grew, more land was needed. The broad shallow basin of the Charles River known as the Back Bay was one of the areas from which new land was gradually being created; and in 1859 Governor Banks, in his message to the legislature, pointed out that the opportunity was favorable to use this properly for "such public educational improvements as will keep the name of the Commonwealth forever green in the memory of her children." Here, at last, came a smile from Opportunity.

In response to this suggestion, a group of scientific and educational societies calling itself the Massachusetts Conservatory of Arts and Sciences, also known as The Associated Societies or Institutions, petitioned the legislature for a reservation of State land in the Back Bay. The petition, hastily drawn up by Dr. Samuel Kneeland as secretary, was presented but not granted. William Barton Rogers' name appears on the list of petitioners, although he was away from Boston during most of the legislative season.

It was determined to make another attempt the following year, and Dr. Rogers was requested to prepare a new petition to the legislature. He drew up a memorial, together with a plan indicating the land desired. This memorial designated four departments or kinds of educational service which would be especially benefited if favorable action on the petition were possible. These were set forth as:

I. Agriculture, including Horticulture and Pomology
II. Natural History, Geology and Chemistry
III. Mechanics, Manufactures, Commerce and Technology in general
IV. Fine Arts and Education

Each of these subdivisions was then skilfully described and explained. The exposition went into considerable detail, and left no doubt in the reader's mind as to the vast and splendid array of public services which could be assured in the course of years if the petition were granted. The document was, in a sense, a complete survey, in simple but often eloquent language, of the practical, educational, and cultural opportunities and values which may be derived by the whole people from visual exhibitions of the wide range of natural fabricated materials, and from the products of art and applied science.[6]

The list of the eighteen signers of the memorial contains names well known in Boston's business and intellectual history. Several supporting petitions were presented simultaneously by the Boston Society of Natural History, the Board of Trade, the American Academy of Arts and Sciences, the Massachusetts Charitable Mechanics' Association, and the New England Society.

The memorial was not immediately successful. It passed the

House fairly promptly, but met opposition in the Senate, and was eventually defeated. It was doubtless thought that the area hoped for, comprising the blocks between Boylston and Newbury Streets and Berkeley and Exeter Streets, and also some contiguous land further to the west, was too much to grant, and that the plans were too grandiose.

Despite this defeat, a sub-committee of the petitioning group, consisting of Dr. Rogers and four associates, E. B. Bigelow, J. M. Beebe, M. D. Ross, and C. H. Dalton, undertook the presentation of a third plan, a more limited one for an "Industrial Institution designed for the advancement of the industrial arts and sciences and practical education in the Commonwealth." This project was set forth by Dr. Rogers in a report entitled: *Objects and Plan for an Institute of Technology, including a Society of Arts, a Museum of Arts, and a School of Industrial Science, proposed to be established in Boston.*[7] This report of Rogers was approved by the legislative committee on October 5, 1860, and became the basis of the Massachusetts Institute of Technology as it exists today.

The report was distributed throughout the city and State in November, 1860. It was sent to all those likely to be interested and was accompanied by a letter from Dr. Rogers, inviting advice and support, as well as membership on a proposed Committee of Arts. The responses were numerous and most co-operative.

In this same month of November, 1860, an application, in the handwriting of Dr. Rogers, was made to the legislature for an Act of Incorporation of the Massachusetts Institute of Technology. It read as follows:

To the Honorable the Senate and House of Representatives of the Commonwealth of Massachusetts in General Court assembled:—

The subscribers respectfully pray for an Act of Incorporation for an Institution to be entitled the MASS. INSTITUTE OF TECHNOLOGY, having for its objects the advancement of the Mechanic Arts, Manufactures, Commerce, Agriculture and the applied sciences generally, together with the promotion of the practical education of the industrial classes, and proposing to attain these ends by the threefold agency of discussions and publications relating to industrial art and science; by a Museum of Technology, embracing the materials, implements and products of the practical arts and sciences; and by a School of Industrial Science, for instruction; by lectures, laboratories and other teachings, in these several departments.

They also respectfully pray that a section of land on the Back Bay may be reserved and granted, on such terms and conditions as may seem needful for the use of said Institute, such section being situated adjoining the sections asked for by the Boston Soc. of Nat. History and the Mass. Horticultural Society.

William B. Rogers *Chairman*
Marshall P. Wilder, Samuel H. Gookin, Alfred Ordway, M. D. Ross, Alex. H. Rice, E. S. Tobey, James M. Beebe, Dr. S. Cabot, Jr., G. W. Pratt, Amos Binney, Dr. S. Kneeland, Jr., Charles L. Flint, B. S. Rotch, J. D. Philbrick, George B. Emerson, R. C. Waterston, Erastus B. Bigelow, Charles H. Dalton, Committee

On November 20, 1860, the Secretary of State approved this application for publication in the *Boston Daily Advertiser*, and then it was forwarded for action by the General Court when it assembled in January. Dr. Rogers' next step was to send out the following letter calling for a public meeting to support the proposed Institute.

Boston, January 7, 1861

Dear Sir,—You have been made acquainted, through the pamphlet and circular which have been addressed to you, with the general 'Objects and Plan' of the Institute of Technology proposed to be established, if practicable, on the Back Bay lands in this city.

It is now proposed to hold a meeting in Mercantile Hall, 16 Summer Street, on Friday evening, 11th inst., at half past seven o'clock, for the purpose of adopting measures preliminary to the organization of the Institute, and in furtherance of a petition to the Legislature for a charter and a portion of the Back Bay lands.

As it is of the highest importance that the industrial and educational interests of the Commonwealth be amply represented at the meeting, we earnestly beg that you will favor us with your presence and counsel on that occasion. Should you be unable, however, to attend, but be desirous of coöperating, as a member of the Institute, in the great public objects we have in view, please affix your signature to the accompanying statement, and return the same, prior to the day of meeting, to the undersigned.

William B. Rogers,
Chairman of Committee

A Great Plan Becomes a Reality 31

The meeting was well attended. Among the speakers were Professor Pierce of Harvard and the Reverend Dr. Gannett of Arlington Street Church. A preliminary organization was set up, pledged to endeavor to establish the Institute, as described in Dr. Rogers' report. A committee of twenty was then appointed to take all necessary steps in its behalf, and to obtain from the legislature, if possible, an Act of Incorporation and a grant of land in the Back Bay for its use and for that of other institutions devoted to the practical sciences.

This committee of twenty, to which Rogers was added as chairman, was the antecedent of the M. I. T. Corporation. It included the following leading educational, professional, and business men of the Boston community, many of whom were staunch supporters of the Institute in the years to come: James M. Beebe, E. S. Tobey, S. H. Gookin, J. C. Hoadley, M. P. Wilder, C. L. Flint, E. B. Bigelow, M. D. Ross, J. D. Philbrick, F. S. Storer, J. D. Runkle, C. H. Dalton, J. B. Francis, Thomas Rice, John Chase, J. P. Robinson, F. W. Lincoln, Jr., Thomas Aspinwall, J. S. Dupee, and E. C. Cabot.

Now that the application for a charter had been made, the former Committee of Associated Institutions also made a fresh appeal to the legislature on January 14, 1861. In support of their application were new petitions from the Board of Trade, The American Academy of Arts and Sciences, The Society of Natural History, The New England Society for the Promotion of Manufactures, and the State Teachers' Association.

At the hearings on the action before the Joint Standing Committee on Education, there was opposition especially from the friends of the School Fund which by previous legislation was to benefit from the sale of the Back Bay lands. The Secretary of the Board of Education, ex-Governor Boutwell, was opposed, but was not fully supported by his Board. Of the newspapers, the *Advertiser*, the *Transcript*, and the *Journal* were especially warm in support of the request, and several Harvard professors were outspoken in its behalf. Rogers had addressed one of the hearings, and E. B. Bigelow and M. D. Ross had spoken at a second. Apparently unsatisfied, the Board of Education desired a third hearing, and Rogers asked the Governor to call a meeting of the Board that the Committee might confer with them.

To this request Governor Andrew responded:

> Boston, March 9, 1861
>
> My dear Professor,—The Board of Education will meet next Wednesday morning. I hope you will come and advocate the claims of the Natural History and Institute of Technology, but no one else should speak. Be thou the advocate. Take time enough. Cover the ground to suit yourself; several speakers would do harm; at least I fear they would. And you may say from me that I wish *one* complete argument, and that no other be made.
>
> Between ourselves I know *you* would have a powerful effect, left to yourself, and I fear some one else might come in and weaken it.
>
> Yours faithfully and fervently,
> John A. Andrew

Ten days later (March 19, 1861) the Joint Standing Committee on Education approved the application. Their report was prepared by Dr. Rogers.

As William reported to his brother Henry, the Act of Incorporation dragged on through the House and passed its second reading in the Senate after an earnest debate, the vote being twenty-six to nine. An amendment required that it be returned to the House for concurrence, which was eventually voted. The "Act to Incorporate the Massachusetts Institute of Technology" was approved by Governor Andrew on April 10, 1861.

Thus, after fifteen years of planning and almost exhausting activity, during which disappointments were frequent and defeat was at times imminent, the great vision of William Barton Rogers and his devoted brother Henry became a reality. So the Massachusetts Institute of Technology was born, to stand as a monument to a leader of remarkable character and to a life of courageous service to American education.

II

The cheering knowledge that the charter had at last become a reality had hardly been received before the whole nation was profoundly shocked by the fall of Fort Sumter. The tenuous hopes that hostilities might be averted now disappeared. The country plunged into war, and national affairs now took precedence over all else.

Bitter as was the disappointment over the delay in advancing the Institute, it was now clear that plans for the organization and development of the school would be greatly impeded and in large measure must be postponed. To Rogers especially this was a heavy blow. During the early war years he did what he could to keep the infant institution alive, but spent most of his time on more pressing public duties.

From the time of his coming to make his home in Massachusetts, Rogers had been constantly active in semi-public as well as in scientific matters. Because of his scientific eminence, and his recognized outstanding judgment and public spirit, his advice and help in public and scientific matters were continually sought. Soon after the granting of the charter, the Legislature of 1861 had passed a bill providing for the appointment of a State Inspector of Gas Meters and Gas, a position for which few scientifically competent men were available. Governor Andrew, sensing the need for an independent and wise man, appointed Dr. Rogers to this then very important post, at a salary of $3,000. Rogers at first declined the position, but was so strongly urged by the Governor and many others that he finally agreed to organize the inspection service and to conduct the necessary studies and tests.

He undertook this work with considerable enthusiasm, and turned it into another opportunity for scientific research as well as public service. For two years he held this position to the great satisfaction of the Governor and of all those concerned with the gas industry. He also served the public as a trustee of the Perkins Institute for the Blind in South Boston, of which his friend, Dr. Samuel Gridley Howe was the head. Here he became acquainted with the marvelous work of Laura Bridgman. He was also one of the organizers of the Union Club, which was founded about this time on the high principles of patriotism and of loyalty to the government. Rogers also took a prominent part in the organization of the National Academy of Sciences which was incorporated by an Act of Congress in 1863. Both he and his brother, Dr. Robert E. Rogers, who had succeeded his brother James as head of the Department of Chemistry of the University of Pennsylvania, were among the fifty distinguished scientists named as the incorporators of this organization. Although he had not had a part in preparing the original act, William Rogers attended the organization meeting and at once became influential in this important national body, which from its beginning in the days of the Civil War to the present has been of great service to the government.

These public services and scientific interests did not deter Rogers from his original and impelling purpose, to carry through the organization of the Institute. The first task was to raise money. The Charter Act passed by the legislature just before the outbreak of war had stipulated that a guaranty fund of $100,000 should be raised within one year. At first the promoters of the school were confident that this condition, although difficult, could be met, but with all the exigencies of war, progress in securing the guaranty fund was very slow. Some small contributions were received, and the first bequest, $3,000, from the estate of Miss Mary Townsend of Boston, was made during this year. It was also encouraging that one distinguished citizen, Ralph Huntington, for whom Huntington Avenue (at first called "Huntington's Folly") and later Huntington Hall were named, wrote to Rogers that by his will the Institute would receive $50,000. On April 2, 1862, John A. Lowell announced that he was planning a school for mechanics under the auspices of the Lowell Institute, of which he was trustee, and now proposed that the courses in this school should be given on the premises of the Institute of Technology should it be successfully established. For this service he promised a sum not less than $3,000 a year. This promise was most encouraging, but, there being no building, it was merely another evidence of future assistance. As the end of the first year approached, the funds in hand were far less than the stipulated guaranty.

There was nothing to do but request an extension of time, and for this quick action was necessary. As chairman of the committee that had been formed earlier, Rogers called a meeting for April 8, 1862, for the purpose of officially accepting the charter, electing a board of trustees (called a "Government"), adopting bylaws, appointing ad-interim officers, and taking such other action as might be necessary to organize the Institute. This meeting voted to petition the legislature for an extension of time in securing the guaranty fund.

A Great Plan Becomes a Reality

On the following day Rogers wrote two letters to the Governor and Council. The first of these was as follows: [8]

Boston, April 9, 1862

To his Ex'y the Governor & the Hon'le Council of
the Commonwealth of Mass.

Gentlemen,—

At a meeting of the Mass. Inst. of Technology held on Tuesday, April 8th, 1862 at the rooms of the Board of Trade, in this city, the Institute having been permanently organized & a Government elected, the following Resolution was adopted.—

"Resolved That the Mass. Inst. of Technology accept the Charter and other provisions of the Act of April 10, 1861, relating to said Institute."

William B. Rogers
Pres. Mass. Inst. Tech.

The second letter of the same date explained briefly the existing circumstances, and quoted the following resolutions passed at the meeting of the previous day.

"*Resolved,* That the members of the Institute are greatly cheered by the fact that, notwithstanding the engrossing claims of the public interests and the anxieties attendant upon the state of the country, they have received the assurance of a prospective fund of upwards of $100,000 for the future use of the Institute.

"*Resolved,* That the government of the Institute be directed forthwith to memorialize the Legislature to the effect that as this prospective contribution is not in a shape to comply literally with the condition of the Law of April 10, 1861, relating to the Institute, an additional year may be allowed them for complying in this respect with the conditions of the legislative grant."

The petition brought prompt action. On April 25, 1862, the legislature passed an act extending for one year the time limit for raising the guaranty fund. Much to Dr. Rogers' relief, the extension of time was thus assured before the first meeting of the new Government.

The first official meeting of the Institute as a corporation was held in the rooms of the Board of Trade on May 6, 1862. Rogers was elected president, and four vice-presidents were also elected, John A. Lowell, Jacob Bigelow, Marshall P. Wilder, and John Chase. Thomas

A. Webb was elected secretary, and Charles H. Dalton, treasurer. On the several committees were men of distinct eminence in the city. At this meeting the carefully elaborated three-fold plan for a Society of Arts, a School of Industrial Science, and a Museum of Technology was adopted.

The phrase *Institute of Technology* now means what M. I. T. has become, but it was originally intended to comprehend a wider variety of public services. The School of Industrial Science, after it opened in 1865, gradually became practically indentified with the Institute, but it was at first only one of three co-ordinate branches, each of which was represented by a committee of the Government and each of which was to have its own officers and members. Rogers was president of the Institute and also principal of the school. He did not officially become president of the school until November 14, 1865.

The ambitious program implied by this three-fold organization could not be carried out at once with war conditions as they were, but the Society of Arts, which was to sponsor "discussions and publications relating to industrial art and science" could be started and thus keep interest in the Institute active until the school and the museum could be financed and organized. The Society of Arts commanded great popular interest in a lecture-going community and did not involve serious expense. Only a large hall for meetings was required, and some simple forms for enrolling members who paid a nominal fee.

A meeting of the Society of Arts, the first public meeting of the Massachusetts Institute of Technology, was held on December 17, 1862, in Mercantile Hall on Summer Street. In an introductory address, President Rogers stated the aims, the character of the reports and communications to be presented, and the great advantage to be derived from a society of arts:

> The present accommodations are amply sufficient for our immediate purposes as a Society of Arts, and nothing is needed for the success of this branch of the Institute but that members and friends shall contribute from their stores of knowledge and invention whatever may give value and interest to the meetings in this hall. From the mill, the farm, the machine shop, the laboratory, the shipyard, from the desk of the engineer

and architect, the chair of science, the workman's bench, the merchant's counting room and all the other scenes where educated industry is at work, we may claim and expect the aid of vigorous thought and coöperative labour; and knowing how mighty is the momentum of the industrial intelligence around us, we can scarcely doubt that the efforts of this branch of the Institute will prove of substantial public interest and advantage. . . .

But let it not be supposed that in improving our opportunity of usefulness in the capacity of a Society of Arts, we are in any way withdrawing our interest from the other and more important branches, the proposed School of Industrial Science and the Museum of Practical Arts. These, it is true, can be carried into effect only in an imperfect and rudimental way without the extensive buildings and arrangements which they require. Still, even now a useful beginning can be made in both, and it should be our aim by such efforts as we can make in each of the departments of our enterprise, to give tangible evidence of its purposes and practical results.

It is, therefore, proposed at an early day to make a beginning in some branches of the School of Industrial Science, and in the collection of objects suitable for the intended Museum . . . we may hope, even thus early in our enterprise, to contribute somewhat to the cause of practical science and industrial education and progress, and be the better prepared for a wise use of the accumulated resources by which our entire plan is to be brought into operation. . . .

The first technical papers ever read before the Society of Arts were also presented at this meeting. R. B. Forbes read a paper on "Sub-Aqueous Gun Firing," followed by one "On the Combination of Wood and Iron in Shipbuilding." He was followed by E. S. Ritchie, the noted maker of scientific instruments, who described his own "Improvements in the Construction of Ship and Boat Compasses." Models of new inventions were displayed, one by C. M. Warren, later a professor in the Institute, whose name is perpetuated in the C. M. Warren Fund of the American Academy of Arts and Sciences.

Meetings of the Society were held thereafter bimonthly, and provided an excellent means of gratifying Rogers' intense interest in publicizing advances in science, invention, and industry through the medium of the popular lecture. From 1864 to 1866 meetings were held in the new Institute's rooms in the Mercantile Library Association Building on Summer Street, and then for many years after the new building on Boylston Street was opened, the Society used one of the larger rooms on the first floor. In 1869 in order to clarify the legal confusion between membership in the Society of Arts and membership in the Institute of Technology, it was found necessary to secure an "Act in Addition to the Several Acts Incorporating the Massachusetts Institute of Technology," which made the Society a distinct organization subsidiary to the Institute, with its own officers, constitution, and bylaws. The same act changed the name of the Institute's governing body from "Government" to "Corporation." The Society had several hundred members and occasionally published its membership rolls in the Institute's catalogue. It maintained a report of its proceedings, which in 1890 was combined with the *Technology Quarterly*, a journal begun by undergraduates in 1888. Membership in the Society of Arts gradually dwindled as specialized scientific organizations increased in number and importance, and since 1917 its only activity has been an annual series of distinctive popular scientific lectures given by members of the faculty especially for students in secondary schools but open to the public.

The Museum of Practical Arts was never established as originally intended, but some of the "instruments and products of the practical arts and sciences" accumulated by Rogers and his followers still survive in scattered exhibits in the M. I. T. corridors, and are controlled by a committee on the Technology Museum.

Just before the first meeting of the Society of Arts in 1862, the 37th Congress passed the Morrill Act providing grants of public lands to the states to "provide Colleges for the benefit of Agriculture and the Mechanic Arts." The act in reality provided funds derived from the sale of western lands rather than donated the actual lands. On December 22, 1862, Governor Andrew brought this act to President Rogers' attention by letter, requesting comments, and suggesting the possibility that the Massachusetts portion of the money might be used for a comprehensive union of all the educational organizations and facilities of the Boston area, or of the state, including the new Institute. As evidence of the Governor's confidence in President Rogers' judgment, the letter contained these significant sentences: "You have gifts of divination in such matters, which I, not

A Great Plan Becomes a Reality

an academician, have not. . . . . . I wish I might have the instruction which I should derive from your reflections and views before writing my address to the Legislature. It meets the first Wednesday in January".

In another letter a week later the Governor requested a report regarding the Institute, so that he could say a good word for it in his annual message to the legislature. To this second letter President Rogers responded with a clear report of what had been accomplished and of the future plans for the Institute, but made no reference to the suggestion in the first letter regarding the combination of all higher educational facilities in one organization.

The Governor's message to the legislature proposed a rather grandiose plan for a union to include "The Bussey Farm and fund, the land grant of the United States, the Institute of Technology, the College at Cambridge, its Scientific School, Museum, Observatory, etc., etc." together with the proposed Agricultural College to be established under the Morrill Act. Naturally enough, Harvard, by virtue of its age, its national reputation, and its abundant resources, would thus become the dominant and controlling unit in this comprehensive program.

A strong but futile effort was made in behalf of this plan in the hearing before the Legislative Committee to which this portion of the message and the whole matter of the land grant had been referred. Arguments presented by President Rogers and other opponents so impressed the committee that it rejected the Governor's plan. It was made clear that from its inception the Institute was determined to stand alone; that its independence was necessary to its success; and that it would accept no grant to interfere with its independence. Governor Andrew yielded in good grace and with respect for Rogers' position.

The special committee recommended that the Massachusetts portion of the fund be divided as follows: "One-tenth of the expected income to be used for purchase of lands for an Agricultural College, and three-tenths to be paid to the Institute as a College of Mechanic Arts. Thus came about the establishment of the Massachusetts Agricultural College at Amherst, later to be known as the Massachusetts State College, and since 1947 as the University of Massachusetts.

Eventually the remaining six-tenths of the fund was also given to the Agricultural College. The report of the special committe giving three-tenths of these funds to the Institute was a powerful aid in the long struggle to fulfill the conditions regarding the guaranty fund, which still had not been completed when the second year was nearing its end.

On March 7, 1863, the Finance Committee of the Institute's Government consisting of Messrs. M. D. Ross, J. M. Beebe, E. S. Tobey, and N. H. Eldridge, issued an earnest appeal for contributions. At the end of the month, however, less than $40,000 had been pledged, and it was feared that it might be necessary to petition the General Court for a second extension of time. At this crucial moment friends showed their loyalty to Rogers and to the struggling institution. Generous gifts came from Nathaniel Thayer and Henry B. Rogers (a close friend but not the brother of the president), and on the very last day of the year of grace a letter to the president announced a gift of $60,000 from Dr. William J. Walker that completed the guaranty fund. The land on Boylston Street was assured.

Dr. Walker should be ever held in grateful memory as the first of the Institute's large benefactors. A reproduction of a part of the document bestowing this first large gift, written by Dr. Walker's own hand, is among the illustrations. By his will a few years later, he generously bequeathed another and much larger sum to the Institute, and his name is perpetuated in the Walker Professorship of Mathematics.

The relief and pleasure of President Rogers may well be imagined. In compliance with a vote of the members of the Institute, Rogers in a letter to the benefactor happily expressed the Institute's thanks and sketched its future plans. He reported the favorable action of the legislature, stating that two bills had been passed, one creating an independent Agricultural College, and the other providing, in view of the land grant to the Institute, that the Governor, the Chief Justice of the Supreme Judicial Court, and the Secretary of the Board of Education of the Commonwealth should be members *ex-officio* of the Government. He closed the letter with these words: "We are now busy planning our building for the School of Industrial Science, and thanks to your munificence, we hope soon to see its foundations laid."

Thus, before the middle of 1863, Rogers was occupied with work on the plans for the building to be erected on the Back Bay land. His brother Henry had kindly sent drawings of the Industrial Institution in Edinburgh, as a possible source of suggestions for the arrangement of the building. Obviously construction would be a slow process, but when President Rogers, in December 1863, reported on the Institute for the annual message of the ever-friendly Governor Andrew, he stated that a building 150 feet long and 100 feet wide had been begun, centrally located on the Boylston Street area next to the new building which the Society of Natural History had completed in 1863.

Before the end of the year, the financial status of the Institute seemed to warrant detailed planning for the courses of instruction in the School of Industrial Science. With the aid of John D. Runkle and Dr. William Watson, who were selected as the first professors, programs of instruction were planned in the fields of applied mathematics, physics, chemistry, and engineering.

The year 1863 was a notable one from many viewpoints. The Institute's charter was assured, and plans for the building and the curriculum of the school were well under way. The progress of the Union cause was so encouraging that President Lincoln had appointed a special day for Thanksgiving in August. The Fourth of July celebration in Boston there included the first great demonstration of the electric carbon light, arranged by the celebrated inventor, E. S. Ritchie, which from the State House dome brilliantly illuminated a large area of the Common, and was enjoyed by a vast crowd assembled there. With his usual interest in such scientific developments, President Rogers made some approximate photometric measurements of the carbon light and estimated it at 12,000 candle power.

Owing to poor health, Rogers resigned his position as State Inspector of Gas Meters and Gas in 1864. On the suggestion of the president of the Boston Gas Company to the Governor, President Rogers was given a furlough to visit Great Britain and the Continent to investigate the state of the art there for the benefit of the Commonwealth.

So came about an absence of six months and opportunity to gain new and helpful experience as well as to renew old friendships.

Although the primary object in undertaking this journey was to recover his health, President Rogers wrote to his brother Henry: "The two matters, which I shall especially desire to look into, when abroad, are (1) the best means of collecting a large suite of models of elements of machinery, of bridges, roofs, arches and other works of civil construction and architecture, to be used as aids in our School of Practical Science, and (2) to examine the recent and best arrangements for working-laboratories and lecture-rooms. Our building will probably be roofed in by next winter, but the arrangement and fitting up of the interior, I shall keep for a later time, when it may be done with a full knowledge of all that is needful to provide for our objects."

Before his departure, a meeting of the Government of the Institute was held on May 30, 1864. At this meeting the detailed "plan for the various branches of teaching, etc.", was presented and adopted, under the title *"Scope and Plan of the School of Industrial Science of the Massachusetts Institute of Technology."* During the absence of President Rogers this plan was published and distributed by Thomas H. Webb, the secretary. When a copy was sent to Dr. Walker it elicited a hearty response and an intimation of his desire to share further in the development of the buildings of the Institute. Other friends were also active for the school during the president's absence. The Corporation had voted the sum of two hundred and fifty pounds toward his expenses, but with characteristic spirit he had sent back the bill of exchange to be credited to the funds of the Institute.

Another detail of the preparations for the opening of the Institute was the choice of an official seal. A committee of which Rogers was a member had studied the problem before his departure for Europe, and during his absence a tentative design was approved by other members of the committee. Records of the Executive Committee show the following entry:

Dec. 26, 1864.
    Voted, To adopt the design recommended by the Committee.
    Voted, That the Seal Committee be authorized and cause the seal to

A Great Plan Becomes a Reality 43

be engraved, and empowered, in their progress of the work, to make such modifications as may be deemed advisable or found necessary.

The four months spent in England and France did much to bring recuperation. President Rogers' letters indicated that the period was a succession of visits in the homes of important people and meetings with men distinguished in science, politics, and the arts, interspersed with visits to gain suggestions for the projected Industrial Museum of Technology. His letters to his father-in-law also showed him in the relaxed and pleasant humor that came with rest and improved health. In one letter from a suburb of Glasgow he wrote: "You would be amused by some of the tavern signs in this region. A little tippling-shop, half way between this and Glasgow, in the village bearing the name of Strathbungo, is adorned by a portrait of *Burns* and a *barrel*, with this inscription:—

> When neebors anger at a plea,
> An get as wull as wull can be,
> How easy can the barley bree
> Cement the quarrel.
> 'T is far the cheepest lawyer's fee
> To taste the barrel."

President Rogers returned to the United States in time to participate in the stirring events surrounding the re-election of Abraham Lincoln, and to arrange the winter program for Institute affairs. On December 1, 1864, the Society of Arts held its first meeting of the year in the Mercantile Library Association Building, which was extensively, even enthusiastically, reported by the Boston papers. The president gave an account of his observations at the scientific schools visited in Europe. He had carefully studied museums in London, Edinburgh, Paris, and Carlsruhe, and concluded that the Polytechnic Institute at Carlsruhe came closer to his plans for M. I. T. than any other foreign institution. At this meeting announcement was made that "The Institute proposes to receive pupils for instruction the present winter. Its friends will have an opportunity of securing for it a munificent donation of $50,000 by subscribing a similar amount before the 1st of January next."

In early January, 1865, an announcement of the "Preliminary

Course of Instruction in the School of Industrial Science of the Massachusetts Institute of Technology" was made public. It read in part as follows:

> The building intended for the use of the School of Industrial Science, now in process of erection, will, it is expected, be in readiness for occupation next winter, when the various departments of the School will be permanently organized, and put in operation.
>
> In the mean time, to facilitate the progress of students who may wish to qualify themselves more completely for entering on the regular courses of study and practice, and to save the time of others more proficient in elementary studies, who may desire to enter, in advance, the second year's course, it is proposed to open some of the classes in February, in the rooms of the Institute, on Summer Street. . . .
>
> The classes proposed to be opened at this time are as follows:
> *Elementary Mathematics, with Practice in the*
>   *Use of the Chain, Level, etc.;*
> *Elementary Physics;*
> *Elementary Chemistry, with Manipulations;*
> *Drawing;*
> *The French Language.*
>
> This preliminary course will cover a period of four months, commencing, it is expected, about the middle of February. The precise date of its commencement, as well as the programme of instruction in the several classes, will be made known as soon as their organization has been determined on.
>
> WILLIAM B. ROGERS
> *President, Massachusetts Institute of Technology*
> By order of the Committee on Instruction of the Institute

The building on Boylston Street was still far from completion, but the realization of the visions, the struggles, and the conquering ambition and spirit of Rogers could not now be far away.

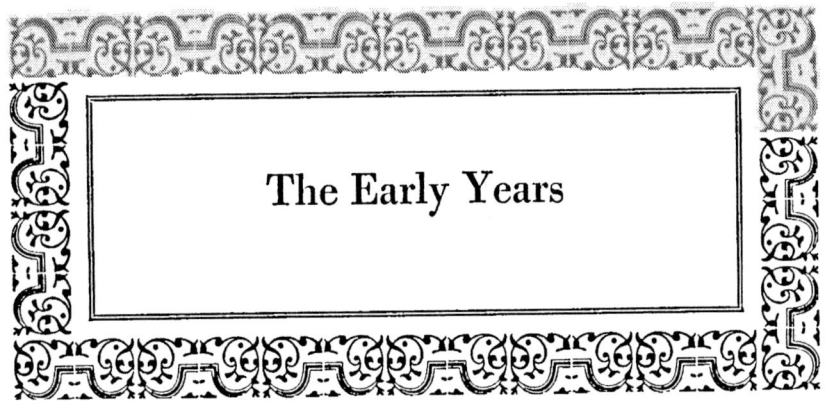

The Early Years

ON THE OPENING DAY of the School, Monday, February 20, 1865, President Rogers made this entry in his diary: *"Organized the School! Fifteen students entered. May not this prove a memorable day!"* The following day he wrote: "At the Institute at 9 A.M. Watson and Runkle met their classes. My first lecture at twelve. Very attentive class." The Institute was launched![9]

On the morning of the second day of the session the following newspaper notice appeared:

School of Industrial Science. The preliminary course of the School of Industrial Science was opened yesterday in the hall of the Society of Arts of the Institute of Technology, by a brief address from Professor Rogers, explaining to the students and their friends the methods of instruction to be pursued in the several classes, pointing out the few simple rules to which the students were expected to conform, and setting before them the value and dignity of the practical professions for which they aimed to prepare themselves. Professor Rogers will have the general supervision of the course, besides taking charge of the department of Physics. The other branches will be given as follows: Mathematics by J. D. Runkle, Civil Construction by William Watson, Chemistry by Francis H. Storer, French by Ferdinand Bôcher, Free-hand Drawing by W. T. Carlton.

The admission requirements for the regular session of 1865-66 had already been fixed and consisted of arithmetic, algebra, plane geometry, English grammar, geography, and the rudiments of French. The program of the preliminary session was planned to meet the needs of boys who had not fully completed these requirements, and also to make it possible for those who had more training to prepare themselves for the work of the second year when the regular session opened in the autumn. It was therefore "a mixed up lot" that attended the preliminary four months' course.

The first applicant for admission to the preliminary session was Eli Forbes of Clinton, and he was soon followed by six other youths, Abraham Bailey, Sam Eastwood, Eben S. Stevens, Joseph Stone, Bryant P. Tilden, and Robert H. Richards. Fifteen were present on the opening day, and the total enrollment reached twenty-three. Of these, eleven completed the entrance requirements for the first year, and ten were able to enter on second-year work in the fall. Six of these continued throughout the upper years and graduated in the first class in 1868. Each year a few men entered with advanced standing, so that the first class to graduate numbered thirteen. Only two of the original group did not return to the school to carry on with the programs they had begun.

Those familiar with M. I. T. of the twentieth century may find it difficult to visualize this little group of students, varying in their previous schooling, assembled in a single room in the downtown Mercantile Library Building. It may be equally hard to see in this simple list of elementary subjects the forbears of the hundreds of subjects which in these days of the 1950's make up the many professional courses, and the long list of other specialized subjects available to the interested student.

The teaching staff for the preliminary session numbered six besides President Rogers, some of whom were to have long and distinguished careers at Technology.

John D. Runkle, the first professor of mathematics, served the Institute as head of the mathematics department until his death in 1902, and as Acting President and President between 1868 and 1878. When the school opened, he was a man of forty-three, who had made his own way from youth. Born on a farm in Root, New York, in 1822, he had attended the district school during the winters, and at sixteen was first introduced to mathematics higher than arithmetic. In the following nine years he mastered the higher branches of mathematics, largely by individual study while working on a farm in the summer and teaching in a district school in the winter. At the age of twenty-five he entered the new Lawrence Scientific School at Cambridge, and graduated with the first class in 1851 with an S.B. degree. Because of his interest in astronomy he was associated with the *American Ephemeris and Nautical Almanac* until 1884. From 1858 to 1861 he was busy building up the *Mathematical Monthly*.

When the filling in of the Back Bay was begun, Runkle with other men, including Mr. M. D. Ross, proposed that an educational institution be located in this new part of the city. When Rogers came to Boston, he soon became the leading promoter of this plan, as we have seen. Runkle was closely associated with Rogers from the beginning, and was as devoted and loyal to him as a son. He had been Secretary of the Committee of Twenty, and it was his pleasant duty to notify Rogers officially of his election as President of the Institute. Rogers deeply appreciated and trusted this able man nearly twenty years his junior, and later picked him as his successor to the presidency. For nearly forty years Technology students knew him as an excellent and kindly teacher, and called him affectionately "Uncle Johnny."

Dr. William Watson, the first professor of mechanical engineering, was a Nantucketer born in 1834. He graduated from Harvard College in 1857 and remained as an instructor in mathematics. After a period of study at the École des Ponts et Chaussées in Paris, he returned to Boston and lectured at Harvard. He was a man of small stature, with a full blond beard and a vigorous personality. He was especially well equipped to share in the work of starting the Institute's program of instruction, and became notable as the first in America to introduce modeling of structural forms in plaster for experimental purposes.

The original instructing staff also included Francis H. Storer in general chemistry, who later was author with Charles W. Eliot of the *Manual of Inorganic Chemistry* widely used throughout the country;

and Ferdinand Bôcher, who became the author of a widely used French grammar. The name of W. T. Carlton, the one remaining instructor, who taught free-hand drawing both here and in the Lowell Institute course, does not appear in any later list of the instructing staff.

Among the students of the small group who began their Institute life in the crowded rooms at the Mercantile Library were some whose names are of special interest. Here we find Eli Forbes, Joseph Stone, Eben Stevens, and Bryant Tilden, all of whom became well known in industry; E. H. Blashfield, the distinguished mural artist; John M. Forbes of the famous shipping family; Joseph W. Revere, grandson of Paul Revere; Samuel Cabot, Jr., whose father had been one of the early supporters of Rogers, and whose brother Godfrey '81, is now the oldest active life member of the Corporation; and Robert H. Richards, the first alumnus to become a teacher at the Institute.

Richards returned to the Institute immediately after graduation in 1868. In two years he became an assistant professor, and a year later was made professor in charge of the department of mining and metallurgy. He was for a time secretary of the faculty, was one of the founders and the first president of the Alumni Association, and served the Institute with distinction for nearly fifty years. He became world-renowned for his knowledge of mining engineering, and especially for his great work on ore dressing. Retiring as professor emeritus in 1914 he lived for thirty years more and died in 1945 at the age of more than 100 years. His autobiography, *Robert H. Richards, His Mark*, contains a most interesting account of those first days of the school and of the struggling early years which followed. Our knowledge of the days at the Mercantile Library depends largely on his reminiscences.

It cannot be assumed that this first group of eager students, although enthusiastic over this new type of education, were paragons of seriousness, or less fun-loving than the students of today. Richards' memoirs show that the students quickly sized up the staff and were not slow to take pleasure in emphasizing their foibles. Rogers was reputed to be so kind and gentle that when a student was referred to him for a rebuke, he would only greet him kindly, and ask him how his mother was. He was also clever in diverting the attention of an unruly boy to some interesting bit of equipment such as a gyroscope. Runkle, although an insistent teacher, was liked for his kindliness, understanding, and sense of humor. Richards tells the following story:

> One day Runkle was sitting on the edge of his lecture table, swinging his pointer up and down. The suggestion of a picture was too strong for Blashfield, the artist of the class. He made a sketch representing Runkle fishing diligently beside a pond with a problem in calculus for bait. Bowditch had just taken a look at the bait and rejected it in disdain. Tryon had come up and was ready to swallow it. The picture, with the faces all startlingly true to life, was passed around the class and received with flattering enthusiasm. Suddenly, Runkle reached for it, and after studying it carefully he returned it with a smile. "Pretty good," he said. This kindly attitude won the boys for the rest of the time.

Storer was appreciated because he made chemistry real and interesting, and Bôcher because he had personality and by bearing and precept taught the ethics of a gentleman. On the other hand, Watson was not especially liked and was the butt of numerous pranks such as enticing an organ grinder into his classroom, gluing his pet eraser to the top of his desk, and letting wet umbrellas drip into his upturned silk hat.

Final examinations in the preliminary course were held in June, 1865. Now that he had actually made a beginning in the School of Industrial Science, Rogers' energies were especially devoted to the consummation of plans for the regular session which he hoped might begin in the autumn in the new but unfinished building on Boylston Street—the building nostalgically known to many generations of Technology men after 1883 as the Rogers Building. Despite summer heat and impaired strength Rogers was busy in revising the architect's plans and supervising the completion of the new building and in securing additional members of the staff. New professorships were desired in architecture, civil engineering, mining engineering, analytical chemistry and metallurgy, and in English language and literature.

The appointment to the new chair of analytical chemistry and metallurgy was offered to Charles W. Eliot, who was well known to

President and Mrs. Rogers. A member of a distinguished Boston family, he had graduated from Harvard in 1853, and remained as a tutor and assistant professor of mathematics and chemistry until 1863. In 1865 he was completing extended study in Europe. Rogers wrote to him at Vienna stating that the bequest of Dr. Walker would bring to the Institute during the late summer approximately $160,000 from which a portion would make possible the establishment of modest chemical laboratories and a salary of $2,000. In a favorable but indefinite reply, Eliot asked for further particulars regarding the new Institute that had come into being while he was in Europe. A long letter giving detailed information was sent to him, and he replied from Paris, July 31, 1865, accepting the position. Thus, the man who was later a distinguished president of Harvard University became the first professor of analytical chemistry and metallurgy at M. I. T., and remained until 1869, when he was elected to the Harvard post. At Technology he was directly associated with Professor Storer, professor of general and industrial chemistry.

Another appointment was that of William R. Ware, a practicing architect in Boston, who had carefully discussed with President Rogers the details of architectural education. He became the first professor of architecture, and remained at the Institute until 1881, when he became head of the department at Columbia University. Three other new professors were secured to complete the staff before the school opened in the autumn.

During the summer, announcement was made that the first regular session of the School of Industrial Science would open on Monday, October 2, 1865, for the full college year of eight months. The announcement stated the scholastic requirements for admission. There were to be no formal examinations for entrance to the first year, and after a month's trial the students were to be divided into an upper and a lower group. The tuition fee was set at one hundred dollars for the year, half payable at entrance, and half in February. Properly prepared special students were to be admitted. Dates were set for conferences with instructors in the rooms at the Mercantile Library Building.

The staff roster was as follows: President, William B. Rogers, LL.D., Principal; John D. Runkle, A.M., Professor of Mathematics

The Early Years

and Analytical Mechanics; William B. Rogers, LL.D., Professor of Physics and Geology; Frank H. Storer, S.B., Professor of General and Industrial Chemistry; Charles W. Eliot, A.M., Professor of Analytical Chemistry and Metallurgy; William P. Atkinson, A.M., Professor of English Language and Literature; Ferdinand Bôcher, Professor of Modern Languages; John B. Henck, A.M., Professor of Civil and Topographical Engineering; William Watson, Ph.D., Professor of Descriptive Geometry and Mechanical Engineering; William R. Ware, S.B., Professor of Architecture; James D. Hague, Professor of Mining Engineering.

The Boylston Street building was not ready for occupancy when the Institute opened in October, and the school, now numbering seventy, had to continue in the crowded rooms at the Mercantile Library Building, and in a few rooms which it was possible to secure in Chauncy Street nearby. Weeks became months, and it was mid-February, 1866, before even one lecture room and a laboratory were in use in the new building, and the school year had ended before a complete transfer could be made.

The first catalogue, printed at the end of 1865, announced that the aims of the "School of the Institute of Technology" were:

First, To provide a full course of scientific studies and practical exercises for students seeking to qualify themselves for the professions of the Mechanical Engineer, Civil Engineer, Practical Chemist, Engineer of Mines, and Builder and Architect.

Second, To furnish such a general education, founded upon the Mathematical, Physical, and Natural Sciences, English and other Modern Languages, and Mental and Political Science, as shall form a fitting preparation for any of the departments of active life; and,—

Third, To provide courses of Evening Instruction in the main branches of knowledge above referred to, for persons of either sex who are prevented, by occupation or other causes, from devoting themselves to scientific study during the day, but who desire to avail themselves of systematic evening lessons or lectures.

The first two years of the curriculum, which the catalogue describes in detail, were the same for all students. In the third and fourth years six professional courses were offered: Mechanical Engineering, Civil and Topographical Engineering, Practical Chemistry,

Geology and Mining, Building and Architecture, and General Science and Literature.

The presence of the sixth course, designed to "furnish such a general education . . . as shall form a fitting preparation for any of the departments of active life," shows that from the beginning the Institute intended to do more than offer specific professional training; it hoped to provide an alternative road to a general education for students not well suited to the traditional liberal arts college. This course never attracted many students, but there were always a few.

In addition to the regular students the school welcomed as special students young men who could attend only for a single year or even a single term primarily to get instruction in some limited field in which interest, aptitude, or previous occupation had brought the ambition to increase their knowledge and prepare themselves for better positions. In the early days of Technology these "specials," as they were called, made up a considerable part of the student body.

As a part of its service to the community the Institute from the first planned to offer evening courses for those who could not afford a full-time education. These were never a part of the regular curriculum, but they were meant to be serious education and not entertainment. "As it is the object of this branch of the school to provide substantial teaching, rather than merely popular illustration of the subjects," the catalogue warned, "it is expected that all persons attending these courses will come with a serious purpose of improvement. . . ." These evening courses as described were never offered by the school, but by a very happy arrangement the Lowell Institute undertook a similar program of evening education. In October, 1865, John Amory Lowell wrote to Rogers:

> I propose to institute evening courses of instruction to be opened gratuitously to the public under such regulations as may be deemed advisable.
>
> It has occurred to me that these courses might with advantage be delivered, in the first instance, under the supervision of the Massachusetts Institute of Technology and by their professors, the programme of course to be acceptable to me. . . .

If such an arrangement would be acceptable to the government I shall be happy to confer with you on the subject.

The evening school began the first year on Summer Street, and was immediately successful. Each year half a dozen courses of lectures or "lessons," open to both sexes, on scientific and literary subjects varied from year to year, were presented by members of the Technology staff, including the most distinguished ones such as Runkle and Eliot. "A course of thirty practical lessons in Chemical Manipulation, by Professors Storer and Eliot" was one of the most famous ones in the early days. The Lowell Institute project was a very important support to the faculty, and the annual payment of $3,000 for the use of Technology's class rooms was a very welcome addition to its income. With a number of changes in policy and organization, these free evening courses have continued to this day.

The *Scope and Plan* made no reference to the training of women, but in 1867 several young ladies who had attended Professor Eliot's evening course in chemical manipulation raised the issue of coeducation at the Institute. On January 30, 1867, one of them requested permission to attend the regular courses, addressing Edward Atkinson, who from the beginning had been one of the Committee on Instruction of the Institute. Her letter was sent to the president on February 1 with this query: "Can there be any objection to ladies entering as special students except possibly want of room in the laboratory?" Two other women made a similar request to Nathaniel Thayer, also a member of the Committee on Instruction. The matter came before the committee, and as a result the president announced that a plan for special instruction in afternoon and evening courses for students who could not attend day classes was projected, but could not at once be put into effect, and further stated that when it was organized the faculty would gladly welcome both men and women as students. The first mention of such courses occurs in the catalogue for 1869-70, and subjects for that year are announced. It seems, however, that the "lessons" given by Technology professors under the Lowell Institute aegis met the immediate needs.

The opening of Technology's doors to women students had an early effect. The first woman admitted was Ellen H. Swallow, a

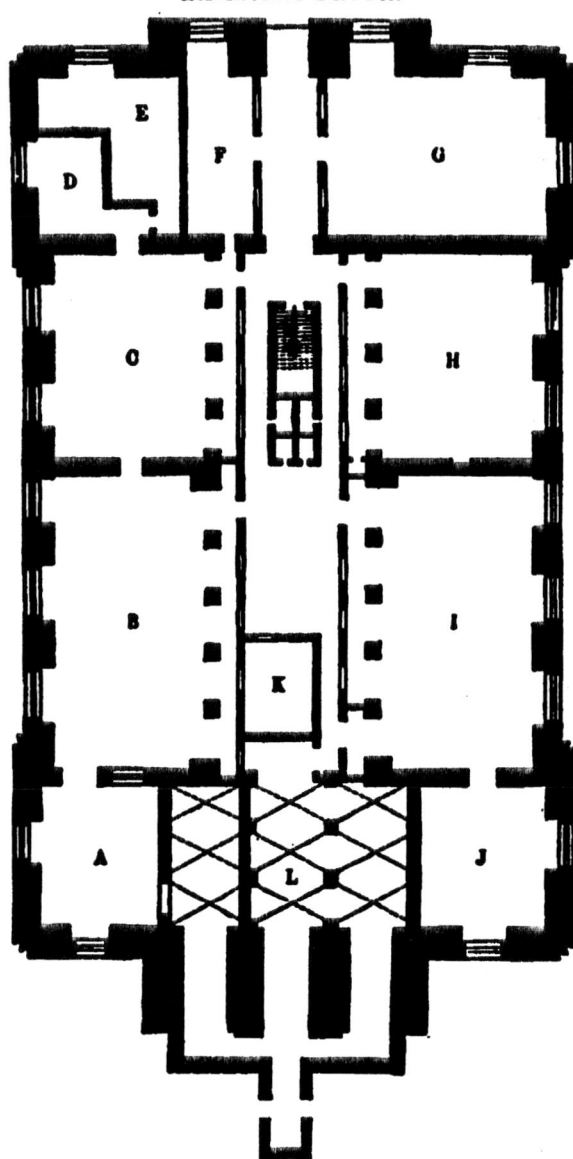

A. Professors' Chemical Laboratory, 25′ 0″ by 22′ 11″.
B. General and Qualitative Chemical Laboratory, 49′ 7″ by 34′ 0″.
C. Quantitative Chemical Laboratory, 35′ 8″ by 34′ 0″.
D. Balance Room, 18′ 0″ by 12′ 0″.
E. Mineralogical and Blowpipe Laboratory, 27′ 8″ by 25′ 5″.
F. Chemical Store Room, 34′ 0″ by 13′ 0″.
G. Work Shop, 40′ 2″ by 27′ 10″.
H. Metallurgical Laboratory, 35′ 8″ by 24′ 0″.
I. Chemical Lecture Room, 49′ 7″ by 34′ 0″.
J. Chemical Lecture Room Laboratory, 25′ 0″ by 22′ 11″.
K. Daily Chemical Supply Room, 14′ 0″ by 12′ 0″.
L. Engine and Boiler Room, 42′ 2″ by 25′ 0″.

From the 1870-71 catalogue, basement plan of the Rogers Building on Boylston Street graduate of Vassar, who became a special student in chemistry during the two academic years 1871 to 1873. Having completed all the requirements for the Institute's S.B. degree, she became in 1873 the first woman graduate. She was a "resident graduate" student in 1873-74, became an assistant to Professors Nichols and Ordway, and soon after married Professor Richards. As will later be noted, she was an important factor in the establishment and operation of the special Women's Laboratory of which mention is made on page 99.

The new building was ready to be occupied in the fall of 1866, a full year later than expected, and the postwar inflation made its cost double the original estimate of $157,000. It had been more than three years since the preparation of plans had been authorized on August 25, 1863, and Jonathan and William G. Preston, a well-known firm that had also designed the building of the Museum of Natural History in the same city block, had been engaged to proceed with its design. The building was an imposing one, a notable example of classical architecture and well suited to the needs of the period. Seventy years later, Walter H. Killam '89, in his admirable book *Boston After Bulfinch* wrote of these buildings: "The harmony of these two buildings set a fine example of regularity in civic architecture which unfortunately was not generally followed." He called the Rogers Building "stately," and all who ever mounted the imposing granite steps and entered the spacious and dignified interior will agree.

President Rogers personally gave special attention to the interior arrangement of rooms to be used for instruction. A commodious basement provided for the work in chemistry and mining, and five floors above the basement housed all the other departments of the Institute. The accompanying floor plans and directory are reproduced from the catalogue for 1870-71. They give a good idea of the scope of the Institute's work in the early years, and will evoke many specific memories in the minds of a thousand alumni who still think of the Rogers Building as the heart of M. I. T. On the first floor the large main lobby, entered from the broad flight of steps, was a spacious room flanked on either side by the administrative offices. A pair of dignified columns on each side separated the front portion

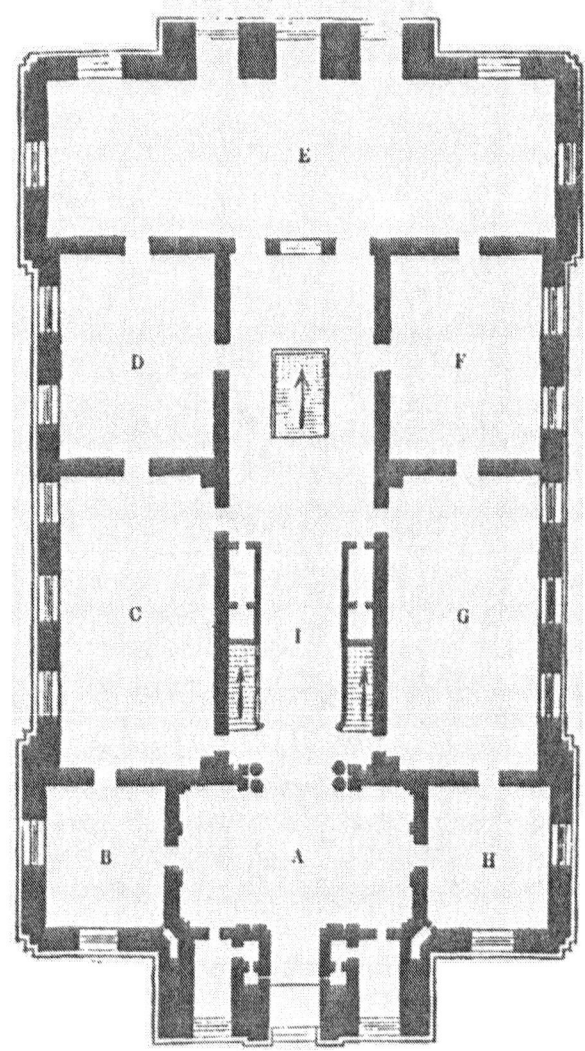

A. Entrance Hall, 42′ 2″ by 25′ 0″.
B. President's Office, 25′ 0″ by 22′ 11″.
C. Physical Lecture Room, 49′ 7″ by 28′ 3″.
D. Physical Laboratory and Apparatus Room, 35′ 8″ by 28′ 3″.
E. Physical Laboratory and Apparatus Room, 92′ 0″ by 27′ 10″.
F. Mining and Geological Lecture Room, 35′ 8″ by 28′ 3″.
G. Society of Arts Room, 49′ 7″ by 28′ 3″.
H. Secretary's Office, 25′ 0″ by 22′ 11″.
I. Stairway Hall, 87′ 3″ by 27′ 10″.

from the central area. Behind these columns broad stairways on each side led up to a wide corridor extending across the building. At each end of this passage were entrances into the great hall, later named Huntington Hall in honor of Ralph Huntington, a generous supporter of the Institute. This hall, extending upward through two high stories, had a large semi-circular platform reached by several steps at each end. From the general floor level there extended backward a sloping floor with fairly comfortable seats arranged in concentric arcs and seating several hundred people.

Huntington Hall was for many years the most dignified and capacious auditorium in the newer residential portion of the city, and it was used for many public purposes as well as for the instruction of Boston Tech students. The great public lectures of the Lowell Institute were held here for two generations, and many men of world-wide reputation spoke from its desk. It is not generally known that for nearly five years while Trinity Church was being built, the Sunday services of that parish were held here, and Phillips Brooks preached regularly from the platform. Bishop Lawrence, writing in the *Church Militant* in 1939, recalls that the barrenness of the hall was relieved by a frieze some eight feet deep depicting the work of the scientist—a chemical laboratory, men standing at furnaces and retorts, a civil engineer with his transit, and others engaged in a variety of scientific and engineering pursuits. Quoting a writer who was apparently a communicant, he says:

> At them [the drawings] we gazed while the anthem was being sung. The two entrances at the head of the staircase faced the congregation, causing every person entering the hall to be gazed at by the worshippers. Phillips Brooks' lectern, which he brought with him from Philadelphia, was taken out of a closet and put in place each Sunday and was the chief ecclesiastical furniture. The choir was a quartette. The slope of the lecture floor and the cramped chairs made kneeling impossible;—yet here, under these conditions and during these four years, Phillips Brooks preached some of his greatest sermons. . .

This frieze, painted about 1870, which had attracted the wandering eyes of thousands of students as well as worshipers, was obliterated when the hall was redecorated in 1898. Later several panels were restored and presented to the Institute by the Class of 1909.

SECOND STORY FLOOR.

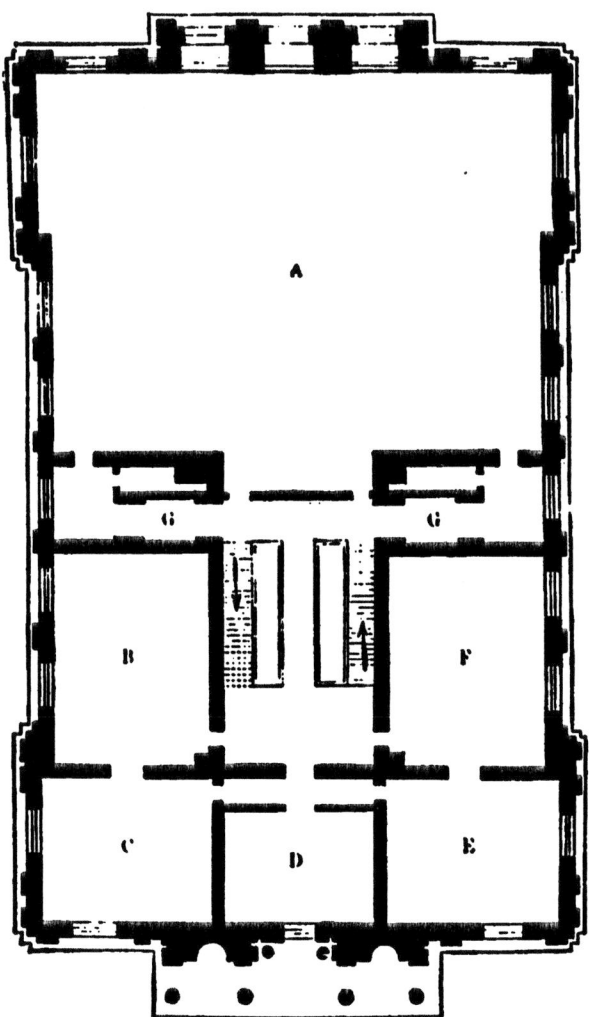

A. Great Lecture Hall, 92' 0" by 65' 5".
B. Mathematical Lecture Room, 34' 9" by 28' 3".
C. Civil Engineering Lecture Room, 32' 2" by 25' 0".
D. Modern Language Lecture Room, 26' 2" by 20' 6".
E. English Lecture Room, 32' 2" by 25' 0".
F. Mathematical and Astronomical Lecture Room, 31' 9" by 28' 3".
G. G. Passage ways to the Great Hall.

At the graduation exercises of the Class of 1883, President Walker announced that the Corporation had voted that the building which William Barton Rogers had planned as the central home and shrine of the Massachusetts Institute of Technology should then and in perpetuity have as its official name THE ROGERS BUILDING. But this building, originally expected to contain all the Institute's activities, had even then been outgrown, and in the following twenty-five years the Institute built or acquired nearly a dozen other buildings in the Copley Square region. After the Institute moved to Cambridge in 1916, the Rogers building was retained and used until 1938. Like the man for whom it was named, it is now only a glorious memory, still dear to the hearts of generations of men who in their youth spent countless hours in its halls of learning.

In addition to his teaching and the other demands on his time President Rogers now had to spend time and strength trying to raise money to meet the deficit on the new building. While he was thus engaged a great blow fell upon him. His brother Henry, who but a month before had been in America on a visit, was stricken with a severe illness while on his return voyage to Scotland in April, 1866, and rapidly became worse. On receiving the news of Henry's dangerous illness in early June, President Rogers and his brother Robert sailed at once for Queenstown, only to be told on their arrival there that Henry had died three days before they had left New York. After a brief stay in Glasgow, the brothers returned to New York, arriving on July 26. Hardly had President Rogers reached Boston when he received news that Dr. Thomas H. Webb, secretary of the Institute, had died suddenly of heart disease. Worn out by his efforts, the weariness of travel, and the deep sorrow caused by these deaths, Rogers went at once to the Savage summer home at Lunenburg, Massachusetts, where he fell ill of a slow and prostrating fever which lasted for many weeks.

It was October before President Rogers was able to return to Boston. Meantime, Professors Runkle and Atkinson had carried on Institute affairs. The school had opened in October, 1866, with increased enrollment, but the financial situation was serious. A letter from Professor Atkinson written in September stated, "I presented

HALF STORY FLOOR.

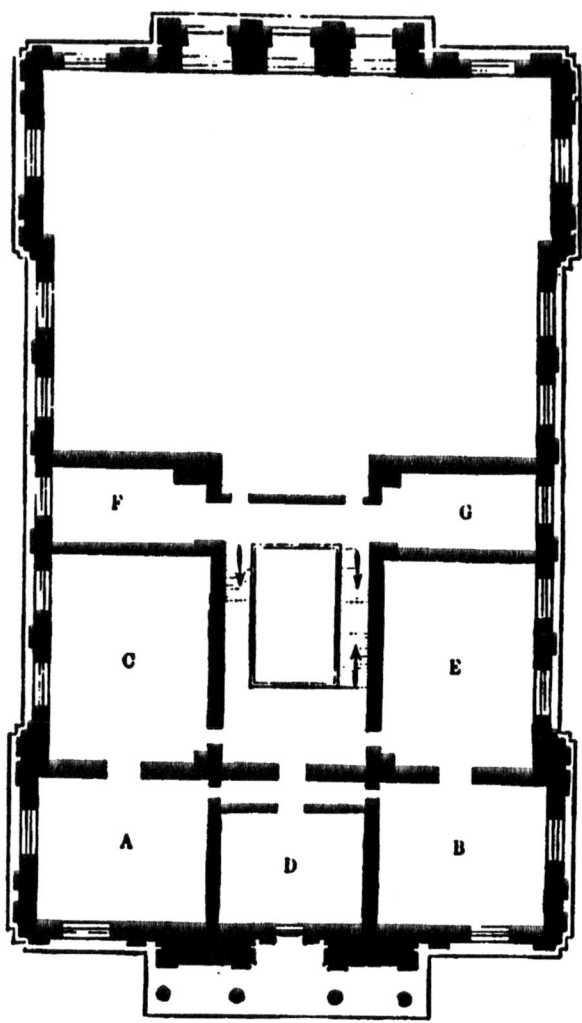

A. Architectural Museum, 32' 2" by 25' 0".
C. Architectural Museum, 34' 9" by 28' 3".
E. Natural History Museum and Lecture Room, 34' 9" by 28' 3".
B. Architectural Library and Study Room, 32' 2" by 25' 0".
D. Plaster Modelling Room, 26' 2' by 20' 6".
F. Prof. Atkinson's Study, 28' 3" by 14' 2".
G. Prof. Osborne's Study, 28' 3" by 14' 2".

THE EARLY YEARS

the bills for our salaries yesterday, but found no funds. Mr. Endicott wanted me to get in the students' fees, but said he would give me his own check if they were not forthcoming fast enough." This was not the only occasion in Institute history when a devoted and loyal treasurer pledged his own resources to meet expenses.

On request of the Committee on Instruction President Rogers prepared the following *Estimate of Annual Expenses of the School of the Institute for the session of 1866-67*:

Estimate of the annual Expense of the School of the Institute on the scale of organisation which will be necessary at the beginning of the Session of 1866-7.

SALARIES

Prof. of Mathematics & Anal. Mechanics	2500.
Prof. of Physics & Geology	2500.
Prof. of General & Indust. Chemistry	25.00
Prof. of Analytical Chemistry & Metallurgy	2500.
Prof. of Mechanical Engineering	2500.
Prof. of Civil Engineering	2500.
Prof. of Architecture & free-hand drawing	2500.
Prof. of Mining Engineering	2500.
Prof. of English Language & Lit.	2500.
Prof. of Modern Languages	2500.
Assistant Prof. of Math. & Intendant of the School	1500.
Assistant Prof. Geol. & Paleontology	
Assistant Prof. Physics	
Prof. Botany either may for the present be paid out of the salary of the	
Prof. of Physics & Geology	
	$26,500.00
Cost of Heating, Ventilating, Lighting, Water, &c.	4,000.
Janitor & other servants	1,200.
Catalogues & other printing for School	500.
Consumption & wear of chemls. & apparatus not charged to students	300.

THIRD STORY FLOOR

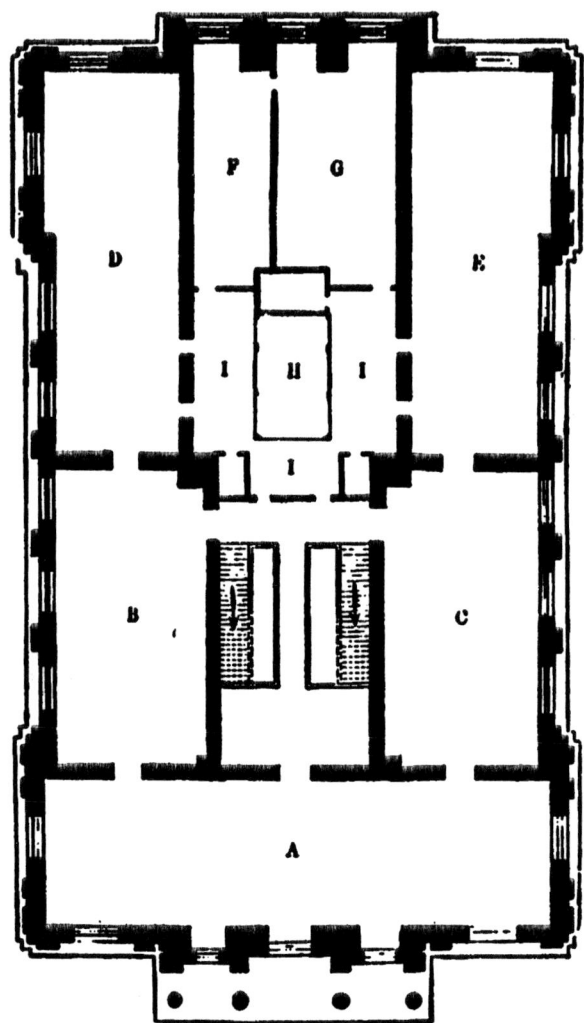

A. First Year's Drawing Room, 92' 0" by 25' 0".
B. Architects' Drawing Room, 49' 7" by 28' 3".
C. Third Year's Drawing Room, 49' 7" by 28' 3".
D. Fourth Year's Drawing Room, 65' 5" by 26' 0".
E. Second Year's Drawing Room, 65' 5" by 26' 0".
F. Mechanical Engineering Lecture Room, 37' 0" by 17' 0".
G. Mathematical and Descriptive Geometry Lecture Room, 37' 0" by 23' 0".
H. Model Room, 21' 0" by 13' 0".
I. I. I. Passage Ways.

Wear of furniture requiring repair . . . . 300.
                                                    ———
                                                    32,800.

Income appropriated to the School, or to be relied
on next Sept. 1st.

Fees of 80 students at 100 . . . . 8,000.
 "   " 80   "   " 125 . . . . 10,000.
From the Trustee of the Lowell fund . . . . 3,000.
From the Walker fund . . . . 10,000.
From Landscrip fund, at least . . . . 1,500.
                                                  ———
                                                  32,500

ESTIMATE OF COST OF APPARATUS OF INSTRUCTION

1. Physical app. & fittings—with a suite of large drawings for
   the lecture room.
      In general Mechanics, Hydrodynamics, Neumatics, Acoustics, Molecular Activity, Thermatics, Optics, Electricity.   15,000.
2. Cheml. fittings, apparatus & agents including [crossed out]
   of specimens for Ind. Chem. & Metallurgy and a collection
   of Diagrams & Models.   9,000.
3. Models of Machinery, with sets of large drawings. . . .   5,000.
4. Instruments for Topograph¹. surveying . . . .   1,000.
   Models & drawings of framing, masonry, &c. . . . . .   3,000.
5. Drawings & Models for Architecture & Building . . . .   3,000.
6. Models & drawings to illustrate Mining—Mining
   Machinery, &c. . . . .   3,000.
7. Minerals—fossils—Set of Models of Crystals—
   Geologic drawings & sections . . . .   6,000.

At this time money received from Lowell Institute was used to help in payment of salaries. Tuition was still $100 for first year students, but raised to $125 for those above first year. As a matter of fact, for this and the succeeding two years the salaries of the professors did not exceed $2,000.

During the crucial year of 1866, two honors came to President Rogers. Harvard University conferred on him the degree of LL.D. on July 18, 1866, *in absentia*. Also during his absence, Governor

FOURTH STORY FLOOR.

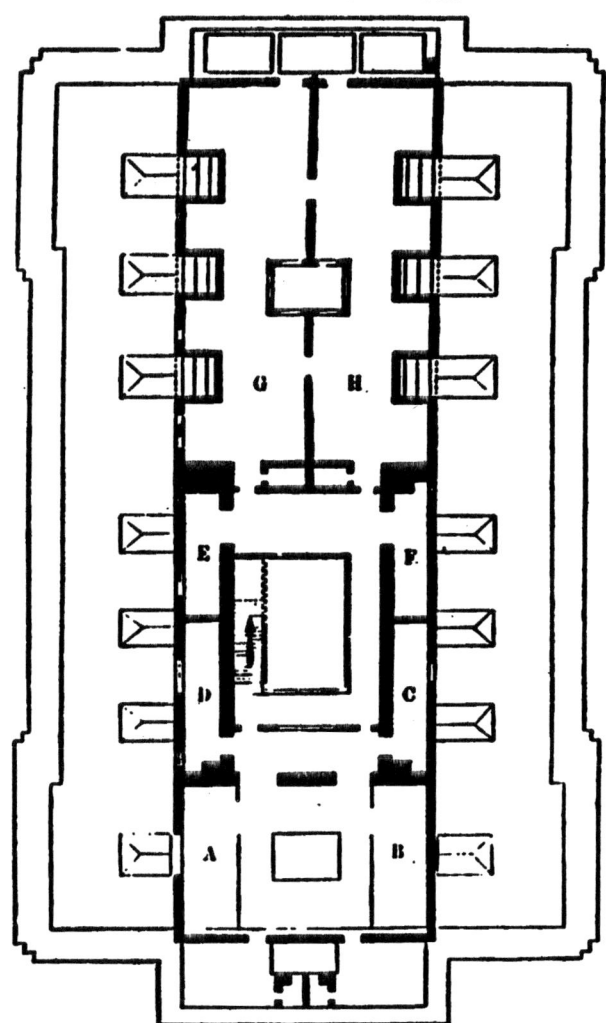

A. Prof. Watson's Study, 24' 5" by 11' 6".
B. Prof. Henck's Study, 24' 5" by 11' 6".
C. Prof. Runkle's Study, 24' 9" by 7' 6".
D. Prof. Ordway's Study, 24' 9" by 7' 6".
E. Assistants' Study, 24' 9" by 7' 6".
F. Prof. Rockwell's Study, 24' 9" by 7' 6".
G. Photographic Laboratory, 65' 5" by 21' 10".
H. Free Hand Drawing Room, 65' 5" by 21' 10".

Bullock appointed him as commissioner or chief representative of the Commonwealth to the Paris Exposition of 1867. When he was able to write to the Governor, Rogers declined the appointment and suggested the name of Charles L. Flint, secretary of the Board of Agriculture, a member of the Government and a staunch friend of the Institute. The Governor was insistent, and after much persuasion President Rogers accepted and at once began active preparations for a suitable exhibit from Massachusetts. He was undoubtedly much helped by Professors Eliot and Storer, and on June 4, 1867, with Mrs. Rogers and with these professors as assistants he sailed for Liverpool en route to the Exposition as Commissioner from Massachusetts.

Rogers' appointment to the Paris post enhanced the spreading reputation of the Institute. It also gave him a brief respite from the worries of raising money for the school. While he was in Paris he received a cheering letter from William Endicott, Jr., the treasurer, which told of subscriptions from ten friends of $5000 each, a total of $50,000, and also a gift of $25,000 from Nathaniel Thayer to endow a professorship of physics. Furthermore, Endicott implied that the new class entering in the fall would probably have one hundred members, so that the new year would open with good promise.

In the midst of his duties in Paris, President Rogers fell ill with pneumonia, but in the late autumn he was able to return to the Institute and resume his lectures in physics and geology. The growth of the school was most gratifying, 175 being enrolled during the year 1867-68. Aside from the chronic financial problem its prospects indeed seemed favorable. The reputation of the Institute had spread throughout the country and beyond the seas. Able men were added to the staff to take up the work of Eliot, who was on leave of absence, and of Hague in mining engineering. At this time George A. Osborne, appointed professor of navigation and astronomy, began a varied and extremely useful tenure of forty-five years before becoming professor emeritus.

The first catalogue to be issued referred to the "degrees or diplomas" to be given in the several departments, and mentioned the requirement of a thesis for graduation. No specific authority had been given in the Institute charter to confer degrees, and as the time for the graduation of the first class, 1868, approached, it became suddenly necessary to petition for such authority. Rogers drew up the necessary document, submitted it to the Chief Justice of the Commonwealth for approval, and then entrusted its introduction to the legislature to Mr. Richard H. Dana on April 29, 1868. Action was prompt, and the right to grant diplomas certifying that the recipients were graduates of the Massachusetts Institute of Technology was readily granted.

The catalogue of the academic year 1868-69 stated: "The form of diploma first given by the Institute is 'Graduate of the Massachusetts Institute of Technology in the Department of ....' "

In June, 1868, thirteen men were granted their diplomas: one in mechanical engineering, five in civil and topographical engineering, six in geology and mining, and one in science and literature. There were no formal graduating exercises. The recipients merely called at the office to obtain their diplomas. Three years later the wording of the diploma was changed, and the designation "S.B. or Bachelor of Science in ...." was introduced. By that time the Corporation had also authorized the degree of S.D. or Doctor of Science, for proficiency in advanced courses of study. It was many years, however, before this degree was awarded by the Institute.

Rogers had for some time wished to relinquish his duties as the professor of physics. Now that the gift of Mr. Thayer made an appointment possible, he recommended that Edward C. Pickering, who had been an assistant professor, be made the first Thayer professor of physics. The appointment was made in July 1868, and for ten years Pickering, later a distinguished astronomer and Director of the Harvard Observatory, held this chair at the Institute.

In October, 1868, President Rogers, who had labored so constantly and devotedly for the school, suffered a slight stroke while attending a faculty meeting. For two months he was unable to work and was then granted leave of absence, and on December 3rd Professor Runkle was appointed Acting President. Rogers spent the winters of '68-'69 and '69-'70 in Philadelphia at the home of his brother, the distinguished Dr. Robert Rogers, and the intervening summer at Newport. He was therefore absent from Boston during the momentous events recorded in the following chapter, but illness and absence did not prevent him from effective participation in them. In the spring of 1870 his health was improving but still uncertain, and knowing that the administration of the Institute was safe in the hands of his devoted friend and confidant, Professor Runkle, he felt that the time had come to resign the presidency. On May 3, 1870, he sent his resignation to the Corporation, and at a meeting on May 17 it was reluctantly accepted. A committee of five prepared a letter on behalf of the Government of the Institute, accepting his resignation with profound regret, with full recognition of the great service he had rendered as president, and with warm hopes for his recovery. This official reply was followed by a letter expressing the loyalty and affection of the faculty, signed by every member.

In 1872 President Rogers' health improved somewhat, and he returned with Mrs. Rogers to spend the winter in Boston with Mr. Savage at the Hotel Berkeley on Berkeley Street, not far from the Institute. The house in Temple Place, which had so long been his home, had been abandoned because of business encroachments. The return to Boston was saddened in March, 1873, by the death of Mr. Savage, always a gallant supporter of Rogers' plans. For the next five years Rogers watched the Institute's struggles from the sidelines. Although he was often physically incapacitated and absent, his interest in no way abated. He was still an active member of the Corporation, and contacts by letter were always possible when his counsel was needed. Finally in 1878, in the Institute's darkest hour, he again took over the helm at the age of seventy-three.

A Declaration of Independence

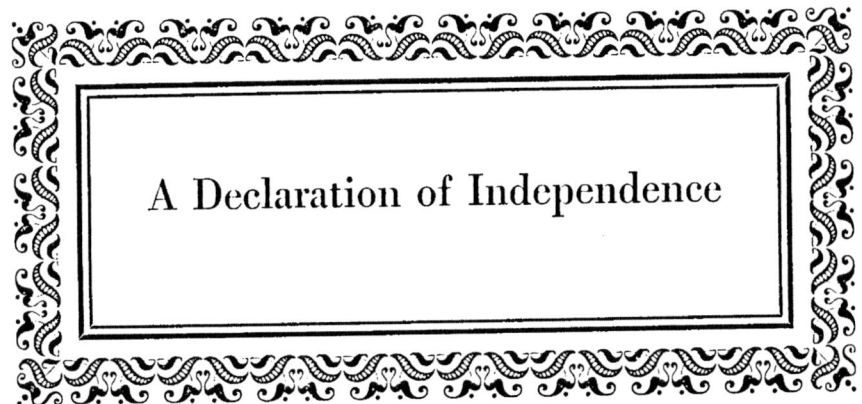

BY THE END OF 1868 M. I. T. was no longer a doubtful experiment, but an established success. It had graduated its first class, its enrollment was steadily rising, and its reputation as Boston Tech was beginning to spread through the country. And now with the founder in retirement, still deeply concerned with the Institute's welfare, but unable to take part in its daily work, the Institute faced a serious threat to its independence.

Early in 1870 while Runkle was acting president, the question of forming an alliance with Harvard arose for the first time. The same question, in one form or another, came up several times again during the Institute's first half century, once during the administration of each of the succeeding presidents. On the surface, the issues in 1870 seemed simple. In the same community there were two schools offering training in applied science, one young and poor in resources but independent and educationally thriving, the other older and comparatively rich, but with an insecure status within the university and apparently unable to attract enough students to justify its existence. A combination that would make one strong school and avoid a wasteful duplication of facilities seemed clearly advantageous to all concerned. But underlying this proposal for co-operation with Harvard, and all the following ones, were two basic issues of educational philosophy and policy: whether the principles and practical applications of the natural sciences formed a proper subject matter for undergraduate education that could for some students take the place of the traditional liberal arts; and whether the technological school should be one of the professional schools within a university or completely independent.

The general educational value of the study of science was thoroughly debated in the 1860's on both sides of the Atlantic, and in America the leaders of M. I. T. were among its most articulate defenders. Rogers gave many speeches on the subject. Dr. Jacob Bigelow, vice-president of the Institute, formerly Rumford Professor in Harvard College, himself a classicist, made a strong plea for the educational philosophy for which the Institute stood, in two remarkable addresses. The first, "An Address on the Limits of Education" was delivered before the Institute's Society of Arts on November 16, 1865, and the second on "Classical and Utilitarian Studies" before a social meeting of the American Academy on November 20, 1866. Dr. Bigelow enjoyed and valued classical studies, he said, but he believed strongly that the aims and educational standards represented by the Institute "conduce most to the progress, the efficiency, the virtue and the welfare of man."

Harvard was officially sympathetic with the ideals of technical education, but it always insisted that "the charge of technical studies belongs with a university." As early as 1847 it had committed itself to education in the applied sciences when it established the Lawrence Scientific School, but it could never quite make up its mind just what the status of technical studies should be within the university. The administration always showed a bias toward the pure rather than the applied sciences, and the prevailing opinion within the university was that professional training should be added to rather than combined with the traditional liberal arts curriculum. In any case, the Lawrence Scientific School never prospered at Harvard and was always a problem to the administration throughout this period.

Rogers, however, stood firm on the ground that the proper place for engineering training was in a four-year undergraduate course and that it could be combined with cultural subjects to make a sound education. After long experience with the higher education of the time and many struggles to raise the prestige of science within the older institutions, he had also become convinced that the school of technology, if it were to play the part it ought to play in American education, must be completely free and independent. He made his position explicit as early as 1861. Fifty years later, in a speech at the Congress of Technology, President Charles W. Eliot of Harvard recalled Rogers' effective opposition to Governor Andrew's plan for a comprehensive union of the state's educational institutions:

> I was present at the beginning of the Institute. I attended a meeting by the invitation of Governor Andrew at his own house very early in the year 1861. It was a meeting which Governor Andrew had himself brought together of moneyed men and teachers, and particularly some of the leaders in the educational institutions already firmly established in Massachusetts, and the desire of the Governor which he stated before the meeting very frankly at its opening, was that the newly chartered Institute of Technology should be united with the Lawrence Scientific School and Bussey Institution and that this combination should rally to its support all the educational forces and moneyed forces of Boston and its vicinity.
> Mr. Rogers was present at this meeting. So was the then President of Harvard University; so was the president of the Lowell Institute, and nothing could exceed the skill and the good temper with which President Rogers met this proposition of Governor Andrew. It did not commend itself to his judgment, but he met it with the utmost tact and skill, and good feeling, and at that meeting Governor Andrew gave up the idea of combining these forces. That was the very first year of the Institute, the year of its charter.

As has been shown in an earlier chapter, President Eliot was mistaken in recalling that Governor Andrew gave up the idea of a coalition of institutions interested in technological education. Eliot himself certainly never gave it up. But Rogers, after a thirty-five-year struggle, had finally concluded that an institution embodying his educational ideals must be free of all entangling alliance. Rogers won his point and stuck to it, but the debate that started at that meeting outlived all the men present, and for fifty years Rogers and his successors had to cope with recurrent proposals for union that threatened the Institute's independence.

The first proposal came in the months following Eliot's election as president of Harvard in 1869. He had been professor of metallurgy and analytical chemistry at the Institute for four years, although sometimes absent for considerable periods in Europe because of his wife's illness. For several months Eliot had been mentioned as a candidate for the Harvard presidency. He was elected by the Harvard Corporation in March, 1869, but opposition within the Board of Overseers delayed the appointment for some time. Many members feared that traditional liberal arts education at Harvard was not safe in the hands of this young innovator with his scientific background, his avowed sympathy with the new technical education, and his reputation as a harsh critic of American colleges for their complacent adherence to a traditional education not well adapted to the needs of America and its people. Finally his election was confirmed by the Overseers, and on July 1 he sent a letter of resignation to Acting President Runkle, at the same time expressing his regret at terminating his associations with his colleagues and the Institute.

Eliot's new position was of course the most prominent educational post in America. His fellow professors at the Institute extended hearty good wishes. President Rogers also sent Eliot a cordial message of congratulation, and in a letter written on July 12, 1869, Eliot replied:

. . . I thank you very much for your kind words about my co-operation at the Institute; but I know perfectly well that I received from the School much more than I ever gave. Your example and precepts, your wisdom and wide experience have not been wholly lost upon me. So far as in me lies, I mean to see that the Institute enjoys the field it has so honorably won, without competition or duplication of any sort at Cambridge. If my position ever enables me to be of any service to you or to the Institute, I trust that you will call upon me without reserve.

This strong expression of good feeling naturally gave Eliot's former associates at the Institute much satisfaction at the time, but it was not long before unforeseen currents disturbed the smooth surface of events. Rumors soon followed by overt action made it clear that the ambitious new president of Harvard, whose aim as he expressed it was "to build here slowly and securely a university in the largest sense," included the Institute in his long-range plans for expansion. He was well aware of the growing strength and reputation of M. I. T.—indeed he himself had made a substantial contribution to it—and he was also aware of the failure of the Lawrence Scientific School to develop as its founders had hoped. In the twenty-three years since its foundation the Lawrence Scientific School had its maximum registration of seventy-nine in 1865. In 1869-70 it was forty-three. The school had produced at least a score of eminent scientists and mathematicians, including Runkle, Crafts, Osborne, Storer, Pickering, Trowbridge, Niles, and Hyatt, who had been on the Institute staff, and others of high reputation. These men had studied under Eben N. Horsford, Louis Agassiz, Asa Gray, and Benjamin Peirce, who at the time were the great leaders in their special fields of science. On the other hand, the gift of $150,000 by Abbott Lawrence and his son James for the promotion of education in engineering and applied science had done little more than to supply a name and a building for the school, which up to 1870 had not been notably successful in the training of eminent engineers. The Lawrence family were clearly disappointed with the progress of the school and were exerting some pressure on the new president. It was only natural therefore that the idea of bringing the Institute into the university as its engineering school should appeal to Eliot as the best way of strengthening the university's work in applied science, and throughout the forty years of his administration he never ceased working toward this end.

In the first months of his presidency, Eliot was apparently quietly discussing his proposal for some sort of union between the Institute and the university. The matter came up definitely in a conversation between Eliot and Runkle at a meeting of the American Academy, which Runkle reported to Rogers in the following letter, dated January 27, 1870:

Last night at the meeting of the Academy I had a long talk with Eliot, & found him still full of the idea of a consolidation of the Inst. and Harvard Univ. He intends to write you and I thought it best to drop you this line in anticipation. He says that James Lawrence is anxious that some arrangement should be made, from which I infer that he is agitating the question.... He said that he had also heard that a subscription was on foot for the Inst. on condition that it should never be united with the Coll. I told him that I had heard of nothing of the kind, & did not believe it. He thought the report came from Mr. J. M. Forbes & Ed.

Atkinson. I told him there was nothing in it; that is the condition—although I know that many would feel in that way.

Now the only way for the Coll. to do is simply to keep all the funds they have, but get permission of the Lawrence heirs & Sam Hooper to use these funds in a little different way, & far more effectively; and let us take care of all the departments of technical education. . . .

Mrs. Rogers, who took care of her husband's correspondence during his illness, decided to bring this letter to his attention. Rogers had apparently heard intimations of such a plan, and this specific proposal caused him great anxiety. From the outset he was absolutely and unqualifiedly opposed to it. On February 1, 1870, he sent a letter to Runkle which strongly expressed not only his personal opinion that such a move would be unwise but also his belief that it would be breaking faith with those who had so loyally aided in the Institute's establishment:

. . . What you say of the convers. at the Academy does not surprise me, though I had begun to hope that the effort in the direction of Annexation would at least be suspended for a while.

Leaving out of view the serious if not insuperable difficulties in the way of changing the application of funds into a channel not originally designed & toward which, it is certain that much of our early endowment would never have been allowed to flow, I can see nothing but injury to the Institute from the projected change.

The Institute has already taken the first place among the Scientific Schools of the U.S. and if *untrammelled* will evidently continue to grow in reputation & numbers. Those who know our History know that this success is due to the Opportunity we have had under the inspiration of Modern ideas.

No kind of Co-operation can be admitted by the Institute which trenches in the least degree upon its independence. What alone is desirable is a friendly working of the two Insts. in their respective spheres. . . .

During the following months the desirability and the legality of a consolidation of the Lawrence Scientific School and the Institute were discussed at length in official circles. Eliot's plan won considerable if not complete support in the Harvard Corporation, but it caused some uneasiness to many members of the Government of the Institute. The Harvard Corporation, officially the President and

Fellows of Harvard College, was a governing body of seven members: Charles W. Eliot, president; Nathaniel Silsbee, treasurer; John Amory Lowell; Rev. George Putnam; Francis B. Crowninshield; ex-Justice George T. Bigelow; and Nathaniel Thayer. All of these men except Thayer were Harvard graduates, and three of them, Lowell, Thayer, and Bigelow, had been on the Institute's Corporation from its beginning in 1862. Lowell and Thayer had been valiant supporters of President Rogers and his educational ideals, but as loyal Harvard men they had also given generously to the Lawrence Scientific School. Judge Bigelow, while Chief Justice, had been an *ex-officio* member, and was elected a life member on his retirement in 1868.

The Corporation of the Institute, then called the "Government" was a much larger body, with nearly forty members. Nine of these were graduates of Harvard or of the Lawrence Scientific School: Jacob Bigelow '66, G. B. Emerson '17, C. L. Flint '44, J. A. Lowell '15, H. B. Rogers '22, S. Kneeland '49, G. T. Bigelow '29, S. K. Lothrop '25, J. D. Runkle, L.S. '51, and C. M. Warren, L.S. '55.

The course of the negotiations in early 1870 is shown in the following correspondence. A few days after their conversation at the American Academy, Runkle wrote to Eliot on February 2nd:

I saw Judge Bigelow today, and a short conversation with him recalled those we have had upon the same subject.

The more I think of it, the more I recognize the importance of some sort of co-ooperation between the Inst. & Har. Coll. But I am more than ever satisfied that if the only alternative is of merging the Institute or its Schools into the Coll., making it a simple appendage, the subject may as well be laid upon the shelf.

From 1847 to 1859 or 60 the Coll. had the field, and if the opportunity had been properly improved, the Inst. would never have had an existence.[10] But, today, in its foundation, number of students and faculty, and facilities, the Inst. is confessedly the first School of its kind in the country, saying nothing of what it may become by carrying out all its plans and departments.

Now, I do not think it at all reasonable to suppose, that under these circumstances, the friends of the Inst. should be willing to turn it over to Har. Coll. and relinquish control of its affairs.

Those to whom it owes its success, naturally feel a just pride in the part they have been able to perform in securing this result.

I think the friends of the Inst. have quite as much reason to suppose that Harvard will be willing to discontinue the two departments of Mining & Civil Engineering, as that the Inst. will be willing to transfer itself to the Coll.

I have no reason to doubt that the Inst. will not willingly listen to any terms of co-operation, which will not virtually sacrifice its independence if not its identity.

I think I have heard you express the opinion that the Coll. should not now, under all the circumstances, some of which I have already alluded to, attempt to occupy the ground so fully possessed by the Inst., and this was one reason why I hailed your election to the Presidency of Har. with so much satisfaction, because I felt certain that you fully recognized the justice of this view of the case.

And, indeed, when we remember that the Inst. is simply what Professor Rogers has made it, I think it safe to say that no one, properly taking this fact into account, will hesitate to accept any opinion which he may have in the matter as final. I do hope, my dear Eliot, that some way may be found to secure a co-operation satisfactory to all and unjust to none.

Eliot replied on the fourth:

I have a moment only; but I want to say one word. Harvard College will propose to discontinue its departments of Mining and Engineering & transfer their funds to the Institute. Also to make the Bussey Establishment a department of the Institute. If its friends preferred to retain the name 'Institute of Technology'—why Amen; though I personally think it would be right to give the combined Institution the name of 'Rogers.'

As to independence, the Faculty of Harvard College has the College in its hands much more completely than the Faculty of the Institute has their school.

The Medical Faculty in Boston is a Completely Independent body, so far as the management of their school goes. The Faculty of the Institute would be Similarly Supreme. It is quite possible to organize a special board of Visitors for the Combined Institution.

Mr. Lawrence has lately written to me urging action. I propose to see Mr. Rogers as soon as possible and after him the Government of the Institute. If you and I could agree on any line of Action, I should be glad.

On February 7, 1870, Rogers wrote the following declaration of independence to Eliot from Philadelphia:

I have been for several days intending to write to you on the subject of your proposed plan of uniting the Inst. of Tech. with Harvard College.

Without in the present letter entering into any detailed argument on the subject, I will frankly say that I am convinced that such a connection would be a decided disadvantage to the Inst., which owes its success in great measure to the fact that it has stood entirely unconnected with other institutions both as to its scheme of education & its government. The development of its plans, in which we have already made such good progress, demands entire independence, and in my mind no contribution of funds would justify us in consenting to a change which would be equivalent to disorganizing the plan which has so eminently won the public sympathy. I see no reason why there should be any conflict between the two Insts.

If it is thought that the Scientific School at Harvard cannot succeed in its present form the simplest solution of the difficulty it seems to me is to devote its funds to scientific scholarships or fellowships, or to some other department in the Univ.

I am expecting to visit Boston soon when I shall be glad if desired to state my convictions more fully on this subject.

In reply Eliot wrote on February 9th:

It is obvious to me from some of the words of your note of the 7th inst. that you have not received a correct idea of the plan, which I (following good Gov. Andrew) cherish, of merging the several schools for technological instruction, which now exist in this vicinity, into the Institute of Technology. The change I would suggest to you will not disorganize the plan of the Institute in any particular, nor will it make the Institute or its School any less independent in reality than it is now. The Institute would have the same organization and general purposes as now, and would hold its property as now. I venture to think that the School of industrial science would be stronger and more independent than now, if the Government of the Institute entered into an arrangement with the University whereby the School of the Institute should become an independent department of the University, established in the Institute's building, and be reinforced with the funds of the Scientific and Mining Schools at Cambridge, and a considerable proportion of the Bussey income. The name of the School would of course remain just what it is, unless you consented to the use of your family name. The Committee of Instruction would become the Visitors of the Combined School. The incorporated body—the Institute of Technology—would remain exactly what it is, and would doubtless carry out its Museum and perpetuate its Society of Arts.

I have, my dear Sir, the profoundest respect for the work you accomplished in building up the School. The change I suggest seems to me not only a great public advantage (by concentrating resources now scattered), but also a magnifying and strengthening of your own work and of your claim to the gratitude of this community. The few near friends of the Institute and yourself with whom I have spoken on the subject have been unanimously of this opinion.

But this subject is one of so many details that I am persuaded that I ought to talk with you about it rather than trust to writing. The whole thing is merely in the first stage of preliminary inquiry. I have been very careful with whom I spoke of it, & have never spoken of it, I believe, except to intimate friends of yours and to the Corporation of the College. I hope, my dear Sir, that you will not give yourself a moment's uneasiness about the matter. Next Sunday I may be in Phila. and will call upon you for a few minutes talk if you allow me. . . .

After having received Eliot's letter, Rogers wrote to Runkle on February 22, 1870: "There seems as yet to be no plan suggested which would not practically commit the Institute to the control of the College, and this I am sure that the friends of the College who belong to our government would not think expedient, even if practicable."

Correspondence of the following months still preserved in the archives of the Institute shows how the alignment of the parties grew more distinct as the plan became more widely known, with Eliot as the vigorous proponent of the plan, and with Acting President Runkle faithfully maintaining the view so ably expressed by Rogers that the Institute must remain free from entangling alliance with the university. Runkle was supported by a majority of the Institute's Government and teaching staff. A number of the loyal Harvard graduates in the Government proved to be among his staunchest supporters. On the Institute staff the men in science and mathematics were for the most part graduates of the Lawrence Scientific School. This list included Runkle, Storer, Osborne, Pickering, Warren, and Trowbridge; Kneeland was a graduate of the college. Of these only Storer was strongly in favor of the plan of union.

The conflict was in part a conflict between principle and expediency. The Institute was extremely poor in funds, but had a fine reputation based on the success of its new type of technical training.

Harvard's school had money, and although connected with the oldest and most renowned college in the country, it had not made training in engineering a noteworthy success. Eliot stressed money in some of his arguments, and also overplayed the suggestion of the great honor the Institute would have in being a part of Harvard.

In May, 1870, Rogers resigned the presidency, and in the five months' interregnum before Runkle was elected, the negotiations with Harvard became tangled with the internal situation at the Institute. The School of Industrial Science by 1868 had become the most important part of the tripartite Institute, and it became necessary to separate control of the School from the Government of the more inclusive Institute including the Society of Arts with its many members. To clarify the relations between the Institute and its two parts, the School and the Society, an act amending the Institute's charter was adopted in March, 1869. Under this act, which changed the name of the Institute's governing body from "Government" to "Corporation," it was possible to modify the committee structure of the Corporation, abolish the four vice-presidencies, and give the president tenure until his resignation or removal for cause. At the annual meeting of the new Corporation on May 23, 1870, delay in electing a president was advocated, and Runkle was re-elected president *pro tempore* with all powers of the president until one was elected. In June, 1870, new bylaws were prepared which provided for three officers, a president, a treasurer, and a secretary. Runkle, as the candidate recommended by Rogers, was almost certain to be elected president. In this situation it was clearly urgent for Eliot to push his plan to completion, if possible, before Runkle could be elected. Some opposition to Runkle developed, largely inspired by Eliot, who let it be known that Runkle was "in his way" and proposed Alfred P. Rockwell, professor of mining engineering, as a candidate for president. Of the faculty members, Storer was violently opposed to Runkle, and Ware nursed a minor grievance because Runkle had found it necessary to reprimand him for making unauthorized expenditures. Rockwell was also probably quietly opposed. There were a few members of the Corporation who, though in no sense unfriendly, were somewhat doubtful that Runkle could maintain the high ideals and loyalties that Rogers had commanded.

On June 20, 1870, the President and Fellows of Harvard College sent the following official communication to the Corporation of the Massachusetts Institute of Technology, John D. Runkle, Acting President.

The President and Fellows of Harvard College, being convinced that the great public interest of professional scientific education would be promoted by a union at the Institute of Technology of all the Schools of Applied Science in and near Boston, respectfully invite the Government of the Institute to consider whether some plan cannot now be devised for the accomplishment of such a union with the consent of the parties interested in the several Schools.

To bring about such a consolidation the President and Fellows will cordially enter into any practicable arrangement, not inconsistent with their legal obligations. . . .

Two days after the receipt of this letter, Runkle wrote to Mrs. Rogers, as follows:

I write to you not knowing just how the Prof. is, & whether his health may not be disturbed by news, which not over important, will still be of great interest to him. I think I told you in my last that the new By-laws were considered at the meeting held on Thursday last, but not finally adopted for want of a quorum. Eighteen were present; but 20 were necessary. Tomorrow another meeting will be held to act if we can get a quorum together, if not we shall go on under our old By-laws for the present.

Yesterday I received an official communication from the President of Harvard Coll., the substance of which is as follows. . . . [Here he quoted the foregoing document.]

So you see Eliot has made his move, & I understand that he intends to accomplish the consolidation, if possible, before our election for President takes place. He says distinctly that I am in his way, & his friends say that after Eliot's plan is carried the Inst. will not need a President.

Tomorrow, after the adoption of the By-laws, & we have decided on the time for holding a meeting for the election under them, I will read Eliot's communication. It may or may not be discussed then—but no action will be taken till the next meeting. The matter is too important to be acted upon, except at a meeting called for the purpose. If the new By-laws are adopted it will need a majority to elect a President—but when elected he is to hold the office until he resigns or is removed for cause. My friends think that there is a large majority in my favor. I now hear of no name but *Rockwell*. He appears to be the Candidate of Eliot—but not as the Pres.—but the Dean of the Faculty under the Consolidation. I do not think he can get a single vote in our Govt. for Pres.

I do not want the Prof. to do the least thing to injure his health—but I am sure that a single line to a few members to use at their discretion will tell. I have seen a letter written by Ware in which he says that the Inst. will surely fail under my management, for I lack all the essential requisites of a good administrative officer. It seems to me that Ware is assuming a grave responsibility by taking such a course. I had occasion to tell him during the term that I should approve no more bills of his contracted without my sanction. This I presume is one of his grievances. Storer, as you may suppose, is rabid. . . . Will you be good enough to write me a line telling me how the Prof. is since his arrival at Newport. I will write again after the meeting tomorrow.

Official negotiations between the Institute and the University were carried on through conference committees, Harvard being represented by Eliot, the Reverend George Putnam, and Judge Bigelow, and the Institute by Runkle, Edward Atkinson, and M. Denman Ross. Several meetings were held at which various slightly modified proposals by Eliot brought no conclusions.

President Rogers, now settled at Newport for the summer, had gained in strength, and as suggested by Runkle, sent letters to various members of the Corporation expressing his absolute opposition to any plan which was likely to be proposed. R. C. Greenleaf's reply, now in possession of the Institute, is typical of the feeling shown by many of the Corporation members:

Your note in relation to the affairs of the Institute of Technology was rec'd just in time to place it in Mr. Atkinson's hand a few moments before the Committee of Conference came to order.

It was exactly in accordance with my views. I have said and done all I could to prevent the absorption of the School into the dead carcass of Harvard's School of Science.

Your letter was very opportune and did much to strengthen Mr. Atkinson in the stand he took in the Committee.

Mr. Atkinson read me his reply to you, and I am sure with such advocates the Independence of the School, which is so dear to you, will be maintained.

Mr. Atkinson's letter is so full that nothing more is needed from me in reply to yours.

Please accept for Mrs. Rogers & yourself my kind regards & earnest wish for your full restoration to health.

By August the conference committees were working on the details of the proposed agreement. The following letters to Rogers from Runkle and Atkinson, two of the Technology committee, indicate the course of events in August and September:

We had another meeting today, Dr. Putnam present, Eliot & Bigelow absent. Putnam went over the old ground, & finally handed the following document, drawn up by Eliot. I copy it for you. It will not go.

"Memorandum of an agreement between Harvard Coll. & the Inst. of Tech. to effect a union of their several Schools of Applied Science.

1. Each Corporation shall continue to hold all the property which it now applies to the purposes of its own School or Schools. This property is

    A. On the part of the College

Scientific School building	$40,000
Professorship of Engineering fund	32,000
James Lawrence fund	50,000
Sturgis Hooper fund	60,000
Bussey farm, (367 acres)	
Bussey building Fund	65,000
Bussey fund for Agr. Dept.	175,000
	422,000

    B. On the part of the Inst.
        Building of Inst. (worth say)
        Unencumbered funds
        Funds held by the State

2. Both Corporations agree to devote the whole proceeds of all the above property to the Consolidated School until this agreement is abrogated by common consent, the Bussey Institution being regarded for the purposes of this agreement as part of said School.

3. Each Corporation engages to devote any funds which it may hereafter acquire for teaching applied science to the use of the Consolidated School, unless such application be incompatible with the terms of the gift.

4. The Consolidated School shall be called the 'Technological School.'

5. The officers & servants of the school shall be appointed & paid by Har. Coll., & the Coll. shall therefore be authorized to receive from the Inst. and disburse the income of the funds mentioned in 1B, & also to collect and use for the purposes of the School the fees for tuition.

6. The Committee on Instruction of the Govt. of the Inst. shall have the right to nominate the incumbents of the Professorships in the Consolidated School which correspond to the Walker, Hayward, and Thayer professorships, the professorship of Mechanical Engineering, and the professorship of Astronomy & Navigation.

The same Committee shall also have the right to inspect at any time the working and general condition of the School, and shall be required to make an annual report thereon to the Govt. of the Inst.

7. The School shall be maintained in the Inst. Building, & this building shall be appropriated exclusively to the School, except that the Govt. of the Inst. & the Committees thereof, and the Society of Arts shall have the right to hold their meetings there.

8. The buildings shall be cared for and kept in repair by the Coll. from the income of the School.

9. This agreement relates exclusively to the School of Industrial Science maintained by the Inst. and has no bearing whatever upon the other objects for which the Inst. was incorporated."

Such is the plan offered us. Shall we take it? It leaves us the initiative in 5 of the 15 professorships and other officers....

Edward Atkinson wrote of the same meeting:

As Prof. Runkle has gone away for a time, it may be that you have had no account of recent conferences and meetings.

At the last Harvard conference only Dr. Putnam was present on that side, the other members being unwell. The Doctor was very earnest and honest in advocating his cause, but I think he was much impressed by our statements, and though he may not have been entirely convinced that we were right, yet under the circumstances he will favor the teaching of pure science rather than applied science at Cambridge.

It may interest you to know that whereas Mr. H. B. Rogers was somewhat doubtful at first, as to the best course to be pursued, he is now most strenuous and earnest against our giving up control, considers it imperative that we shall administer our own trusts and that our Government knows better what is needed in our school than the College Authorities are ever likely to know!

I find that Mr. Beebe has been very anxious lest we should not keep the trust imposed upon us by Dr. Walker. The following members of the Government are absolutely opposed to any transfer of our control and will maintain the absolute independence of the Institute:—

Messrs. Runkle, Kneeland, Endicott, Atkinson, Lincoln, Little, Dalton, Emerson, Beebe, Forbes, Fuller, Rogers, H.B., Tuxbury, Francis, Bigelow, E. B., Greenleaf, Ross, Cummings, Hoadley, Bowditch, Warren, and yourself.

As it is possible that you may not have had Pres't. Eliot's memo I send you a copy which please return.

The question is settled and need give us no more uneasiness. I have had a private talk with Ware and we need not fear any resignation from him. He has been very out-spoken but will be loyal to us after the question is absolutely decided. I let him understand that we should not be troubled if Storer resigned but that we should miss him if he took the same course.

I think we have decided upon an excellent plan for the hall. The estimate (not including heating) is only $13,000.—We asked for $15,000. and $2,000.—for other rooms and shall go on at once. Preston will have nothing to do in the matter.

I have been deputed to get up a permanent book of record of all deeds, wills, or grants by which we have been benefited and I have asked Messrs. Beebe & Tobey to furnish a written statement of Dr. Walker's views and wishes.

I now doubt not the election of Runkle as soon as the summer days have passed, and I am very sure that the late discussions have consolidated and strengthened the Institute.

Atkinson added a brief letter dated August 17, 1870. It reads:

I only included in my last those about whom I was absolutely sure. I have no doubt about Flint, White, Edmands, Fay, and several others.

In fact the real Harvard strength consists only of three Bigelow, Thayer and Lowell and when Mr. Lowell examines the question in its legal aspect I doubt his being in favor of the Harvard plan.

A further bit of good news was reported two days later by Atkinson in a postscript to a letter dealing with the book of record which he had been "deputed to get up":

I believe your brother's library and cabinet were given to the Institute by bequest. To whom shall I apply for a copy of that portion of his will to enter upon our record book.

P.S. Mr. A. H. Rice is very heartily on our side and for the complete independence of the Inst.

From existing records and letters it seems clear that Dr. Putnam's memorandum was not the final one acted upon by the committees, for another memorandum in Runkle's handwriting, undated but presumably presented about a month later, was sent to Rogers with an accompanying letter. This memorandum varies, in many respects quite widely, from the previous one. It reads as follows:

Memorandum of an Agreement between Har. Coll. and the Mass. Inst. of Technology to effect a union of their several schools of applied science.

I. The Inst. of Tech. shall maintain, conduct and control its School of Industrial Science substantially as now organized for the year 1869-1870, subject only to the provisions hereinafter contained.

II. The Corporation of the Coll. shall have the right to inspect at any time the working and condition of the school, and to make such examinations as they may see fit, and to give all degrees to such candidates as may be recommended therefor by the Corporation of the Inst. in such form as may hereafter be mutually agreed upon.

III. Changes in the courses and departments of instruction, and in the conditions of admission & graduation shall be made by the Inst. subject to the approval of the Corporation of Har. Coll.

IV. The President of the Coll. shall have the right of attending any stated meeting of the Corporation of the Inst. for the purpose of making any communications or suggestions deemed important by him or by the Corporation he represents.

V. So long as this agreement shall be in force the Corporation of the Coll. shall not maintain any School of Applied or Industrial Science other than the school of the Inst. except so far as is necessary to comply with the conditions of the Bussey donation for instruction in practical agriculture.

VI. The Corporation of the Coll. shall pay over to the Corporation of the Inst. as often as once in six months the income of all property which it now holds for the instruction in applied science, & of all funds which it may hereafter acquire for the same purpose, except such as must by the terms of grant be differently appropriated.

VII. The Corporation of the Inst. shall faithfully apply all the funds received from the Corporation of Har. Coll. to the purposes of instruction of applied science in its school, annually rendering to the Coll. an account of the expenditure thereof.

VIII. The Corporation of the Inst. engages to maintain in its school so long as this agreement remains in force, a Lawrence Professorship of Engineering, a Lawrence Professorship of Chemistry, and a Sturgis Hooper Professorship of Practical Geology: and the appointments to these Professorships shall be made by the Corporation of Har. Coll. subject to the approval of the Corporation of the Inst.

IX. In consideration of the foregoing it is mutually agreed that the School of the Mass. Inst. of Technology shall be held and considered as the School of Applied Science maintained in connection with Har. Coll.

X. This agreement may be abrogated by the vote of either Corporation, but its termination shall not take effect except by common consent, until at least one year from the date of the communication of such vote by either Corporation to the other.

Runkle's letter to Rogers commenting on this memorandum follows:

I send you a copy of the points passed upon today by our Committee as a first rough approximation of what may possibly prove a basis of union. I do not like III. I shall not go for it. It virtually gives Harvard the power of controlling our courses of study, & indeed the whole policy of the school. This, with the graduation, would not leave us very much after all. I am not in favor of IV: but it may not do any harm.

We must find out just how much Har. will be able to pay over to us now; & how much will be left after paying the Professors we take by the new arrangement.

If a few of the objectionable points can be removed, it will probably be as good a plan as can be devised—the question still remaining whether it will be for our ultimate good to have anything at all to do with Harvard. The interest of Mr. Thayer & Mr. Lowell in the union is not to be overlooked. If some plan satisfactory to both parties can be found these men will have no divided feelings. I am anxious to know how this matter strikes you. It is something to give up the graduation of our students: but the fact of educating them is of more importance.

I hope you will not allow this matter to trouble you: for I do not think our Govt. will be willing to adopt any plan which will substantially put our School in the hands of Har. Coll.

If the articles of agreement can be so drawn as to secure the control to us without any future question, I should be willing to entertain this plan provided it shall be found that the income from the Harvard funds do not fall much below $25,000 per annum.

If we do not unite, & do not get the means from other sources to raise salaries we shall lose all the Professors we have whom we could least afford to spare.

If you can send me a note which I can get by Tuesday morning next I shall be glad. We have another meeting on that day. After that I suppose any plan we may decide upon, if any, will go to the joint Committee....

There can be little doubt as to the nature of Dr. Rogers' reply, although no copy of it has been found. Of the Institute Corporation Edward Atkinson, M. Denman Ross, John D. Philbrick, Richard C. Greenleaf, John M. Forbes, William Endicott, Jr., and John Cummings, Jr., were so actively opposed to any form of combination or union that would make the Institute the Technological School of Harvard University that they readily convinced a large majority of their colleagues, and when the definite proposal made by the Harvard President and Fellows was voted upon, it was defeated. When a counter proposal was made by the Institute to the Harvard Corporation it was never answered.[11] The wisdom of Rogers and the great service of Runkle, Atkinson, and his other associates eventually brought about the complete collapse of Eliot's ambitious plan to absorb the Institute.

Lean Years

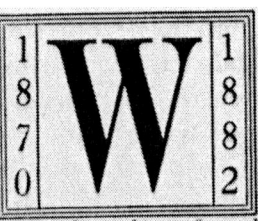

WHEN the time came to choose a new president in October, 1870, John D. Runkle, who had led the Institute through the critical negotiations with Harvard, was elected. No other choice could have been so wise. Runkle had worked so long and so intimately with Rogers over the plans for the development of the Institute that the two men thought almost as one. After the election there was no trace of dissension on the part of the few members of the Corporation who had at first been favorably disposed toward the combination of the Institute with the Lawrence Scientific School. Mr. Lowell and Mr. Thayer showed neither disappointment nor resentment, but continued as effective and valued members of the Corporation. For them it had been largely a question of the best way to carry out the Rogers idea of scientific and technical training. With the decision against a union, these men gave their wholehearted support to the Institute under the new bylaws and were among the most active in service on the committees. The only dissatisfaction with Runkle's election was apparently on the part of two members of the faculty. Storer had been intensely partisan to President Eliot's scheme, and resigned in rather bad temper. Shortly afterward, he was appointed professor of agricultural chemistry in the Bussey Institution, and so continued his long association with Eliot. Ware had only a temporary personal grievance, and his disaffection soon disappeared.

When the bylaws were changed in 1870, the Corporation of twenty-six members was organized into four committees, which were responsible for the School of Industrial Science, the Museum, the Society of Arts, and Finance. The Committee on the School of Industrial Science, which was most actively concerned in the Institute's educational program, was a strong group of able men. John A. Lowell was chairman, and Dr. Rogers an influential member, even during his period of illness and convalescence. Phillips Brooks, later Bishop of Massachusetts, was a member from '72 to '75, and Edward Atkinson, George B. Emerson, Samuel K. Lothrop, Henry B. Rogers, John D. Philbrick, J. Elliot Cabot, and J. Baxter Upham were all active in support of the new president during the early years of his administration. Most of them were still on the Committee during the difficult financial period between 1874 and 1879 and on into the next decade. The treasurers of the Corporation, William Endicott, Jr., and his successor John Cummings, were towers of strength and splendid examples of loyalty to the school throughout these trying years.

In the first three years of Runkle's administration the Institute grew steadily in numbers, in reputation, and in the scope of its work. Students now came in increasing numbers from outside New England and even from far western points. The enrollment rose from 224 in 1870 to 261 in 1871, and to 348 in 1872-73. After this period of growth came a long struggle with poverty in the lean years following the depression of 1873, during which enrollment dropped year by year to a low of 188 in 1878-79. Yet even during this trying period when the Institute's material fortunes were at their lowest ebb, Runkle and his loyal staff continued to make notable educational progress and lay the foundations for future triumphs.

During the five years of growth following the graduation of the first class in 1868, able young men whose later careers showed the wisdom of their selection were added to the instructing staff, which rose from eighteen in 1868 to thirty-four in 1873. John M. Ordway took the place made vacant by Eliot's resignation. Edward C. Picker-

LEAN YEARS

ing had already become the first Thayer Professor of Physics. The following young men, all in their twenties, were notable new appointments: John Trowbridge in physics and drawing, who later became head of the department of physics at Harvard; James M. Crafts, noted research chemist, who became a professor and later president of the Institute; Robert H. Richards '68, who three years after graduation became professor in charge of the department of mining and metallurgy; William Ripley Nichols '69, who as professor of general chemistry at the Institute achieved fame for his work in sanitary chemistry; Eugene Létang, the first of the distinguished Beaux Arts men to teach architectural design in America; Gaetano Lanza, a brilliant young mathematician and engineer, who succeeded Watson in 1872 as head of the department of mechanical engineering; and Charles R. Cross '70, who was made instructor immediately after graduation, assistant professor the following year, professor in 1874, and in 1879 the Thayer Professor of Physics. Cross became known to many generations of Technology men as the distinguished head of the department of physics and founder of the department of electrical engineering. In this period also came the appointments of T. Sterry Hunt in geology, Alpheus Hyatt in paleontology, and William H. Niles in physical geography and geology.

It was a brilliant, hard-working, and enthusiastic group of men, for the most part in their twenties or early thirties, that served under Rogers and Runkle and gave the Institute a fine start as a great school of science. Most of them were trained at the Institute, for in those days only the occasional college graduate sought special training in engineering or science either for teaching or for industry. A few had studied abroad, generally in Germany or Switzerland, countries which were already giving much attention to technical education. So it happened that the development of a strong staff had to come about largely by molding it from able men who had themselves gone through the Institute's rigorous training. Most of these men remained at the Institute for twenty or more years after this time, and many graduates now living will recall with pleasure and gratitude their fine qualities of friendliness as well as their skill as teachers.

In the early years hard-working and capable men like Richards, Nichols, and Cross, when appointed to the staff were given large responsibilities, and within two years after graduation were made assistant professors, and promoted to the rank of full professor in less than five years. The title of associate professor had not been adopted, the ranks being professor, assistant professor, instructor, and assistant. The staff in 1873-74 numbered thirty-eight, of whom twenty-three were of professorial grade. Of these, three were members of the original staff selected by President Rogers, and ten others had been in continuous service for at least ten years. Four of them, Richards, Nichols, Cross, and Whitaker were graduates of the Institute.

In the hard times that followed the panic of 1873 the staff was somewhat reduced. Promotions were extremely rare, and new appointments to faculty grade non-existent. Nevertheless a few careful appointments of instructors and assistants were made in order to maintain the high standards of teaching which Runkle and the administration were determined to continue during these difficult years. One of these, Jules Luquiens, a Swiss by birth, who came to America after extended graduate study in Europe, taught at Yale and elsewhere, and became an instructor in modern languages at the Institute in 1874. A man of broad culture, he was a very successful teacher and had acquired an expanding reputation for his excellent textbook. In 1884 he became associate professor, and later full professor. He was later called back to Yale to a special professorship. His going was deeply regretted, but his good fortune was a source of pleasure to his colleagues.

The scope of the Institute's educational work widened during these years. Soon after the school opened in 1865-66, its work was departmentalized for the professional training, but the departments, as they always have, taught numerous subjects for students in other departments as well as their own professional curricula. All students took the same subjects for the first two years, and then chose a professional course. The list of six professional courses that appeared in the first catalogue remained unchanged until 1871. Then a seventh department was added, called "Natural History," with a program for those who wished to prepare for medicine or for professional work in agriculture, geology and mineralogy, or rural economy. Natural history was the precursor of biology and the numerous applications of the biological sciences which developed in later years with the rise of bacteriology.

In 1873 a rearrangement and expansion of the professional courses took place. New departments of physics, metallurgy, and philosophy were established, and the students began their specialization at the beginning of their second year. The following professional courses were offered in 1873-74. The numbering system is already beginning to look familiar:

    I   Civil and Topographical Engineering
   II   Mechanical Engineering
  III   Geology and Mining Engineering
  IV   Building and Architecture
   V   Chemistry
  VI   Metallurgy
 VII   Natural History
VIII   Physics
  IX   Science and Literature
   X   Philosophy

It is significant that a technical school reputedly devoted only to practical science and engineering maintained from the earliest days studies in literature, philosophy, and modern languages; required all students to take subjects in this area in all four years; and from the outset offered one or more complete curricula that combined general science with the humanities.

The establishment of the laboratory of physics at M. I. T. at this time was an important contribution to American technical education. Before President Rogers' severe illness in 1868, he and Professor Pickering had given much thought to the establishment of a physical laboratory. It was impossible to discuss this matter with the president while he was so seriously ill, but Mrs. Rogers was kept informed on most matters connected with the School, and relayed the information quietly to her husband. Professor Pickering proceeded with the plans, which were approved by the Committee on Instruction on May 11, 1869, and the first physical laboratory in America was set up in time for the opening of the school year in September, 1869.

On February 14, 1872, the Corporation passed the following resolution:

> Resolved, that as a slight recognition of the eminent services which Professor William B. Rogers has rendered the Institute of Technology, the Physical Laboratory of the Institute shall be designated and hereafter known as
> 'The Rogers Laboratory of Physics.'

A copy of this vote was transmitted to Rogers by Secretary Kneeland. When Rogers was able to reply, three months later, he accepted the honor modestly. He told of his original reasons for planning such a laboratory, and gave Professor Pickering credit for its organization and direction. Somewhat later he directed that his own valuable collection of physical equipment, much of it acquired at his own expense when he was in Europe in 1867, should with certain small reservations be formally presented to the physics department.

In 1868, a two-year program in design, construction and professional practice was established in the department of building and architecture for men desiring only intensive work in these special fields. Students taking this work were commonly called "partial architects" to distinguish them from the much smaller number in the four-year course. Many architects who subsequently achieved high distinction had their training in this program. Later the broader, longer, and more scientific training of the regular course was regarded as essential for men who would be responsible for the design and construction of the large buildings and skyscrapers which were then appearing in the cities, and the two-year program was abandoned in the late nineties.

Eugene Létang's teaching in design made the partial course highly successful. Létang was the first of the eminent graduates of the École des Beaux Arts in Paris to participate in the training of architects at M. I. T. He brought to the work of the department much of the French grace and beauty of design and was a very effective teacher. He came to the Institute in 1871 as an assistant to Professor William R. Ware, the first head of the department, was made an instructor in 1879, and the following year was promoted to the grade of assistant professor. The department had acquired high reputation by 1881, when Professor Ware resigned to become head of the new school of architecture at Columbia University. Theodore M. Clark, a Boston architect, was made head of the department as his successor.

The most important contribution of President Runkle, the mathematician, to the Institute's educational program was his insistence on practical experience in laboratory, shop, and field as a necessary supplement to the study of the principles of science and engineering. The beginning of practical shop work for students came early in his administration. In July, 1869, he reported that by courtesy of Commander Rogers of the Navy Yard, seven of the students of the Institute in mechanical engineering had been granted free access to the machine shops at the Charlestown Navy Yard, and were pursuing their work there to great advantage. In the early seventies a plan was developed to enable students to visit important engineering operations in various parts of the country during the summer vacation. Expeditions were organized under the leadership of one or more staff members, and students of the three upper years who could meet the expense involved were eligible to participate.

In 1871, Professors Runkle and Richards conducted an excursion of fifteen students interested in mining and geology to the new mining regions of Colorado, Utah, and Wyoming. The following year W. E. Hoyt, instructor in civil engineering, with a dozen students in civil and mechanical engineering visited the Baldwin Locomotive Works in Philadelphia, the bridge and iron works at Phoenixville, and the steel, coal, and oil regions of Pennsylvania. This group also observed the construction of the great railroad bridge over the Ohio at Cincinnati and the building operations for the Mississippi bridge at St. Louis. On their travels they saw many of the principal bridges in the area between the Ohio and Mississippi Rivers and the Hudson. In 1873 came trips to the small mines and chemical works of New England and New York state, and in 1874 Professors Ordway and Richards led a group to the rapidly developing mining region near Lake Superior.

These summer excursions, forerunners of more highly organized summer schools, made the school widely known as a source of technical knowledge and of professionally trained young men. They were therefore of great value to the Institute and to industry as well as to the students.

An important extension of the intimate relations between the Massachusetts Institute of Technology and the Lowell Institute took place in 1872. Beginning in 1865 the Lowell Institute had supported free evening lecture courses given at Technology by Technology professors. The much more widely known public lectures of the Lowell Institute, frequently given by distinguished men from abroad, had been given at its hall in a Washington Street building. In 1872 this building was torn down, and an arrangement was made with President Rogers to have them given thereafter in Huntington Hall in the Institute's building on Boylston Street. The annual rental of $2500 was a great help to the struggling Institute. This arrangement lasted more than fifty years. John A. Lowell, the trustee of the Lowell Institute, now desired to go further and establish as a part of its public service a school devoted to the promotion of industrial art in New England. He carefully discussed the matter with President Runkle, and the Lowell School of Practical Design was established. It was supported by the Lowell Institute, but housed and administered by M. I. T., not as a part of the School of Industrial Science, but as a separate entity. The textile industry was chosen as the most appropriate field for the new school, and Charles Kastner, a man highly accomplished in fabric design, was appointed director. A drawing room and a weaving room were provided in the upper story of the main building, in which students could work their designs into actual fabrics of every variety in commercial sizes.

The school opened auspiciously in the autumn of 1872 with twenty-five students. In 1883 it was removed to the building erected on Garrison Street. It remained a free school until 1901, when it was found necessary to require a small tuition fee, and the school was put under the direction of C. Howard Walker, for many years a lecturer in the department of architecture, and transferred to the Massachusetts School of Design under the management of the Museum of Fine Arts School.

From the beginning military training was a part of the curriculum, as required by the Land Grant Act. The most exciting episode in the Institute's military history was the Great Fire of 1872, which

Lean Years 97

swept away sixty acres of buildings in the part of Boston where the Institute first held its classes. The school's only loss was its interest in certain fire insurance companies, amounting to about $6,400. The student battalion was mobilized and encamped on the Common, and remained on police duty for several days.

Up to 1873, the military training was not very effective, and students had come to regard it as a waste of time. When Lt. E. L. Zalinski of the 5th U.S. Artillery became instructor in military science in 1873, he endeavored to make it both interesting and educational. He organized the students into military units, not as fighting men but for civilian service and physical welfare. In his three years in charge he put military training on a sane and effective basis, and created a new respect for this branch of instruction.

In 1874 a special committee of the Corporation consisting of Alexander H. Rice, John Cummings, and Edward Atkinson studied the whole problem of military training at the Institute, and joined Lt. Zalinski in recommending a new building designed to be used as a drill hall and gymnasium. With financial aid from Corporation members and about thirty interested companies and other citizens, in 1875 a combination drill hall and gymnasium was built on the part of the Boylston Street land near Clarendon Street. This building was of wood construction covered with corrugated iron and a slate roof. In addition to the drill hall and armory, a room at one end contained the first lunch room—"Jones' Lunch"—established by the Institute, and here professors and students and their friends could obtain lunches and dinners at very reasonable cost, reputed to be not in excess of 25 to 35 cents for a hearty dinner. In 1883 in order to make room for the "New Building," later called the Walker Building, the drill shed was moved to Exeter Street, where the Hotel Lenox now stands. In this location it was used for more than three decades, until the student body became too large.

The great Centennial Exposition at Philadelphia in 1876 was an important event in the Institute's life. In June a detachment from the student battalion under Lt. Zalinski maintained a camp, named "Camp W. B. Rogers," near the buildings of the University of Pennsylvania, which apparently served as M. I. T. headquarters. Dr. Rogers had been nominated as one of the Massachusetts commissioners, but was unable to serve. President Runkle represented the Institute and spent a good deal of time in Philadelphia studying the technical and educational exhibits, especially the Russian exhibit showing the stepwise training of young men in fundamental procedures which the engineer needs to know and showing how manual training could be co-ordinated with education for the mechanical industries. Runkle became convinced that this type of teaching would be invaluable in the training of mechanical engineers.

Runkle took back to Boston some samples of work done by Russian students, and plans of the shops in which the work was done. He then prepared a report for the Corporation suggesting that a flat-roofed, one-story building 125 by 40 feet could be built for $3,000 to house a new School of Practical Mechanism based on the Russian plan and at the same time to provide space for the laboratories of industrial and organic chemistry and for a proposed women's laboratory. The Corporation approved the report at a meeting in August, 1876, and voted to establish the school as soon as funds could be had. A gift for this purpose was secured, and the rest of the money was eventually appropriated.

The new building, a brick structure called the "Annex," was erected alongside the Rogers Building and was ready in the fall of 1876. Here the School of Mechanic Arts began offering a two-year course with instruction in elementary mathematics, English, drawing, and shopwork. This school, later moved to the "new" shops on Garrison Street, with enlarged facilities for wood and metal working, was the best and probably the first special shop for manual and machine training in the country, and was the origin of much of the later interest in manual training as an important element in education. It supplied the pattern for high schools of mechanic arts and strongly influenced the state agricultural and mechanical colleges set up after the Hatch Act. The School of Mechanic Arts—unlike the Lowell School of Design—was a specialized division of the Institute designed to train factory technicians and shop managers. Students pursuing this program were registered as "specials." In 1889, when other vocational institutions were arising, the school was discontinued, but training in shopwork continued to be given to regular and special students in the engineering departments.

LEAN YEARS

The Women's Laboratory, mentioned on page 55, began to function in 1876, and shared the Annex with the School of Mechanic Arts. Its establishment had been made possible by a generous contribution from the Women's Educational Association of Boston which in 1875 had made urgent request to the Government that a special laboratory for women be opened, "to afford instruction in chemical analysis, industrial chemistry, mineralogy and natural history." The great energy and organizing talent of Mrs. Ellen (Swallow) Richards were probably a major factor in its establishment and practical success. The new laboratory was placed under her direction and became the training ground for more than a hundred special students, some of whom later received the Institute S.B. degree. In 1883, when the mechanical shops were removed to a new location on Garrison Street, the Annex was torn down. A new building later known as the Walker Building, had been erected, and better opportunities for the higher education of women in scientific pursuits became available in the Kidder Laboratories of Chemistry and in the physical, biological, and other laboratories of the Institute. A special room, the Margaret Cheney Room, named for an early student, was set aside for the use of women students. When these changes were made, in 1883, the Women's Laboratory with its splendid record of service ceased. From this time properly qualified women were admitted to any of the professional courses of the Institute on the same basis as men.

In 1874 Runkle introduced the first official graduation exercises. Degrees had been authorized in 1868 by legislative act, and Runkle felt the need of some simple and dignified method of awarding them. The class of '74 was the first to receive them as a part of an organized but not a public ceremony. Strangely enough, this innovation was not mentioned in any catalogue or president's report of the years immediately following, and it was not until four years later, 1878, that graduation or commencement day became a public function at which parents and friends could witness the awarding of the hard-earned S.B. degrees. Thus began a practice that has been maintained ever since with increasing elaboration of program.

Another important development was the formation of the Alumni Association in 1875.[12] At the first annual reunion of the class of 1873, meeting on January 24, 1874, at the Parker House, George W. Blodgett moved that a committee of three be appointed to consult with other classes about the formation of an alumni association, and to report at the next annual meeting. The motion was approved, and three men were elected: Blodgett, William A. Kimball, and Webster Wells, all of '73 (and incidentally all graduates in civil engineering).

Kimball was most active in carrying on the work of the committee, and in October, 1874, addressed a questionnaire to the 102 graduates including the newly graduated class of 1874. He "earnestly requested" the graduates to meet on January 29, 1875, at 2 P.M. At the specified time twenty-seven men appeared. Professor Robert H. Richards '68, was chosen chairman of the meeting, and Kimball secretary, although the actual minutes of the meeting were kept by Professor Charles R. Cross '70. Kimball then outlined the numerous desirable functions of such an association, and the necessary details of organization were discussed. Cross '70, Richards '68, and Kimball '73, were nominated as a committee on the constitution. An organization meeting was held and officers *pro tempore* were chosen.

At the first actual annual meeting, held on January 27, 1876, balloting confirmed the election of Professor Richards as president and Professor Cross as secretary for two years. Isaiah S. P. Weeks '71 was elected vice-president, and C. Frank Allen '72 and Francis H. Williams '73 were elected to the Executive Committee. At this first annual dinner, on January 27, 1876, the assembled group passed the following resolution:

"Whereas, the Alumni Association of the Massachusetts Institute of Technology has perfected its organization, and thus completed the final step in the plan of the founder of the Institute, who with so much zeal and unselfishness devoted the best years of his life to its cause:

"*Resolved*, that we take this occasion to express our love and gratitude to Professor William B. Rogers, the father of this great and worthy enterprise."

Professor Richards sent a copy of the resolution to Dr. Rogers with a letter declaring the purpose of the Association to help build and strengthen the Institute. In a gracious reply Rogers expressed his appreciation, and his belief in the great potential value of the Alumni Association.

After several years of encouraging growth, if not prosperity, dark clouds appeared. The widespread depression following the panic of 1873 had serious effects on the Institute, not so much by actual losses in investments as by a reduction in the flow of small gifts to the school, and especially through a gradual falling off in the number of students due to lower incomes, higher entrance requirements, and an increase in tuition to $200 per year.

During these lean years President Runkle was constantly harassed by financial worries and the problems of retaining his loyal staff. As a result of the vigorous growth in the early seventies the faculty and instructing staff had been enlarged, and the additional salaries became a serious burden. Before the end of 1874 the treasurer reported that expenses already exceeded income. The finance committee of the Corporation voted to pay the debts, but also voted to recommend to the Corporation a most urgent attempt to secure a balance between expense and income. Members of the faculty proposed reductions in their already small salaries, and reductions in staff. Even the abolition of professorships was considered.

It was voted not to reduce the salaries of the staff, but new appointments were limited to young men with the rank of assistant. To help meet a threatening situation an anonymous donor generously gave $25,000 toward the payment of salaries. In one of the darkest periods, John Cummings, the treasurer, again proved his faith in the school by pledging his personal fortune in its behalf.

The spectre of poverty stalked the Institute. In 1877 President Runkle reported that "without immediate relief we must either discontinue some of the departments or cut down the salaries, already too small, or, more probably, both." A year later, worn out by constant anxiety and responsibility, President Runkle felt that he could no longer continue in the presidency, and resigned. Freed from responsibility, he was given leave of absence and spent nearly two years in Europe for rest and the study of industrial education abroad. At the opening of the year 1880-81 he resumed the Walker Professorship of Mathematics.

For eight years, at least five of them the most critical in the history of the Institute, he had given, as Dr. Rogers said, "unflagging devotion to its welfare." Fortunate, indeed, was the Institute to have had this devoted man in the presidency through this period of stress and anxiety. In days of somewhat less stress and brighter outlook it was also fortunate in having his service for more than a score of years as the revered senior professor in the department of mathematics.

President Runkle's resignation in 1878 brought a new problem to the Institute. Who should or could be his successor? All minds turned again to Dr. Rogers, and at the earnest solicitation of the Corporation, he reluctantly consented to resume the presidency of the Institute *pro tempore*, but only until a suitable successor should be found. In accepting this responsibility, however, he imposed two conditions: that the duties of the office should be lightened until a new president should be appointed, and that the Corporation should raise $100,000 to be added to the Institute funds by the beginning of the next school year. On December 10, 1879, Rogers was formally elected president for the second time.

Rogers immediately set to work to reduce expenses and to help raise money. With much regret Professor Howison's department of philosophy was discontinued, the teaching staff was cut, and salaries were reduced. Dr. Kneeland resigned as secretary so that the Institute would not have to pay his salary. Still the fees from students were insufficient to meet salaries, and professors were spending their own money for necessary apparatus. Happily by the end of the school year the tide began to turn. Subscriptions to capital funds had passed $60,000, and $2500 additional income was obtained through the rental of Huntington Hall for the Lowell lectures. Rogers began to see a ray of hope, and the following year his anxiety was lightened still further by excellent prospects and increased attendance at the opening of the school in the fall of 1880. He was also happy that his "dear Runkle" was back in his chosen work.

In this period, Rogers had also been carefully considering men who might become his successor. His choice soon rested on General Francis A. Walker, professor of political economy in the Sheffield Scientific School at Yale, and at this time actively engaged in Washington as Superintendent of the Tenth Census (1880). Rogers found an opportunity to hold some conversation with General Walker in the spring of 1880, and was deeply impressed. Thereupon, on June

12, acting with the authority of the Committee on the School, he wrote to General Walker, offering him the position of president, and characterizing him as "the person whom we may consider to be best fitted by scholarly training, zeal and administrative ability, to carry forward the educational plans of the Institute."

In a straightforward reply General Walker said, ". . . I can now say that I confidently anticipate being so far advanced in my Census work as to be able to leave in the hands of a deputy whatever may remain undone at the beginning of the collegiate year 1881-82, and that I entertain no doubt that I should then, with great satisfaction, if it were still desired on your part, transfer myself and all my work to the Institute of Technology, with the single desire to devote my time and energies to its interests. All my thoughts of the position you so kindly propose are agreeable, and I see nothing in the future which I would prefer to do. . . ."

Although it would still be a full year before General Walker could come, a great burden was lifted from President Rogers by this response. On May 20, 1881, the Corporation formally elected General Walker as President Rogers' successor. The election was at once reported to the faculty. In a letter to the retiring president a committee of the faculty voiced the faculty's appreciation of his great services, their loyal affection for him, and their assurance that his successor would carry forward the designs and ideals for the school he had so nobly developed.

For the last time as president, Rogers awarded the degrees at the graduation of the class of 1881. The new president took office in the fall without a formal inauguration, and Rogers continued to assist in the administration of the Institute during Walker's necessary absences in Washington. An inaugural ceremony was planned as a part of the graduation exercises of the class of 1882 on May 30, in which the ex-president should formally hand over to the actual president all the responsibilities and the metaphorical keys of the Institute. By order of General Walker, who declared that "He would not have his young men leave their *alma mater* under a symbol of mourning," the United States flag, which usually on Memorial Day floated at half-staff over the Institute, was this day flown at the top of the staff.

But mourning came all too soon, for on that day occurred the most tragic event in the history of the Institute. Huntington Hall was crowded with the graduating class, parents and friends who had come to attend the simple ceremonies, and others who sought this opportunity to hear the two outstanding leaders of the Institute, the founder, Dr. Rogers, and the energetic new president, General Walker. At the designated time on the program, President Walker arose, and with emotion and eloquence, introduced his predecessor as the great leader who had established a new era in higher education. Dr. Rogers, visibly affected, rose to reply. To use General Walker's own words: "His voice was at first weak and faltering, but as was his wont, he gathered inspiration from his theme, and for the moment his voice rang out in its full volume and in those well-remembered, most thrilling tones. Then, of a sudden, there was silence in the midst of the speech; that stately figure suddenly drooped, the fire died out of that eye ever so quick to kindle at noble thoughts, and, before one of his attentive listeners had time to suspect the cause, he fell to the platform instantly dead. . . ."

In that tragic but triumphant moment came the climax of a great life. For thirty-six years since he first promulgated his "Plan for a Polytechnic School in Boston," Rogers had battled ill health, disappointments and sorrows, financial depression, and the difficulties of establishing a new type of educational institution against the inertia of academic tradition, and had triumphed through sheer force of idealism, character, and personality.

Three days later, on Friday June 2, 1882, simple funeral services were held in the same hall. No other place could have been more appropriate, for William Barton Rogers' life had been built into this structure. The assemblage included the staff and student body of the Institute, many distinguished citizens of Boston, and representatives of the many organizations he had served and his membership had honored: the National Academy of Sciences, the University of Virginia, the American Academy of Arts and Sciences, the American Association for the Advancement of Science, the Boston Society of Natural History, the Appalachian Mountain Club, Harvard University, Yale University, and other colleges and societies.

The Reverend Dr. George E. Ellis, an intimate friend, conducted the simple service and spoke briefly and movingly of the great man whose active life was ended. The Reverend S. K. Lothrop added an eloquent tribute to the glory of Rogers' character and his remarkable personality and ability to command the interest of men. Colonel Theodore Lyman spoke of Rogers' love of nature and of his patience and ability in studying the secrets of the physical world. They were all simple and sincere tributes, spoken with deep affection as well as admiration for his clear vision, the power of his intellect, and the perfection of his character.

Thus ended the career of a great and good man, a marvellous leader who had seen his vision turned to reality, his ambition crowned by success, his life-long struggle victorious. He had lived to know that the project he had created was in safe and strong hands which would enlarge and ennoble the ideals he had conceived.

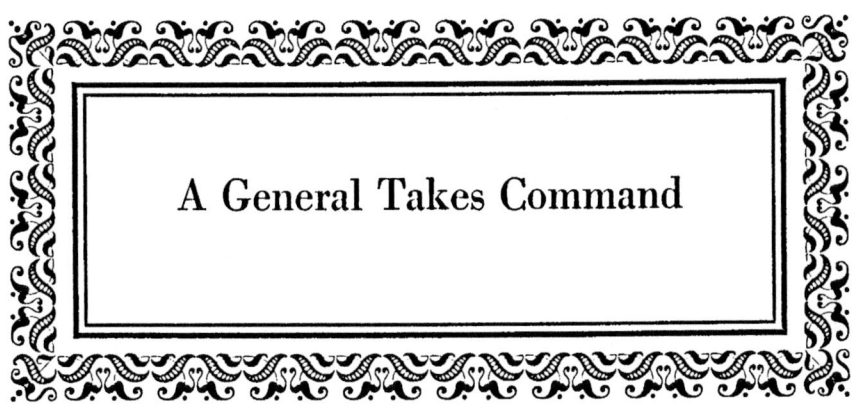

A General Takes Command

FRANCIS AMASA WALKER, although formally elected on May 20, 1881, actually became president of the Massachusetts Institute of Technology on November 1, 1881. Because of his responsibilities as Director of the Tenth Census (1880) he had been unable to give full time to the affairs of the Institute hitherto, and in fact, thereafter had to go to Washington frequently to supervise the completion of the voluminous reports. As we have seen, Dr. Rogers had offered to carry on the administration in the interim. There was therefore an overlapping of two eras, that of the organization and early development headed by a distinguished scientist—a man who had grown old in the long struggle to bring to reality his life-dream, and a new era of hope, revived courage, and the prospect of a great future under an able economist in the prime of life who had already been a brilliant soldier and was an administrator of proved and exceptional ability. Nothing could better have demonstrated the judgment of Rogers and his associates than the selection of General Walker to carry on the Institute's ideals and to build it into a great national institution.

At the age of forty-one when he took over the presidency, Francis A. Walker was already a distinguished and notable figure. He was born in Boston, June 2, 1840. His father, Amasa Walker, was a Boston merchant with a high sense of public duty; and his mother, born Hannah Ambrose, the daughter of a New Hampshire merchant, was a woman of great force of character. Soon after the birth of Francis, his second son, Amasa Walker gave up business life, moved to North Brookfield, Massachusetts, and devoted himself to public service and the study of economic problems. In 1842 he was elected a professor at Oberlin College and lectured there on political science without pay. For many years he was lecturer on economic problems at Amherst College, from which he received the honorary degree of LL.D. He published two notable books, *The Science of Wealth* and *The Nature and Uses of Money and Mixed Currency*, which gave him an international reputation. As a member of the American Peace Society, he attended peace congresses in London and Paris in 1843 and 1849. He served in both branches of the State legislature and for some years was Secretary of State for the Commonwealth. In 1860 he was a national elector voting for Lincoln, and the following year became a member of Congress.

Brought up in this stimulating intellectual atmosphere, young Francis responded readily to its influences. At the age of seven he began the study of Latin at a private school and later attended the academy in the neighboring town of Leicester, where he was prepared for college at fourteen but remained an additional year in the study of Latin and Greek. In 1855 at the age of fifteen he entered Amherst College expecting to transfer to Harvard after one year, but he continued at Amherst. In the middle of his sophomore year serious eye trouble forced him to withdraw for practically a year, but on recovery he joined the class of 1860 and completed his courses with that class. During his college years he was notable for his scholarship in economics, history, and philosophy, and for his ability as a writer and speaker. He won the Sweetser Essay Prize and the Hardy Prize for Extempore Speaking and was elected to Phi Beta Kappa. With apparently tireless energy he took part in various undergraduate activities, literary and otherwise. He was one of the editors of *The Undergraduate Monthly*. In 1857 when he was only seventeen, his "Thoughts on the Hard Times" was printed in the *National Era* of Washington, D. C., and in the following year the same journal printed four of his articles, one of which was entitled "Why are We a Manufacturing People?" He also assisted his father with various economic writings. Although the youngest member of his class, he was also the most influential and his opinions were the most respected. He was a leader in his fraternity, Delta Kappa Epsilon, was chosen junior orator, and in his senior year was elected president of his class. One of his classmates wrote of him: "He was a good scholar, a ready writer, a forcible speaker, an all-round athlete, and excellent chess player, a steadfast friend, and universally popular." He also excelled in boxing and was praised by a well-known prize fighter for his quickness. One weakness which he often mentioned in later life was a hasty, almost ungovernable temper which in his youth gave his family much anxiety, but which during his college years and thereafter he got increasingly under control although its fires were by no means dead.

Upon graduation he entered the law office of Devens and Hoar in Worcester, the senior partner of which was subsequently the famous General Charles Devens of the Civil War, and later attorney general of the United States in the Hayes administration, while the junior partner, George Frisbie Hoar, later was for many years the able U.S. senator from Massachusetts. During the critical winter of '60-'61 young Walker was drilling as a member of a rifle corps in Worcester. When the first call for the "Three Months Troops" came in April, 1861, he was eager to enlist, and even went so far as to equip himself with a uniform of Major Devens' 3rd Battalion of Rifles. An older brother had already enlisted but Francis was still a minor, and his father objected to having both his sons among the first 75,000 volunteers. The young man had to wait impatiently and unhappily for three months, until his twenty-first birthday gave him the legal power of decision. As the time approached, he wrote to Governor Andrew modestly expressing his desire to be commissioned in one of the companies to be organized for the war, and stating his previous training and education. His letter ended as follows: "I beg you, however, not to believe that I make a Commission the condition of my service for I hold myself ready for the humblest and hardest work in the sacred cause." On the same day he wrote to the adjutant general of the Massachusetts Volunteer Militia, whom he had apparently met at Amherst, urging his good offices with the governor. He closed his letter thus: "I believe I should make a reasonably good lieutenant; at any rate, I should like to try it, south of Mason and Dixon's line."

His patriotic aims were not immediately realized. After two disappointments in securing an expected commission, and after days of uneasy waiting became weeks, one day General Devens, who had already been at the front and had returned to recruit the Fifteenth Massachusetts Volunteers told him of a vacancy as sergeant-major in his regiment, but advised him not to take it, since it meant being an enlisted man with practically no chance of promotion. Walker had already ordered a second lieutenant's uniform, which was ready for delivery on that day. On calling for it, he asked the tailor to take off the shoulder straps and put on the chevrons of a sergeant-major. The decision made, he returned to the general's office, and on August 1, 1861, began his military career by reporting for duty as sergeant-major of the 15th Massachusetts Regiment. Shortly afterward, without his own knowledge or that of General Devens, he was honorably discharged from the service and immediately thereafter appointed captain and assistant adjutant general under General D. N. Couch. His habit of doing with diligence and intelligence the work he found to do, without asking whether it was in keeping with his education and social position, had brought an unexpected reward.

This is not the place to recount in detail General Walker's career as soldier. His war record was unusual, and may be summarized in his own transcript of his military titles:

August to September, 1861, Sergeant-major 15th Mass. Vols.
September 14, 1861 to August 10, 1862, Capt. and Assist. Adjutant General, U.S.V.
August 11 to December 31, 1862, Major and Asst. Adjutant General, U.S.V.
January 1, 1863 to January 12, 1865, Lieut. Colonel, Asst. Adjutant General, Headquarters Second Army Corps.
August, 1864, Brevet Colonel, U.S.V.
March 13, 1865, Brevet Brigadier General, U.S.V.

Throughout the war he was a staff officer with the Army of the Potomac in a highly responsible position. First under General Couch, later under Generals Hancock, Warren, Burnside, and Hooker, and eventually under General Grant, he was engaged in many battles and exposed to many dangers. Once his horse was shot under him but he was uninjured. At the battle of Chancellorsville he was so badly wounded by a bursting shell that he was obliged to go home for nearly three months; as soon as his wounds were healed he returned to active duty. In the following year while on his way to deliver a confidential message in the darkness of night, he was captured, and with other prisoners started the next day on the long march towards Richmond. With a companion he escaped into a swamp. When night fell he sought the Union lines, which could be reached only by swimming the Appomattox River. Stark naked, he was dramatically recaptured as the current took him to an enemy outpost. Then, ill and weakened by exposure, he was taken to Libby Prison and remained there with vitality at a low ebb for two months before being exchanged. He returned to North Brookfield to recover, but strength did not return, and he resigned on January 21, 1865. Two months later he was breveted brigadier general "for gallant conduct at Chancellorsville and meritorious services during the war."

He had entered the army, as he said, a "green boy" of twenty-one, and emerged a mature man, a brigadier general at twenty-five. During the next three years, with health partially restored, he taught Latin, Greek, and mathematics at Williston Seminary in Easthampton, Massachusetts, and at the same time assisted his father in writing *The Science of Wealth,* an occupation which broadened and intensified his interest in economics. In 1865 he married Miss Exene Stoughton of Gill, Massachusetts. He left Easthampton in 1868 to join the editorial staff of the strong Springfield *Republican.* He soon acquired a solid reputation and was sought as a lecturer in economics at Amherst College to succeed his father, who had gratuitously served the college for some years. As the census year 1870 approached, he was offered and accepted a federal appointment as Chief of the Bureau of Statistics and Deputy Special Commissioner of Internal Revenue, and was immediately made Superintendent of the Ninth Census. He carried out this difficult assignment so successfully that the *Report of the Ninth Census* excited the admiration of statisticians throughout the world. A noteworthy innovation was the "Atlas" showing by maps and graphs the great mass of statistical data which otherwise might have been merely a collection of important but unexciting tables of figures. Work on the census was delayed by the irritating inefficiency of politically appointed enumerators and collectors of data. It was several years before all divisions of the census were actually finished, and Walker was not entirely satisfied with it.

Before this work was finished, President Grant appointed him Commissioner of Indian Affairs, a post that required a scrupulously honest and fair-minded administrator. In this office from November, 1871, to his resignation on December 26, 1872, General Walker performed one of the great public services of his career. His wisdom in dealing with the problems involved was unfortunately not perpetuated by his successors.

Because of the needs of his growing family, Walker decided to resign from government service, and enter the shoe manufacturing business with his brother-in-law. Early in 1873, after he had prepared his belongings for shipment from Washington to North Brookfield, came the wholly unexpected offer of the professorship of political economy and history in the Sheffield Scientific School of Yale University, at a moderate salary. He at once rejected the prospect of a prosperous business career for the more congenial profession of teaching. Later in the year a similar offer came from his *alma mater,* Amherst, but he had already committed himself.

The next seven years, from 1873 to 1880, Walker spent in the highly successful administration of the department of political economy at the Sheffield Scientific School and in numerous incidental public services. For five of these years he was secretary of the Governing Board of the School. He served five years on the New Haven School Committee, and four on the State Board of Education. His life at New Haven was an extremely active one. Carefully groomed, and generally wearing a glossy silk hat, which accentuated his erect, military bearing, he became a conspicuous figure. He took the deepest interest in the academic and social welfare of the students, and as a lecturer commanded the profound respect of his hearers. Professor W. T. Sedgwick, who was one of his students at "Sheff" and later was brought by Walker to the M. I. T. faculty, more than once described to the writer how when "warmed up" the General would pace back and forth like a caged lion, at the same time presenting his lecture with such vigor, clarity, and even eloquence that every student listened with interest and admiration to the flow of his speech and ideas.

While a professor at Yale, Walker wrote constantly on economic subjects, and was in demand as a speaker before important groups. Offers of professorships in other universities and editorial posts on important newspapers, a request to allow his name to be put up for the presidency of Amherst, and many other opportunities were rejected. But the request that he serve as the Chief of the Bureau of Awards of the Philadelphia Centennial in 1876 appealed to his sense of national duty. He accepted the post, with the approval of the college, and performed the many and varied services to the complete satisfaction of exhibitors, commissioners, and foreign representatives. In 1878 he went to Paris as United States delegate to the International Monetary Conference, and presented his views on sound money with vigor. He was State Railroad Commissioner in 1879.

When a new law was passed making possible the improved system of statistical treatment which he and General Garfield had advocated ten years before, Garfield, now President, insisted that Walker should become Director of the Tenth Census (1880). Again it was a public duty that faced him, and in 1880 he left New Haven to assume this monumental task. His successor, Carroll D. Wright, said, "The contributions of the Tenth Census to social science constitute the most colossal official contribution that had ever been made by any government."

General Walker, at the age of forty-one, in vigorous health, was the perfect type to succeed William Barton Rogers. With a magnetic personality, a highly efficient organizing mind, a varied experience in responsibilities of the highest order, he had the reputation of being America's leading economist, and had developed a deep appreciation of technical and scientific education although his own training had been in the classics and the political sciences. In physical appearance he was a man of medium height, with broad shoulders and compact body. His erect, soldierly carriage and somewhat florid countenance dominated by keenly observant but kindly hazel eyes commanded instant attention. A carefully trained dark moustache, which became iron gray and was somewhat clipped as he advanced in years, added further distinction to his features. He was a marked man in any assemblage. He kept himself physically fit, and dressed with meticulous care. He usually wore a cutaway coat and dark striped trousers, but invariably put on a frock coat ("Prince Albert") for official meetings or occasions when he was to speak in public in the daytime. It may be doubted whether he possessed a sack coat for service outside his home. He generally wore a silk hat, always in perfect condition, which made him appear slightly taller than he really was. When the Walkers came to Boston there was a delightful but extremely busy family life. Seven children, five sons and two daughters, enlivened the household. Four of the sons attended the Institute in the years between 1883 and 1899. But for all young men the father had a genuine interest, from which sprang his desire to do all that was possible for the welfare of the students during his presidency.

On November 5, 1881, General Walker was formally introduced by President Rogers to the faculty, and on the 10th he attended his first meeting of the Corporation, when the retiring president introduced him to the members and he took the chair as president. At this meeting William Barton Rogers was made professor emeritus of physics and geology, the first appointment of this kind in the history of the Institute. In the first six months of his incumbency President Walker had to spend considerable time in Washington, and during this period Dr. Rogers assisted in administrative matters, with the internal details of staff administration handled by the newly appointed chairman of the faculty, Professor Ordway.

The precarious state of the Institute at the time of Walker's coming has already been indicated, and the lean years continued for nearly half of the new president's administration. But the leadership of a man with so many remarkable attributes brought unbounded hope and assurance to all. He was not unaware that in 1878 a second attempt at union with Harvard had been frustrated only by the self-sacrifice of Rogers in resuming the presidency, and the zeal and almost incredible labor of his associates in raising the $100,000. Although little documentary evidence exists, subtle attempts to compromise the Institute's independence were made, and Walker was well aware of them, as is recorded in the remarkable

A General Takes Command 115

biography of Walker [13] written by James Phinney Munroe '82, who for nine years was his constant associate and confidant. With characteristic vigor Walker championed absolute independence. From the beginning, Walker recognized four important problems: the broadening of the curriculum; the relief of the great congestion in the Rogers building, where practically all subjects were taught; the much needed enlargement of the staff; and the upbuilding of the physical, social, and moral welfare of the student body.

With characteristic energy General Walker not only assumed the arduous duties of president, but also plunged into work as an enthusiastic teacher, and gave a course of lectures on the principles of political economy, attended by all third-year students and many "specials." These lectures were very popular, and the students soon realized they were listening to a master of his subject. While occasionally hesitant at the beginning of a lecture, in a few minutes he would become so fluent and give such graphic illustrations, generally relating to current or historical affairs, that the subject pulsated with vitality.

With the wide range of new problems with which he was faced there was much need of discussion and consultation with members of the staff and even with the students. In these matters he was always approachable and while it might be his duty to determine policies he was invariably ready to receive comment and suggestion. The door of the president's office, on the left of the main entrance hall of the Rogers building, was almost always invitingly open when he was within. Anyone desiring to consult him, whether high official, professor, or lowly student, was free to enter and talk, briefly if possible, of his problems, and could be sure of an interested and courteous hearing. The president's large table was about midway in the room, facing the door, and always burdened at each end with piles of official papers, journals, and reports.

It was an office that betokened constant activity rather than leisure, and its occupant was a prodigious worker. He carried on a voluminous correspondence, and for the first ten years his letters were generally written by his own hand at home at night. During this period a public typist occasionally assisted him. Then one young lady, Miss Julia Comstock, was appointed as an assistant to the office staff of the Institute, and spent part of her time in the president's office as a personal assistant.[14] One of her duties was using the telephone—there was only one in the Institute—which the president absolutely refused to touch.

Although one of the busiest of men, the president always seemed to find time to welcome a visitor cordially and then to give close consideration to the matter on which the vistor wished to consult. The memory of a moment when as a timid freshman the writer sought presidential advice on some trivial matter of statistics and the kindliness and gracious attention given in those few minutes has been a happy one for three score years. It was entirely in keeping with Walker's inborn kindliness, his high sense of duty, and his desire to give help to any who needed it. The editor-in-chief of *Technique,* the college annual then published by the Junior class, once stopped to make an inquiry just at the end of the afternoon period, when Walker was about to leave the office. After greeting the young man the president rose, took his silk hat, and accompanied by the student passed down the granite steps and toward Berkeley Street discussing the matter as they walked along. On the sidewalk they were accosted by an elderly and ill-clad woman, who had apparently become confused and lost her way. Instantly, the president raised his hat with characteristic courtesy and directed the poor woman to her destination. It sometimes happened that the illness of a student not living at home came to the president's knowledge. In such a case, he would at once go to the boy's boarding house to assure himself that proper care was given, and then possibly write to the parents.

It was acts and events like these and hundreds of other evidences of the president's interest, thoughtfulness, and sincerity that made him a heroic and beloved figure, an ideal in the minds and hearts of the students. But they also learned that he could be stern and incensed by misbehavior. One day in the later years of his presidency, hearing unusual commotion in the lobby, he dashed from his office to break up a "rush" which a large group of sophomores had started when the freshman class emerged from a lecture room on the first floor. Without a word, but scarlet with anger, he entered the fray, threw the trouble makers right and left with startling speed, demonstrating with well-directed blows his skill as a trained boxer. In short order, he broke up the fight, and then "with forceful language reminiscent of the army," gave the cowed and surprised students a lesson in college manners which was not soon forgotten. This episode became a lasting memory and tradition that added to his prestige in the eyes of the admiring student body.

Next to the dynamic effect of his personality, his selection of men of character and vision to fill educational posts in the various professional fields was President Walker's most memorable contribution to the Institute. In 1881 the faculty, including the president himself, ex-president Rogers, the first professor emeritus, and ex-president Runkle, numbered but twenty. Among them Professors Runkle and Osborne in mathematics; Richards in mining and metallurgy; Cross in physics; Niles in geology; and Lanza in mechanical engineering constituted a popular group who had pioneered in the earlier years but who were also destined to continue into the twentieth century their outstanding service to the Institute. Their early colleagues on the faculty, Atkinson, Nichols, Henck, Ware, Ordway, Whitaker and Luquiens, had not been held in less esteem by the students of the period but were sooner to be lost to the Institute through election to other institutions, resignation, and death. A serious loss was that of Professor William Ripley Nichols '69, a remarkable teacher and pioneer in sanitary chemistry. After years of work while suffering from an obscure and apparently incurable malady, he had gone to Germany for treatment, and died in Hamburg in 1886 following an operation. In addition to the professors who constituted the official faculty, the instructing staff also included nine with the rank of instructor, seven of whom, H. K. Burrison '75, Ellen H. Richards '73, Silas W. Holman '76, W. O. Crosby '76, G. F. Swain '77, W. H. Pickering '79, and Charles L. Adams, later became known to many generations of students. There were also eleven assistants, so that the total instructing staff numbered forty.

President Walker recognized that the Institute's growing reputation was perforce closely related to the strength and quality of the teaching staff, and that to maintain its standards it was now imperative to make a number of new appointments because of the marked increase in number of students and the broadening and diversification of the work of the school. With many new applications of science and engineering already foreshadowed or definitely under way, it was necessary to have a faculty staffed with additional men of the type able to foresee and promote the development of important new fields, such as electrical engineering which was recognized at M. I. T. in 1882 by the establishment of a professional course in the subject, the first in the country.

In the first two years of President Walker's administration, the number of professors and assistant professors had been increased to twenty-three. In these two years had occurred the death of Dr. Rogers and the resignations of Professor Ware and Professor John M. Ordway. Ordway had been elected as head of all chemical and related work at Tulane University in New Orleans. His going was deeply regretted, for he had for fifteen years rendered great service as professor of industrial chemistry and metallurgy.

In 1883 Walker began the series of strong appointments to the staff that did much to determine the future history of technological teaching not only at the Institute but throughout the country. The upward trend in numbers, begun in 1880, now seemed certain to be continuous and to promise stability. Because of the rapid expansion in the range of subjects which must be taught to provide the best professional training, President Walker was insistent that only the most promising men should be selected. For new instructors and for laboratory assistants, some of the best men of the graduating class or from recent classes were found to be most satisfactory, since they already knew the Institute and its standards. The ranks were soon to be further strengthened, both by promotions from within and by the appointment of outstanding men from outside who brought new inspiration and enthusiasm into the staff.

Practically all departments were urgently in need of additional personnel. Fortunately, some appointments and several promotions had been made in his first two years which had partially met the need. Silas W. Holman '76, a brilliant physicist and admirable teacher, was made an assistant professor in 1882. His career at the Institute was one of outstanding service for more than twenty years, especially as an associate of Professor Cross in electrical engineering and theoretical physics. In the early nineties Holman suffered a gradually increasing paralysis which completely inactivated him in 1897. His

A General Takes Command

keen mind was not impaired, and even when he had to be moved in a wheel chair he came daily to the Institute and was constantly consulted by eager and admiring students. Greatly mourned, he died in 1900. Another graduate in the famous class of 1876, William O. Crosby, who had become a recognized authority in geology and mineralogy, and achieved fame for his thorough exposition of the geology of the Boston basin, was appointed assistant professor in 1883. His career at the Institute covered a span of fifty years and all grades from assistant to full professor.

In addition to these men, six new assistant professors were appointed in 1883. George F. Swain '77, now recognized as possibly the finest teacher-engineer of civil engineering the country has produced, was instructor in civil engineering from 1881 to 1883, as the chief helper to George L. Vose, who had succeeded John B. Henck, Sr., as professor in 1882. The brilliant Swain was made assistant professor in 1883, and in 1888, after the retirement of Vose, he was made Hayward Professor of Civil Engineering in charge of that department. At that time the expansion of railways had created a great demand for civil engineers, and the department was the largest in the Institute. Swain's influence at the Institute was immediate and powerful, his career a brilliant one, and his reputation national. In 1909 he was finally induced to become the McKay Professor and head the department of civil engineering at Harvard University, but was again associated with the Institute as a teacher in the five-year period of joint activity, 1914-1919.

The growing importance of the field of industrial chemistry led to the appointment of Lewis M. Norton as instructor in that subject in 1882. Six years before, while a special student at the Institute in the class of 1875, he had been a laboratory assistant in chemistry. After several years of practical industrial experience, he had two years of graduate study in Germany. He was an excellent teacher, an extremely industrious worker, and a man of warm personality. He was promoted to an assistant professorship in 1883, and from then until his untimely death from pneumonia in 1893 he was untiring in his service to the Institute. As one of his last group of students, the writer pays tribute to his ability, kindness, and fine character. It was he who proposed and was the compelling force in the establishment of the course in chemical engineering, the first of its kind in the world, which was opened to students under W. H. Walker in 1888 and graduated its first class in 1891. In its more than sixty years of existence, this department has become one of the largest, most widely known, and nationally important departments of the Institute, and students have come to it from all parts of the globe.

Also in 1883 William T. Sedgwick was appointed assistant professor of biology and at once took charge of the department of natural history, one division of which prepared students for the study of medicine. Sedgwick had graduated at the Sheffield Scientific School at Yale in 1877. While an undergraduate in biological chemistry expecting to study medicine, he had sat spellbound at the brilliant lectures of Walker, then professor of political economy at Yale. That they should later be associated as professor and president and as close friends was a happy turn of the wheel of fate. Sedgwick worked his way through "Sheff" as a tutor and as a laboratory assistant to Dr. R. H. Chittenden, the distinguished pioneer in biological chemistry. He then attended the Yale Medical School for two years, at the same time serving as a teacher in Chittenden's absence abroad, after which he was awarded a fellowship in biology at the new Johns Hopkins University, where he obtained his Ph.D. degree in 1881.

From this time, teaching was Sedgwick's chosen profession. After two years as associate in biology at Johns Hopkins, his service at the Institute began. The original name of the department—natural history—was officially changed to biology in 1889. Sedgwick completely reorganized the work, and for a time taught practically all the biological subjects himself. As a teacher he was without a peer. He really founded a new department, which always remained small but extremely useful. In later years, it had great influence on the development of public health and sanitary engineering not only at M. I. T. but throughout the country. Sedgwick himself became the outstanding leader in public health in America, and many of his students became distinguished in sanitary engineering and in public health administration. His influence on his students was remarkable. He should be remembered also for the editorial help given to Mrs. Rogers in the preparation of the two notable volumes, *The Life and Letters of William Barton Rogers*.

A General Takes Command

Webster Wells of the class of 1873, who had been made instructor, and for a time bursar, was another of this group of men promoted in 1883. He was made assistant professor in charge of first year mathematics and served also for a year as secretary of the faculty. His textbooks in algebra and geometry were widely used in secondary schools as well as in the colleges. He was a very quiet and reserved but not unfriendly man, and although he lacked the saving sense of humor to a large degree, he taught with faithful thoroughness.

A different type of personality was exhibited by Peter Schwamb, a graduate in mechanical engineering in the class of 1878, who had worked for four years in the plant of a locomotive manufacturing company as a draftsman and designer. He came in 1883 as an instructor and director of the shops of the School of Mechanic Arts, which had been established by the efforts of President Runkle, and in 1883 he became assistant professor of mechanism. This basic subject, fundamental to advanced work in machine design, he taught with enthusiasm and skill. He was a man of inventive capacity and sound theoretical and practical knowledge, and also a kindly and patient teacher who liked students and would spend hours helping those who needed it.

Three other appointments, originally made in the School of Mechanic Arts but later transferred to the regular staff in mechanical engineering, should here be mentioned. In 1884 James R. Lambirth, for years affectionately known as "Pop," became instructor in forging, and Theodore B. Merrick instructor in wood-working. In 1886 Robert H. Smith began his long career in charge of the machine tool laboratory. Merrick remained on the staff until 1915. Both Lambirth and Smith were very popular with their students, and both reached retirement age in 1932, and were thereafter listed as emeritus professors.

Several others who came in as instructors in the early years of Walker's administration subsequently played an important part in the development of the Institute or in the advancement of science in America. One of these was the distinguished astronomer, William H. Pickering, a graduate in 1879, an assistant and an instructor in physics from 1880 to 1887, and thereafter associated with the Harvard Astronomical Observatory, especially as the head of the great South

American Observatory established at Arequipa, Peru. Another was Cecil H. Peabody '77, who was one of the early American teachers in Japan, where he spent two or three years teaching mechanical engineering at Sapporo. He then returned to America, and after a year at the University of Illinois, he became instructor in steam engineering at M. I. T. and was made an assistant professor in 1884. He should be remembered as the organizer and first head of the department of naval architecture and marine engineering, a department which has for fifty years had a memorable and continuous history, and is especially noteworthy for its service as a graduate school for the naval constructors sent from the U.S. Naval Academy.

Another and an especially highly regarded man of this group was Alfred E. Burton, a graduate of Bowdoin College in the class of 1878, and for four years an assistant on the U.S. Coast and Geodetic Survey, where he had a broad experience in exploration and observation. In 1882 he had been appointed instructor in topographical engineering, and in 1884 was promoted to an assistant professorship.

Burton's genial personality combined with his varied and interesting professional experience and his skill as a teacher made him a great favorite with his students, and indeed with all students at the Institute. He liked and understood young men, appreciated their problems, and could deal with them with common sense and sympathy, for he was one of the friendliest of men. He was one of the organizers of the first summer school in surveying and related aspects of civil engineering in 1887, a project which later became an important part of the school work, and was greatly broadened when a large tract of land was acquired for a permanent summer camp on Gardner Lake in Maine, and its excellent equipment was made possible by interested alumni. It is not surprising to find that Professor Burton, with his eminent qualifications for the position, eventually became the first dean of students at the Institute.

One of the most distinguished members of the Institute's staff throughout this period was Ellen H. Richards (Mrs. Robert H. Richards), who had the rank of instructor in chemistry from 1878 until her death in 1911. During her lifetime she was the only woman on the instructing staff. As Ellen H. Swallow she had graduated at Vassar College in 1870 and then came to M. I. T. as a special student to study chemistry. She completed the requirements for the S.B. degree in 1873 and as previously recorded, was assistant to Professors Nichols and Ordway. She married Professor Richards in 1875, continued her chemical work, and was director of the Women's Laboratory from 1876 until it was discontinued in 1883. She was then appointed as an instructor on the regular Institute staff and thereafter for many years she shared in the teaching of all students of food chemistry and sanitary chemistry, and in these fields became the foremost authority of her sex in the world. In the middle eighties she was noted for her investigations of water supplies, especially those of Massachusetts, in association with Professor Thomas M. Drown. As a result of her work she became nationally famous as the founder of the "home economics" or "domestic science" movement, and the pioneer in the study of the technology and economics of home management, with emphasis on a broad study of foods and nutrition. In this field her writings were considered law and gospel, and she lectured with tireless energy before women's clubs and colleges throughout the country. Her professional work in the Institute's laboratories helped to give Technology a reputation as the leading center in America for the study of sanitation of water, food, and air. In addition to carrying on her own professional work and maintaining a hospitable home, she was of great assistance to her husband in his field. She helped him with his examination papers, his reports, and his books, for by accompanying him on summer excursions to all sorts of mining operations, she had acquired a wide knowledge of mining and metallurgy. A bronze tablet now in Building Four bears testimony to the great contribution of Ellen Swallow Richards, the most remarkable woman in Technology's history, and one of the great women of the country.

President Walker was quick to recognize special ability in the students of the upper years. In James P. Munroe of the class of 1882 he saw a keen and particularly capable senior with a special gift for the type of work demanded of an executive secretary of the faculty. On his graduation the appointment was made, and then began the long association of Mr. Munroe with the administration of the Institute. As one of the founders of the college paper, *The Tech*, in 1881, Munroe had acquired a broad knowledge of student and alumni affairs, which was constantly drawn upon and expanded in the seven years he served as clerk, registrar, and secretary of the faculty. When Mr. Munroe felt impelled to withdraw officially to enter his father's business in Boston, he remained closely in touch with Institute affairs and was highly influential in them. In 1897 he was elected a member of the Corporation and served as its secretary from 1907 to 1929. His close association with President Walker led to his writing a biography, *A Life of Francis Amasa Walker*, published in 1923. The service of Mr. Munroe to the Institute was lifelong. His influence in the decades following President Walker's death will be considered later.

Another alumnus of that era closely associated with President Walker, was Harry W. Tyler of the class of '84. Although he was graduated as a chemist, his main interest was in mathematics, and he was at once appointed assistant in that department. In 1887 he went to Germany for two years of graduate study, and on his return in 1889, he taught mathematics and succeeded Mr. Munroe as secretary of the faculty for a year. In this work he was so successful that in 1891, a year after his appointment as assistant professor, he again became the secretary of the faculty, and although he was also made head of the department of mathematics in 1902, he carried the two positions with great success until 1906, when he resigned as secretary of the faculty.

One other appointment in the first five years of General Walker's presidency is a particularly notable one. In 1885 Dr. Thomas M. Drown, a graduate of the Medical School of the University of Pennsylvania, and an analytical chemist of great distinction, was made head of the department of chemistry as the successor to Professor John M. Ordway, whose resignation to become department head at Tulane University has been recorded. Professor Drown brought expert knowledge and service not only to the Institute but also to the State of Massachusetts. He and Professor Sedgwick served the State Department of Health as consulting chemist and consulting biologist respectively in the epoch-making studies on water supply and sewage disposal carried out at the Lawrence Experiment Station, which stimulated much work elsewhere in the United States and brought the highest recognition from experts in these fields in England and on the Continent. Indirectly this work is closely related to the history

A General Takes Command 125

of scientific research and education at the Institute. In 1895 Dr. Drown resigned to become president of Lehigh University.

The second five-year period of the Walker regime was, like the first, one of continuous growth in numbers of students and in reputation. Within this period the student body approached the thousand mark and exceeded it in 1891-92. Growth, however pleasing, also meant added and even more rapidly growing expense and responsibility. Still further accessions to the staff were needed, partly as replacements for old men who had died or retired but largely to meet the educational demands in the growing professional fields and in the broadening general education that was a part of the program established by the faculty for the professional courses.

Sound, even if comparatively limited, training in English and history, economics, or what was then called political economy, and foreign languages was insisted on as a part of the mental equipment of the man who was to have the Bachelor of Science degree of M. I. T. It was natural that President Walker, himself a social scientist, should take the lead in strengthening this part of the Institute's educational program by giving his vigorous and brilliant lectures on political economy. Greatly strengthened by these lectures, the courses in science and literature and elective studies were amalgamated in 1882 into a course in general studies, known for many years thereafter as Course IX. This course demanded two years of basic work in the sciences and mathematics, but in the upper years placed its main emphasis on the fields of economics, political and industrial history, public or business law, English, and modern languages. Although never one of the large courses, it had a marked influence in the school for many years. Most of its graduates went at once into teaching, law, or business, and many attained leadership in their fields. To strengthen the staff in this area, now called the humanities, the most important appointments were those of Charles H. Levermore in history, George R. Carpenter and, somewhat later, Arlo Bates in English, Charles F. A. Currier in history, Alphonse van Daell in modern languages and Davis R. Dewey in economics. Within a few years, Professor Levermore was called to head Adelphi College in Brooklyn, and Professor Carpenter to become the head of a department at Columbia. Professor Bates served with increasing distinction until his lamented death in 1918.

Professor Charles Otis, long head of the modern language work, a great friend to students and an excellent teacher, died during the school year 1888-89. He had been a professor at M. I. T. since 1873. His place was taken a year later by Professor Alphonse van Daell, a native of Belgium, an experienced teacher and a man of pleasing manners and wide learning. His students found in him a wellspring of inspiration, humor, and a generous desire to add to their cultural appreciation and social adjustment. The writer happens to be one of that group.

In 1887, Professor Calvin Francis Allen joined the staff of the Civil Engineering Department. Professor Allen had graduated at the Institute in 1872 and after lengthy experience in the work of railway construction in the west, especially with the Sante Fé, during which time he also became a lawyer, he returned to teach railway engineering at the Institute. He was active in the Alumni Association and for several years its secretary, and was one of the founders of the Society for Promotion of Engineering Education. His deep interest in these matters continued throughout his long life until his death at age ninety-seven in 1948.

Another man who joined the civil engineering staff in the middle eighties was Professor Dwight Porter, who had been known to President Walker at Yale and in connection with the Census of 1880, on which Porter had been a special commissioner on water power and hydraulics. This experience gave him expert knowledge in this field, and his teaching was highly effective. He also was in direct charge of the course in sanitary engineering, the first of its kind anywhere, which had been established in 1889 as an autonomous division of the department of civil engineering. This useful division, which was closely associated with special branches such as bacteriology and sanitary chemistry in the departments of biology and chemistry was wisely administered by him throughout his whole period of service, until he retired in 1921.

In 1888 Francis W. Chandler, who in the early seventies had been an assistant, returned to M. I. T. as the head of the department of architecture, which had already established its reputation as the leading American school of architecture. Professor Chandler's years of rich experience especially as supervising architect for the Treasury Department, his deep knowledge of the various types of architectural development, and his remarkable personality now added greatly to the reputation of this department and attracted many students who later became leading men in their profession.

Another professor who joined the staff in the Walker period and who wielded great influence in his own department was Professor Heinrich O. Hofman, a native of Heidelberg and a graduate of the Royal Prussian School of Mines. He later had wide experience in metallurgy in Germany and in various parts of America. He thus added to the already high reputation which the mining department had gained through the outstanding work of Professor Richards and his associates.

If William Barton Rogers and the men who so valiantly served with him in the first fifteen years of M. I. T. history may be regarded as the pioneers who explored the realm of the new education, cleared the land, and planted the first seed, Francis A. Walker and the group he appointed in the following ten years may be thought of as those who still pioneered but also carefully tended and enriched the fields of technical education and brought them into an era of broadened usefulness. These two groups exerted a definitive and continuous influence on the Institute's educational aims and philosophy. The results of their painstaking deliberations and discussions in an active faculty, debating problems of education from various angles, broad in their possibly varying viewpoints and yet generous, co-operative, and harmonious in arriving at constructive ideas and modes of action, have largely determined the whole course of the educational policy of the school.

An Era of Development

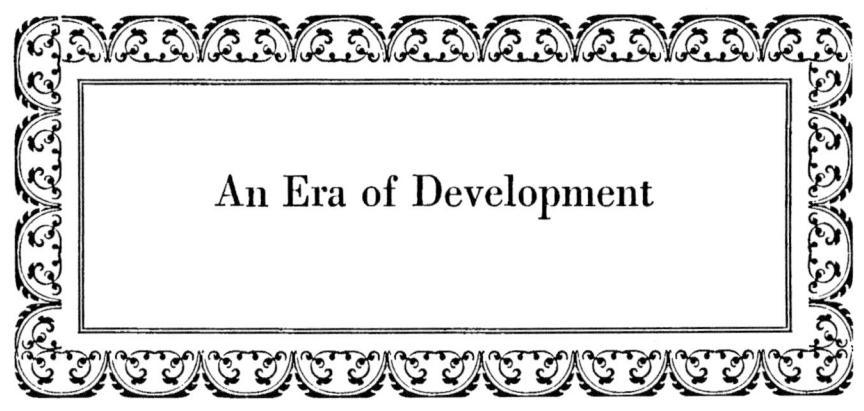

THE fifteen years of the Walker administration (1881-1897) were an era of great development, both for the Institute and for technical education in America. When General Walker assumed the presidency in 1881 he found a school with extremely slender resources, a small but extremely loyal and overworked faculty, and a student body of about 300 with a strong tradition of hard work. By the time he died in 1897, the Institute had become a truly national institution, the leader of the new type of education in America, with an enrollment of 1200 students, a staff of acknowledged leaders in the technical professions, and a well-developed and universally recognized philosophy of education.

The growth of the Institute measured in terms of numbers of students and staff is indicated by the graph on page 130. In 1878 the enrollment had dropped to 188, the lowest point since 1872, but had shown some increase in the next two years, until in 1881 it touched three hundred. Of these only about half were regular students, the rest being "specials," most of whom did not expect to complete the requirements for a degree and who often did not stay in the school more than a year or two. After 1881 enrollment grew steadily. It had doubled by 1887, and doubled again by the time of

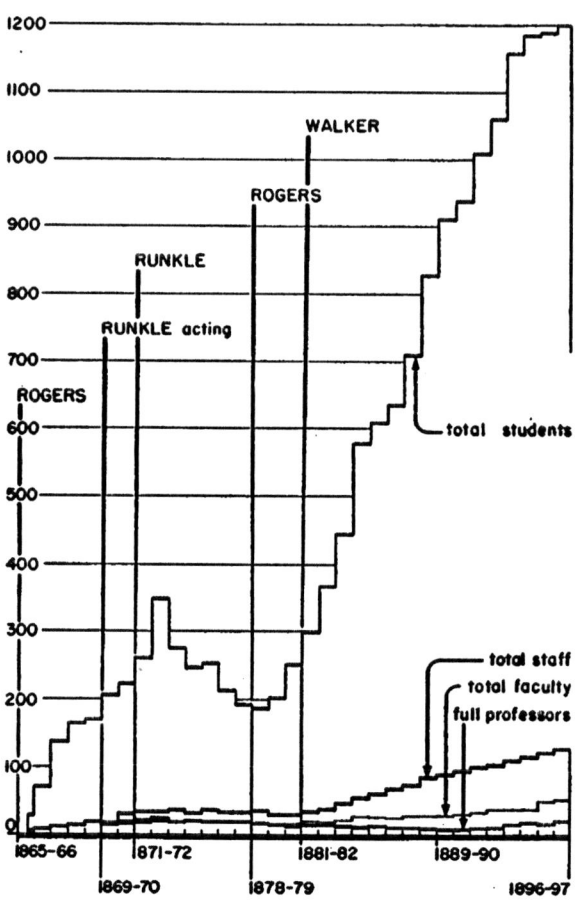

Walker's death. During this period the total staff grew from 38 to 128, of whom 52 were faculty members.

In the task of seeking funds to provide the necessary physical equipment and staff for this development Walker was aided by devoted members of the Corporation. In 1881 the Corporation numbered thirty-three, including the three representatives of the Commonwealth. It still contained nine men who had been on the original committee of twenty, and nine others who had been on its roster since the middle sixties. Eighteen of the Corporation members had thus been active almost from the beginning and had grown old in its service. As time passed, some of the original group had died or resigned. Notable among the losses were John Amory Lowell, ever a great friend of the Institute, Dr. Samuel Kneeland, long its secretary, C. H. Dalton, the first treasurer, Ralph Huntington, E. B. Bigelow, J. M. Beebe, E. S. Tobey, R. C. Greenleaf, J. I. Bowditch, and S. P. Ruggles, who had been strong supporters in the difficult years. Their places had gradually been taken by other well-known and highly competent men, including Augustus Lowell, Henry P. Kidder, Howard A. Carson '69, Charles Fairchild, Samuel D. Warren, and Edward S. Philbrick. The ever faithful and loyal John Cummings was still treasurer, and the representatives of the Commonwealth were Governor John D. Long, Chief Justice Marcus Morton, and John W. Dickinson, secretary of the State Board of Education.

By the end of 1882 it became clear to the president that, with the growth of the school, and the increasing frequency of its problems which needed careful discussion and prompt decision, it was quite impossible to have matters handled promptly and effectively by the Corporation as a whole, or even by the large Committee on the School of Industrial Science, many of whom through business demands, age, or physical disabilities rather than waning interest, could not maintain the activity of earlier years. With the changes then taking place quick action was often necessary, and absenteeism made difficulties in administration when questions of policy had to be met and financial problems settled. Sensing these difficulties, Walker set up an Executive Committee, consisting of the president and treasurer, *ex officiis*, and five other members, continuity being provided by the annual choice by the Corporation of one of its members to serve for five years. This Executive Committee, meeting frequently at stated intervals, was given the power to deal with immediate problems, major and minor, including teaching appointments, with committee action subject to confirmation by the whole Corporation. This radical change in administrative policy, while somewhat startling to the conservative, was a powerful factor in the extraordinary development of the school under President Walker.

Another immediate problem confronting President Walker was more difficult to solve. More space for the work of the Institute had been needed even in times of lowest attendance, but now with increasing numbers, the need was critical. The physical plant consisted of the main building on Boylston Street, which was already crowded; the one-story brick structure (it could hardly be called a building) built by President Runkle to house the School of Mechanic Arts and the Women's Laboratory, which was outgrown and totally inadequate; and the drill shed at the Clarendon Street end of the block. There were no funds for further building on the Boylston Street site.

Back in 1873 the Institute had petitioned the legislature for a grant of a small plot of about 12,000 feet of the Back Bay lands located in what is now the central part of Copley Square in front of Trinity Church. Here it had been proposed to erect a building for the use of the departments of chemistry and mining. The petition was successful, but the buildings were not erected for lack of funds. Now eight years later President Walker, carefully surveying the gravity of the situation, declared his intention to work for the immediate erection of a building on this area, which the Institute controlled without restriction. Trinity Church had been built and was in use in 1877. The proposal to build immediately in front of the noble façade of Trinity was naturally very disturbing to its communicants, but the relations with Trinity remained friendly, as they had been from the beginning. The eventual outcome, and one in harmony with the public interest, was the advantageous sale in 1882 of the land to become part of a public square. The money received was to be used towards a new building on the same block with the main Technology building.

Although the proceeds of the sale were grossly inadequate for the purpose, the president boldly proceeded to move the old drill shed to a plot of land leased from the Boston and Albany Railroad on Exeter Street, and to have plans prepared for a new building to take its place on the Claredon Street end of the block. Construction was begun on faith that the necessary money could be secured afterward. It was a distasteful situation, for Walker abhorred begging and exploiting himself, but there was no other way, and with the assistance of some of the men on the Corporation he undertook the task of raising funds for the building.

The New Building, as it was called, completed in 1883, was externally no architectural gem, and contrasted most strikingly with the beautiful classic building with which it shared the grounds. President Walker recognized its unlovely exterior, but there was insufficient money for both adornment and utility, and he had insisted that internally it should be especially well adapted to the purposes for which it was to be used. Some years later, by vote of the Corporation, this useful building was named the Walker Building.

In 1882 a few lots of land on Garrison Street, next to the railroad, were purchased. On a part of this land a two-story building was quickly erected to provide space for the mechanical shops on the first floor, and for the Lowell School of Industrial Design on the upper floor. This building replaced the temporary building—the Annex—that since 1876 had housed the shops and the Women's Laboratory.

The first seven years of President Walker's administration were indeed lean years, and he often said that he never could be quite sure of not finding the building locked and in the hands of creditors as he came to his office in the morning. The New Building had cost about $165,000, and the shops on Garrison Street about $30,000 more. The William Barton Rogers Memorial Fund of $250,000 had been secured through the exertions of two members of the Corporation, but this could not be used for construction, and so did not remove the great need for additional endowment. In his report for 1884, Walker explained the urgent need of early and large endowments. "Shall funds be wanting," he asked, "to place this school, whose unsurpassed usefulness among the educational institutions of the country stands acknowledged by the unprecedented accession of students from every part of the land, upon an assured basis, and to give it the means fully to meet the growing demands of the community?" He pointed out the need of endowment as a reserve against hard times, as security against financial disaster or the possibility of temporary internal mismanagement. He declared it "a perilous position for an educational institution that it should depend so largely upon tuition fees as to draw one-half its revenue from this source. Yet five-sixths of the income of the Institute of Technology will be thus derived the current year." Funds were needed, he said, for free scholarships, for lowering tuition fees, for making it possible to make salaries of the teaching staff at least as high as the salaries in classical colleges, to meet the progressive demands of industrial education, and to provide for original research. This earnest and broad presentation of the need for endowment, coupled with his wholehearted belief in the great value of the Institute to industry in the community and throughout the country was reiterated and expanded in his reports of 1885 and 1886.

In the second five-year period of President Walker's administration came a few rays of sunlight to dispel the financial gloom that had hitherto beclouded his presidency. The first of these was the bequest of $100,000 in 1887 under the will of Richard Perkins of Boston. Before becoming a confirmed invalid, Mr. Perkins had frequently visited the Institute and observed the students at work in laboratories and drawing rooms. His interest in the school did not diminish in spite of eight years of continuous invalidism. The whole sum thus obtained was to be maintained as a permanent fund, half the income to be used in assisting needy students, the other half to be at the discretion of the Corporation.

In December, 1886, the Corporation found it necessary to petition the State Legislature for a grant of $200,000 from the public treasury to strengthen its financial condition. The legislature of 1887 voted to appropriate one-half the amount requested, to be paid in two annual instalments on the 1st of December, 1887, and the 1st of December, 1888, but imposed two conditions, that $100,000 from other sources should be added to the funds of the Institute prior to the first payment by the state, and that twenty free scholarships should be established and maintained under conditions imposed in the law.

After strenuous effort led by William Endicott the $100,000 demanded as conditional to the state appropriation was secured from previous contributors to the Institute. But the condition requiring twenty free scholarships was not easy to accept, since it actually would impose an additional financial burden on the school. It was therefore decided to ask the legislature at its next session to increase the amount of the authorized grant by the further sum of $100,000. President Walker presented the matter earnestly and brilliantly to the appropriate committees of the General Court, and the additional amount was voted.

An Era of Development

What this effort cost President Walker in strength and nervous energy is beyond estimate. As he more than once remarked, it had "shortened his life by ten years." The grant was a great relief to the administration and an encouragement to the faculty. The Corporation was able to pay the debts incurred by the construction of the New Building, and to meet certain other obligations, including the appointment of more staff members. Ten state scholarships were granted to deserving young men for the year 1887-88, and ten more were to be awarded the following year, after the second payment by the state.

Another act of the Legislature of 1888 was significant in Institute history. On petition of the Corporation, the original statute which limited the Institute's authority to hold real and personal estate to an amount of which the clear income might be $30,000 was replaced by an act authorizing the Institute to hold property to an amount that would yield an income of $100,000, to be devoted exclusively to the purposes and objects set forth in the original and additional acts of incorporation. The action of the Corporation in seeking the change was a farsighted and important one. In at least one instance a similar legal limitation had prevented a university from accepting a large bequest. In the case of the Institute the restriction was not harmful at the time of the change, but it might become so, and eventually (1905) it was entirely removed.

The grant of state aid was a great help in meeting past obligations, but it did not provide for the future growth and security of the Institute. In his annual reports Walker continued to stress the need for endowment funds so that the Institute would not have to rely to such a dangerous degree on tuition fees and state aid, and so that it could safely meet the demand for expansion of its work in the various branches of science, engineering, and industry.

By the fall of 1888 the School of Industrial Science had 827 students and a faculty of twenty-nine professors of all grades, thirty-two instructors, and eighteen assistants, and the need for more space for classrooms and laboratories was again urgent. In the early summer of 1888 the Executive Committee by authority of the Corporation had purchased some 19,000 square feet of land on Trinity Place, at a cost of more than $76,000, as a site of new a building. It was decided that this building should be devoted largely to the departments of mechanical and civil engineering, and should be of especially strong mill construction, capable of supporting heavy machinery without the jarring and tremors so familiar in the Rogers Building.

The building and equipment were completed before the end of the calendar year—a six-story building, with the two lower floors for the laboratories of the department of mechanical engineering, the next two for its drawing rooms and classrooms, and the two upper floors for the department of civil engineering. This at once became known as the Engineering Building (later Engineering A). Its completion made possible extensive space changes for overcrowded departments which had previously been housed in the Rogers and New Buildings. For the first time in many years several of the departments of the school had breathing space, but even now none had really enough to provide the best conditions for teaching or study, and research space was practically non-existent.

The second five-year period of President Walker's administration ended in 1891. In the ten years he had, by great administrative ability, indomitable energy, and unremitting industry, combined with a rare and compelling personality, welded Corporation and instructing staff into a great and efficient organization, and brought the Massachusetts Institute of Technology to world-wide reputation and a dominant position in technical education. It was far from rich in financial resources—in fact it probably operated each year with a deficit—but it had wealth of character because Walker and his associates on the Corporation and on the faculty had wealth of character, faith, ability, and a courage which could not dream of failure.

The remainder of General Walker's presidency, beginning in 1891, was a period of comparative calm. The growth of the student body, percentagewise, now became slow. When Walker assumed the presidency there were 302 students. At the end of his first five years there were 637, a gain of 335, or over one hundred per cent. During the second five years (to 1891) the gain was 374, or sixty per cent, to a total of 1011. This was the first year that registration exceeded a thousand students. Thereafter, the enrollment rose by

An Era of Development

variable but small increments to 1,198 in 1896-97, the year of the president's death.

But the registration figures supply a very inadequate basis for showing the real growth of the institution. A far better criterion is the expansion in the professional courses or the new departments of professional work and in the physical resources, the buildings and laboratories of the Institute. The course in electrical engineering had been established in 1882 as an offshoot of the department of physics. Chemical engineering followed in 1888, under Dr. L. M. Norton, as a combination of industrial chemistry and mechanical engineering; natural history had become the much broadened course, biology; the course in sanitary engineering began in 1889 with co-ordinated work in civil engineering, biology, and chemistry; and geology was set up as a professional course in 1890. Moreover, great expansion in special fields of interest had taken place in all departments, so that by 1891 an overcrowded condition again existed.

To relieve the department of architecture which had completely outgrown its quarters in the New Building and to allow for the expansion of electrical engineering, physics, and chemistry, another building was erected alongside the Engineering Building on Trinity Place. It was occupied in 1892, largely by the department of architecture, and was known as the Architectural Building.

The small yearly increase in registration was carefully discussed by President Walker in his annual report to the Corporation for 1894. Expressing surprise and satisfaction that there was not an actual loss instead of a slight gain in numbers, he recounted certain causes which might reasonably have brought a falling off in numbers. First, the period of hard times beginning in 1893 seriously affected the income of all classes in the community, and was especially felt at the Institute since most of its students came from families of limited or moderate means. The depression prevented many new students from entering and forced the withdrawal of some who had already registered but could not meet the tuition payments of $200 a year.

A second but perhaps minor reason was that more advanced admission requirements in mathematics had this year been put into effect, and some preparatory schools had been unable to meet these requirements at once. A third cause, which might be expected to produce a falling off in attendance at the Institute was the remarkable increase in technical schools or departments in state universities and colleges in many parts of the country which were now offering courses of instruction more or less like those given at the Institute, and at lower cost to the student. Walker was pleased rather than alarmed at this growing competition. The greater the desire for scientific education, he said, the greater the constituency to which the Institute could appeal, and the greater the need for the Institute's leadership.

Nevertheless the annual deficits showed that the financial situation was serious. An appeal to have the Franklin Fund, which had grown to more than $350,000, devoted to the permanent endowment of physics and electricity at the Institute was rejected by the trustees of the fund. The Franklin Institute in Boston, a high-grade trade school, was established instead. This decision though disappointing was not entirely unexpected. Then the Corporation, on December 12, 1894, voted to appeal again to the legislature for an annual appropriation to the Institute for a brief term of years. This was the first appeal for State funds since 1887 and 1888.

The petition presented to the legislature at the 1895 session was for $25,000 per annum for the next six years. It recited the numerous reasons for the imperative need, the exceptional expenses for apparatus and machinery for teaching purposes, the services which could be rendered to the manufacturers of the state now in a serious situation from outside competition, and the interest of the Commonwealth that this school, the first institute of general technology founded in this country, should not fail for lack of means. The appropriation was voted by the legislature with an amendment appropriating two thousand dollars a year during the same term for ten free scholarships in addition to those established under the acts of 1887 and 1888. The aid received by this action of the legislature was timely and most gratefully received by administration and instructing staff.

The new building for the department of architecture had not been occupied for more than a year when the need for additional space was acutely felt by several departments. Again lack of funds prevented immediate action. Fortunately, a few bequests and gifts had come to the Institute in the late eighties and early nineties so that the general tension had been slightly relieved, and the president and Corporation began to discuss the possibilities of additional building. In 1893 the Institute purchased the land on Clarendon Street then occupied by a skating rink and later by the Grundman Studios, and the vacant land lying between the Institute's property on Trinity Place and the Providence Railroad yards, a total of fifty thousand square feet, at a cost of $299,000. On a part of this land a new boiler house was built, and the inadequate steam pipes from the Rogers Building were removed. Although there were no additional funds in sight, it was finally decided to proceed with plans for a new educational building to be located on Trinity Place next to the Architectural Building with faith that the money would be found. In 1896, a few months after the decision was made, the faith was justified, for it was learned that Henry L. Pierce, a member of the Corporation who had been head of the company owning the great chocolate mills in Dorchester (now a subsidiary of General Foods), had made an unrestricted bequest of $750,000 to the Institute.

The news of this sudden fortune, coming after so many years of continuous anxiety, filled President Walker's cup of happiness to overflowing. It semed to be the reward for his years of toil and worry, of faith and optimism, and unshakable belief in the future. The Pierce bequest was used for the new building, which was named the Pierce Building. By the irony of fate, President Walker did not live to see it completed. When it was occupied in the fall of 1898, it added twenty-five per cent to the classroom space of the Institute, and housed the departments of biology, geology, and architecture, and the laboratories of industrial chemistry. The building originally built for the architectural department was then used for engineering work and became known as Engineering B.

From the beginning of his presidency General Walker had determined to promote the physical welfare of the students and to provide a finer social atmosphere. Interest in young men was one of the dominant elements in his character, and even when immersed in the most exacting matters of endowments, new buildings, and faculty appointments, he never failed to give aid and encouragement to students who sought worthily to add variety and spice to their serious preparation for a professional career. To help the students towards a broader outlook and more complete or well-rounded development was one of his objectives quite as definitely as that of keeping the Institute in a position of leadership in technical education.

When Walker came in 1881, nearly two-thirds of the 302 students lived in Boston or in the cities and towns within commuting distance. From nearby suburbs they walked or came by horsecar daily, and from the outlying towns by train to one of the half dozen stations in the city, whence they generally walked to the school. Students came daily from as far as Worcester, Newburyport, and Lawrence, or even farther. To make a nine o'clock class they had to rise with the lark, snatch a hasty breakfast, and hurry to the depot to get an early train. At the end of the day they got home in time for a late supper, with work for the next day still to be done. Whatever diversions or social life these students had were likely to be in their home town rather than at "the Tech."

Since there were no dormitories, students from more distant points had to find quarters in South End rooming houses or private homes throughout the city, for the vicinity of the Institute was sparsely settled in the early years. The full class schedules and the time spent in travel left very little opportunity for diversion or organized recreation. Furthermore many students were "specials," often older men primarily interested in pursuing the work in some specialized field in which they had already had some experience, and not candidates for a degree. Many of the most successful and loyal of M. I. T.'s alumni were in this group. In the seventies less than half of the students were taking the full schedule of subjects, and as late as the middle nineties only sixty-one per cent of all students were "regulars." With the emphasis so largely on a full-time program of classes and laboratory work, and with so many commuting and special students, "college spirit" developed slowly. It was generally assumed that Tech students were quite different from the students in the older or "liberal" colleges. They came largely from families of limited means and no traditional college loyalties, and they came with serious and immediate objectives. For many of them association with fellow students was confined to class and laboratory exercises and military drill, with occasional meetings between classes or at the noon period. There was no lunch room for students until 1876, when a small one was provided at one end of the drill shed, and there were never any chapel exercises, either voluntary or mandatory. Yet somehow a general acquaintanceship developed, despite slow trains and long days, and from the beginning the hard-working students developed pride in being Technology men and acquired something of the spirit that had made M. I. T. possible. Even those who remained for only a year or who fell out of the ranks before graduation absorbed a feeling of loyalty which was often evident in later years.

In the early seventies when attendance at the Institute was approaching its first peak, the beginnings of an institutional spirit found expression in the establishment of a student publication, *The Spectrum*, a monthly of a few pages, which first appeared in 1873. No list of editors was given, and the brief essays on current events and the occasional verse throw no light on the identity of the authors. Its articles were varied and brief, with little relation to the student life in the school. One article decried the lack of opportunity for social diversions because of the severity of the studies. The paper apparently had a difficult career, and succumbed at the end of its second volume. The Treasure Case of the Institute library contains several numbers of the two incomplete volumes — the only ones known to exist today — donated by W. E. Nickerson '76, who quite probably was one of the editors. Thereafter the depression years brought a rapid falling off of students, and unfavorable conditions for the cultivation of the institutional spirit which had begun earlier.

It is clear that in comparison with modern times there was very little of what may be called student activities before President Walker's time. The Alumni Association, formed in 1875, served as a rallying point for the graduates, but its efforts were for the institution rather than for the undergraduates. When once again better times began in 1880, and students from widely scattered areas came in greater numbers, interest in undergraduate activities rose. General Walker sensed the need for a richer student life and early turned his attention to the physical and social side of student life. He was sympathetic to all moves by student groups to enlarge their range of interests in both the social and the athletic fields. The M. I. T. Athletic Club had come into existence, but there was no other attempt at organized athletics prior to Walker's time. Temporary baseball teams played wherever a vacant lot could be found. There was also a combination gymnasium and drill hall in the shed-like building on the sand lot at the corner of Boylston and Clarendon Streets, but its equipment was extremely meagre. One of Walker's first moves was to take up the matter of an appropriation for improving the gymnasium and for a tennis court near the building. He was at heart an athlete himself, but since his college days his life had been so crowded with great responsibilities that his only participation was in attending occasional baseball or football games, especially those between Harvard and Yale, where as a former Yale professor he always gave enthusiastic support to the Blue. He was therefore sympathetic to the limited development of these games as a source of enjoyment and exercise. Interest in athletics grew somewhat as the student body increased. A Football Association was formed in 1884, and an intercollegiate association organized in 1886 included Williams, Amherst, Tufts, and Technology. This reached its climax in 1889 when Tech's uncoached team won the intercollegiate pennant. Football had not then reached the dominant position it later assumed in college life, and games were played for enjoyment, without expensive equipment or coaches. The game persisted lamely at Tech until 1906, when student government decided that M. I. T. men had neither the time for training nor the means to keep up intercollegiate competition. On the other hand track athletics, which gave opportunity to more men in special types of athletic activity, became increasingly popular, and M. I. T. teams competed with a fair share of success.

The most quoted—and probably the most widely misunderstood—words that President Walker ever wrote were these: "This is a place for men to work and not for boys to play." These words aroused considerable discussion at the time they were first used, and they have since been quoted out of context by hundreds of alumni proud of their rigorous training at M. I. T.

Actually these words were originally part of a plea for better athletic facilities.[15] Walker was never opposed to recreation and sport;

he believed thoroughly in their physical and mental value and their broadening influence if used wisely. In fact he strove mightily to dispel the popular opinion that Technology men were badly overworked, and that only the most brilliant could succeed. In his many discussions of American education, however, he did protest against indifference to real attainment and against the excessive dominance of athletics and social and club life as he had seen them developing in many of the colleges in the country, possibly as the result of the swing to an elective system which made it possible for a student to elect "snap courses" that might be entirely unco-ordinated. Walker noted with apprehension that a college course might be extremely enjoyable socially but lacking in substantial basis for human service. Since an engineering or technical training aims especially to prepare students for serious professional responsibilities, the president felt that the student's *work* should receive first consideration. "The four years spent at the Institute," he said in his president's report in 1886, are "spent in the work, not of decoration, but of construction; not in polishing the surface, but in building up the substance of mind and character." Nevertheless he encouraged student activities conducted in a rational way as a help rather than a hindrance to good scholastic development.

In spite of the lack of facilities and time, numerous clubs and societies came into existence to satisfy the gregarious instincts and the professional interests of the students, some short-lived, and some more permanent. The 2G Society was formed in 1881 by the students in mining engineering; an Architectural Association served similarly for the students in architecture, and a Mechanical Engineering Debating Society soon followed. The K_2S Society was limited to students interested in chemistry, and a Civil Engineering Society drew the students of that department. In addition a number of clubs brought together congenial men for dining or for special interests: a glee club, an orchestral club, and several regional and language societies. Some of the transitory organizations of this period had amusing or mysterious names, such as Dy/Dx, Hammer and Tongs, K.O.S., Mandamin, and Pi Kappa. One dining club known as T.L. had as its motto *Semper Macaroni Terrapinque*. These clubs were not large in membership and generally represented the more well-to-do men in the school.

The first fraternity, Sigma Chi, was founded in March 1882. Within three years Theta Xi and Alpha Tau Omega were chartered (1885). The club known as The No. 6 Club from its house at 6 Louisburg Square soon became a chapter of Delta Psi and within the next six years Technology had chapters in Phi Gamma Delta, Delta Tau Delta, Delta Kappa Epsilon, Chi Phi, and Delta Upsilon, and a local, Phi Beta Epsilon, which has maintained its independent status for over sixty years. The fraternities, although few, were extremely useful in providing living quarters for congenial groups of men in limted numbers, but in the eighties and nineties they comprised only a very small part of the student body.

In 1881 a new student paper, *The Tech*, was founded. It began its long career on November 16, 1881, under an enterprising and loyal group consisting of H. Ward Leonard '83, President, H. E. Ross '82, W. B. Snow '82, H. B. Gale '83, H. G. Pratt '84, I. W. Litchfield '85, and A. D. Little '85. The first editorial board was composed of A. W. Walker '81, editor-in-chief, G. W. Mansfield '82, G. J. Foran '83, F. F. Johnson '84, H. S. Chase '83, G. T. Snelling '82, C. H. Tompkins '83, and R. T. Gibbons '83. In 1883-84 the president of the committee was H. W. Tyler '84, and in 1884-85, I. W. Litchfield '85.

The Tech was active in promoting a larger degree of student government, and the formation of the Institute Committee in 1893 was in part due to its excellent editorial boards in the early nineties. The Institute Committee, with its original membership composed of the president and two members of each of the classes, and its purpose to promote the interests of the Institute at home and abroad, has had a large and salutary influence on undergraduate affairs ever since its inception.

A different kind of periodical more in the nature of a technical journal was *The Technology Quarterly* begun by students in 1887. It was taken over in 1890 by the Institute as an official publication under the editorship of James P. Munroe '82 publishing the proceedings of the Society of Arts, papers presented to the Society, and accounts of research work done at the Institute. From 1892 until it ended in 1908 Dr. R. P. Bigelow, the Institute librarian, was editor.

An Era of Development

In 1890, a lunchroom was established under the excellent management of Mrs. Ellen A. King in the basement of the Rogers Building. Her husband having died, Mrs. King bravely began a new career to support herself and two small daughters, and by hard work, skill, and unusual character, she made the project a great success and became a personage commanding the highest regard of presidents, professors, and everyone else at the Institute. This kindly, cultivated, and remarkable woman was the motherly friend of hundreds and possibly thousands of students in the eighteen years that "Mrs. King's lunchroom" existed. Untrained in business matters, she quickly won the help of professors in her bookkeeping and in other matters, and the lunchroom became a real social center for staff and students at the midday period. She was a real friend to all, but especially to scores of boys who found her a sympathetic and wise adviser in days of stress, and a person with whom they could discuss books and poetry in hours of leisure. In 1898 the lunchroom was moved to larger quarters in the basement of the Pierce Building, and it was finally supplanted in 1908 by the new Union Building. In tribute to Mrs. King's character and loyalty to the Institute she was elected an honorary member of the Alumni Association on her retirement in 1908, a deserved honor which she deeply appreciated to the end of her long life.

The Student Co-operative Society was established in the 1890's to sell books and supplies at as near cost as possible. In the same period the Technology Y. M. C. A., the forerunner of the broader Technology Christian Association, undertook the useful work of locating suitable rooms for students. The facilities for social activities in the Institute buildings were still very meagre at the end of Walker's administration. In the very early years, the faculty once granted the use of the "gym" for a dance, over the protests of a more strait-laced committee of students, which had refused to sanction its use. Finally in 1896 The Technology Club was opened on Newbury Street nearly opposite the Rogers Building, with alumni, staff members, and senior students eligible for membership. It was a highly useful organization during all the years the Institute remained in Boston, and became the general headquarters of alumni activities. President Walker was one of the promoters of the club, and believed whole-heartedly in its great value to the Institute as a place where students and staff could daily meet on equal terms for luncheon or dinner, or for the numerous social gatherings and entertaining talks by well-known speakers that were held under its auspices.

One of the most striking characteristics of the Walker regime was the continuously increasing accession of students from many remote parts of the United States and from foreign countries. This had actually begun in the early seventies when the aims of the school, as so brilliantly set forth by President Rogers, had attracted attention far beyond the bounds of Massachusetts. Walker did much to attract able students from all over the country by arranging for entrance examinations in several large cities, and by offering summer instruction to students from other colleges who wished to qualify for advanced standing. In his first report to the Corporation in 1883, he pointed out that of the total of 443 students registered that year, sixty-five per cent were from Massachusetts and nearly seventy-eight per cent from New England, and that twenty-two states and territories including the District of Columbia were represented. Four foreign countries sent eight students. In the senior class of that year twenty-five out of the twenty-nine men were from Massachusetts. In 1891, the first year that student population exceeded one thousand, thirty-nine states as well as the District of Columbia were represented, and twenty-two foreign countries sent thirty-eight students, the largest number until after the turn of the century. Walker's last report (1896) recorded that 60.9 per cent of the students were from Massachusetts, that forty of the forty-four states were represented, and that twenty students came from twelve foreign countries. Boston Tech had indeed already become an international as well as a national institution.

By the 1890's President Walker was known throughout the civilized world as a leader in economic thinking and in the development of technological education. His annual president's reports, which included careful statistical analyses of the student body—studies of age, geographic origin, quality of preparation, and distribution among the technical fields—and equally careful presentation of his views on higher education in general and technological training in particular, are important documents in the history of American education. Their vigor, sound reasoning, and high idealism make them stimulating reading today. Walker had a great and inspiring faith in the new type of education that M. I. T. stood for, in which vigorous technical courses of study were combined with what he regarded as equally important liberalizing courses in English, economics, and languages, and he saw in it great potentialities for the future of America. Commenting on the increasing popularity of technological education in the report for 1894, he said:

It has been stated that not less than one hundred colleges and universities in the United States are to-day offering technical instruction. There is now not a State in the Union without an institution in which more or less of a course in Engineering is laid out. Some of these are classical institutions of long standing and high repute, which are as rapidly as possible transforming themselves to meet the wants of the age. If, indeed, "imitation is the sincerest form of flattery," those who originated the earlier schools of science and technology have reason to pray that their heads may not be turned, as one classical college after another throws overboard studies and exercises which thirty years ago were declared to be absolutely essential to mental discipline and culture, without which no one could become a thoroughly educated and cultivated man, to make room for studies and exercises which, even down to recent days, have been stigmatized as interested, mercenary, and of a base flavor. Certainly the surviving founders of the Massachusetts Institute of Technology, who, from 1857 to 1865, supported President Rogers and Dr. Jacob Bigelow in the demand for an educational system better adapted to the wants of modern life than the mediaeval and monastic culture then alone offered to the aspiring student, have reason to rejoice that the battle of the New Education is won. . . .

. . . I have no fear of any decline in the relative importance or influence of our school. There will be as much need of leadership in this department of education as ever, even as in the early days when the Faculty of the Institute of Technology first developed the laboratory of General Chemistry, the laboratory of General Physics, the laboratory of Economic Metallurgy, the laboratory of Applied Mechanics and the laboratories of Steam, Hydraulic, and Electrical Engineering. And the more highly the educational value of scientific study and practice is appreciated, the whole land over, the larger, and not the smaller, will be the number of those who will desire to obtain that instruction and training under the very best conditions.

Early on the morning of January 5, 1897, President Walker died from a stroke of apoplexy at the age of fifty-six. Everyone connected with the Institute was dazed by the calamity. Messages expressing the great loss to state and country and to education poured in from official sources, and from many individuals throughout the United States and England who had been associated with him in military or governmental life, or in the field of political economy, in which he was the recognized leader.

His funeral, held in Trinity Church, was crowded with distinguished citizens, state and city officials, college presidents and professors, and perhaps most impressive of all, the whole student body, unashamedly weeping as the casket containing the form of the man they had idealized was borne from the church on the shoulders of a group of senior students. It was an event of great sorrow and solemnity, but an occasion surcharged with the deep consciousness of the triumphant ending of the life of a truly great man.

Two days after the untimely death of President Walker a mass meeting of students was held in Huntington Hall to adopt resolutions expressing the grief of the undergraduate body. At this meeting it was voted that a committee of three make arrangements for a student memorial to the late president. Wilfred Bancroft '97, president of the senior class and chairman of the meeting, appointed the committee of which Charles-Edward A. Winslow '98 was made chairman. A year later on the anniversary of Walker's death, at a great meeting in Huntington Hall, President Crafts presiding, Mr. Winslow, president of the senior class as well as chairman of the student committee, made the presentation of the memorial. He spoke as follows:

The committee decided to secure the erection of a bust as the most fitting memorial within their power; and, for its execution, turned to Mr. Daniel Chester French as an eminent sculptor and as a personal friend of General Walker.[16] The committee wish to express their special gratitude to Mr. French for what has been, in a large measure, a labor of love. . . .

The funds for the monument the committee wished to obtain entirely from the undergraduate body; this was done before the end of the term, the sum being completed by a generous gift from the Class of '97.

During the summer the bust was modelled; the autumn has been taken up in casting it and in constructing the tablet and the bracket upon which it rests. The completed monument now stands in the corridor below; and the committee are prepared to-day, in the name of the students of the Massachusetts Institute of Technology in the classes of 1897, 1898, 1899, and 1900, to present it to the Corporation of the Institute.

This bust is not needed, sir, as a monument to President Walker. President Walker's monument is found in something more enduring than marble or than bronze, in the great school which he built up until it led the world. President Walker's monument is found in something more beautiful than any creation of the sculptor's art, in the strong and noble characters which have drawn their inspiration from him, and moulded themselves after his example. The students of the Institute can erect a true memorial only by living after the manner of him who held that the mission of education was to make men, and by exhibiting increasing loyalty to the school which he believed was better equipped than any other to fulfill that mission. . . .

And we ask you to let this bust of President Walker stand in the corridor, Mr. President, because we want the students of the future to know something of his presence as we knew it. General Walker, while he lived, was not content to be merely a great name to his pupils; he must not become so now. His personality, which knit every Institute man to itself with special individual bonds, must never fade from memory.

As you look upon the enduring bronze below, transfigured by the touch of a compelling art, you will feel that this personality is with us once again. You will see in that eloquent face the courage which was undaunted by the rout of Chancellorsville; the energy which revolutionized the United States Census; the broad, clear vision which established an epoch in Political Economy; the loyalty and devotion which built up this institution; the modesty, the hopefulness, the enthusiasm, which made President Walker our ideal of all that we hold true and manly. . . .

After a formal acceptance speech by President Crafts, the audience, deeply moved, passed to the corridor below, where the bronze rested upon its marble bracket. Here the flag, which had till then concealed the bust, was drawn by Ambrose Walker '91, a son of the president. During the ceremony the Glee Club sang with beautiful solemnity "Integer Vitae."[17]

In this same year the Alumni Association also appointed a committee to make plans and collect funds for a more substantial memorial—a gymnasium and social center for students. By 1902 over $100,000 had been subscribed and the Corporation set aside land for the building, but because of a proposal to move the Institute plans for the building were suspended and the Walker Memorial was not completed until 1917. A different type of memorial was a biography of President Walker published in 1923. It was written by James P. Munroe with a deep understanding and knowledge that came from years of intimate contact.

The death of General Walker ended the second great era in the history of M. I. T., an era of strengthening and expanding the institution built by the educational vision of the founder. In the half century from the time when William Barton Rogers had put into words his great concept of a polytechnic school in Boston, which he and his brother Henry had so carefully planned, and in a little more than thirty years from the time this vision of a new education came to its embryonic realization in the opening of the school in the old Mercantile Library Building on Summer Street, the Massachusetts Institute had become the leading school of engineering and applied science in the Western Hemisphere, and possibly without a peer in the whole world. Within a single generation as men count human existence, the Institute had grown from less than a score of students taught in a few bare rooms, to more than a thousand who daily went to their classes in four large and well equipped but crowded buildings in the best part of Boston.

Here was the monument of three men whose names must never be forgotten by those who have been students in its laboratories and classrooms. Rogers, the seer, the man of broad and prophetic vision, the eloquent orator who could sway the thoughts of men, had founded something even greater than he could have known. Runkle, loyal, able coadjutor and kindly and devoted teacher, had nobly supported the founder and had led the Institute through its darkest hours until his strength was exhausted. Then Rogers again took the helm for two difficult years, and in this time found a new and incomparable successor. Walker, brilliant soldier and administrator in war and even more brilliant in the service of his country in peace, by his dynamic personality, unremitting toil, wisdom, and unflinching faith, had brought the school through years of financial stress and established it firmly in its position of leadership.

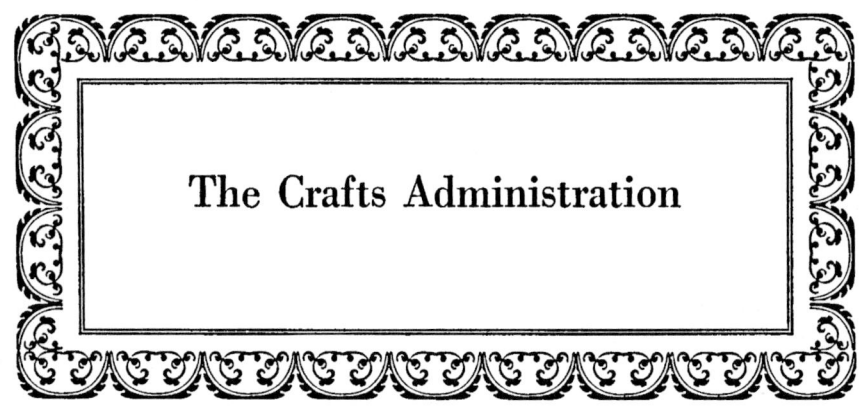

The Crafts Administration

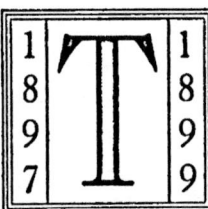

THE sudden death of President Walker brought the difficult question of the choice of a new leader for the Institute. On January 13, 1897, eight days after President Walker's death, Professor James Mason Crafts, senior professor in chemistry, was elected chairman of the faculty, to carry on the administrative functions for the remainder of the academic year. During this period careful thought could be given to the selection of a successor to President Walker.

Undeniably men of the type of Rogers or of Walker are so rare that few appear in a single generation. But it would seem quite natural that among the chosen associates of a great leader there would be men of fine qualifications and more than ordinary calibre, who could succeed to topmost positions of responsibility and leadership. Fortunately, at this critical juncture, there were on the faculty of the Institute a number of men of recognized leadership in educational and professional work in science or engineering, who had been in long and intimate contact with the late president and with the school, and who had the ability, the judgment, and the loyalty to its ideals, to serve as its head, if this service should be required of them. Men like Swain, Sedgwick, Tyler, and Dewey, as well as the older and internationally known Crafts, were in this group. But there was no early intimation that one of these men might be chosen, and no trace of competition for consideration or preferment.

On October 20, 1897, the Corporation elected Professor Crafts as the fourth president of the Institute.

The career of James Mason Crafts was an unusual one. He had a world-wide reputation in his special field of organic chemistry, since his most important researches and discoveries had been made while he was working in Europe, much of the time on leave of absence from the Institute. He was born in Boston, March 8, 1839, of old New England family. His father, Royal A. Crafts, was a successful merchant and pioneer woolen manufacturer. His mother was the daughter of Jeremiah Mason, a famous lawyer in Boston, and often the legal opponent of Daniel Webster. His early schooling was at well-known private schools for boys, Mr. Kidder's in Bowdoin Square and Mr. Sullivan's near Park Street Church. Then for a time he attended the Boston Latin School, and was later tutored by Dr. Samuel Eliot. His early predilection for experimental science, especially chemistry, led to his attendance at practically all the scientific lectures so popular at this period in Boston, and it was thus that he fell under the spell of William Barton Rogers. He was even more influenced by Rogers through meeting him at his grandfather's house, where Rogers was a frequent visitor, and where the two men held long conversations on scientific subjects, much to the boy's edification. He also listened eagerly to Professor Josiah Parsons Cooke, professor of chemistry at Harvard, and to Louis Agassiz, the great naturalist who first came to America in 1846 to lecture at the Lowell Institute.

Under these influences, the youth's mind developed a strong scientific trend. After his preparatory years he gave up his earlier intention of going to Harvard College and entered the Lawrence Scientific School, from which he was graduated with an S.B. degree in 1858. The following year he studied in the engineering department of the school, and the next six years he continued his studies in foreign universities. He first went to Freiburg to study mining engineering, then, as chemistry became his compelling interest, to Heidelberg, where he became the friend and for a time private assistant of the great Bunsen. In 1861 he went to the École de

Médicin in Paris to study, and there worked with Würtz, one of the greatest of organic chemists, for four years. Here he met Charles Friedel, with whom he was later to be associated in research. In 1865 he returned to America and spent a year traveling in Mexico and California, being interested especially in silver mining. He then established a private research laboratory in Professor Eben N. Horsford's old house in Cambridge.

When Cornell University which was founded in Ithaca by Ezra Cornell, opened its doors in 1868, Crafts, at the age of twenty-nine, was called to the chair of chemistry, and became dean of the chemical faculty, in charge of the department. Pioneering in a new school developed his organizing ability and gave him experience in administration as well as in teaching. While at Cornell he published a short course in qualitative analysis. In 1870 he accepted the professorship of general and analytical chemistry at M. I. T. made vacant by the resignation of Professor Storer, and the following year was appointed professor of analytical and organic chemistry. In 1875 he was made professor of organic chemistry. Unfortunately, four years after his first appointment his health became impaired so that he was obliged to give up continuous work. Therefore, in 1874 he again went to Paris, where, as his health improved, he became associated with Friedel in research work in organic chemistry. Between 1874 and 1879 he was teaching at the Institute only intermittently, and in the academic year 1879-80 was given leave of absence and began a long residence in Europe. From 1880 to 1890 he lived chiefly in Paris, occupied in research at the École des Mines. With Professor Friedel, who had succeeded Würtz as director, he investigated the ethers of silicium (now known as silicon) and its compounds with organic radicles, and together they perfected the method for the synthesis of many organic compounds by the use of aluminum chloride, a procedure which bears their joint names. This was for him a period of great scientific activity and much accomplishment.

His own researches were not confined to organic chemistry but also extended into physics. He invented a hydrogen thermometer, and later developed a method for improving the accuracy of mercurial thermometers which won for him the Jecker Prize of the French Academy of Sciences. Other honors also came to him, and the

French Government made him a Chevalier of the Legion of Honor. As a result of his research work he was elected a Corresponding Member of the British Association for the Advancement of Science, and after returning to Boston in 1890, he was elected to membership in the National Academy of Sciences. While living in France he had been elected to many of the European chemical societies, and his scientific papers were published chiefly in the *Comptes Rendus* of the French Academy of Sciences.

On returning to Boston, he resumed his research in the chemical laboratories at M. I. T. On June 3, 1890, he was elected a life member of the Corporation, and in 1892 he again became professor of organic chemistry, serving also as acting head of the department of chemistry, after the departure of Professor Drown to become the President of Lehigh University. The students to whom he lectured were the seniors in chemistry and chemical engineering, with perhaps a few graduates, possibly fifty or sixty students in all. The main body of undergraduates had little opportunity to know him other than as a noted scientist who after years of residence abroad had come to add further distinction to an already highly effective faculty. Although so much of his life had been spent in advanced and exceptionally productive research, he had no degree other than his original S.B. from the Lawrence Scientific School until Harvard University conferred on him the honorary degree of LL.D. after he had assumed the presidency of M. I. T.

Since he was a man of great learning and a world figure in the field of organic chemistry, the students attending his lectures naturally had great respect for him, and admiration for his mastery of his field and for his experimental skill. In view of his cyclopedic knowledge, it is not surprising that Professor Crafts' lectures were sometimes difficult for the less brilliant students to follow clearly and absorb immediately. This was the more difficult, as his old students will remember, because of his way of writing his long and complicated equations on the blackboard as he lectured, sometimes with his back to the class, while erasing almost as rapidly with his left hand the first part of what his right hand had written. This procedure often added materially to the difficulties of the over-eager student in his note-taking, but the kindly professor was always willing to repeat if requested, or to explain privately to the slow student. In the exposition of his subject and its ramifications, his carefully prepared lectures were models of excellence. His scientific papers were also clearly written and, if delivered at a scientific meeting, excellently presented. It would be difficult to find a more scholarly address than the one he made at the inauguration of his successor, in which he exhibited a breadth of knowledge ranging from engineering to poetry that stamped him as a man of unusual learning. When he presided, he did so with great dignity and fine presence rather than ease, and was disposed to brevity and reticence in his remarks. As a public speaker he was not the equal of the facile and brilliant Rogers, nor of President Walker, whose speeches whether prepared with much effort or given extemporaneously, were always impressive and often eloquent.

President Crafts was a tall and handsome gentleman, kindly in manner, but dignified and reserved. In 1867 he had married Miss Clemence Haggerty; they had a family of four daughters. Their Boston home was at 59 Marlborough Street.

As a foremost scientist, and a man of broad culture and cosmopolitan experience, well aware of the history and needs of the Institute, Professor Crafts at the age of fifty-eight was splendidly equipped to maintain the prestige established by the earlier presidents. It must have been with deep regret that he gave up the satisfactions of research and teaching, which he had so brilliantly pursued for more than thirty years. As president, his duties became very largely administrative. His presidential reports show his interest in technical education, and his belief in the educational ideas expressed by Rogers, Runkle, and Walker. He advanced no new theories and sought no radical changes in procedures. A man to suggest rather than to dictate, he believed that internal educational problems, as they had been in the past, should be carefully discussed and decided by the faculty over which he presided.

To aid him in administrative matters, Crafts inherited the invaluable service of the two committees of the Corporation which had aided his predecessor, a strong Executive Committee consisting of Dr. Francis H. Williams, Thomas L. Livermore, Augustus Lowell,

Alexander S. Wheeler, and Howard Stockton; and a Finance Committee the members of which were William Endicott, David R. Whitney, Charles C. Jackson, Nathaniel Thayer, and Samuel Johnson, all wise and experienced advisers. Fortunately, with but a single change they continued throughout the three years of President Crafts' administration.

President Crafts' first two reports to the Corporation give a picture of the developments at M. I. T. during those closing years of the nineteenth century. His first report must have been a difficult one to write, for in addition to his tribute to his predecessor, he had to record the resignation of John Cummings, who had loyally served the Institute as treasurer for thirty-four years, and the deaths of three long-standing and valued members of the Corporation. Lewis W. Tappan, Jr., died April 7, 1897. Mr. Tappan was the first bursar appointed and was later treasurer of the Institute, and part of the time secretary of the Corporation. He had a very intimate knowledge of Institute history and deep regard for it. Henry D. Hyde died ten days later, April 17, 1897, and William H. Forbes, who had succeeded his father as member of the Corporation in 1893, died October 11, 1897. The president also reported the retirement and the appointment as professor emeritus of Silas W. Holman, a brilliant physicist and a gracious and successful teacher. These were severe losses.

On the other hand it was a satisfaction to report receipt of the munificent bequest of three-quarters of a million dollars from the estate of Henry L. Pierce, the largest bequest up to this time, and to report progress on the construction of the new Pierce Building. It was also gratifying to record the contribution of $50,000 from the John W. and Belinda L. Randall Charities Corporation together with several supplementary and minor gifts, and the reduction of the debt from $150,000 to $120,000.

In the following year the president reported gifts of more than $175,000 to the general funds of the Institute, and of nearly $450,000 for scholarships and aid to teachers in pursuing advanced work. Of this large amount, the largest contribution was a bequest of $400,000 from Edward Austin, who had spent much time in Asia, and whose fortune was made in the East India trade. Mr. Austin had been a friend of William Barton Rogers, and in the early days gave the department of natural history its first microscope. By his will he also gave generously to Harvard and several other educational institutions. His bequest to the Institute was made with the instructions that the interest should be paid to needy meritorious students to assist them in paying for their studies.

One of the high lights of the Crafts administration was the gift in 1899 from Augustus Lowell, who had long studied the needs of the Institute, of $50,000 to initiate a fund for the benefit of members of the instructing staff who were prevented by illness or disability from performing active duties as teachers. Mr. Lowell was a generous friend of the Institute of long standing. He had been a member of the Corporation since 1873, and a member of the Executive Committee since its establishment by President Walker in 1883. Mr. Lowell expressed the wish that this money should become the nucleus of a larger amount to which others might contribute for the purpose he had in mind. It was not a pension fund in the ordinary sense, and its administration was left freely in the hands of the Corporation. The thoughtful and generous character of this eminent man was again demonstrated when following his death a few months later, it was found that by a bequest he had duplicated the amount he had previously given. This most useful fund is still carried in the treasurer's report under the name of the Teachers' Fund.

The administration of President Crafts, though brief, was a significant one. For the first time in its history the Institute had an opportunity to develop without overhanging financial clouds. The endowments, invested funds, and value of the educational plant increased from $1,798,763.47 to $3,339,441.42. Libraries and laboratories expanded, the Pierce Building was constructed and occupied, and there was a distinct increase in the number of graduate students and an expansion in educational programs. During the last decade of the century the internal development of the Institute was more impressive than the gain in enrollment, which fluctuated slightly with a net increase of 118 students. The number of seniors graduating increased from 103 in 1891 to 185 in 1900; twenty Master of Science degrees had been conferred in that period; and the faculty had increased from thirty to fifty-four, and total instructing staff from eighty-nine to one hundred and thirty-six. The growth in the educational power of the Institute and in its usefulness to science and industry was even more significant. The newer professional courses of chemical engineering, sanitary engineering, naval architecture, and geology were now sending out graduates with thorough training, and the older departments were expanding and strengthening their work. At the turn of the century the Institute offered thirteen courses, with names and numbers now fairly well stabilized:

     I. Civil Engineering
    II. Mechanical Engineering
   III. Mining Engineering and Metallurgy
   IV. Architecture
    V. Chemistry
   VI. Electrical Engineering
  VII. Biology
 VIII. Physics
   IX. General Studies
    X. Chemical Engineering
   XI. Sanitary Engineering
  XII. Geology
 XIII. Naval Architecture

In many of the departments new subdivisions, or "options" as they were called, were gradually evolving, which made it possible for the advanced student to gain increased knowledge of special technical applications within his chosen field. In mechanical engineering, for example, an option dealing with the problems relating to heating and ventilation of large structures had been set up; advances in electrochemistry had led to a carefully planned program in that branch of physics; in architecture, an engineering option had been in successful operation for two years; and a landscape option was offered which may be regarded as the forerunner of the course in city planning.

Few problems demanding unusual action arose during President Crafts' administration. Although the war with Spain came during the first year of his administration, no special service by the Institute was requested. The sinking of the *Maine* brought about a great wave of patriotic emotion among the students. Many were eager to join the military or naval forces, but for the most part they were restrained by advice of older and cooler heads to continue their studies until there was evidence that they would be needed. Nevertheless, some who were already associated with military organizations such as the state militia, and others whose zeal for service could not be held in check, left the Institute before the end of the spring term. About a hundred alumni and students were active in various capacities from brigadier general to private in this short war in which typhoid fever killed more men than Spanish bullets.

The revived interest in the Navy that came at the time of the Spanish War led ultimately to a very successful program of training in ship construction for naval officers. A course in naval architecture had been started at M. I. T. under Professor Cecil H. Peabody in 1893, an outgrowth of the work in marine engineering in the department of mechanical engineering.

In 1898 Professor Peabody took a very active part in an interchange of ideas with the Navy concerning an appropriate program of studies for a three-year course in naval construction, with particular emphasis on the building of warships, to be taken by certain graduates of the Naval Academy. A preliminary conference was followed by a letter from the Chief Naval Constructor, Commodore Hichborn, stating that he was instructed by the Secretary of the Navy to ask the Institute to submit a scheme for the technical education of naval cadets assigned to the Corps of Naval Constructors. After careful consideration by the faculty, and after some further conferences with members of the Board of Naval Constructors, a program of studies was sent to Commodore Hichborn early in September, 1898.

A member of the Board of Navigation was then ordered to visit the Institute on September 20th. Because he arrived without notice in the latter part of the vacation period, he saw only the secretary of the faculty, Dr. Tyler, and Professor Peabody. Furthermore, all models, appliances, and equipment had by then been packed for removal to new quarters of the department and could not be well inspected. The report that the visiting captain made to his chief unfortunately contained numerous misconceptions about the Institute. "There is no method by which students can be kept up to their work by any means of discipline at the disposal of the Institute," it said, and recommended that the government establish a postgraduate course at the Naval Academy. Final decision on the matter was deferred, but some postgraduate work was begun at Annapolis.

The position taken by the Institute was that technical training in such a specialized field can best be carried out in an institution with broad and varied engineering programs and a large and highly trained staff, each member of which is competent in his own specialty, where mature students are brought in contact with many other advanced students in all branches of engineering accessory to the problems of naval construction.

The discussions between Professor Peabody and the officials of the Navy Department were continued, and came to a satisfactory conclusion when in 1900 a definite plan for an advanced course of instruction of naval constructors at the Institute was submitted, and after careful study and full discussion, was approved by the Navy and made effective the following year.

Professor Peabody, representing the Institute, and a representative of the U. S. Navy Department negotiated with Commander (later Captain) William Hovgaard, of the Danish Navy, recognized as the world authority on warship design, to take charge of this work. President Pritchett, as one of his first official acts, approved this selection, and Hovgaard was invited to become a professor at the Institute.

Professor Hovgaard accepted the appointment, and arrived in 1901. In that year the Navy Department assigned its first group of high standing graduates of the Naval Academy to the Institute for a three-year program in naval construction covering the professional work of the third and fourth years of the M. I. T. course in naval architecture, and a year of graduate work, which led to the degree of Master of Science. Thus began an arrangement which with constant improvement has been in effect for nearly fifty years, with the result that practically all warships built by the Navy for the past thirty or more years have been designed and constructed under the supervision of men trained at M. I. T.

This superior training was in no small degree the work of the brilliant and competent Professor Hovgaard. For more than thirty years he gave instruction in warship design, and his reputation in this field was international. His influence at the Institute was outstanding. For many years even after he became professor emeritus, he served the department, and was called upon by the Navy and by shipbuilding companies for expert advice. His interests were not confined to his specialty, for he was also an able mathematician and had a comprehensive knowledge of world affairs.

The Massachusetts Institute of Technology was one of two institutions which were requested by the United States Commission for the Paris Exposition of 1900 to exhibit the work in higher education in the United States. Through the efforts of the faculty and of Institute graduates resident in Paris, a splendid exhibit was prepared, which won a number of awards, including the *grand prix* in the class of Special Industrial and Commercial Education, and gold medals in the classes of Higher Education; Special Education in Fine Arts; Architecture; the Working of Mines, Ore Beds, and Stone Quarries; and Mining and Geology. The Student Co-operative Society was also awarded a gold medal. A request was later received from the École des Beaux-Arts for the presentation of a number of the large architectural designs representing the work of students and alumni that were a part of the Institute exhibit. This exhibit was seen by people from all over the world and added greatly to the prestige of the school.

The part played by the Institute's alumni, as individuals and as the Alumni Association with its many branches and clubs, has always been a useful one. In the closing years of the century the organization of the alumni was improved, and they began to take a more active interest in the development of the Institute, the maintenance of its ideals, and especially in the promotion of the welfare of the students.

As has already been recorded, the Alumni Association was organized as early as 1875, when the number of graduates was only 173, for the purpose of maintaining the members' interest in each other and in the school. In 1878 it formalized its interest in the welfare of the school when it voted "that a permanent Committee on the School be appointed from the alumni, whose duty shall be to keep itself informed as to the courses of instruction, management, and policy of the School, and to render a report on the same at each annual meeting." This was done over a long period, in fact until 1905. Another traditional function of alumni—to support their *alma mater* by contributing money—also began in the early years, although the highly organized campaigns for regular gifts did not come until the twentieth century. In the eighties many alumni were among the loyal contributors to the William Barton Rogers Scholarship Fund, a revolving fund for loans to worthy and needy students. The number of students so aided was never large in any single year, but the fund was a demonstration of a double desire, to honor the memory of the founder, and to aid the deserving student in his efforts to secure the best of professional training.

Membership in the Alumni Association was at first confined to those who held the degree of the Institute, but in 1898 it was opened to the much larger number of men who had studied for shorter periods as special students, or who had left before completing the full requirements for the Institute's diploma. In that year the number of actual graduates was 1980, but the total number of former students was about 8600. Numerous strong local organizations in areas away from Boston had also grown up, the earliest, largest, and most prominent of which was the Northwestern Association, with headquarters and regular meetings in Chicago. By 1899 other strong alumni groups were active in Denver, New York, Springfield, Philadelphia, Pittsburgh, and Buffalo.

The opening of The Technology Club in Boston in 1896 greatly stimulated alumni activity and began a new era of more effective organization of the alumni and more intimate relations with the school. The club house at 83 Newbury Street, nearly opposite the Rogers Building, became the nerve center for all alumni activities as well as a general social center for alumni, staff, and senior students. Although its house was small and its facilities as a social club could not compare with clubs like the St. Botolph or the Algonquin, it made a unique contribution to the life of the Institute, and by bringing together staff, alumni, and students created a new Tech spirit.

One of the first acts of the new club was an invitation by its executive committee to all secretaries of classes to meet informally to discuss plans by which the class spirit and interest of the graduated classes could be maintained and strengthened. The result was the formation on November 4, 1896, of the Association of Class Secretaries, the sole officers of which were a secretary and an assistant secretary. Its object was "to promote class spirit and the welfare of the Institute, and to systematize all matters pertaining to class organization and record." The membership of the association automatically included the secretaries of all graduated classes, to which were added the secretary of the Alumni Association, the president of The Technology Club, the secretary of the Institute, the president of the senior class, and a representative of the undergraduate Institute Committee. The first action of the association was to provide a plan for uniformity of class organization and class records. The class secretaries provided a ready means of reaching practically all former students and eliciting their interest and aid in projects for the welfare of the Institute. Plans were prepared for suitably inducting new classes into the Alumni Association at its annual meetings, and for other kinds of service to the school.

For many years the Association of Class Secretaries, with headquarters at The Technology Club, was the dynamo that activated interest in all the classes that passed through the Institute. One of its most important contributions was the founding of *The Technology Review*. Under the guidance of a publication committee, consisting of Arthur D. Little '85, C. Francis Allen '72, and James P. Munroe '82, the first numbers appeared in 1899. For more than fifty years now the *Review* has united the alumni and upheld the reputation of the school. It has sometimes been characterized as the outstanding alumni publication in the country.

With a journal, a club house, and an effective organization the alumni by 1900 were well prepared for the great services they were to render to the Institute during the first fifteen years of the new century—to mobilize against a threat to the Institute's independence and to raise the money necessary to support the old Boston Tech and under President Maclaurin's leadership to build the new Technology.

The Association of Class Secretaries and The Technology Club have both been inactive for many years, but curiously enough neither has been officially disbanded. When at the end of the academic year in June 1915, the date for the removal of the Institute to Cambridge was determined as but a year ahead, the inadvisability of attempting to maintain The Technology Club at the house on Newbury Street became clear. After the transition, faculty members from across the river as well as down town alumni would no longer find it a convenient lunching place. A favorable opportunity to sell presented itself and was accepted. The Engineers' Club, which already had fifty or more Technology members, offered to take in all Technology Club members in good standing at no increase in club dues. The offer was quite largely accepted, especially since the University Club at 270 Beacon Street, already overcrowded, could not make a similar offer. It was hoped that eventually the club might have the privileges of the Walker Memorial when it should be built, but the enlarging student population for whom it was intended seemed to make this improbable, nor was a student center likely to be well adapted for use as a club for alumni. The charter of the club was never surrendered and the hope was expressed that at some not too distant future The Technology Club might again resume its activities.

During President Crafts' administration another attempt was made to bring about an arrangement with Harvard that would allow the university to participate in the management of the Institute and influence the type of education it should give. It may be recalled that the first attempt had been made not long after Professor Eliot had left the Institute to become president of Harvard. A second proposal was made in those dark days when the request for state aid had failed during the Runkle administration three years before General Walker became president of the Institute. The plan at this time had been frustrated only by Professor Rogers' resuming the presidency, and by the labor of his associates in raising $100,000. When General Walker became president, he saw that the danger still persisted, and promptly made it clear that he believed a technical school should develop in its own way, free from entangling alliances and untrammeled by traditions of the classical college.

Now, nearly twenty years later, when the Institute was much more firmly established, the possibility of a co-operative arrangement with Harvard arose again and gave deep concern to those who had struggled for years to build the Institute as an absolutely independent educational institution of applied science and engineering. In the president's report for 1898, Crafts explained the negotiations as follows:

> A letter was addressed from the Corporation of Harvard College to the Chairman of our Executive Committee asking for a conference. A committee of five was chosen at a meeting of our Corporation, and they held conferences with two members of the Harvard Corporation during the summer and autumn of last year. Your committee reported results to you at your stated meeting, March 9, 1898, and I will briefly recapitulate the substance of this report. The question under discussion was the possibility of avoiding a duplication of courses of instruction in industrial science in the two neighboring institutions. The desirability of this end was recognized by both committees, and finally the terms of a proposed agreement were signed by all the members in conference, with the understanding that they would be submitted to the Corporation of Harvard College, as a first step toward further action.
>
> The proposal for agreement provided for the transfer to the Institute of Technology of the courses in Civil, Electrical, Mechanical, and Mining Engineering, Metallurgy, and Architecture, now given at Harvard, as well as the use of the income from certain funds destined to the support of these courses. It was provided that the five Fellows of Harvard College should have a place among the fifty members of the Corporation of the Institute, and that two of them should be added to the present seven members of its Executive Committee, making a committee of nine. The presence on the governing board of the Institute of the above-named Fellows of Harvard College was in consequence of the use of funds belonging to the University, and of the alliance of the two bodies for the purpose of technical education. No further change in the form of government, and no changes of title or of independence of action on the part of the Institute were agreed to by the joint committee.

The proposal failed because the Harvard Corporation attached conditions to the agreement looking toward a closer union, which made it unacceptable to the M. I. T. Corporation. Underlying the disagreement was a basic difference in educational theory, Harvard believing that "the charge of technical studies properly belongs with a university," and the Institute insisting on the "absolute independence of its government."

The negotiating committees parted amicably. The M. I. T. committee reported to the Corporation:

Although the result has disappointed our expectations, we still feel convinced that as friends and earnest promoters of instruction we can so direct the course of our respective institutions that they shall mutually help one another and avoid duplication of work.

It is possible that such a result may be better attained by a friendly interpretation of our common purpose than by any attempt at a formal agreement.

The negotiations ended with the following message from the Harvard Corporation:

The President and Fellows regret that the alliance with the Massachusetts Institute of Technology, proposed by them in a communication dated April 12, 1897, has failed.

The President and Fellows cordially recognize the friendly spirit of the letter of the Committee of Conference of January 10, 1898, and will at any time meet the authorities of the Massachusetts Institute of Technology in consultation, for the purpose of avoiding unnecessary duplication of instruction.

On October 24, 1899, President Crafts, having passed his sixtieth year, and still cherishing an intense desire to return to the chemical researches which he had been forced to curtail or omit entirely during his presidency, presented his resignation to the Executive Committee. It was accepted with regret on December 26, and announced to the whole Corporation at its meeting on January 1, 1900. In his letter he wrote feelingly of the conflicting desires which had stirred him, and of the impelling wish to return to research which had been so important in his life in the years before he became president. On June 5, 1900, at the end of the school year, he resigned from the Corporation and the faculty with the deepest respect of his colleagues. For several years thereafter he continued to use his laboratory in the Walker Building for his own research in high-temperature thermometry.

President Crafts died in 1917. He was one of the great scientists of his era, who strongly influenced the development of organic chemistry. His reserved, shy manner had never made him a beloved hero to the students, but they all had a deep-seated admiration and regard for him as a great investigator, a true friend, and a president who had continued the interest in student welfare which had characterized his three predecessors.

At the Turn of the Century

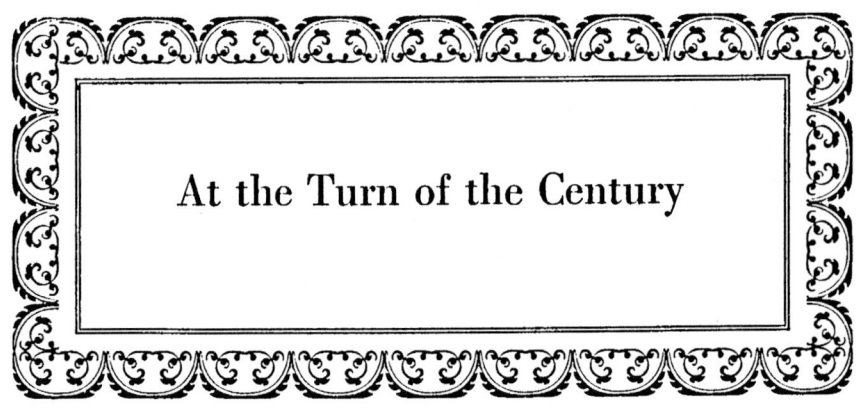

IN THE middle of the last year of the nineteenth century Henry Smith Pritchett became the president of "Boston Tech." In scope and reputation the school had now fulfilled if not surpassed the great vision of its founder. Already four men, each a leader in his own branch of learning, had espoused its cause, administered it wisely, dominated its early and struggling years, and brought it to a position of eminence among American institutions. Rogers the geologist, Runkle the matematician, Walker the economist, and Crafts the organic chemist, had each left his imprint on the character of the school. Now a leader skilled in his field of astronomic and geodetic science, was called to its presidency by the Executive Committee. Dr. Pritchett had been for the past three years outstandingly successful in a difficult assignment as Superintendent of the United States Coast and Geodetic Survey. He was a man, said Colonel Livermore of the Executive Committee, ". . . of eminent repute at home and abroad for scientific attainments and work . . . with a genius for organization. . . ." Dr. Pritchett was officially elected by the Corporation on March 15, 1900, and took office on July 1.

The new president was born in Fayette, Missouri, April 16, 1857, the son of Carr Waller and Betty (Smith) Pritchett, both of whom were Virginians by birth and lineage. He was the first of Technology's presidents to be born in the great middle section of the country west of the Appalachians. His boyhood and youth were spent in Missouri in the exciting years before, during, and after the Civil War when feeling between Northern and Southern partisans in that state was at fever pitch. His father had a dramatic and unusual career as teacher, preacher, and astronomer. A man of strong Union sympathies, he had been obliged to leave his home and family in 1864 with his life in danger. He succeeded in reaching Union lines and eventually arrived in Washington, where through his astronomer friend, Asaph Hall, he was enabled to join the Sanitary Commission. After the war he returned to Missouri and became the organizer and head of the Pritchett School Institute, later called Pritchett College, at Glasgow, Missouri, where by the munificence of a cultured and generous woman, Miss Berenice Morrison, an astronomical observatory had been established.

Young Henry Pritchett entered this school in 1866, and was graduated in 1875 at the age of eighteen with an A.B. degree. Doubtless influenced by his father's interest in astronomy, he went to Washington, where he studied for two years with Asaph Hall, his father's friend, at the U. S. Naval Observatory. In 1878 he was appointed assistant astronomer, a position he held for two years. He then returned to Glasgow and became director of the Morrison Observatory. In 1881 he was elected assistant professor of mathematics at Washington University in St. Louis. The following year he obtained leave of absence and joined the astronomic commission to New Zealand to observe the transit of Venus, an event of great astronomical significance. When his fellow astronomer became ill, he single-handed made the work of the commission a successful project. He then made important pendulum studies in Java, China, and Japan. In 1883 he returned to St. Louis as professor of astronomy and director of the observatory at Washington University, a position he held until 1897. For sixteen years he gave remarkable service to this university.

In 1894 he again was given leave of absence to study and travel in Europe. His first wife having died in 1891, he took his two older sons with him and settled down for an extremely busy year under the distinguished Seeliger at the University of Munich. His work was highly regarded and he was granted a Ph.D. degree in 1895, *summa cum laude*, an unusual honor to be attained in a single year of study and research.

In 1897, two years after his return to the university, he received a letter from Lyman J. Gage, the Secretary of the Treasury under McKinley, requesting him to come to Washington for an interview. The outcome was the offer of the position of Superintendent of the United States Coast and Geodetic Survey, which for the previous three years had been so badly managed under a political administration that it was no longer scientifically respectable.

Dr. Pritchett accepted the post. His predecessor was dismissed on November 30, 1897, and Pritchett assumed the office on the following day. He reorganized the survey, planned its work for a ten-year period, and administered it efficiently. During the Spanish-American War it supplied accurate information, maps, and charts which were of great value in the military and naval operations. It also provided the maps and data used in the long controversy over the Alaskan boundary, finally settled in 1903. The scientifically important Department of Terrestrial Magnetism of the Carnegie Institution of Washington was created at Pritchett's suggestion. Another notable recommendation of his was that the Office of Standard Weights and Measures, which had been a subsidiary division of the survey, should be set up as an independent branch of the government's scientific work. Secretary Gage asked Professor Samuel Wesley Stratton of the University of Chicago to submit a report on what the functions of such an organization should be. As a result Congress created the National Bureau of Standards in 1901, and Stratton was appointed the first director, a position he held until 1921, when he became president of M. I. T.

Life in Washington, with its wide social and professional contacts through the Cosmos Club and other organizations, was particularly enjoyable to Pritchett, and his work at the head of the survey was notably successful. But when the offer of the presidency of the Massachusetts Institute of Technology came, he accepted, sensing an opportunity for a broader service to professional education.

His inauguration as president took place in Symphony Hall, Boston, on Wednesday, October 24, 1900, with appropriate and colorful ceremonies. It was the first academic event of its kind in Institute history. Elaborate arrangements had been made for music and entertainment for the distinguished guests. Dr. Francis H. Williams '73, secretary of the Corporation, was chief marshal, assisted by a large corps of marshals and aides. Sixty undergraduates served as ushers. The academic procession of college presidents, representatives of the Federal Government and the Federal and State Courts, the Governor of Massachusetts and delegates from both branches of the legislature, the Mayor of Boston, and representatives of important mercantile associations filled the platform. The invocation was given by Bishop Lawrence, and addresses by Colonel Livermore, Professor Crafts, and Senator Henry Cabot Lodge preceded the inaugural address of President Pritchett. A reception at the Rogers Building terminated the formal ceremonies, and in the evening a torchlight procession of students passing the president's residence added a touch of gaiety and informality to the welcome to a new chief.

President Pritchett entered upon his work with enthusiasm. Three aspects of Institute affairs engaged his close attention: student welfare, the reputed inbreeding of the faculty, and the organization of administration. The new president at once manifested a keen interest in the welfare of the student body, and proceeded to study minutely this aspect of Institute life. His first report to the Corporation, made but two months after his accession to office, stressed the desirability of giving more attention to the physical welfare of the student, and strongly recommended that there should be a department of physical culture, to which a trained physician familiar with student life should give full time. It was his belief that the proposed Walker Memorial building would be admirable as the headquarters of such a department. A resolution to this effect was passed by the Corporation on December 26, 1900, with a request that the faculty confer with representatives of the alumni on this matter. The Corporation voted to set aside land for the site of a building if the alumni would raise $100,000 toward the project before July 1, 1901. The president's further recommendations may be summarized as follows:

1. Every student entering the first year should be required to have a strict physical examination, and be given careful advice as to diet, exercise, and health preservation.

2. Each student so examined should spend a prescribed amount of time in open air exercise in good weather and in a ventilated room in stormy weather.

3. Competitive sports that give outdoor exercise and opportunity for individual skill should be encouraged rather than those requiring expensive and time-consuming team work.

Pritchett's predecessors had also been interested in student health and welfare, of course, but their efforts had always been hampered by financial stringency. For at least a dozen years Professor Sedgwick had given valuable health talks to new students. But Pritchett's proposal of *complete* medical supervision was an important step forward. The trend of events and the changes in Institute affairs made it impossible to bring President Pritchett's excellent ideas to fruition at this time. Nevertheless a beginning was made in 1901, when Dr. Franklin W. White '90, a graduate of the Institute and a well-known physician in Boston was appointed medical adviser and maintained office hours twice weekly at the Rogers Building.

Another evidence of the expanding interest in the well-being of the students was the gift from Samuel Cabot in 1900 to provide medals, one each of gold, silver, and bronze, to be given as individual prizes each year to the three undergraduates who by their regular attention to healthy living and to work in the gymnasium had made the greatest physical improvement. These medals, annually presented, have been of distinct service, and are always highly valued by the recipients. Also in 1900 the trustees of the Massachusetts General Hospital authorized the Corporation of M. I. T. "to nominate a student patient to a free bed at the General Hosptal at any time during the ensuing five years."

In addition to the formal athletic program that had begun in the 1880's, there had always been a good deal of informal athletic activity that provided an outlet for interclass rivalry, especially between the freshmen and the sophomores. A football game and a cane rush in the fall and a baseball game in the spring had become annual events. The most important contest in the early days was the cane rush, which as years passed became a very rough game. With masses of several hundred students struggling for possession of the cane, minor injuries were frequent. The increasing size of the classes made the cane rush more and more dangerous, and finally in 1900 a freshman was trampled to death. Greatly saddened, the upperclassmen undertook a serious discussion of the whole subject of athletics in an effort to find more suitable kinds of competition between the two lower classes. As a result, the whole student body voted to abolish the cane rush and to withdraw from intercollegiate football. The only football game remaining was to be an annual contest between sophomores and freshmen. A new program of supervised competitive events was developed, and Technology Field Day became a well regulated and recognized holiday in the first term of the college year. The initiation of this change by the students themselves drew the warm approval of the faculty and administration.

Boston Tech students, like college boys everywhere, enjoyed intercollegiate rivalry, and shared the political excitement of the community. Torchlight processions, for example, were common in this era, especially during presidential campaigns. Hastily organized battalions of students from the Institute, Harvard, Tufts, and other colleges, provided with bands, banners, and flags, and enrobed in cheap cotton gowns of their college colors, would form at Scollay Square and march down Beacon Hill and through the Back Bay area to Copley Square. The Harvard and Technology contingents would then have a "scrap" in front of the Rogers building, with Tech men guarding the sacred steps and each group trying to secure the opponent's banners and gowns, or some fragments of them, as trophies of battle.

In 1902 the increasing interest in student welfare was finally recognized in the administrative structure of the school with the appointment of Professor Alfred E. Burton as the first dean. The function of the dean at Technology was unique. He had no authority over staff or curricula. The faculty as a whole decided all questions of curriculum, on recommendation of the department head. The dean was the general adviser and supervisor of the student body, a sort of father who was consulted by boys having trouble with their work or needing counsel in personal affairs. Burton's love of youth, his appreciation of their problems, and his wisdom as a father himself, were instantly effective. A boy might be overworking and discouraged, or devoting his time unwisely; he might be in a course for which he had no real aptitude; or he might be shirking, and exerting a harmful influence on his fellows. Burton was keen to sense these matters. He could stir a boy's pride, or persuade him to change to a department where his real interest lay. He could give real sympathy and helpful fatherly advice, or the severe scolding that a case might seem to require. It was his duty also to take disciplinary action in the occasional cases where punishment, probation, or even suspension or dismissal were indicated.

It was also the dean's business to be generally helpful to the students in their management of undergraduate affairs. Student activities had always been initiated and controlled by the students themselves, and the creation of a dean's office did not change the policy of student self-government, which has always been a valuable part of the M. I. T. tradition. The dean's function as Pritchett and Burton saw it, was to develop self-reliance and responsibility in the students. Pritchett's wise choice of the first dean was a landmark in Institute history.

In 1902 the upper rooms over the mechanical laboratories or "shops" on Garrison Street, formerly occupied by the Lowell School of Design, were converted into a social center for student activities known as the Tech Union, which served as a temporary substitute for the proposed Walker Memorial Building. At the Union was a large common room, pleasantly decorated in deep red and white, which could readily be converted into a large dining room. A smaller committee room, tastefully furnished in green, and a kitchen provided with all the appliances needed for serving simple dinners completed the suite. A steward was in constant attendance, ready to furnish dinners for class meetings, professional societies, or any other social gatherings of students.

The first dinner there was given by Governor Eben S. Draper '78 to the freshmen and sophomores who took part in the Field Day games, about 150 attending. Guests were President Pritchett, the Advisory Council on Athletics, Dean Burton, Major F. H. Briggs, the great friend of Tech sports, Dr. Francis G. Peabody of Harvard,

Professor Harry W. Tyler '84 and "Jimmie" Munroe '82. The Cabot loving cup, yearly inscribed with the numerals of the winning class, was passed from hand to hand, and each student gave his name as he passed it on.

The president and the dean were both interested in the Tech Union as a means of promoting social life and a sense of solidarity among the students. President Pritchett had been deeply impressed in Munich with the gaiety and good fellowship enjoyed by the German students on their nights off from serious study when they would gather in the beer hall, eat inexpensively, sing their songs, and drink their Muenchener beer. With his encouragement, the "Tech Kommers," an informal gathering of students at the Union every Saturday night, with beer, sandwiches, and music, soon became popular. Of course, many students were at first enthusiastic. Some were doubtful, or even shocked, and most of the instructing staff were somewhat disturbed at the innovation. Many of the citizens of the community were critical, and letters appeared in the public press. In reply to a formal protest from a group of ministers, Pritchett defended the meeting as pleasant and harmless, with only a half pint of beer consumed per student. ". . . Shall students be allowed to come together," he wrote, "in informal gatherings for discussion of topics of technical and general interest, in buildings under my control, with instructors present, where an inexpensive and simple lunch is served and the drinking is restricted to a moderate use of beer, or shall they be sent to hotels and restaurants where expensive dinners are the rule and all restrictions removed? In my judgment, the first position is the truthful one, and that which will help the boys to temperate and clean living." As usual in such cases, the matter soon ceased to be of public interest, and student groups harmlessly continued to have their refreshments in the Union, although probably some members of the staff did not entirely approve. Dean Burton and Bursar Rand stimulated interest in the Union and did much to make it a general meeting place with special opportunities for Saturday night gatherings with inexpensive dinners and entertainment. Class dinners were held, and student professional societies and many other undergraduate organizations met there regularly, with professors or instructors frequently appearing as speakers or guests. In 1908 the Union was moved to better and more convenient quarters on Trinity Place and continued its very important function until Technology moved to Cambridge and the Walker Memorial was built to take its place.

Three years after the Union had been started, a new gymnasium was built on land owned by the Institute on Garrison Street alongside the shops and the Union. The long lease of the land on Exeter Street where the old gymnasium and drill shed had stood for more than twenty years had terminated. President Pritchett induced the Executive Committee to authorize at once the construction of a structure 90 feet by 160 feet with one high room for the main gymnasium, with plenty of light and air and suitable equipment for gymnastic exercises, and floor space available for winter practice for the track teams. An ell 60 feet by 30 feet had locker room for three hundred students, showers, and dressing rooms on the first floor, and offices for the gymnastic instructor and the track coach on the second. The building was completed and put in use in December, 1905. Regular gymnastic training was available on an optional basis with a full-time instructor for the first time (there had been a part-time one since 1891). Physical examinations were now required of all students participating in the athletic program. The gymnasium was a vast improvement over the dark and ill-ventilated old drill shed, and marked the beginning of organized physical training, which three years later became a required subject for all freshmen.

In his efforts to provide a richer social life for the students, Pritchett was ably supported by his wife. After being a widower for ten years he had married, shortly before coming to Technology, Miss Eva McAllister of San Francisco, an attractive woman of fine personality who quickly won the affection of the student body. The president and his wife took a special interest in students who lived in the South End and Back Bay rooming houses, and were often helpful to boys who were lonely or sick far from home.

On one occasion, soon after the Pritchetts had become established in Boston, the students showed their appreciation for the new president and his wife. At the end of a political torchlight parade, the Technology battalion marched to the Pritchetts' house on Marlborough Street and called them out by loud and prolonged cheers. When President and Mrs. Pritchett appeared with some guests, the regular M. I. T. yell was heartily given. As it ended some one shouted, "What's the matter with Dr. Pritchett?" and the crowd roared the appropriate response, "He's all right!" Describing the event years afterward, a student who was in the group wrote, "I can see Mrs. Pritchett's tall figure now, in her white dress, . . . and on that cheer she seized a light scarf from her shoulders and waved it. One of the marshals caught her spirit and called out, 'What's the matter with Mrs. Pritchett?' 'She's all right!' *And she was.*"

President Pritchett's immediate interest in the social and physical welfare of the students did not deter him from giving equally serious consideration to other aspects of Institute affairs. He had assumed the presidency at a time when the Institute seemed about to enter on a new period of development, which created important problems for faculty and administration. On some of these he apparently had preconceived ideas, for in his first report to the Corporation, after two months in office, he said: "Later, with longer acquaintance, I shall ask your attention to certain recommendations regarding the work in the departments, which I feel at this time I am not prepared to make."

With the rising tide of students which had set in at the turn of the century and the widening range of technical subjects in the thirteen professional courses, the problem of maintaining an adequate teaching staff had again become serious.

In the late nineties the criticism began to be whispered in certain quarters that the preponderance of its own graduates on the teaching staff was making the Institute educationally narrow and complacent, and that with an inbred staff the Institute could not expect to maintain indefinitely its position as leader in the field of engineering education. By 1900 there were probably a hundred institutions in the United States offering some engineering instruction. A number of engineering schools and many of the large state universities and colleges which had early benefited by the Morrill and subsequent acts now had highly reputable departments of engineering, but the Institute with its strong faculty and greater range of courses, unquestionably was still first in the field. The problem of securing the best staff and facilities to maintain this position was not a simple one, especially with competition from the rapidly growing and liberally supported State universities on the one hand, and from growing industrial organizations which could offer higher pay and possibly greater opportunities on the other.

It was a fact that a majority of the teachers of professional subjects at the Institute were M. I. T. alumni. From the early years, capable men who had themselves been through the mill and had then expanded their technical knowledge by professional research and practical experience were appointed to permanent positions on the small faculty in somewhat larger numbers than were men from elsewhere. Professors Richards '68, Cross '70, Swain '77, Peabody '77, Schwamb '78, and Allen '72, represented this type of teacher in engineering, and Norton '76, Holman '76, Crosby '76, and Wells '73 in science and mathematics. When the period of extremely rapid growth came in the eighties, able graduates from the various courses were year by year appointed as assistants or instructors as were also men from other institutions. By 1900 a strong group of these men were members of the faculty, including H. W. Tyler '84, W. L. Puffer '84, E. B. Homer '85, A. H. Gill '84, A. L. Merrill '85, H. P. Talbot '85, H. E. Clifford '86, A. A. Noyes '86, E. F. Miller '86, and W. H. Lawrence '91. These men would have constituted a strong group on any faculty as their subsequent careers amply show.

On the whole, then, this criticism was unsound. In the first place, certainly before 1890, M. I. T. graduates were often the best and sometimes the only men available in their fields. Furthermore a study of the staff in 1899-1900 shows that it was a broadly trained and diversified group of men. Of 97 men on the teaching staff 51 had had their basic training at the Institute and 46 elsewhere. But of the 51 Institute graduates at least 39 had greatly expanded their technical knowledge by advanced study abroad or by extensive research on problems in applied science or engineering, or had joined the staff after active professional experience. It is also significant that a seventh of the staff here considered was teaching non-technical subjects, including English, modern languages, economics, and history, and that a group of 30 or more special lecturers added widely varied contributions to student instruction.

Before he accepted the presidency, Dr. Pritchett had probably heard these vague charges of educational provincialism and was inclined to accept the opinions of the critics. Although generally urbane in manner, he formed positive opinions, and he was clearly determined to bring about certain changes in the administrative structure and the personnel of the Institute. Perhaps by nature, or possibly as a result of his administrative experience in Washington, in his dealings with the staff he sometimes evinced some of the characteristics of both a dictator and a reformer. As he proceeded to carry out his ideas, he sometimes gave the impression that his judgment as an administrator was swayed by personal likes and dislikes.

Whatever may have been President Pritchett's estimate of the Technology faculty when he arrived on the scene, he readily concurred in the recommendations of department heads in the spring of 1901 when a number of new appointments and promotions were requested. More than half of the men proposed for advancement were graduates of the Institute. The president had by this time evaluated the qualities of these men and had discovered that they were neither technically unqualified nor narrow in their educational vision. Among those now elected to the rank of assistant professor were George V. Wendell '92, Louis Derr '92 (also Amherst, A.B. '89 before entering M. I. T.), Willis R. Whitney '90, Frank H. Thorp '89, Charles L. Norton '93, Charles E. Fuller '92, William A. Johnston '92, and Charles F. Park '92. All these men made notable contributions to the Institute. Wendell, Whitney, and Thorp had all taken Ph.D. degrees in Germany, and the later brilliant career of Wendell as professor of physics at Stevens Institute and Columbia, and of Whitney as the first director of the Research Laboratory of the General Electric Company at Schenectady may be mentioned in passing. William H. Lawrence '91, who had organized the new course in architectural engineering, the first of its kind in the country, was promoted to the rank of associate professor, as was also William L. Puffer '84 in electrical engineering. William Z. Ripley '90 was promoted to a full professorship in economics, but resigned shortly after to accept a special professorship at Harvard.

In 1902 two distinguished scientists were appointed non-resident professors. No such appointments had been made since Professor Crafts nearly thirty years before had been given the title for a limited period. The men now honored were Elihu Thomson, long-time head of the Thomson-Houston System, and Percival Lowell, founder and director of the Lowell Observatory at Flagstaff, Arizona. Both were life members of the Corporation. As a special lecturer at the Institute since 1894, Mr. Thomson had become highly regarded by the staff and by the students who flocked to hear him. Mr. Lowell, one of the donors to the fund for the Lowell Building, had lectured occasionally, and had stirred great interest in students because of his discoveries and his theories regarding the canals on the planet Mars. The names of these men added prestige to a faculty list which already included men of national reputation.

In the earlier years of the Pritchett administration four new heads of departments were appointed. In 1901 Professor Henry P. Talbot '85 was made head of the department of chemistry, which at this time also included the work in chemical engineering. Dr. Thomas A. Jaggar, Jr. was secured from Harvard in 1902 to take the place of the retired Professor William H. Niles, in charge of geology. In the same year Dr. Louis Duncan was secured as head of the new department of electrical engineering. John Bigelow, Jr., who at one time had been professor of military science was appointed head of the department of modern languages in 1904 on the resignation of Professor Rambeau.

The first administrative change President Pritchett made, the appointment of Professor Alfred E. Burton as the first dean of the Institute, had the warm approval of the whole Institute family. For twenty years he served as dean to the great satisfaction of students and staff. In 1905 he was granted a leave of absence to study methods of teaching descriptive geometry in the great engineering and architectural schools, especially in France. At the request of the President he also attended as a delegate from M. I. T. the Fiftieth Jubilee Meeting of the Society of German Engineers in Berlin, and visited the great technical school at Charlottenburg. On his return in 1906 Burton made an interesting and valuable report. During his absence Professor Allyne L. Merrill '85, was acting dean. In 1906 Merrill began his long tenure of twenty-eight years as the efficient and greatly respected secretary of the faculty.

The second change was a division and reassignment of the work done by Dr. Harry W. Tyler, '84, as secretary of the faculty and registrar. This step was taken without consulting the faculty and perhaps without reference to antecedent history. With two competent assistants, Dr. Tyler, whose mind always worked with mathematical precision, had not only organized and administered all the work incident to the office of secretary of the faculty, including matters of registration and student records, with dictatorial efficiency, but he had also been a wise general adviser to students, and his knowledge of the present and past student body was cyclopedic. In addition he had been invaluable as clerk of the Executive Committee at their stated meetings. It was the president's view that these varied and important activities required too much of a man who was also helping in the executive work of a department, as Dr. Tyler was in the mathematics department, and doing his full share of teaching as well. With an ordinary man this would certainly have been true, but Tyler was exceptional in his capacity for such work and enjoyed its organization and smooth routine. It was a case of clash of personalities— Greek met Greek. The arbitrary way in which the change was ordered offended many of the staff, who felt it to be a personal rebuff to Tyler, but the ultimate outcome was entirely salutary.

Walter Humphreys '97, who for two or three years had been a valuable assistant to Tyler, was appointed registrar. O. F. Wells, who had also assisted Tyler, was made recorder. Humphreys had an unusual flair for the work which he now undertook, and for nearly a score of years developed it with great success and general satisfaction. A year after his resignation in 1922 to accept an important industrial position, he was elected a member of the Corporation, and in 1929 became its secretary.

Dr. Tyler continued as secretary of the faculty and likewise carried on brilliantly his increasing duties as head of the department of mathematics until 1906, when, by presidential fiat, Professor Dana P. Bartlett '86, was appointed acting secretary of the Institute, to be succeeded two years later by Professor Allyne L. Merrill '85, who served until his retirement.

One example of the keenness of Tyler's memory for students may be cited. In 1883 a student named Howard L. Coburn from a small town in Maine had entered the Institute and remained for two years as a member of the class of '87 in mining engineering. Financially unable to return to the school, he then worked in positions of increasing significance until 1896, when he decided to continue professional study and obtain the Institute's degree in mechanical engineering. Recognizing that many changes in requirements had taken place in eleven years, he went to consult Dr. Tyler. As he entered the office, Tyler looked up, greeted him by name, and referred exactly to his earlier status in the Institute. Surprised at being recognized and placed so definitely without reference to office records, he stated his desires, and registered as a junior in the class of '98. Coburn became a leader in student affairs and completed his course with high credit. He was one of the most loyal alumni, probably the only one to hold membership in two classes eleven years apart. He often related the incident as an example of Tyler's uncanny memory for details.

A third notable change was an appointment to the office of bursar. Albert M. Knight, who for eleven years had held this post, was forced by ill health to resign. A strange, shy, elderly man, kindly at heart, he had carried on his work with extreme parsimony, as perhaps had been necessary in the dark days of the Institute's poverty. Merciless toward the careless student, he sometimes had compassion toward the hard-working boy who was earning his way and found difficulty in meeting his tuition or laboratory bills when due. He was equally strict in his scrutiny of bills and in inquisitorial demands on professors asking for equipment or service that he did not personally authorize. Anything smacking of extravagance was anathema to him.

An amusing episode illustrates this characteristic. Professor Noyes was in need of some very accurate weights for a chemical balance used in a particularly delicate research in physical chemistry. He therefore went to the bursar with a requisition for one set of gold-plated weights. The word "gold-plated" at once stirred Mr. Knight's suspicion, and he asked severely, "Why gold-plated, Dr. Noyes?" In his quiet patient way Noyes replied: "Because solid gold costs too much."

As successor to Mr. Knight, Frank H. Rand was appointed bursar in 1902. He had been recommended by George Wigglesworth, an able business man who for more than ten years had been treasurer of the Institute. The bursar's office was transformed. Rand had a fine personality, was co-operative, always helpful to the staff and department heads, and at once became deeply interested in student affairs.

Frank Rand was a self-made man from Vermont who began his business career at fourteen as a candy boy on the steamers on Lake Memphremagog. At sixteen he was chief telegraph operator at Wells River. Between times he attended a business college, then read law in the Vermont attorney general's office, and later was graduated from a law school in Albany and was admitted to practice in New York and Vermont. He became superintendent of a manufacturing plant in New Jersey, and thereafter for thirteen years held a bank position in Boston, resigning to become bursar at the Institute. Here he introduced new office methods, unification of purchases, and a simplification of the complicated system of bookkeeping. He gave special lectures on business administration, established a system of banking for the students, and became manager of the Tech Union, the students' club and lunchroom.

The bursar was no longer just a man behind a window, or a task master keeping a sharp eye on students' financial obligations. He was a vital human being with a warm sense of helpfulness and sympathy, who knew which students were hard pressed to meet their bills or were actually suffering from lack of food or working too many hours at night to earn their way. To these he was a friend and confidant. He was appointed assistant treasurer of the Institute a few months before his premature death in 1913. After his death the students collected funds for a memorial which three years later when Walker Memorial was built took the form of a fireplace in Litchfield lounge bearing the inscription, "Dedicated to the memory of Frank Henry Rand, Bursar at Technology, and a Loyal Friend of All. Presented by Students 1904-1913."

The growth of the Institute brought acutely to the front the need for other changes, the most urgent of which was the need for space for physics and for the rapidly developing work in electrical engineering.

Ever since electrical engineering had been set up as a professional course in 1882, it had thrived under the able direction of Professor Cross, and he had built a strong staff of assistant professors and instructors. The work largely centered in the Walker Building, which housed the activities of physics and of chemistry, except for industrial chemistry, which had been transferred to the Pierce Building in 1898. Here also most of the classes in modern languages were held. The Walker building was now intolerably crowded, and Professor Cross had repeatedly shown that electrical engineering could not be properly developed without commodious quarters in a new building. He also recommended that this branch of the Institute work should be more fully recognized by being made a separate department, under other leadership than his own.

The urgency was so great that in 1901 the Executive Committee recommended that a new building designed to meet the needs in electrical engineering should be at once erected on a part of the remaining land on Trinity Place, and voted to authorize the construction of a new building.

At this juncture came the generous action of the sons and daughters of Augustus Lowell, for nearly thirty years a member of the Corporation and a notable benefactor of the Institute, who had died in 1900. His two sons, A. Lawrence Lowell and Percival Lowell, now also members of the Corporation, and their sisters, Miss Amy Lowell, Mrs. William L. Putnam, and Mrs. T. J. Bowlker, jointly made a gift of $50,000 in memory of their father. To this sum George A. Gardner added $10,000 and Mrs. W. S. Fitz and Charles C. Jackson $5,000 more. With this amount in hand a new building was planned, to be known as the Lowell Building in grateful recognition of the services of Augustus Lowell. By new and improved construction methods the building was sufficiently advanced during the summer of 1902 to permit occupancy by the new department of electrical engineering.

It was the president's belief that the new director of the department of electrical engineering should be brought from the ranks of practicing engineers rather than from the academic world. Without consulting faculty members, he found the man of his choice in Dr. Louis Duncan, a consulting engineer in New York, and a man highly regarded professionally, who had pioneered the course in applied electricity in Johns Hopkins, had twice been elected president of the American Institute of Electrical Engineers, and was at the time the electrical engineer of the New York City Transit Commission.

President Pritchett's recommendation that Duncan be elected professor of electrical engineering and head of the department at the Institute was readily acted on by the Executive Committee. Dr. Duncan assumed the position at the opening of the academic year, with the cordial welcome of the staff. Since he continued to carry on extensive consulting work, the administrative tasks of the department fell largely and increasingly on the shoulders of Associate Professor Harry E. Clifford, '86. As the months passed, Duncan's outside activities and his absorption in consulting work seemed to erase his interest in teaching and the training of students, and after the second year he resigned. Clearly his had been an unfortunate appointment, and the high reputation of the department was maintained only by the co-operation, pride, and loyalty of the staff.

On Duncan's resignation in 1904, Clifford was appointed acting head of the department, and for two years more administered its affairs with outstanding success. As a teacher he was in the first rank. His relations with colleagues and students were exceptionally fine. He was gifted and witty, but his rapier-like thrusts in argument or repartee sometimes struck more deeply and were more stinging than he intended. It was generally expected and hoped, not only in the department but also in the faculty as a whole, that he would be appointed official head of the department. The president must have recognized Clifford's ability, for he requested Clifford to visit the University of Wisconsin and observe the work there, and especially to report to him regarding a very successful professor, Dugald C. Jackson, as a possibility for the Institute staff. Clifford submitted a highly favorable report, and a few months later, without further discussion with Clifford, the president announced that Professor Jackson had been elected head of the department of electrical engineering.

Jackson accepted the appointment, but because of the importance of a technical case on which he was engaged was unable to come at once to the Institute, and Clifford continued to act as the administrative officer of the department for several months. Jackson began his duties at Technology early in 1907, and then began his long tenure, which, as subsequent history shows, was increasingly successful, for he was an able executive and a skillful teacher and director of research as well as a widely known consultant. As the years passed he contributed greatly to the reputation of the department and of the Institute.

The cavalier treatment of Clifford by the president reflected no discredit on Jackson in any way, but at the time it caused much resentment, and was without doubt the main reason that Clifford accepted the McKay Professorship of Electrical Engineering at Harvard in 1909.

The Pritchett administration also marks the establishment of modern research laboratories properly staffed and equipped for an educational program leading to a doctor's degree. As far back as 1872 the Institute had been authorized to give the Doctor of Science degree. Research was carried on more or less sporadically for many years, but it could not be extensively developed because of lack of money and heavy teaching loads. The first announcement of a program leading to a master's degree appeared in the catalogue for 1884-85. Before 1900 only twenty-two master's degrees had been granted and no doctor's degrees.

The first master's degree was given in 1886 to Frederick Fox '85 in chemistry, and the second in 1887 to Arthur A. Noyes of the class of 1886. After graduate study in Germany, Noyes returned to the Institute and began a brilliant career in the field of physical chemistry, with such associates as Dr. Willis R. Whitney '90, and Dr. S. P. Mulliken '87. In 1901 Noyes submitted a plan for a research laboratory to President Pritchett with a request for a modest appropriation for the promotion of this work. Since the question of the relocation of the Institute was at the time under discussion, action on his request was postponed. On January 12, 1903, Dr. Noyes wrote again to President Pritchett, renewing with some modifications his earlier request. One paragraph from that letter demonstrates the generosity, the earnestness, and the administrative foresight of Dr. Noyes. He wrote:

... I will give to the Institute each year for a period of three years, with the expectation of further continuance, the sum of $3,000.00, in case the Institute will establish Research Laboratories of Physical Chemistry, which shall be independent of existing departments and under the charge of a director, assign to them adequate space, equip the laboratories (at a cost estimated at $6000); appropriate annually the sum given by me and an additional sum of equal amount for the maintenance of the laboratories and payment of research workers in them, and give recognition and standing to the latter by suitable appointments as regular members of the Institute staff. . . .

On February 10, 1903, the Executive Committee voted to establish the proposed laboratory. Funds were provided by the Institute, by Dr. Noyes, by grants from the Carnegie Institution, and through George E. Hale '90 by a contribution from the William E. Hale Fund for Scientific Research. Dr. Noyes was appointed director and given an independent budget. To house this laboratory and also to provide more room for the departments of naval architecture and of geology, which were also in great need of space, the Executive Committee authorized the construction of a temporary two and a half-story building on Trinity Place. The upper part of Engineering C, as the new building was called, provided a drafting room for the naval architects and a room for the mineralogical collections, while the lower portion was devoted to physical chemistry.

Here the Research Laboratory of Physical Chemistry opened on September 20, 1903, and for several years carried out the researches that gave the laboratory and its directors a world-wide reputation. Here also was carried out the work of graduate students leading to the first Ph.D. degrees given by the Institute. A group of brilliant research men composed its staff. Of the two men chiefly responsible for this important laboratory Dr. Noyes later became the acting president of the Institute, and Dr. Whitney became the first director of the great Research Laboratory of the General Electric Company at Schenectady. When Dr. Noyes took over the duties of president, Dr. William D. Coolidge became director until he was appointed assistant director at Schenectady, and later followed Dr. Whitney as director. The remarkable record of the Research Laboratory of Physical Chemistry constitutes a brilliant page in Institute history.

Research was coming into its own. A graduate school of engi-

AT THE TURN OF THE CENTURY

neering research was proposed and authorized in 1902, but was not further developed. A new Research Laboratory of Applied Chemistry with a separate organization, however, was established under the able direction of William H. Walker, professor of industrial chemistry. A Sanitary Research Laboratory, under the general direction of Professor William T. Sedgwick, was made possible by annual gifts from an anonymous donor in 1903 and 1905. This laboratory was devoted to year-round research in special problems relating to sewage disposal and its bacteriology and chemistry. Not primarily a teaching laboratory, although a few advanced students had summer employment there, for several years it carried on highly important work in the field of sanitation, and its ten special reports were widely demanded. Professor C.-E. A. Winslow '98 and Professor E. B. Phelps '99 were directly in charge of the investigations, and each gained national recognition from this work.

In 1900 A. Lawrence Lowell, later president of Harvard and for many years a member of the Corporation of M. I. T., became the trustee of the Lowell Institute, which from the beginning had always been intimately associated with Technology. The Lowell lectures were still popular and useful, but Mr. Lowell felt they were not meeting the educational needs of the people in the way the original donor intended. He discussed with President Pritchett ways of making more effective use of the funds, and suggested a plan for training able working-men already in foremen's positions for better places in the industrial world. Pritchett recommended that Professor Charles F. Park '92, make a survey of the situation. His report was so satisfactory that the school recommended was established, and Professor Park was invited to become the director.

The Lowell Institute School for Industrial Foremen, as it was called, was not an integral part of the Institute, but its classes were given in the evening in the rooms and laboratories of M. I. T. with members of the Institute staff as instructors. This school, later known simply as the Lowell Institute School, has been for fifty years an important member of the educational community of New England.

Between 1904 and 1907 promotion to the rank of full professor came to a group well known for teaching ability, for authorship of excellent textbooks, or for prominence in the administration of scientific accomplishment. The group consisted of Professors Frank Vogel in modern languages; Charles F. A. Currier and John O. Sumner in history; Frederick S. Woods; Dana P. Bartlett '86; and Frederick H. Bailey in mathematics; Harry E. Clifford '86, in electrical engineering; William H. Walker in industrial chemistry; Harry M. Goodwin '90, in physics and electrochemistry; Henry Fay in analytical chemistry; William O. Crosby '76 in geology; and Allyne L. Merrill '85 and Edward F. Miller '86 in mechanical engineering.

On December 7, 1904, a convocation was held in Huntington Hall to commemorate the one hundredth anniversary of the birth of the founder, William Barton Rogers. It was not a great public celebration, but a more intimate memorial ceremony, largely restricted to the Institute family. The audience was composed of Corporation, faculty and staff, graduate and undergraduate students, and a few invited guests. Most honored of these was Mrs. William Barton Rogers, who throughout her long and useful life had been particularly devoted to the Institute and its welfare. Two other special guests were President Lyon G. Tyler, of the College of William and Mary, and Professor Francis H. Smith, professor of natural philosophy at the University of Virginia, who, in addition to President Pritchett, were the speakers of the day, chosen because of the early personal association of Dr. Rogers with the institutions they represented.

President Pritchett presided. In his introductory address he recalled his special satisfaction when as a young man of twenty-three he attended the meeting of the American Association for the Advancement of Science in Boston in 1880, to read his first scientific paper, and had the privilege of meeting and grasping the hand of Dr. Rogers, and added, ". . . I shall never forget the charm of his face and of his manner. . . ." He then discussed briefly the Rogers plan for the Institute of Technology. "It is worth our while on this Anniversary Day," he said, "to look again at the original conception which the founder of the Institute had, not only because such a remembrance gives a just view of his power and originality, but because it will also show that his plan was one so far-reaching, so original in conception, and so practical in its details that it has taken the world years to catch up with it...."

President Tyler brought greetings from William and Mary College in Virginia, where Rogers had been a student, and had succeeded to his father's position as professor of natural philosophy. William and Mary, second oldest college in what is now the United States, said Dr. Tyler, had been recognized long before the Revolution as having the most thorough system of intellectual training in the colonies, and it was here that the lecture system, the elective system, and the honor system had their inceptions. All the advantages of this training he said, were reflected in the character of Rogers, in the free and independent spirit of inquiry, the high sense of honor, and a "scorn of all low and disingenuous artifices." Dr. Francis H. Smith spoke as an old pupil of Rogers in the University of Virginia. He remembered Rogers as a great teacher who so stirred his listeners that they believed he had no equal. Of his effect on the university, Dr. Smith said: "... More than fifty years have rolled away, yet Professor Rogers is still a living force with us. His name is carved on one of our buildings. His portrait looks down on our students in our chief hall. His bust is in our Physical Laboratory. Apparatus which was used by him and experiments devised by him are exhibited year by year, and never without respectful mention of his name. That name is a household word in our School of Geology. His fame is one of our college heirlooms...."

An account of the earliest years of the Institute was given by Professor Robert H. Richards '68, who had been one of the earliest, in fact the seventh, of the students to be enrolled at its opening in 1865. With warmth and loyalty, he recounted the early years, the development of new methods of instruction, and the high idealism and faith, and also the difficulties that seemed to block the way. He told with simple force, and with some humor, of the great gifts of Rogers as a teacher and leader of students, who demanded much but gave infinitely more. "... To have divined the need of the coming age," said Richards, "to have persuaded a whole community to accept and support the new conception, to have influenced and moulded students and teachers into a working model, so that consciously or unconsciously the superstructure is imitated by every successful scientific school in the English-speaking world,—this was the genius, this the title to fame, of the founder of the Massachusetts Institute of Technology. . . ." The convocation closed with the reading by an undergraduate, Norman Lombard '05, of extracts from the brilliant *Memoir of William Barton Rogers* written by General Francis A. Walker in 1887.

This convocation was a small episode in the history of a great institution, but it illustrates the extraordinary power of one man's ideas and personality. In each generation since Rogers' death, when the leaders of the Institute have turned to the founder's ideas for guidance, they have found his conception of technological education a sound one.

Courtesy of Mrs. William Stanley Parker

James Savage, Sr., and his family, photographed in the library of his home on Temple Place in Boston. William Barton Rogers and his wife, Emma Savage Rogers, are standing. Seated by his father is James Savage, Jr., between whom and Rogers were strong bonds of affectionate regard; writing to the younger man during the Civil War service that culminated in Savage's death October 22, 1862, from wounds suffered at the battle of Cedar Mountain, Rogers signed his letters "God bless you, Jim. From your loving brother, 'Bill.'"

The first page of the basic document from which the Massachusetts Institute of Technology was to take its origin is reproduced here. Known as "A Plan for a Polytechnic School in Boston," it was written on March 13, 1846, by William Barton Rogers in answer to the request of his brother Henry. William began it in the morning and broke it off with a promise to write more "tomorrow," but resumed the task later in the evening and brought it to completion. The full text is printed in Appendix I.

Boston, April 9, 1862.

To his Ex'y the Governor & the Hon'ble the Council of the Commonwealth of Mass.

Gentlemen —

At a meeting of the Mass. Inst. of Technology, held on Thursday April 8th 1862 at the rooms of the Board of Trade, in this city, the Institute having been permanently organized & its Government elected, the following Resolve was adopted —

Resolved That the Mass. Inst. of Technology accept the Charter & other provisions of the Act of Ap. 10. 1861. relating to said Institute.

William B. Rogers
Pres. Mass. Inst. Tech.

William Barton Rogers, as President of the Massachusetts Institute of Technology, writes to the authorities of the Commonwealth for the "Government" of the newly formed Institute, formally accepting the Charter granted by Act of the General Court on April 10, 1861, fifteen years after he had drafted the germinal plan for such a school in Boston.

The work of the Massachusetts Institute of Technology was begun in 1864 in rooms in the Boston Mercantile Library building on Summer Street, here shown as depicted in a contemporary print.

Occupied in 1866, and named in 1883 for William Barton Rogers, the Rogers Building was the Institute's center for sixty years.

William Barton Rogers
President 1862-1870, 1878-1881

John Daniel Runkle
Acting President 1868-1870
President 1870-1878

Francis Amasa Walker
President 1881-1897

James Mason Crafts
President 1897-1900

Henry Smith Pritchett
President 1900-1907

Arthur Amos Noyes
Acting President 1907-1909

Richard Cockburn Maclaurin
President 1909-1920

President Maclaurin at his desk in the Rogers Building; on the wall, progress photographs of construction of the new Technology in Cambridge.

Dr. William J. Walker of Newport, R. I., whose gift of $60,000 in April, 1863, saved the day for the Institute by enabling it to meet conditions set by the Legislature.

Ralph Huntington of Boston, whose bequest of $50,000 in 1866 came as deeply valuable assistance to the Institute in its early days of financial difficulty.

T. Coleman du Pont, '84, whose gift of $500,000 in 1911 was the central factor in solving the problem of a new site for the Institute, and was stimulation for other gifts.

George Eastman, whose benefactions to the Institute, totaling nearly twenty millions, made possible at the outset the construction of the Institute's Cambridge home.

Know all men by these presents:

That I, William J. Walker of Newport in the State of Rhode Island do hereby give and grant to the Massachusetts Institute of Technology, the proceeds in money of six hundred shares in the Old Colony and Fall River Rail Road Company, belonging to me, provided that there shall be subscribed or pledged by persons of supposed responsibility on or before the tenth day of the present month of April, an amount of money for the benefit, use, and endowment of the aforesaid Institution, which, when added to the sum hereby granted and given by me, shall together amount to not less than one hundred thousand dollars, and thus enable the said Institution to comply with the terms and conditions of an Act of the Legislature of Massachusetts so far as to acquire and make available for the purposes of said Institution a certain parcel of land located in Boston in the State of Massachusetts, and which has been granted by said Act to said Institution.

In testimony of the foregoing instrument, I, William J. Walker, have hereto affixed my signature and seal in Newport aforesaid on this second day of April in the year Eighteen Hundred and Sixty Three.

In presence of
E. M. Nicolai
E. S. Tobey

William J. Walker

The opening and the final paragraphs of Dr. William J. Walker's deed gift of April 2, 1863.

1 Temple Place
Boston May 4. 1863

Dear Sir,

At the risk of repeating what may be already known to you, I feel it to be a most agreeable duty to tell you of the favorable action of the Legislature on the two subjects connected with our Institute which have come before them.

If the information has not already reached you, I am sure you will be glad to hear that they have repealed the ungracious condition accompanying the grant of land on the Back Bay, and that we are now released from all possible liability connected with the sales of the surrounding land.

We are now busy planning the building for the School of Industrial Science, & thanks to your munificence we hope soon to see its foundation laid.

Believe me dear Sir
with great respect,
Yours truly,
William B Rogers.

Dr William Walker.

The opening and the final paragraphs of President Rogers' reply, indicating better days in sight for the Institute.

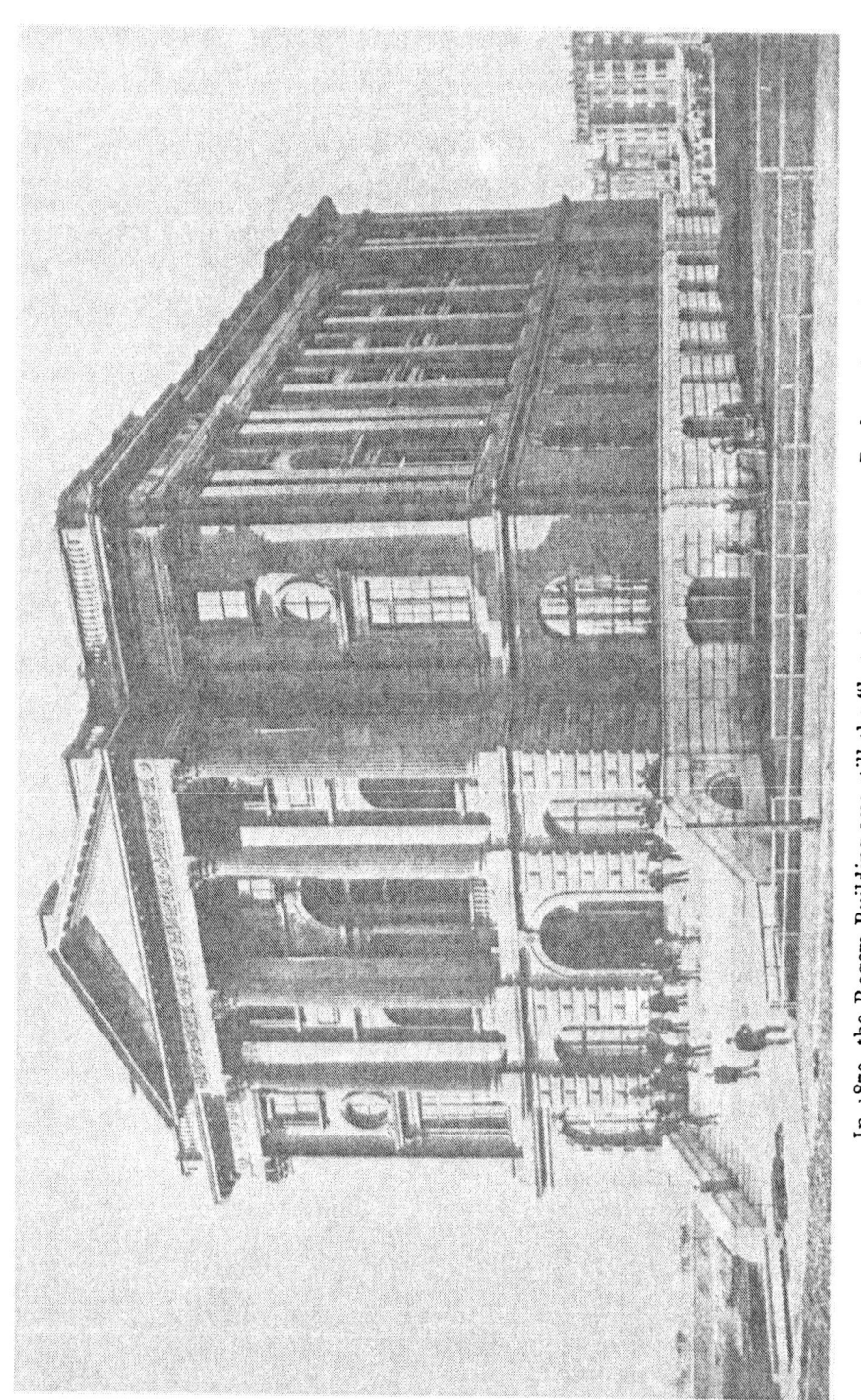

In 1872, the Rogers Building was still the "last structure west on Boylston Street."

In its earliest days, the Great Court in Cambridge had a similarly pioneering look.

Not many months later in 1916, the first plantings began to suggest pleasantness to come.

Two aspects of undergraduate life appear in this photograph of *The Tech's* office in Room 30 of the Rogers Building, taken in April, 1893. The banner is for the 1888 Eastern Inter-Collegiate Foot Ball League Championship, won by M. I. T.

Pea soup, clam chowder, boiled halibut, baked beans, brown bread, and cold corned beef were on the menu in the Rogers Building lunch room March 27, 1893.

Growing Pains

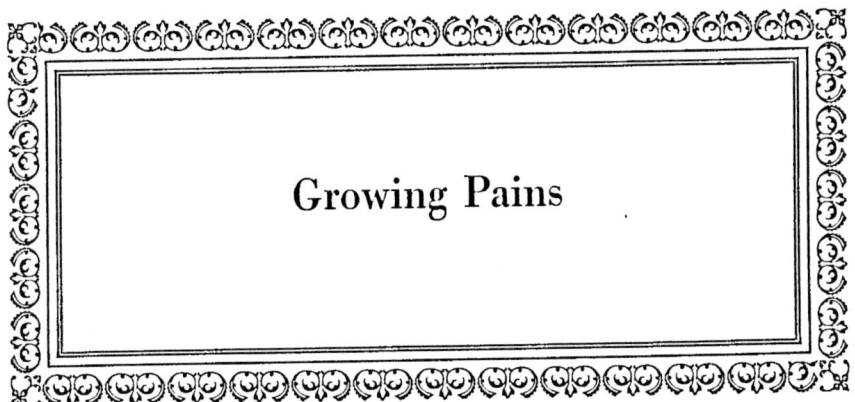

IN THE 1890's the student body had passed the thousand mark, but had shown only small fluctuations, reaching 1277 in 1900, with an average for the ten years of 1128. In the three opening years of the next decade a marked upturn took place, each of these years bringing an increment of more than ten per cent. A considerable part of this increase was due to the influx from areas outside New England, and the rising number of graduate students. In three years the number of graduates of other colleges at the Institute had increased more than fifty per cent to a total of nearly two hundred.

This growth was gratifying evidence of the high reputation of the school, but the accompanying need for expansion of facilities was a source of immediate and serious concern to faculty and administration. Growth involved an increase in teaching personnel on the one hand, and the familiar problem of making adjustments to meet space requirements on the other. The matter of increase in staff was carefully considered and cautiously met, principally by increasing appointments in the ranks of instructors and assistants. The faculty, i.e., professors of all three grades, numbered 63 in 1900; in 1903 it was but 69. In the lower ranks, however, instructors increased in this period from 44 to 66, and assistants from 32 to 51. The problem of space and facilities for teaching and research was more difficult.

In his report for 1901 President Pritchett referred to a suggestion that it might be desirable to establish a limitation of numbers. While arguing strongly against any geographic limitation, he suggested that at some time it might be advisable to limit the number of undergraduate students admitted. This action was not found necessary at this time. After 1903 the number of students declined, possibly in part because a rise in the tuition charges had been found absolutely necessary to increase the Institute income. A second cause may have been the development of other technical schools and the growth of engineering departments in colleges and state universities. The lower registration temporarily relieved the situation somewhat, but the real problem, that of space, was merely postponed.

Even if the Institute had had money for new buildings, it could not have built them because the necessary land was not available. With the construction of the Lowell Building and the one known as Engineering C, almost every foot of land owned on Trinity Place was utilized. The Grundman Studios occupied the rest, nearly 24,000 feet, which would be available on termination of a lease, but even this would be far from sufficient for the projected Walker Memorial and other needed facilities. Legal restriction prevented further building on the Boylston Street site. The legislature agreed to remove restrictions and to give the Institute title in fee simple, but legal action by the abutters indefinitely postponed building plans, and the ultimate sale of the land was long delayed. In this period no new buildings were erected on the original site.

A radical solution of these problems, first proposed in an article in the *Technology Review* for July, 1902, and endorsed in the president's report for 1902, was that the Institute should move away from the Copley Square neighborhood entirely, and find a new location with ample space for present needs and future growth.

Widespread and vigorous discussion followed. The rising value of land and the encroachment of retail trade made the old site undesirable, it was said, and the noise and vibration that came with growing traffic made teaching and experimental work increasingly difficult. A suitable new location would give room for the new educational buildings now necessary, and would make it possible to establish a dormitory system and to develop an intellectual and social center for the students worthy of a great institution. It would certainly be unwise to put the proposed Walker Memorial on Trinity Place if the Institute were to be moved within twenty-five years. On the other hand, opponents of the move urged legal difficulties, the loss of time in the erection of new buildings, and the loss of moral support that would come if the Institute abandoned its focal position in the heart of Boston and moved away from its educational neighbors and the industrial and mercantile interests that had been its main support. Furthermore, where could ample space be found that would be accessible and near enough to Boston's libraries and museums? How could such a comprehensive plan be financed?

These and other related questions occupied the Corporation, faculty, friends, and alumni of the Institute almost continuously for the next ten years, without a satisfactory answer until the new location of the Institute was finally determined in 1911. In the meantime no long-range plans could be made with any assurance. The result was a postponement of building plans and a resort to temporary expedients to meet the most pressing needs.

Early in 1904 the removal issue became suddenly entangled with a revival of the old proposal for some sort of union with Harvard. In January of that year the Institute staff was startled by an announcement in the *Boston Daily Advertiser* of a proposal for an alliance or "merger" of the Massachusetts Institute of Technology with Harvard University, followed a few days later by a lengthy article on the subject, stressing particularly the advantages of the proposed union. Two days later the same paper published interviews with members of the Institute Corporation, preceded by a brief account of the scheme and the conditions proposed. On the same day an editorial appeared in the *Boston Evening Transcript,* strongly presenting some objections to such a combination. Thereafter for a time these newspapers had almost daily editorials on the subject.

This attempt to effect a union—the fourth during Dr. Eliot's presidency—was precipitated by the announcement in November, 1903, of a bequest to Harvard from the estate of Gordon McKay for the promotion of applied science, especially mechanical engineering, amounting in a few years to a million dollars, and eventually to much more. The Massachusetts Institute of Technology, although it was the leading technical school in America and not without resources, was greatly in need of funds for further development, especially if it were to remove its plant to a new location. On the other hand, the Lawrence Scientific School up to that time had not become an outstanding school of engineering. Its replacement by M. I. T., or the union of these schools under the proposed merger, was therefore looked upon favorably by President Pritchett and some members of the Corporation as a means of improving the financial position of the Institute. The chief arguments for the merger were that there was undue waste of effort and money if two competing schools of engineering and applied science were to continue in the Boston area, and that education at the Institute would be humanized by association with the liberalizing and broadening influences of the university. These arguments although plausibly and cleverly presented were not convincing, and they have not withstood the test of time.

The newspaper accounts aroused a storm of protest from the faculty, staff, and alumni of the Institute. Should the Institute now, after nearly forty years' struggle, give up its hard-won independence, sacrifice its fundamental principles, and yield a leadership won the hard way to come under the partial or complete domination of Harvard in the hope of monetary advantage?

The Association of Class Secretaries at once went into action. The Association several months earlier had conceived the idea of a great general reunion of alumni in Boston in 1904, the centennial of the birth of William Barton Rogers, to provide an occasion for renewing old friendships and discussing some of the special problems facing the school, such as the removal issue. Committees had been appointed, and plans for the reunion were already well under way. At a meeting of the Association in February the available details of the newly proposed merger were discussed with great care, and the following resolution was unanimously adopted and transmitted to President Pritchett. "Resolved: That it is the sense of the members present that they are opposed to any plan of union with any other institution which might in any way impair the absolute independence of the Massachusetts Institute of Technology." At another meeting of the Association on April 26, 1904, the chairman, Walter B. Snow '82, again brought up the matter of the merger. It now seemed important to follow the original policy of the Association by bringing the matter to the attention of Institute men generally. It was therefore voted: "That there be appointed by the chair a committee consisting of the chairman and seven others, said committee to have full powers to take such action as it deems necessary toward securing for presentation to the President and Corporation expression of opinion of the alumni in the matter of the relations of the Institute with Harvard University."

The committee of the Association of Class Secretaries at once sent the following circular and postal-card petition to over 3700 graduates and former students:

Boston, Mass., April 27, 1904

Dear Sir,—There is evidence of a renewed and determined effort to secure closer relations between the Institute and Harvard University. Believing that this will lead to the sacrifice of the independence of the Institute, which would be disastrous to it and contrary to the public interest, the undersigned, a committee of the Association of Class Secretaries, invite their fellow-alumni to join them in signing the accompanying petition for immediate presentation to the President and Corporation.

Announcement will be made of such further steps as may be taken by the Association or its representatives.

Very truly yours,

W. B. Snow '82, Chairman
C. T. Main '76
R. A. Hale '77
E. C. Miller '79
I. W. Litchfield '85
E. G. Thomas '87
J. A. Collins, Jr. '97
F. H. Fay '93, Secretary

Committee of the Association of Class Secretaries

The enclosed postal card read:

"We, the undersigned, alumni of the Massachusetts Institute of Technology, respectfully petition the Corporation to entertain no proposition to unite, ally, or associate itself in any way, financial or otherwise, with any other educational body."

Signature _____ Class of _____

By May 12, a total of 1637 alumni had returned their petitions. Of these 1557 were positive, eight expressed belief in a union with Harvard, and twenty-five thought some combination of effort might be possible. The remaining forty-seven advocated independence but thought the petition too sweeping, or were willing to rely on the Corporation.

In May, 1904, presumably at the suggestion of President Pritchett, a resolution was passed by the Corporation of the Institute, as follows: "That the Executive Committee be requested to ascertain whether any arrangement can be made with Harvard University for a combination of effort in technical education such as will substantially preserve the organization, control, traditions, and the name of the Massachusetts Institute of Technology." The Executive Committee at once appointed a conference committee of two, consisting of President Pritchett and Dr. A. Lawrence Lowell, to confer with a similar committee from the Harvard Corporation, Dr. Henry P. Wolcott and Charles Francis Adams, II. Thus all except President Pritchett were prominent graduates or officials of Harvard University.

The conference committees met, and as a result of their deliberations agreed upon a tentative plan of alliance which they were to recommend to their respective Corporations. A brief statement regarding the informal completion of this "Tentative Plan of Co-operation between Harvard University and the Massachusetts Institute of Technology" was made in the president's report for 1904-05 before it was submitted to the Corporation. The full text of the document was presented in the president's report for 1905-06, together with certain revisions made after the agreement had been subjected to careful legal scrutiny. The legal opinion pointed out certain difficulties involved in the use of funds of the university which were or in future would be held in trust, and held that a favorable decree from the Supreme Judicial Court would be necessary before such an alliance could be consummated.

Although the tentative plan asserted that the Massachusetts Institute of Technology would still nominally retain its charter, name, organization, and general objects as a technical school, in reality it would lose its absolute independence and become integrated with Harvard University as its engineering school. It would essentially replace the Lawrence Scientific School and absorb its faculty. Three members of the Harvard Corporation would be added to the Corporation of the Institute and to the Executive Committee. Degrees were to be conferred by both the Technology and the Harvard Corporations, so that all alumni would henceforth be graduates of Harvard as well as of Technology.

Under the proposed plan the Institute would also be obligated to move to a new location on the Boston side of the Charles River opposite Harvard Square. Anticipating the success of the plan, a group of men including Andrew Carnegie and Henry L. Higginson had acquired a tract of land adjoining Soldiers Field in Brighton, now the site of the Harvard Business School. One part of the agreement read:

> The site of the institution shall be in Boston on the right bank of the Charles River, as nearly as practicable opposite to Harvard Square, and the Massachusetts Institute of Technology shall there erect, furnish, and equip buildings having the capacity of at least its present buildings. But the Institute shall not be required to proceed with such purchase and construction until it shall have sold a sufficient part of the land which it now owns. Provided, however, that this agreement shall be avoided, if at the end of four years from the time when this agreement goes into effect the Institute shall not have purchased said land and proceeded to a substantial extent with such construction.

At the alumni reunion held June 6-8, 1904, the proposed removal and merger provided the main topic of conversation at all gatherings and the theme for the speeches at the alumni dinner at the Hotel Somerset that ended the celebration. President Pritchett spoke at length on the subject, expressing his belief that co-operation with the university would safeguard the Institute's ideals of leadership in engineering and technical education. He mentioned the increasing competition from other institutions and especially the great state universities in western states, with the income and resources of the states to support them, and said that he believed it better to co-operate with Harvard and share in the benefits of the great bequest which had recently come to the university rather than to have two institutions of technical training (one of which would be well endowed) in competition in the same general community. He emphasized his own belief that under the proposed form of alliance the Institute would lose none of its strength or prestige or traditions and could enter into such an arrangement with courage and assurance and without fear. This earnest address, which was received with respectful attention if not conviction, ended with the promise that any plans of co-operation with Harvard that might be formulated would be communicated to the faculty and the alumni, and that their opinions would be considered before final action was taken.

The next speaker, President Gunsaulus of the Armour Institute of Technology in Chicago (the first of the institutions to copy the name Institute of Technology) expressed the great obligation of his own institution to M. I. T. Then he related the circumstances of a visit made by Mr. Armour and himself to the Institute, where they talked with President Walker. It was this visit that determined Mr. Armour to increase his gifts to the school he had endowed, and to change its name to the Armour Institute of Technology. The speaker predicted that to prevent a union with Harvard the alumni would come to the support of the Institute and that this nation would eventually realize that it owes more to the Massachusetts Institute of Technology than to any other educational foundation. Quoting Nehemiah, civil engineer of Jerusalem, who said, "I am doing a great work, and will not come down," he said to the audience, "You can't come down to any lower ideals. The Massachusetts Institute of Technology cannot come down. We look upon this institution, all of us, as the one that shall be the pioneer in research."

Colonel Thomas L. Livermore of the Corporation next spoke, commenting on the Corporation members and their devotion to the Institute. He mentioned that fourteen of the forty-six members were graduates of Harvard alone, and nine were graduates of Technology, but gave assurance that all members were equally sincere in their desire to preserve and not to destroy the Institute. The origin of this whole problem, he said, is financial. Then he electrified his hearers by the suggestion that concerted effort on the part of the alumni is what is needed to insure what is uppermost in the hearts of most of you, if not all of you." He recommended that former students make pledges of contributions "for the Institute, to keep it at the best, and to make it in the future the leader of all technical institutions in this country."

Dean Alfred E. Burton then spoke eloquently for the faculty, although as yet no definite proposition had been presented to them. The faculty's views, he said, were not based on any prejudice against Harvard, or against Harvard professors, or against Harvard ideas. In fact Harvard men on the faculty were even more definite in their ideas as to the unwisdom of entering into any arrangement with their *alma mater*—for which they had the deepest love and loyalty—than were the graduates of Technology. For himself he felt it would be wiser to continue to follow as a purely independent institution the general plan of education which Rogers laid down, rather than to change the old system for a new one merely because of the possible financial advantage of the McKay bequest. As dean he felt that one of the strongest arguments against the proposed affiliation was its relation to the social life of the students themselves, and their feeling that now they are an integral part of a single strong institution.

The next two speakers in this long evening of brilliant and earnest discussion were Isaac W. Litchfield '85, representing Chicago, and Proctor L. Dougherty '97, of Washington. Each spoke of the intense feeling of loyalty which alumni in the associations they represented had for the Institute, and of their desires to see it go on to greater success and to greater glory as the school without a peer in this country.

The final speaker, and the one who spoke with greatest brevity but a maximum of eloquent intensity and loyalty to the ideals of Technology, was James P. Munroe '82, president of The Technology Club and a life member of the Corporation. Mr. Munroe spoke of his personal association with John Cummings, who had sacrificed his own savings to prevent the Institute from being absorbed by Harvard earlier in its history, and recalled the righteous anger of Francis A. Walker whenever it was proposed that there should be any pause or change in the magnificent development of the Institute. He spoke of the spirit of Rogers, which is the Tech spirit, which the faculty and alumni hold as a sacred trust. His impassioned speech ended with these words: "And if we alienate it or diminish it or lose our courage in the matter of that trust, if we do not hand that trust on to our successors as it was given to us by those great men to whom I have referred,—and if we do not hand on that trust undiminished, untarnished, then I say we are traitors to those men and to the Institute."

The first great Technology reunion ended on this note. It was permeated to the very core by the sense that here was a great problem which must be met, a possible peril that must be encountered with all that the alumni had of loyalty, courage, and resourcefulness.

President Pritchett had promised that before final action was taken by the Corporation the whole matter would be placed before the faculty and the alumni, and in December the Corporation voted to authorize the president to seek the opinions of the faculty and the alumni on the proposed plan. The Executive Committee of the Corporation, on March 24, 1905, received the report of the conference committee. The plan was discussed then and again on March 30, but no action was taken other than to vote again that the question be referred to the faculty and alumni, and their opinions be reported to the Corporation not later than June 1, 1905.

The matter finally came before the faculty on May 5, 1905, with full attendance except for Professors W. T. Sedgwick and H. W. Tyler, both of whom were in Europe. After exhaustive consideration and debate a vote was taken, and a comprehensive report was adopted declaring the proposed agreement educationally unsound and prejudicial to the development of the Institute. The vote was decisive, fifty-six to seven. Of the opponents of the plan eight were graduates of Harvard, fourteen were graduates of other colleges or universities, and thirty-four were graduates or former students of the Institute. It was well known that the two absent professors were both strongly in opposition to the merger. Of the seven who voted in favor of the merger none were Harvard men and but two were graduates of the Institute. Majority and minority reports were prepared, and were printed in full in a special number of the *Technology Review*.

Approximately 3200 graduates and former students of the Institute were also asked to vote on the proposal, and some 2900 responded. A total of 1351 graduates voted against the plan, and 458 in favor of it. Of former students not graduated, 684 voted against the agreement, and 376 for it. Thus of those alumni whose votes were determinable, 2035 voted against the alliance, and 834 for it.

In the face of this alumni opposition, the Corporation on June 9, 1905 voted twenty-three to fifteen, that "The Executive Committee be requested, when they may ascertain that the Institute has power to sell the land on which it now stands, to propose to Harvard University an agreement upon the terms of the tentative plan now before this Corporation."

Here the matter rested until a decision of the Supreme Judicial Court on September 6, 1905, denied the Institute a title in fee simple to its property on Boylston Street and specifically enjoined it from either selling or building on the two-thirds of the area not at the time occupied. This decision made it impossible to carry out the agreement, for without selling its land the Institute would not have the money to build on the proposed location. The Corporation therefore directed President Pritchett to notify President Eliot of Harvard that it would be impossible to proceed with the plan for the proposed alliance. The independence of the Massachusetts Institute of Technology was thus again assured.

Dr. Abraham Flexner in his biography of President Pritchett implies that the opposition to the merger plan in the teaching staff at the Institute was concentrated in the younger men. This misconception should be corrected. No vote was taken of the opinion of instructors and assistants except as they were alumni. The faculty members only were especially polled, and the senior members of the faculty, with a single exception, were strongly in opposition. Most of them had taught at the Institute for many years and had shared loyally in its early periods of distress. They had faith and pride in the Institute and believed with its founder that it had a special mission in education and that it should remain absolutely independent and free to develop in its own way. The younger men shared this view.

It is not to be supposed that the proposed merger was unanimously acceptable at Harvard. Few opinions were publicly expressed. Most antagonistic of all the professors there was Dean N. S. Shaler, a grand old man who had been in charge of the Lawrence Scientific School since 1891, and had been for years the close friend, confidant, and adviser of Gordon McKay. In January, 1904, Shaler and his wife had left Cambridge for a sabbatical vacation in Egypt, Greece, and Italy. Professor James Lee Love in his history of the Lawrence Scientific School writes:

> . . . Only the shadow of repeated proposals to surrender all applied science work to the Massachusetts Inst. of Technology lurked to disturb him; he had won confidence that this could be defeated, and he hoped that time would dispel this shade forever. But, instead, bitterness and shock came forth when he least expected it. . . . Professor Shaler heard of the proposal to merge the two schools in Italy, and hastened home to oppose it. The Harvard Faculty was, officially, silent. The Faculty of the Institute was strongly and openly against the measure. The Alumni of the Institute supported its Faculty; and Dean Shaler, with their aid, again prevented the merging of the Lawrence Scientific School with the Institute of Technology. He was not in any sense against, or critical of the Institute, which he trusted and honored as an unexcelled technical school. He fought because he knew that the Lawrence Scientific School deserved to win, and that the merger was a violation of Mr. McKay's wishes and a breach of the trust that Harvard had assumed in accepting the endowment. He believed that there was not only ample room for the utmost that both schools could do for technical education, but also that there was a great need and demand for the kind of technical education that could be given within a great university. . .

It is clear that this grand old fighter carried the burden of the opposition to the merger at Harvard. That the president of the university and others in power were against him made him a saddened and disillusioned man, although the ultimate result must have given him some comfort.

The merger battle was in some respects reminiscent of the first attempt to unite the Institute and the Lawrence Scientific School in 1870, but was much more far-reaching in its educational significance. Then M. I. T. was a very young and struggling school; now it was a great and well established institution with thousands of graduates to attest its merit. No problem which had ever arisen in Institute history had so deeply stirred the loyalties of faculty and alumni and even of the Corporation, in which there was sincere division of opinion. It would be untruthful to say that this long and intense controversy was carried on without heat, or without engendering pronounced and lasting feelings of distrust in the motives of those who were most active in attempting to bring about the alliance. Many of the faculty felt that the president had not been entirely frank in some of his statements to that body. With his strong determination and self-assurance, and the aloofness which he sometimes manifested, he perhaps did not feel that it was necessary to be specific or to attempt seriously to reconcile the differences of opinion among his staff.

President Pritchett painfully realized that his faculty would not follow his leadership in this controversy, and in letters to some of the alumni he expressed regret that there had been suspicion as to his motives, and distrust in his judgment and leadership. What personal ambitions he had are not known. The generous and perhaps the just assumption is that fundamentally he was actuated by a powerful and sincere desire to see Technology expand under his leadership, and that he believed that technical education in America could be better promoted by combinations and associations of educational resources than by adherence to the established traditions of singleness of purpose and independence.

Except for a few individuals, this intense battle of ideals was conducted without personal bitterness, and there was never resort to vituperative personalities. Normally friendly relations were in general quickly restored, and the amicable relations between the faculties of the two great schools were entirely unimpaired and have so remained throughout the more than forty years since this struggle was at its height. On one occasion in the mellowed years after Dr. Pritchett had retired from the Carnegie Foundation, he was in Cambridge and spoke with cordial feeling to the faculty at Technology. In this friendly address he stated that as president he had made mistakes, and had not been as wise as he had thought.

The alumni reunion of 1904, apart from its significance in the merger controversy, proved to be a momentous occasion that set the pattern for later great Technology reunions, two of which fall within our period. It was a three-day celebration planned to include participation in the ceremonies accompanying the end of the school year; class and fraternity dinners; a "Tech Night" at the Pops; a day's outing at Nantasket; a banquet with serious addresses by the president, distinguished guests, and alumni; and plenty of provision for informal gatherings to reunite long-separated classmates, to meet old professors, and to review old scenes.

On the appointed day, June 6, 1904, 1600 alumni from all parts of the country arrived in Boston. A reception by Mrs. William Barton Rogers to greet returning alumni provided a fitting introduction to the reunion. This was followed by class dinners, after which came a reception by the Corporation and faculty at which the early graduates were enabled to pay their respects to Mrs. Rogers and Mrs. Francis A. Walker as old friends, and to meet Mrs. Henry S. Pritchett for the first time. This great reception, a notable social event attended by many prominent Boston people as well as hundreds of alumni, was held at the Museum of Fine Arts in Copley Square, where many treasures of the museum added beauty and splendor to the decorations. It was a brilliant affair in an unusual setting, and possibly the last of its kind held in that building.

Graduation day followed with its usual dignity. Quite in contrast, "Tech Night" at the Pops opened as a gay and uproarious affair of cheers and songs including an improvised song to the tune of *John Brown's Body,* which asserted that "You can't make crimson out of cardinal and gray." The evening was soon to become notable for the music conducted by the beloved but frail Frederic Field Bullard '87, who had so skillfully matched his music to the words of the *Stein Song* written by Richard Hovey of Dartmouth. On this occasion under his baton, the *Stein Song* was more than a college song—it was a hymn of praise. It was Bullard's last of many services to his *alma mater,* for on June 24 he was stricken fatally by the physical disabilities that he had borne so manfully from his early youth.

The day at Nantasket was one of especial gaiety and fun with a parade and class stunts on the beach and a luncheon at the Atlantic House. The evening brought the climax of the reunion at a great alumni dinner at the Hotel Somerset, presided over by Dr. Samuel

J. Mixter '75, president of the Alumni Association, who welcomed the returning alumni, as well as the new class of 1904, and read letters of congratulation from former President Grover Cleveland; President Drown of Lehigh (former head of the chemistry department at M. I. T.); Rev. Edward Everett Hale; Dr. Charles D. Walcott of the U. S. Geological Survey; and Andrew Carnegie. Then came an array of speeches, all bearing on the matter that was deepest in the hearts and minds of the hundreds in attendance—the proposal for alliance with Harvard which has been discussed.

To those who were fortunate enough to share in the events of those days in 1904, it seemed that they were surcharged with prophetic vision, with a spirit of optimism that would not be denied, and with a loyalty to ideals which was irrepressible. The reunion ended with a deep and unanimous conviction that now the alumni must show generosity, unremitting work, and self-sacrifice to preserve, maintain, and promote through the future years the glorious traditions of a magnificent institution founded on a great ideal, which had struggled through years of poverty, discouragement, and sacrifice to its high position, and which could, given the proper resources, go on to still greater heights.

Colonel Livermore's earnest speech at the reunion dinner had made clear to the alumni the financial problem at the heart of the merger controversy. "It would take a pledge of not a great sum from each individual of the 3,000 alumni," he said, "to make the Institute feel as independent as it ought to be. It is not money for the benefit of the board of government, or for any individual, but for the Institute, to keep it at the best, and to make it in the future the leader of all technical institutions in this country. . . ."

On the very next day a group of former students from widely separated parts of the country gathered at The Technology Club and began the plans for an organization to raise a Technology income fund to relieve the pressing financial needs of the Institute. Numerous meetings were held, headquarters were established at The Technology Club, and a plan for a general appeal to all former students was developed, asking for contributions on a five-year basis. The work was undertaken with great enthusiasm, and a man from each class served as its representative in the work of canvassing alumni. The reunion had shown the loyalty of past students, and here was the opportunity to demonstrate it by action.

The plan was heartily endorsed by President Pritchett. Three members of the Corporation, William Endicott, chairman of the Finance Committee; Colonel Thomas L. Livermore of the Executive Committee, and General Charles J. Paine were glad to serve as an advisory committee. An executive committee of Dr. Francis H. Williams '73, chairman, Professor Robert H. Richards '68, James P. Munroe '82, and Professor Francis W. Chandler of the faculty; and an income fund committee of Everett Morss '85, chairman, E. G. Thomas '87, C. M. Spofford '93, and L. P. Wood '01, secretary, were set up. Many alumni throughout the country were soon working on local committees.

The response was almost instantaneous. Within a few weeks contributions began to arrive, and pledges were received in amounts varying from one dollar to a thousand dollars annually, from men scattered from Alaska to Mexico and from Maine to California. The birthday of William Barton Rogers was suggested as an appropriate time for tribute to be paid to him by this form of loyal service, and in the seventeen days preceding December 7, 1904, pledges amounting to more than $60,000 were received. Before the end of December, six months after the campaign had begun, the pledges amounted to about $200,000. In the first three years cash turned over to the treasurer amounted to approximately $42,500, $35,700, and $41,100 respectively. It is interesting to note here that before the end of the five-year period the amount of money paid over to the treasurer of the Institute was approximately $196,000, a very high percentage of the pledges. In addition the Walker Memorial Fund, begun in 1898, now amounted to over $131,000.

This prompt action by the alumni had an immediate and salutary effect. The Institute's income from tuition had dropped several thousand dollars as the number of students had now fallen below 1400. The yearly payments made possible the carrying out of certain plans for construction and for the discharge of debts that had been contracted for building the Tech Union and the new gymnasium on Garrison Street. Other gifts in the closing years of Pritchett's administration had helped to relieve the financial stringency. In the period from 1904 to 1907 a bequest from the estate of Ednah Dow Cheney brought about $14,000 for the maintenance of the Margaret Cheney Room for women students; Nathaniel Thayer gave $25,000 to the permanent funds; and bequests of $25,000 each came from the estates of Charles Merriam and Macy S. Pope, and a bequest of $5,000 from Alexander S. Wheeler. Dr. Charles G. Weld before resigning from the Corporation gave $15,000 to the permanent funds and an additional sum for the department of naval architecture. There were also a number of lesser gifts for special purposes.

One result of the controversy of 1904-05 was the recognition of the inherent right of the alumni of an institution to participate in the discussion of such major questions of policy as the proposed removal and merger. The formal recognition of the claim of the alumni to a voice in the administration of the Institute came in 1906 with a change in the bylaws of the Corporation that provided for the yearly election of three alumni to membership on the Corporation for five-year terms. The background of this change in policy goes back to 1878, three years after the Alumni Association was formed, when the Corporation, through the Executive Committee of the Alumni Association, invited a nomination of an alumnus for election to the Corporation. Howard A. Carson '69, already an outstanding civil engineer and later to be widely known as chief engineer of the first Boston Subway, was nominated and duly elected. He thus became the first graduate on the Corporation. A few other men who had been students at the Institute and had risen to positions of eminence were elected to the Corporation at irregular intervals, but the Alumni Association had not been officially asked to make nominations after the first instance.

For many years the Alumni Association had also appointed, it may be remembered, a Committee on the School, charged with the duty of reporting annually on the condition of the Institute. While both this committee and the Corporation through its special committees had worked for the common good of the Institute, their activities had not been clearly co-ordinated and some annual reports of the committee to the Alumni Association had probably not been officially transmitted to the Corporation. There had been a growing feeling in the Alumni Association for some time that its members might advantageously have a larger share in the responsibilities of the Institute, but it was a matter in which the first official move should logically come from the Corporation. Through the diplomacy of the president of the association, Frank L. Locke '86, and its Executive Committee in co-operation with a committee of the Corporation, the matter was brought before the Corporation, and a plan for the nomination and election of the so-called term members was considered with most favorable results. At a stated meeting of the Corporation held December 13, 1905, the committee on nominations presented a plan for amending the bylaws to provide for term members to be elected from lists submitted by the Alumni Association. After discussion the amendment was adopted, by practically unanimous vote. The amendment made possible a gradual change in the personnel of the Corporation by the following procedure:

1. No new life members were to be elected until by death or resignation the number of members in this group was reduced below thirty-five. The number of life members thereafter was to be limited to thirty-five.

2. In addition to life members fifteen members were to be elected for terms of years as specifically provided.

3. The corporation would thus eventually have the following composition: Thirty-five life members; three *ex-officio* members, the president, the secretary, and the treasurer, and fifteen term members nominated by the alumni and elected by the Corporation, making a total of fifty-three.

To put the plan into immediate operation it was further specified that at the regular March meeting of 1906 nine alumni should be elected from a list of fourteen nominated by the Alumni Association, with staggered terms of five, four, and three years; and that annually thereafter three should be elected from a list of five nominees, for a term of five years.

At the time this plan was acted upon by the Corporation there were forty-four life members of the Corporation. Of these eight were actual graduates of the Institute and four others had been former students but had not taken the degree of the Institute. All were men of distinction in their special fields of business or professional activity. In addition to Howard A. Carson '69, the first alumnus on the Corporation, the others were, in the order of their election to life membership: Francis H. Williams '73, physician and professor at Harvard Medical School, elected in 1882, and elected secretary of the Corporation in 1891; James P. Tolman '68, president of Samson Cordage Company, elected in 1883; Samuel M. Felton '73, later president of the Chicago & Alton R. R., elected 1887; Charles W. Hubbard '76, manufacturer of chemicals, Boston, elected 1889; Samuel Cabot '70, head of Samuel Cabot, Inc., elected 1889; A. Lawrence Rotch '84, proprietor of Blue Hill Observatory, elected 1891; John R. Freeman '76, head of Manufacturers' Mutual Insurance Company and distinguished engineer, elected 1893; James P. Munroe '82, manufacturer and publicist, elected 1897; Eben S. Draper '78, head of Draper Corporation and later Governor of Massachusetts, elected 1898; Robert S. Peabody '68, head of Peabody and Stearns, architects, elected 1898; Charles A. Stone '88, president of Stone & Webster, elected 1902.

The nine alumni elected to term membership in 1906 were: T. Coleman du Pont '84, president of the du Pont Powder Company, Wilmington, Del.; Charles T. Main '76, consulting engineer and builder of textile mills, Boston; Frederick W. Wood '77, president of Maryland Steel Company, Sparrows Point, Md.; Frederick K. Copeland, '76, president of Sullivan Machinery Company, Chicago; Joseph P. Gray '77, vice-president of Boston Manufacturers' Mutual Fire Insurance Company, Boston; Frank L. Locke '86, superintendent of factories, Boston Rubber Shoe Company, Malden; Frederick H. Newell '85, chief engineer, Reclamation Service, U. S. Geological Survey, Washington; Eben S. Stevens '68, president and treasurer of Intervale Mills, Inc., Quinebaug, Conn.; and Richard H. Soule '72, consulting engineer, Boston.

Two important changes in the personnel of the Corporation took place at the annual meeting in 1907. James P. Munroe '82, was elected secretary, succeeding Dr. Francis H. Williams '73. Dr. Williams had been a most active and loyal member of the Corporation for twenty-five years. He had aided valiantly throughout the dark years in President Walker's administration and the periods of stress and danger when the Institute's independence had been threatened. He had the deep respect and affection of the faculty. He had served with zeal as chairman of departmental committees, especially in chemistry and biology, in which he had both a general and a professional interest. For sixteen years he had been secretary of the Corporation. Relinquishing this office to the equally devoted Munroe meant no diminution of his almost parental affection for the Institute.

At the same meeting, George Wigglesworth, who had also served for sixteen years as a most valuable and efficient treasurer, resigned his office. The skill with which he had administered the financial affairs of the Institute through these difficult years was phenomenal. He was succeeded by Francis R. Hart '89, a loyal alumnus who had had a wide financial experience both in the United States and in tropical America, and was an official of one of Boston's strongest banks. He was an admirable man for this important post.

In the spring of 1907 occurred the death of Alexander S. Wheeler, who had served M. I. T. for twenty-five years and had been a member of the Executive Committee from its inception until 1902. Despite this and other recent losses of senior members, the Corporation was greatly strengthened in its relations to science and industry by the incoming group of term members. The three alumni term members elected in March, 1907, were George E. Hale '90, the brilliant astronomer and physicist; George W. Kittredge '77, chief engineer of the New York Central Railroad; and Frank G. Stantial '79, superintendent of the Cochrane Chemical Company at Everett.

With this election the Corporation consisted of fifty-four men at the end of the academic year 1906-07, of whom twenty-six had at some time been students at the Institute and therefore were representative of the alumni, either as term members or as life members. Three ex-officio members represented the Commonwealth, and the remaining twenty-five life members were prominent in business or industrial life, and deeply interested in the welfare of the Institute.

Throughout his busy years as president of the Institute Dr. Pritchett followed the example of his predecessors in devoting a part of his time and energy to important public services. He was the superintendent of awards of the Buffalo Exposition in 1901; he became one of the trustees of the Franklin Fund, created by Benjamin Franklin's gift of $1,000 to the City of Boston, which by 1904 had increased to over $400,000. The trustees proposed to use the fund to found a school devoted to the teaching of various trades, but legal complications prevented immediate action. President Pritchett also was chairman of a state commission to consider the advisability of constructing a dam across the Charles River, to maintain a basin free from tidal fluctuations. This important improvement was completed in 1910. President Pritchett served on this project until 1908.

In the summer of 1904, President and Mrs. Pritchett went to the British Isles for a few weeks' vacation. While there they were invited to visit Andrew Carnegie at his summer home, Skibo Castle, in Scotland. The outcome of this visit was of great importance to Boston and eventually to President Pritchett himself. At this time the subject of the Franklin bequest came up, and the proposed plans for an endowed evening training school were discussed. Mr. Carnegie asked why the trustees hesitated. President Pritchett replied: "For lack of adequate funds." Thereupon Mr. Carnegie said: "I'll match Ben Franklin," and gave the money, amounting to $408,396. Thus the Institute's president was largely instrumental in making possible the establishment and maintenance of the Franklin Union, the name of which was later changed to the Franklin Technical Institute.

According to President Pritchett's biographer, this visit was of transcendent importance in another way. When Mr. Carnegie asked about his errand in Scotland, the president replied: "I am trying to get a $25,000 professor for a $7,500 salary." Mr. Carnegie's experience as a trustee of Cornell had made him aware that professors were underpaid, and the subsequent discussion started a train of thought that led to his decision to do something to assist professors in their old age. The result was the Carnegie Foundation for the Advancement of Teaching, with its provisions for pensions for retired professors. The Foundation, with its endowment of $10,000,000, was announced in 1905, and M. I. T. was one of the fifty-two institutions originally recognized as entitled, by reason of standards and courses of study to participate in its benefits.

Mr. Carnegie decided that President Pritchett was the right man to head the new Foundation. Pritchett accepted the invitation, and in December, 1905, resigned as president of the Institute. On the urgent request of the Corporation, the resignation was postponed for a year, and an arrangement was made that allowed President

Pritchett to spend half his time in New York in the work of organizing the Foundation. Early in 1906 he and Mrs. Pritchett established their home in New York, and he came to Boston for essential Institute business. During this period, many of the responsibilities of the president were capably carried on by Dr. Arthur A. Noyes '86, who in response to duty relinquished the directorship of the Research Laboratory for a year to serve as chairman of the faculty.

Meantime, search was being made for a new president. None of the obviously willing candidates appeared to be wholly acceptable to the Corporation. On October 5, 1906, however, the Executive Committee of the Corporation invited Professor Andrew F. West, dean of the Graduate School at Princeton University, to become president of the Institute. On October 30, Professor West sent a cordial and appreciative letter declining the offer, and expressing his belief that it was his duty to remain at Princeton to carry on the work he had begun in building up the Graduate School. Finally at the end of the academic year, in order to give the Corporation more time to find the right man, Dr. Noyes was appointed acting president, and served most successfully in this post for the next two years.

In the history of the Institute, President Pritchett's regime was characterized by several notable administrative changes and faculty appointments. But his name will be most appreciatively remembered for the great interest which he with Mrs. Pritchett took in student welfare, which really opened a new era. The appointment of Professor Burton as the first dean was a matter of prime importance. The establishment of the "Tech Union" in the rooms over the Garrison Street shops brought a new feeling of social unity in the student body. Even the hostility to the beer-drinking "Kommers" was quickly dispelled. The honest difference of opinion in regard to the merger with Harvard, although causing temporary barriers to complete understanding with his opponents, left little permanent bitterness and distrust. In the busy days of his presidency Pritchett was inclined to be somewhat aloof, according to memories of the younger men of the staff, and did not have the mellowness of his later years. But he made many student friendships, some within the faculty, and probably more among leading citizens outside his academic circle, and in the clubs to which he was elected.

He had the zeal of the missionary and the temperament of the reformer. His opinions were positive; his speech was generally direct and vigorous, but not always persuasive. His administration must be remembered as a period when problems of the greatest moment to the Institute had to be faced. The road taken at this important turning point has led to great things, and in after years President Pritchett was generous in expressing his opinion that right judgments had prevailed. Now fifty years later, his greatest contribution seems to have been his interest in the social welfare of the student. Even for this alone, he will be gratefully remembered as a successful president.

The Noyes Administration

THE DISTINGUISHED service of Professor Arthur A. Noyes as chairman of the faculty and as director of the Research Laboratory of Physical Chemistry as well as in other ways both within the Institute and in national scientific societies, made his appointment as acting president especially satisfactory to all connected with the institute. It is now known that he had been asked if he were willing to accept the presidency. His devotion to his research work, his modesty, and the feeling that as a bachelor he lacked the social qualifications he deemed essential in a president, influenced him to decline this honor as, with characteristic loyalty to the Institute, he expressed willingness to serve as acting president until the right man could be found. He assumed the office on July 1, 1907, and in order that he might have no other compelling responsibilities, he shortly after withdrew from the directorship of the Research Laboratory until he should be free to re-assume it. Professor Gilbert N. Lewis, who had been closely associated with Dr. Noyes in the Laboratory, was appointed its acting director.

Arthur Amos Noyes was born in Newburyport, September 13, 1866, of pioneer English stock, his forebears having settled in Newbury, Mass., in 1635. His father, Amos Noyes, was a scholarly and able lawyer in Newburyport, and his mother was a woman of culture and fine personality. He attended the public schools in that city, and having there acquired an absorbing interest in chemistry, he prepared for the Massachusetts Institute of Technology. A year after graduating from the high school, he entered the second year class of M. I. T., having by his own efforts completed all freshman work except drawing. He excelled in chemistry, and was graduated in 1886, before reaching the age of twenty. He returned for a year of advanced work and was the second man to receive the Institute's Master of Science degree, which he obtained in 1887.

The following year he spent as an assistant in chemistry at the Institute. He then devoted two years to advanced study in Germany, and obtained his Ph.D. degree at the University of Leipzig in 1890. Here he worked in organic chemistry under Wislicenus and carried on his *arbeit* for the doctorate under Ostwald, the leader of the new field of physical chemistry, with such brilliance that Ostwald always regarded him as one of his most notable disciples.

The next ten years Noyes spent at the Institute in teaching and research in analytical, organic, and physical chemistry. He also prepared a small book entitled *Notes on Qualitative Analysis* which was especially helpful to Technology students and widely used elsewhere. He was appointed assistant professor of organic chemistry in 1894, associate professor in 1897, and professor of theoretical chemistry in 1899. From the beginning of his professional career he was undoubtedly the leading exponent of physical chemistry in America, but his interest in chemistry was not narrowly confined. He early became active in the American Chemical Society, of which he was president in 1904, and he was the virtual founder of the Northeast Section of this national society. A large number of research papers presented at its meetings emanated from his laboratory.

Since physical chemistry was his chosen field, it became his principal ambition to establish at the Institute a research laboratory of the highest grade. Toward this objective he worked unceasingly, and with the generous determination to devote as much of his own earnings as possible to its development. As director of the Research Laboratory of Physical Chemistry, which was established in 1903,

Dr. Noyes was exceptionally successful. Young men of outstanding ability from far and near became research workers or graduate students under him. The names of most of these early workers are now, or have been, in the highest echelons of scientists. By the biblical standard, "By their fruits ye shall know them," the men trained in this laboratory prove the greatness of Dr. Noyes' character and leadership.

From the beginning of his career as a teacher of chemistry, Dr. Noyes was outstanding for the clarity of his lectures, the helpful, even inspirational, quality of his contacts with students in the laboratory, and the interest in scientific and cultural fields he was able to develop in students doing research under his direction. They were greatly influenced by his friendliness, his quiet sense of humor, and the breadth of his interests outside his professional orbit, which made him an ideal leader of young men. From youth he had been interested in good literature, and had been especially fond of poetry, although this hobby was not generally known. Having spent his boyhood within sight of a river long famous for its ships and small boats, he was a sailing enthusiast, and in short summer vacations cruised along the New England coast with members of the Research Laboratory as crew and companions. On these happy excursions they learned more intimately the thoughtful and cultured side of their chief.

The recognized soundness of Dr. Noyes' views on technical education, the capacity he had shown in the development of the Research Laboratory, and the high esteem in which he was held by his colleagues led to his election as chairman of the faculty in the spring of 1906. It was an especially important position in the final year of the administration of President Pritchett, whose time and energies were divided between the Institute and the newly established Carnegie Foundation for the Advancement of Teaching. On assuming his new position as acting president in 1907, Professor Noyes devoted himself assiduously to the broad problems of development of the Institute. It was a time when Technology was in a period of self-examination, readjustment, and expansion after the issue of the proposed merger with Harvard had become settled. Now the main problem was to readjust to a definite policy for the next few years, until the matter of moving could be settled.

As a professor concerned with the broad training of young men, as chairman of the faculty, and as acting president, Dr. Noyes devoted much time and thought to the fundamental problems of technological education, and also to the reformulation of the educational ideals and policy of the Institute. When the merger with Harvard was proposed, he was one of the most earnest and sagacious in opposition. His cogent arguments for independence on educational grounds were presented before the faculty, and published in an important article called, "The Ideals of the Institute" in the *Technology Review* in 1905. At the opening of the school year in 1906, at the request of Dean Burton, he addressed the first year class and other new students, welcoming them to Technology and convincingly presenting the ideals for which the aspiring young scientist or engineer should strive in his conduct of professional life. He stressed the thorough scientific background necessary, and also the breadth of character and ideals that may be cultivated through general study and reading good literature. This "Talk to First Year Students," as it was called, was published in the *Technology Review* for January 1907, and was read by many hundreds of alumni.

In another notable talk at a convocation of the instructing staff late in his first year as acting president, he discussed teaching as a high and rewarding calling, and insisted that good teaching and thorough research constituted a perfect unity. The following year, while still acting president, in an address of welcome to his successor, he gave an admirable restatement of his views of the educational philosophy of the Institute, as it had developed through time and experience. The expression of these educational ideals, so well exemplified in his own daily life, was one of Noyes' most important contributions.

Noyes' first president's report stressed the primary and indispensable function of the Institute as an undergraduate school insisting on thorough fundamentals in science and engineering, combined with liberalizing courses, as it had been from the beginning in the much simpler days of Rogers. Naturally, in the intervening forty years the extremely rapid advances and the ramification of the sciences had created new problems of adjusting these older fundamental ideas to the new needs and demands. Insistence on more extended training in the secondary schools helped, but merely to raise the entrance requirements was not enough. One of the methods suggested as a next step was that a period of summer work in semi-professional subjects be required in the summers following the first and second years, in order to broaden the base and permit more advanced courses or additional subjects in the later terms. As a result of such a program the student completing his four-year course would have more actual knowledge, greater breadth of view, and a more highly developed sense of professional responsibility, so that he could successfully meet the ordinary demands in a professional or industrial field without claiming to be a highly trained specialist. A five-year program leading to the Bachelor of Science degree was also proposed and actually established for students who desired to broaden their courses on the literary and cultural side.

The first report also called attention to a change in the teaching of mathematics designed to give the student a more logical and unified introduction and a clearer conception of the whole subject instead of dividing it into the traditional isolated parts such as advanced algebra, analytic geometry, and the two divisions of calculus. The new system made it possible for the student to economize time and effort and to visualize more easily a large number of concrete applications.

One of the early official acts of Dr. Noyes was to approve a reorganization of the faculty to make it more effective in handling its educational business. The faculty now having increased to a total of eighty-six, it semed desirable to have special committees to give detailed study to various problems and make reports suggesting appropriate faculty action rather than to expect the whole group to pass on all matters of detail in the monthly meetings. The reorganization plan provided for a chairman of the faculty, elected yearly, to preside when the president could not attend, a permanent secretary, and a series of standing committees, of which the committees on faculty business, on courses of instruction, on undergraduate scholarships, on petitions, and on graduate students were typical. This arrangement greatly facilitated the faculty's control of the whole educational program. Dr. Noyes was unanimously elected chairman in each of the two years of his incumbency as acting president.

Although Noyes insisted on the primary function of the Institute as an undergraduate school, he also foresaw and was preparing his own students for the time when much more than an undergraduate training would be demanded in order to provide the highest leadership in American industry and science. History has demonstrated the soundness of his thinking.

The first report of the acting president called attention to the provision by all departments for a fifth year of work leading to the Master of Science degree. Another provision made it possible for college graduates who had the essential background in the sciences to be admitted to graduate status at once for a two- or three-year program leading to the master's degree. Previously such students had been required to complete the M. I. T. requirements for the S.B. degree before attaining actual graduate status. The next year a bulletin entitled "Advanced Study and Research" was issued, and during this period the Institute began to attract graduates of other colleges in substantial numbers for both graduate and undergraduate work. Sixty of the 208 graduates in 1907 had previously been students in other colleges.

Dr. Noyes himself had taken the lead in establishing the facilities for advanced study and research leading to the doctor's degree to meet the demand for a smaller number of exceptionally trained men whose careers would probably be on the frontier of scientific and engineering research. This period seems to have been the first when men could earn the doctorate in a school of engineering and applied science in this country, instead of having to go to Europe. In this type of graduate work the Research Laboratory of Physical Chemistry was a pioneer. "Noyes' Laboratory" was widely recognized as outstanding in its special field, and was a potent force in the awakening of other American institutions to their opportunities in graduate work.

In the mid-century period of the 1950's it is difficult to realize that up to 1904, when for the first time the Master of Science degrees were awarded to the naval constructors coming to the Institute from the Naval Academy, M. I. T. had given only forty-one master's degrees. By June, 1953, the number, in four categories, was nearly 8551. The Ph.D. degree was awarded for the first time in 1907, to three students, all in physical chemistry under Dr. Noyes. By 1953, M. I. T. doctorates numbered 1947. It is evident that before 1910 the school had gradually found the means and was awakened to its opportunities in this area, and to Dr. Noyes belongs much of the credit.

Noyes' interest in the social welfare of the students was no less sincere than that of his predecessors. The establishment of the Tech Union on Garrison Street had been a forward step of first importance. For five years the Union had been extraordinarily successful, but its remote location somewhat limited its use. Dr. Noyes in his first report to the Corporation, dated December 11, 1907, warmly praised President Pritchett's great service in making the Union possible, in rationalizing the athletic system, and in the appointments of Dean Burton and Dr. White, the Medical Adviser. He went further, however, and urged the appointment of a corporation committee on welfare of students, and that a larger and more central place be provided as a student center until the Walker Memorial could become a reality. The committee was appointed, and on its recommendation the Executive Committee of the Corporation voted to build at once a new Union on the unoccupied space between the Pierce Building and Engineering C. Here a new building sixty feet square and two stories high was erected. Space in the adjoining buildings was taken for kitchen and serving room and other needed conveniences. This building, furnished amply and attractively, was essentially a small modern club that provided on the first floor a large dining room and lunch counter capable of feeding a thousand students a day, and on the upper floor a large and attractive social room, a library, and two or three smaller rooms. The large dining room supplanted the lunch room in the basement of the Pierce Building which for ten years had been admirably conducted by Mrs. Ellen A. King, who resigned in 1908.

During Dr. Noyes' administration a number of notable changes took place in the faculty. Professor W. O. Crosby '76, who had become extremely deaf during his long tenure of more than a quarter century, was retired at his own request, and became the first Institute professor to benefit from the Carnegie Foundation. Four resignations, much regretted throughout the Institute, were those of George V. Wendell '92, associate professor of physics, and an extraordinarily able and popular teacher, to become head of the physics department at the Stevens Institute of Technology; Associate Professor Frank P. McKibben '94, who for ten years had been a strong right hand to Professor Swain, to become head of the department of civil engineering at Lehigh University; Assistant Professor Richard W. Lodge '79, who retired to do consulting work in mining; and Assistant Professor Douglas W. Johnson, whose growing reputation in geology led to a professorial appointment at Harvard, where he had taught on a part-time basis.

To lose these men after they had been for years a part of a smoothly running mechanism was something of a shock. Wendell was an unusual personality and a tower of strength to the physics department, a man so universally liked that his going seemed almost catastrophic. But his greatest service to Technology was yet to come. McKibben had a combination of theoretical and practical knowledge gained by many summers of actual work on large projects that made his teaching especially effective. Lodge, with long practical experience before becoming a teacher, had certainly given to mining engineering students a sense of "know-how" and the details of operating problems not to be learned from books. To them "Dicky" Lodge was a personal friend, confidant, and valued adviser. These were all severe losses to the Institute, but to the men concerned they meant well-won professional advancement.

New men entering the faculty were Reginald A. Daly, an outstanding scientist from the Geological Survey of Canada, as professor of physical geology; the versatile and brilliant Dr. Edwin B. Wilson from Yale University as associate professor of mathematics, who served the Institute for fifteen years in varied ways with high distinction; Lewis E. Moore from the University of Illinois as assistant professor in civil engineering; and Edward E. Bugbee '00, from the University of Washington at Seattle as assistant professor of mining engineering.

These new appointments and the recent promotions more than maintained the quota of full professors. Other promotions within the faculty were also notable. The names of Gilbert N. Lewis; Henry G. Pearson; Ralph R. Lawrence '95; Harrison W. Smith '97; Leonard M. Passano; Charles B. Breed '97; George L. Hosmer '98; Henry L. Seaver; Miles S. Sherrill '99; Earle B. Phelps '99; Maurice de K. Thompson '98; and George E. Russell '00, are certainly familiar and pleasant ones for the students of that period to recall. Every one of these men went forward to a high position either within the Institute or elsewhere.

Two of Technology's ablest men, Professors Clifford and Swain resigned in 1908 and 1909. Professor George F. Swain '77, who had been the head of the department of civil engineering since 1887, accepted an appointment as the first Gordon McKay Professor of Civil Engineering in the Harvard Graduate School of Applied Science, where the salary and the freedom of time to carry conulting work were much greater than at the Institute. Professor Swain was famous and highly respected for the extraordinary quality of his teaching. His work was largely with advanced students, and he was noted for his insistence that they "think through" every problem before committing themselves to an answer. He was impatient with a student who he thought was indolent, and he was likely to be sharp in criticism if a student jumped at conclusions. His favorite comparison of a student's mental capacity with that of "my black cat" was a by-word among the seniors. Regardless of, or perhaps because of these characteristics he was a remarkable teacher, and the students had for him a sort of adoration despite the fact that the sensitive ones were sometimes deeply wounded by his sarcastic remarks. Swain's fame and skill as a teacher were matched by his extraordinary record as a consulting engineer on many important projects, especially those concerned with structures. As senior member of the Boston Transit Commission in 1895, for example, he was of decisive influence in the plans for the Boston Subway and the East Boston Tunnel, and in the selection of H. A. Carson '69, as the Chief Engineer of the Commission. Swain had made the civil engineering department one of great strength and reputation, and his interest in engineering education is shown by his election as president of the Society for Promotion of Engineering Education in 1894. He was likewise prominent in professional societies, in Canada, Great Britain, and Germany as well as in America. In 1913 he was president of the Boston Society of Civil Engineers, and was the first professor to be elected president of the American Society of Civil Engineers. He had also been awarded the much prized Lamme Medal.

Swain's resignation became effective at the end of the college year, but most fortunately it was possible to secure as his successor one of his ablest pupils and earlier subordinates, Charles M. Spofford '93, who had taken post-graduate work under Swain following his graduation, had been an engineer with the Phoenix Bridge Company for two years, and had taught under Swain for nine years at M. I. T. After this professional experience he had been appointed head of the department of civil engineering at Brooklyn Polytechnic Institute, where he made an extraordinary record. On February 26, 1909, he was appointed Hayward Professor of Civil Engineering at the Institute, to assume his duties at the beginning of the next school year. He became head of the department of civil and sanitary engineering in 1911.

On January 21, 1909, it was announced that Professor Harry E. Clifford '86, had been offered and had accepted the position of Gordon McKay Professor of Electrical Engineering at the Harvard Graduate School of Applied Science, and was to begin his teaching there in the autumn. This resignation, like that of Swain, caused sincere regret at the Institute. Professor Clifford had been in the first regular group to graduate as electrical engineers, and had at once been appointed as an assistant in physics. A brilliant mathematician, an excellent lecturer, and a close student of mathematical physics, he established a high reputation for his knowledge of theoretical electricity and its applications. As a teacher he was of the highest rank. After electrical engineering became a separate department, he was responsible for the administration of the department during most of the time until Professor D. C. Jackson came in 1907. He was a notably successful administrator, and built a strong staff. His own thorough knowledge, increased by extensive summer travel to visit important electrical installations abroad, and his wide acquaintance through his membership in the principal engineering societies, made him an admirable leader in the growing department.

It is a high tribute to Clifford and Jackson, both men of exceptional ability and strongly developed individuality, that for nearly two years they worked side by side with the single purpose of assuring the best training possible to the young men who enrolled in this rapidly expanding field. Each had his own inherent qualities of leadership and large capacity for administration. With Jackson as head of the department, it was not surprising, therefore, that when the invitation came to Clifford to take the highest position in his own professional field at Harvard, he accepted it at once. The position gave him unusual opportunities and much freedom of action, and he could still be in fairly intimate contact with his close friends and former colleagues at the Institute.

Noyes, himself an alumnus (the first to act as president, and the only one until 1948) was naturally interested in alumni affairs and fostered the increasingly intimate relations between the alumni and the administration of the Institute. The ties that bound faculty, administration, Corporation, and alumni together were greatly strengthened during this period. Relations with secondary schools, the state, and the public were also improved. Isaac W. "Ike" Litchfield '85, who had for years been an energetic and loyal alumnus, now devoted his full time to this service. Dr. Noyes in his last year as acting president also assisted in the reorganization of the Alumni Association that established the Alumni Council, which proved to be a most important means of fostering close relations between former students and the school, and participated in the plans for another great Technology reunion to take place in June, 1909.

The part played by the Alumni Association in Institute affairs in the first decade of the century was of vital importance in the history of the Institute. The improved organization, the Income Fund, and the term-membership plan were the beginning of far greater things in the next decade, when the alumni, under the leadership of a great new president, made it possible for the Institute to continue its outstanding contribution to technological education on a larger scale in the new plant in Cambridge, and to give a national service unexcelled in the annals of American educational institutions.

From the day when Dr. Noyes took the position of acting president he had insisted that his tenure should cease as soon as the right man for the presidency could be found. With characteristic modesty he said in an interview, "I have no hesitation in saying that I would rather be president of the Institute than to hold any other position in the country, provided I felt myself well fitted to fulfill the duties of the place. I have, however, clearly recognized that this would not be for the true interests of the Institute; for it needs at its head a man with a larger working capacity, with a greater aptitude for the public and social sides of the work, and with certain other important qualities more highly developed." Toward the end of the year 1908 it was his great pleasure to recommend to the Executive Committee of the Corporation the name of a man admirably suited in all respects to be the new president. The man was Richard C. Maclaurin, who had come from New Zealand to be a professor at Columbia University. Maclaurin was discovered by George V. Wendell '92, who had recently left M. I. T. to become head of the physics department at Stevens Institute. His election was confirmed by the Corporation in November, and he was to take office at the end of the college year.

In the two years of his tenure, Dr. Noyes had carried on his work with as great distinction as if he had been actually a president rather than an acting president, and he should be regarded as one of Boston Tech's great leaders. His unselfishness and his deep but unostentatious interest in the students as well as his broad vision and scientific eminence made his administration a notable one. Possibly some of the most satisfying moments in his career came in the last days of the spring term in 1909.

At the final regular faculty meeting of the year the following resolution was adopted by a unanimous rising vote:

Resolved, That the members of the Faculty of the Massachusetts Institute of Technology desire to express to Dr. Arthur A. Noyes, upon his concluding his work as Acting President, their deep sense of the service he has rendered by his admirable executive ability, his power of initiative, his untiring labor, his unfailing tact and his contagious enthusiasm. Under his skillful management a period which might easily have been one of discouragement and detriment has been marked by distinct and constant advance in the affairs of the school and by the inception and progress of new and excellent measures in its administration. They also wish to declare their admiration for the unselfishness with which he has laid aside for the time being the original work in which he has gained such distinction, in order to devote his energy to the interests of the Institute as a whole; and they thank him for the kindly and helpful spirit which has marked all his relations toward them, both official and personal.

Possibly an even greater and more triumphant happiness came to him a few days later. At a convocation of the student body James H. Critchett, president of the senior class, acting as spokesman for the whole student body, presented Dr. Noyes with a silver loving-cup bearing this inscription: "Presented to Dr. Arthur A. Noyes by the Undergraduates of the Massachusetts Institute of Technology in gratitude for his faithful and efficient service, his warm-hearted sympathy and his unselfish devotion as Acting President, 1907-09." Practically every student in the Institute had contributed to the purchase of this cup.

On June 4 the Corporation passed the following resolution:

The Corporation of the Massachusetts Institute of Technology desires to place upon record its cordial appreciation of the exceptional service, as Acting President, rendered to the Institute by Professor Arthur A. Noyes since July, 1907. Giving up temporarily that work of research which was especially congenial and through which he had brought high credit to Technology, Dr. Noyes undertook the duties of administration at a time when that responsibility was unusually difficult. He performed those labors not only with characteristic fidelity, but with distinct ability and success. To the task of finding a permanent president he brought special knowledge and untiring zeal. Not satisfied with the simple maintaining of established policies, he instituted new ones, and carried them so far and so well forward that he places the Institute in the hands of his successor in a condition not only excellent in itself, but full of the promise of immediate and important growth.

Relinquishment by Dr. Noyes of the duties of acting president ended a period of Institute history but by no means ended the service of this great alumnus and scientist to the Institute. He was undoubtedly proud to have served as a matter of duty, but he was happy to return to his cherished work as director of the Research Laboratory of Physical Chemistry, and to rejoin his colleagues in the scientific investigation which was his real professional life. To this he gave his full time for four years, and then in 1913 in response to an appeal from George E. Hale '90, to aid in the transformation of Throop College in Pasadena into the California Institute of Technology, he gave a part of his time to that constructive service. It was again a call to duty. For seven years he divided his time between the Institute in Cambridge and the newly reorganized Institute in Pasadena. In 1916 he organized, built, and became director of the Gates Chemical Laboratory there.

In 1920 Noyes resigned as a professor at M. I. T., and for the sixteen years thereafter he shared in the development of a great sister technical school the breadth of a continent away from the scene of his earlier triumphs, with unlimited opportunities for research and for the application of the ideas he had developed. Having contributed an unforgettable chapter to the history of his *alma mater* in his twenty-six years as professor and administrator at "Boston Tech", he duplicated that triumphal service in helping to make "Cal Tech" a school with similar ideals of service to science, to industry, and to national life.

During his career many honors had come to him: LL.D. from the University of Maine in 1908; Sc.D. from Harvard in 1909; and from Yale in 1913; and LL.D. from the University of Pittsburgh in 1915. The Willard D. Gibbs Medal was awarded him in 1915, the Davy Medal from the Royal Society in 1927, and the Theodore W. Richards Medal in 1932. He was president of the American Association for the Advancement of Science in 1927. He was for many years a member of the American Academy in Boston and of the National Academy of Sciences, and during World War I was in Washington as chairman of the National Research Council. His death on June 3, 1936, brought genuine sorrow especially to all who had been associated with him at the Institute. A portrait of him, one of the finest in the Institute, is in the Moore Room in the Eastman Research Laboratories, and no one who knew him can look upon it without the feeling that this modest man was a great character and a great president.

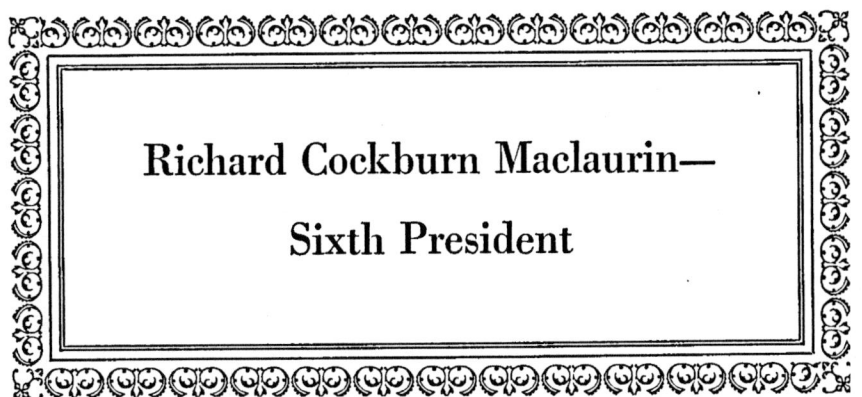

Richard Cockburn Maclaurin— Sixth President

THE INAUGURATION of Richard Cockburn Maclaurin as the sixth president of the Institute in June, 1909, was an important educational occasion of interest to three widely separated portions of the globe. The British Isles and the far-off islands of New Zealand could proudly claim him as a distinguished scholar and educational leader, and America was equally proud to have him as a new adopted son.

For the Institute the splendid inaugural ceremony was the principal event in the celebration of the second great All-Technology Reunion of June 7-9, 1909. Hundreds of sons (and daughters) of Technology from all over the land came to Boston to affirm anew their allegiance to M. I. T. and their loyalty to its aims and traditions. It was an added satisfaction to welcome the distinguished man of science who would be its next leader, and pledge to him their constant support.

Except to the very few who at the time of his election knew of his professional work in physics, Maclaurin was a relatively unknown figure from the antipodes with a reputation for notable accomplishments. The whole Institute, from Corporation to student body, was eager to learn more intimately of his early life, his personality, and his unusual background. Here was a president-elect of foreign birth and training with a unique and world-wide experience in educational affairs. What sort of man was he, and what had been the varied experiences of the thirty-nine years of his life?

Richard Cockburn Maclaurin was born in the little village of Lindean in Roxburghshire, Scotland, June 5, 1870. His father, Robert Maclaurin, had been a minister of the United Presbyterian Church, but because of lack of sympathy with its strict doctrines he decided at the age of fifty-four that life for himself and his large family would be happier in a new land where outlooks were broader and more liberal. His wife was "bonnie Martha Spence," daughter of an eminent surgeon in the Shetland Islands, and a woman of varied interests and fine character. She was undoubtedly the greatest influence in the sensitive life of her brilliant young son, the most studious and serious-minded of the ten children of the family.

Early in 1874 Robert Maclaurin left Scotland with two of the older sons for far-off New Zealand. Late in November of that year the mother with seven of the children left Glasgow, where the family had lately lived, and on the barque *Ada* began the three months voyage to New Zealand. Nine months later an aunt bringing one of the small daughters made the family group complete.

The father had secured a place for the family at Alexandria (now Pirongia) close to the lands reserved for the Maoris. Here he had begun a service as a missionary-preacher on a long, hard circuit. In 1877 he became a teacher in the newly established public school system. In the work of teaching the pupils of all ages who came to his school from the widely scattered farms he found enjoyment and success. He also continued the study of botany and geology begun in his university days in Scotland, and added to his meager teacher's salary by giving lectures in nearby settlements. The family life was busy and full of interest, with the father teaching his own children and joining with them in their sports. One can discern a sort of parallel to the way in which Patrick Rogers had shared so largely in the training of his sons nearly a hundred years earlier.

In this beautiful environment young Richard spent his boyhood, sharing in a somewhat limited way the pioneer life, for he was delicate in health and unable to endure fatigue and excitement. Intense in his emotions, he was nevertheless gifted with a keen sense of humor and a love of work. Hautapu, where the family lived, was nearly a hundred miles from Auckland, and was served daily by a mail coach. The post office was under the Maclaurin roof, and young Richard, not yet nine years old, took over the work of supervising the arrival and dispatch of mails. Later, when a government grant of land to the family at Te Aroha demanded the work of his father and older brothers, he went along, at the age of eleven, and undertook to supply the camp with food, even though it often meant a five-mile walk to the nearest settlement.

In 1884, just before reaching the age of fourteen, young Richard entered the Auckland Grammar School. He had won a scholarship awarded by the Board of Education for which there had been one hundred and fifty other contestants. This gave him twenty pounds and free tuition, and was the first of the many scholarships by which his education was financed. He had the highest standing in the school and won all the prizes. Since other members of the family were also studying in Auckland, their father bought a house in the city, selling his grant of land in order to pay for it. Seven years of Richard's life were spent at the Grammar School and at University College, where he was accompanied by his brother James, six years his senior. Both worked for honors, James in chemistry and Richard in mathematics.

The father was taken ill and died while Richard was in the midst of his examinations for his B.A. degree, but his brothers helped him financially to complete his honors course. In 1891, after waiting several months for examination papers to be graded in England, Richard learned that he had passed with first class honors in mathematics and mathematical physics and had won his M.A. degree at University College. On advice of his professor of mathematics, W. S. Aldis, who was himself a Cambridge man of distinction, it was planned that he should go to England for advanced study, trusting that he could finance his way by scholarships. Accordingly he left New Zealand in time to matriculate at Cambridge in October, 1892. His first act on arrival was to take the examination for a scholarship known as "open exhibition," which was held one morning by Emmanuel College shortly before the beginning of the term. On the afternoon of the same day a similar examination was held at St. John's and he took that also. He won scholarships in both places, and chose St. John's because it was larger and was particularly famous for mathematics. The scholarship or grant-of-aid for thirty pounds, with remission of room rent, was of great help, and gave him nearly enough to meet his college bill for the year.

At Cambridge Richard was a "working man," as students were called who gave their time almost exclusively to study rather than to social diversions or athletics. He practiced the strictest economy, buying no fuel and taking care of his room himself. A similar financial situation gave many of the colonials a common bond of fellowship. One of them with whom he became especially friendly was a young Boer, Jan Christian Smuts, a student of law of his own age, but with a year of residence when Maclaurin arrived. After an extremely brilliant career at Cambridge, where he won a "double first" in law, Smuts was to study at Strasbourg and then return to South Africa, to make an equally brilliant record in legal, military, and administrative affairs. His close friendship with Smuts undoubtedly turned Maclaurin's thought to the law after he had won distinction in mathematics and physics.

Maclaurin did not study incessantly, of course. Some of his long vacation periods he spent in walking trips in England with other impecunious colonials. Once he went to the Shetlands to visit his only relatives in Britain, the Spence aunts. On another occasion, with two Boer students, he went to Strasbourg to visit Smuts, and on the way stopped at Antwerp to see the sights and to visit the exhibition then in progress there. He was tremendously impressed by the great Rubens masterpiece, *The Descent from the Cross*, at the Cathedral. His love of beauty and art was deep and persistent.

His next scholastic goal was that of senior wranglership. For two years he took the unusual course of working without a tutor, but with competition especially keen, he engaged tutorial assistance for the half year preceding the examination. Unfortunately he had serious trouble with infected teeth, and also suffered an attack of influenza just at the time of the eight days of examinations, but with great courage kept to his program. As a result his name was twelfth rather than first on the list of men taking the B.A. degree with honors in mathematics in 1895. He continued for a fourth year of study in mathematical physics, and undertook a research problem which he planned to work into an essay for a Smith's Prize, the winning of which would identify him as a man of ability as a professional mathematician. He finished this year in the top group of men in mathematical physics.

Maclaurin had now completed with honors the program he had first set for himself at Cambridge, and was in doubt as to what he should do next. This question was unexpectedly answered by the appearance of James Ross, a rich Canadian engineer, the builder of the Canadian Pacific Railway through the Rockies, who was seeking a tutor for his son, then a junior at McGill. Maclaurin was chosen at once. He spent a congenial and prosperous winter at Montreal, tutoring not only young Ross but other McGill students, and finding opportunity to complete and submit his essay for the Smith's Prize. After a brief visit to the United States, he returned to Cambridge in May, 1897, and at the June announcement of awards was listed as a Smith's Prizeman.

Having been convinced by Smuts and by his own reflection that law was more concerned with human behavior and human service than mathematics, he decided to embark on study for the bar, and became a member of the Honourable Society of Lincoln's Inn. Once more he aimed for the highest honor, the Yorke Prize of one hundred guineas, which in law was comparable to the Smith's Prize in mathematics, and which required a thorough piece of research. After careful study he decided to investigate the nature and evidence of title in realty. The essay was highly commended and in December, 1898, won the Yorke Prize, given for the first time since 1893.

While his studies in Cambridge had been prospering, interesting events were taking place in New Zealand. Plans for a college at Wellington had been dormant for some time, but in 1897, the sixtieth year of the reign of Queen Victoria, the new institution named in honor of the Queen was established, and the agent-general of the Dominion in London advertised for candidates for four professorships. This possible opportunity again brought Maclaurin to a point where he must make a critical decision. While he had been eminently successful in preparing for a career in law, the chance to help establish a new institution of learning made a great appeal to him. Moreover, it would bring him back to what he thought of as his own land, and to his family ties there. He made application for the professorship in mathematics and mathematical physics, and set about securing the needed credentials. The list of those recommending him was a famous one, including many of world renown. The committee reported Maclaurin's qualifications as unique. On January 12, 1899, he received his appointment and twelve days later signed a contract at the office of the agent-general. On January 19, Cambridge awarded him the degrees of Master of Arts and Master of Laws. A long period of preparation for his life work was ended. Possibly the Latin proverb: *Alia initia e fine* came into his mind now, as it did at a later time and half a world away.

As one of the four foundation professors at the new Victoria College in Wellington, Maclaurin found an unusual opportunity to apply the knowledge he had acquired in the traditional education of the old world to the building of a new university in a young country. At first the college had no buildings, and the classes were held in rooms and laboratories of the two high schools of the city late in the day after they had been vacated by the regular pupils. The new professors were strangers; even Maclaurin found no welcoming friends in this commercial city. As the only New Zealander of the group, he was elected chairman, although he was the youngest of the quartet of professors. To make the program varied, each was asked to teach some subjects other than his specialty without extra pay. Maclaurin offered jurisprudence and constitutional history, since the college was also to become the university law center, and a man was already secured as lecturer on law. In his mathematical courses the work was necessarily elementary and the number of students small, but the courses in law were more popular. As chairman he helped the 115 students organize a students' association and a debating society, and was helpful in other ways. Although there was delay in securing from the government the site and the money for buildings, it soon became clear that staff and students are what make a college.

It was a special pleasure for Maclaurin on returning to New Zealand to renew the warm relations with his brothers and sisters and their families. Having no family responsibilities of his own he lived at the Wellington Club, where he met men of importance in the city and numerous visitors from elsewhere, and had an opportunity for the kind of conversation that he enjoyed. For similar reasons he joined the Masonic fraternity and rose high in that order. (Hence the Richard C. Maclaurin Lodge established at M. I. T. in later years.) He shared in the deliberations of groups interested in social legislation and the creation of a new type of government, and in this was greatly aided by his knowledge of matters of law. After his years of self-imposed restrictions while at Cambridge, he found much pleasure in his new and enlarged social contacts with important legal, scientific, and literary men. New opportunity to enjoy outdoor life, fishing, tramping, and mountain climbing improved his health, and he renewed an old interest in the native Maoris and their ways of life.

One of Maclaurin's first duties, aside from his teaching, was to publish his *Title to Realty*, as required by the terms of the Yorke Prize. Since he did not have the facilities to revise it as he had intended, it was published in London in 1901 in its original state, and won not only excellent reviews but also in 1904, recognition by Cambridge University, which conferred on him the degree of LL.D.

At an evening party in Auckland in 1902 Maclaurin met a young lady whose charm stirred him deeply. The following day he took occasion to visit the gallery where she was studying art and met her again by chance, but without learning her name or home. Some months later, in January, 1903, he accidentally met her on a boat from Auckland to Wellington and learned that she was Margaret Alice Young, daughter of a Scotch merchant who had for some years been living in Auckland, and that she was to leave for England within two days to continue her art studies. He lost no time in cultivating the friendship and securing permission to write to her. At the end of the college year, ostensibly to study educational matters, Maclaurin embarked for England via the United States. He visited the newly established Leland Stanford Jr. University in California, lunched in Washington with President Theodore Roosevelt, and visited Boston, where he saw the Massachusetts Institute of Technology for the first time. Upon his arrival in England he at once went to Newcastle, where Miss Young was spending Christmas with an aunt, and the result was a happy one for both, for their engagement soon followed. After a short visit he returned to New Zealand, and prepared a series of scientific papers on light, which were later published in the *Proceedings* of the Royal Society, and eventually as a book, *Theory of Light*. Miss Young returned after a year's study in England, and the wedding occurred on December 27, 1904.

The following two years were busy and happy ones. Again science and law each beckoned to him, for with the establishment of a Law School at the college early in 1907 Maclaurin was made its dean, but continued to give instruction for honors mathematics under the title of professor of astronomy. Six months later, most unexpectedly, came the offer of the chair of mathematical physics at Columbia University in New York. Although a complete surprise to him, this appointment had been in the making for at least two years, and came as the result of a long search by Ernest Fox Nichols,[18] professor of physics at Columbia. While spending a year at Cambridge, England, Nichols had been commissioned by Columbia University to find a professor of mathematical physics, and after two years of searching, had received a letter from Sir Joseph Larmor of the Royal Society strongly recommending Maclaurin.

The offer of the position at Columbia reached Maclaurin in July just before the birth of his first son. Again he was at a fork in the road. One branch continued the way he had already begun to travel. The other led to new experiences and perhaps greater opportunities in a land foreign to him, but nearer to the England that had been the center of his academic interests. He accepted the offer, and on September 18 resigned from Victoria University College, notwithstanding the urging of his friends to remain in New Zealand. His work at Columbia was to begin at the opening of the second term, about the first of February, 1908. He arrived in New York Sunday, January 26, promptly got in touch with Nichols, and soon met his new colleagues in the physics department.

On the day of his arrival or on the following Sunday, Maclaurin with Professor and Mrs. Nichols had supper at the home of George V. Wendell '92, a loyal and enthusiastic alumnus who had resigned as associate professor of physics at M. I. T. the preceding June to

Richard Cockburn Maclaurin—Sixth President 237

become head of the physics department at Stevens Institute of Technology. He and Mrs. Wendell were fascinated by the brilliant New Zealander, and it struck them both at once that here was the right man for the presidency of M. I. T. During the next month Wendell saw Maclaurin often, talked freely about the Institute and its problems, and persuaded him to take a trip to Boston to look over the situation. They set off for Boston on March 18, visited the Institute, went through its laboratories, met some of the faculty, and discussed the whole situation with Dr. Noyes. Maclaurin was impressed by the men he met, and not greatly disturbed regarding the serious problems confronting the Institute. He returned to New York ready to take calmly whatever decision might be the outcome of his visit.

As soon as his term's work at Columbia was ended, he hurried to England, where Mrs. Maclaurin and their son had already arrived. Together they went to Cambridge for the installation of Lord Rayleigh as chancellor, and at that celebration Maclaurin received the degree of Doctor of Science in recognition of Part I of his book *Theory of Light*. Unfortunately both he and the child contracted diphtheria. Both recovered and spent the rest of the summer recuperating.

During all these months Dr. Wendell had been quietly at work promoting his candidate, and had kept Dr. Noyes fully informed of developments. Maclaurin returned to New York in September, and soon had a number of apparently casual meetings with men on the M. I. T. Executive Committee, Charles A. Stone '88, Francis R. Hart '89, and Frederick P. Fish, then president of the American Telephone and Telegraph Company. By the end of October he had been offered and had accepted the presidency of the Massachusetts Institute of Technology. On the 23rd of November his election was confirmed by the Corporation.

On December 15, 1908, the president-elect addressed a crowded convocation of students in Huntington Hall. He was greeted with heartiest enthusiasm when introduced by Dr. Noyes. That evening he was entertained at dinner by the Corporation and faculty at the new Tech Union where welcoming addresses were made by Dr. Noyes, who presided, by George Wigglesworth for the Corporation,

Dean Burton for the faculty, and Walter B. Snow '82, for the Alumni Association.

A month later on January 14, 1909, Dr. Maclaurin was the special guest and one of the speakers at the annual alumni dinner, and was greeted for the first time by several hundred cheering and enthusiastic alumni. The man from the antipodes at once commanded both the respect and the liking of his audience. Dr. Noyes made a happy speech with many kind words for his successor; and Eben S. Draper '78, who had been elected governor of Massachusetts two months earlier, brought the felicitations and promised the assistance of the Commonwealth in so far as he could have influence on Beacon Hill.

Notwithstanding this exciting series of episodes, Maclaurin carried on his work at Columbia throughout the year, and in addition gave a course of ten public lectures on light at the American Museum of Natural History on the Jesup Foundation. His object was to explain the methods and the findings of science in non-technical terms, and to demonstrate that, as he expressed it "modern science is an elaborate work of art." This series showed his talent for making modern science understandable to the layman by endowing it with human attributes, and appealing to the spiritual and esthetic senses. Although his official associations with Columbia were but of three semesters' duration, he left his mark there as many tributes show. From these brief but brilliant achievements he came to Boston for inauguration as president of M. I. T. and the supreme services that marked his career.

Long before Maclaurin had come to America, the Alumni Association had planned June 7 to 9, 1909, as the time for the second great All-Technology reunion. After the election had been made known, the Corporation gladly assented to the proposal that the inaugural ceremonies should fall within this period as the first feature of the gathering.

The inauguration exercises took place at 11 o'clock on the morning of June 7, 1909, in Symphony Hall, a worthy setting for the dignified and impressive convocation. More than 2500 alumni, faculty and staff members, senior students, and numerous invited guests filled the floor and the balconies to overflowing.

Frederick P. Fish, former president of the American Telephone and Telegraph Company, and a member of the Executive Committee of the Corporation, was the presiding officer. In the first row on the stage with him were the speakers of the day: Dr. Richard C. Maclaurin, the president-elect; Dr. Arthur A. Noyes '86, the retiring acting president of the Institute; Dr. Henry S. Pritchett, president of the Carnegie Foundation for the Advancement of Teaching, and former president of the Institute; Right Rev. William Lawrence, Bishop of Massachusetts; Eben S. Draper '78, Governor of Massachusetts; Hon. James Bryce, British Ambassador to the United States; Dr. A. Lawrence Lowell, president of Harvard University; and James P. Munroe '82, secretary of the Corporation. Other members of the Corporation and the committee in charge of the exercises of the day were seated immediately behind them. Then, banked row on row were the presidents and academic delegates from several hundred universities and colleges, in colorful academic robes and hoods, and representatives of learned societies, Federal and state departments, and important scientific, literary, and mercantile associations.

After the playing of a Bach prelude and fugue on the organ, and the singing by the assemblage of an ode written for the occasion, Bishop Lawrence offered the invocation. Mr. Fish made his opening remarks as chairman of the day by first quoting the famous entry in Rogers' diary on the first day of the Institute's academic life, and then referring to the pioneering work of the Institute and of the many institutions which have followed the pattern thus laid down. Then came the formal announcement: ". . . it gives me great pleasure to notify you that we have selected Richard Cockburn Maclaurin, A.M., LL.D., Sc.D., as President of the Massachusetts Institute of Technology." Then, turning to Maclaurin, he added: "I do not go too far to say, . . . , that all here and all we represent pledge you, President Maclaurin, our loyal support."

Brief and impressive addresses followed. Governor Draper, speaking officially and also as an alumnus, appreciatively mentioned the great service the Institute had rendered in many lines and brought the cordial greetings of the Commonwealth. Former President Pritchett referred with warm feeling to his admiration for the Institute, and from personal experience commended to the new president all its component groups from Corporation to student body and the many fine associates in science, law, and industry that he would meet in the community. James P. Munroe, speaking for the alumni, eloquently outlined the growth of the indomitable spirit of Technology and the part it had played in the development of the nation's resources. Turning to the new president he said: "Of this Technology spirit you, sir, are the appointed guardian. The Institute Corporation, under state authority, gives you today certain definite powers and responsibilities. With no less solemnity and with hardly less authority, we of the alumni place at the same time in your keeping this intangible force which, we believe, is the essential soul of Technology. . . .

President Lowell praised the contribution of Technology graduates and of professors to the public welfare, and then extended the warm greetings of the "university across the river," and, "the right hand of fellowship," and "a personal word of congratulation [to the new president] upon your acceptance of the great trust confided to your hands."

Ambassador Bryce expressed his deep satisfaction that the new president was, like himself, a Briton, a Scotsman, and a fellow member of the ancient Legal Society of Lincoln's Inn, brought Britain's greetings, and stated that only to the United States would she willingly give up so great a leader. Then referring to America and to the Institute he said: ". . . As you know, British students have been so long accustomed to come for first-rate teaching to this Institute of yours that we cannot but feel deeply interested in its prosperity. Between you and us there has always been a free trade in men. . . . You have set no protective tariff on ideas themselves nor upon the men who produce them. . . ."

Dr. Noyes then welcomed the new president as a successor and colleague, outlined the Institute's traditional and present aims, and emphasized his belief in the form of education typified by the Institute, "in which efficiency for highest service to the country and the formation of sound habits of thought and of work must take first place, while in no way underestimating the significance of that culture which rounds and makes a whole man."

Following these cordial addresses, Dr. Maclaurin presented his inaugural, first expressing his feeling of being honored by his election, and his appreciation of the warmth of his welcome to Technology and to Boston. He then declared his firm belief in the practices and the ideals he had found here, and his intention to sustain and promote its great aims. His own creed as an educator, he asserted, comprised three principles, simply stated but sometimes difficult to apply: first, that the end of education is to fit men to deal with the affairs of life honestly, intelligently, and efficiently; second, that science rather than the "older learning" should take the leading part in higher education for the larger section of the community in order that the problems of industrial, social, and international affairs may be better understood and met; third, that we should always bear in mind that science and culture must go hand in hand to produce the broad and liberal outlook that marks a really educated man. As a possible fourth principle in his creed he emphasized that teachers in technical fields should have breadth of view and freedom from prejudice so that the scientific spirit may be joined to an appreciation of those things which lead to soundness of health, soundness of mind, and soundness of morals. ". . . clearly, we cannot make architects and engineers by doing nothing," he added. "Work, and hard work, too, must always be the leading feature of a technical institute; but I see not the slightest reason why we should not have all the advantages of a rational social life among the students and work as hard as ever. . . . In social matters, tradition is all-powerful, and we are fortunate above all else at the Institute in having a tradition that is thoroughly wholesome. There is a tradition of seriousness of purpose and hard work, and there is little or no tendency to set up a wall of caste which is not an inconspicuous feature in the college life of the older world and may perhaps be observed even here, [America] and which, if allowed to stand, is a menace to true citizenship and true democracy." [19]

The impressive inauguration constituted a landmark in Institute history, but it did not end the functions of this eventful day. In the afternoon Class Day exercises were held in Huntington Hall, and in the evening Governor and Mrs. Draper held a brilliant reception at the State House for more than two thousand alumni and many invited guests. The State House was ablaze with lights, from the gilded dome to the pillared portal, and on Beacon Street there was an endless stream of carriages and automobiles. The governor escorting Mrs. William Barton Rogers headed the procession from the Executive Chamber to the celebrated Hall of Flags, followed by President Maclaurin and Mrs. Draper, and attended by the governor's staff. Ambassador and Mrs. Bryce, President Lowell, many of the academic delegates, and many more of the prominent citizens of Greater Boston came to pay honor to Technology and its new leader. So, in a blaze of glory, ended the day of the inauguration.

The next day President Maclaurin, in his first official act as head of the Institute, awarded the degrees at the graduation exercises of the Class of 1909 in Symphony Hall. Although the scene was the same, the circumstances were far different, and President Maclaurin's thoughts, as he skillfully conducted the simple proceedings, with an audience composed largely of the parents and friends of the graduating class, must have been quite in contrast to those on the preceding day when he was receiving the plaudits of the vast audience at the colorful and moving ceremony.

The ceremonial impressiveness of inauguration, the simple dignity of graduation exercises and the triumphal splendor of the governor's reception were made the more memorable by the gaiety and jubilation of the other episodes of the All-Technology reunion which shortly followed. As at the reunion of 1904, the plans provided opportunity for entirely informal pleasures, for visiting old and beloved teachers, for mixing with old friends and acquaintances, for luncheon meetings of classes, and also for general jollification on a mass scale. The first of these larger occasions for celebration was the "Tech Night at the Pops," in the evening of graduation day, when with music, songs, and cheers the newly graduated class was heartily welcomed into the fellowship of the alumni.

Once again the place of gathering was Symphony Hall, but it was a place transformed. Banners and flags of cardinal and gray were prominently displayed. On the front of the organ a parti-colored electric sign blazed T E C H. On each of the hundreds of tables occupying the floor was a banner with numerals of the class that would soon crowd around it. The balconies were filled with wives and guests. At the appointed moment the central entrance to the floor was opened. The classes, led by 1908, entered in reverse order of age, and took their places at the designated tables. Each class as it filed in was heartily cheered. When Governor Draper entered at the head of his class, '78, the entire audience rose and made the hall resound, but the climax seemed to be reached when three representatives of '68, Professor Richards, Eben S. Stevens, and Eli Forbes, entered bearing aloft the banner of the oldest class. Then, after a momentary pause, even more tumultuous applause greeted the newly-graduated class of 1909, nearly three hundred strong, as it marched to the position of honor assigned to it. It was a record night at the Pops. Never before had floor and galleries held such a mass of enthusiastic people. When all the classes were in their places, Dr. Noyes escorted President Maclaurin to his seat at the front of the hall. The cheering and applause were almost deafening. Then the alumni recognized Mrs. William Barton Rogers as she was escorted to a front seat in the balcony, and the cheers for her throbbed with affectionate regard.

The orchestra entered into the spirit of the occasion with a pleasing program including Tech songs. Between the numbers the classes saluted each other with half-forgotten class yells, and joined in the regular M. I. T. yell for beloved professors and prominent alumni present. For the finale, the whole audience stood and sang the *Stein Song*. It had probably never before been sung with such volume and fervor.

After the concert some 1400 men marched to the Rogers Building and massed on its familiar steps and the area in front of the building. Led by E. M. Hager '93, president of the Northwestern Association, they gave vociferous M. I. T. cheers for all the presidents from Rogers to Maclaurin, with a friendly and appreciative crowd of listeners packing Boylston Street.

On Wednesday, the final day of the reunion, the informal jollification begun at the Pops concert continued at an outing and banquet. Twenty-five hundred enthusiastic pleasure seekers left Boston at 9:30 on two chartered steamers for Nantasket. On arrival the alumni immediately hastened to the oceanside and gathered around the class banners that had been set up along the strand for a half mile or more. Then, assembling in military formation, with two bands in attendance, they paraded along the beach coming to rest at the reviewing stand. Luncheon at the Atlantic House followed, after which stunts on the beach were performed in order by each class, beginning with '68, (Professor Richards solo) and ending with 1909 (en masse.) At four o'clock sharp the steamers sailed on the return trip. The early start gave time to prepare for the alumni banquet in the evening, the climax of the reunion, in itself an occasion to be remembered, and the perfect ending for a remarkable reunion.

No Boston hotel being able to accommodate the number desiring to attend the banquet, Horticultural Hall had been secured long in advance, and here the hundreds of alumni and guests were well served in attractive surroundings. President Edwin S. Webster '88, presided and served as toastmaster for the after-dinner speaking. At the head table with him were President Maclaurin; Dr. Noyes '86; Governor Draper '78; Samuel J. Elder, representing Yale University; Speaker Joseph Walker of the House of Representatives; Professor Francis H. Smith of the University of Virginia; Secretary George H. Martin of the State Board of Education; Arthur D. Little '85; Everett Morss '85; T. W. Robinson '84, president of the Commercial Club of Chicago; Colonel Charles Hayden '90; Colonel Thomas L. Livermore of the Corporation; Frederick P. Fish of the Corporation; Professor Gaetano Lanza; Professor George F. Swain '77, vice-president of the American Society of Civil Engineers; Ralph W. Pope, representing the American Institute of Electrical Engineers; Calvin W. Rice '90, secretary of the American Society of Mechanical Engineers; Willis R. Whitney '90, president of the American Chemical Society; and James P. Munroe '82, secretary of the Corporation.

The after-dinner speeches were brief and suitable for the time and the occasion. In his welcoming speech Mr. Webster aroused much enthusiasm by stating that action on a new site was now imperative and that the alumni must all help in securing the best possible location. Governor Draper emphasized the industrial significance of technical education of varied kinds in relation to the state. Dr. Maclaurin was received with tremendous applause and rounds of cheers. He took this occasion to express his appreciation of the hearty support shown by the alumni, and then spoke of the problems he would be facing, especially in the selection of the new site and paying for it, and the importance of securing ample space for the strong development of the Institute which he predicted. The greatest applause came when he said: "There will be no more talk of merger with Harvard, but I think we should be false to every precept of decency if we did not reciprocate most heartily the genuine expression of good will that President Lowell has so recently made. And I think we should be equally false to every precept of common sense if we failed to do our utmost to co-operate with Harvard wherever such co-operation is possible. I believe that in the domain of applied science there is much that we can do for our mutual help, but, to make co-operation real and practical, we must be strong enough for independence. May this be the great practical result of this great reunion." His speech throughout showed a clear conception of the work to be done, and was surcharged with optimism for the future. Possibly few realized that a definite type of co-operation with Harvard was already gestating in his mind.

Dr. Noyes, speaking from his recent personal experience, discussed the fine spirit of the student body in their extracurricular activities as well as in their professional work. Finally, Samuel J. Elder, speaking as a Yale man, but also as unofficial representative of the colleges of this country, warmly welcomed President Maclaurin to America to share in its work in education and to find satisfaction in the enthusiasm of our college graduates. Of the M. I. T. men he said: "In the far-flung battle line of our industrial life, in the mines, in the canals, in the gigantic public works of the day, there are Tech men everywhere. They return in magnificent numbers and with intensest loyalty to their academy halls. There is no disintegrating force in their highly specialized studies." And of the relations between alumni and their colleges throughout America, he concluded: "Loyalty to them dominates us, compels us, owns our lives."

On this high plane this reunion came to an end, leaving in Technology men the deepest satisfaction over the impressive events of the three crowded days, and a high sense of the greatness to come. The spirit of courage and optimism, and a great devotion to the Institute had pervaded the whole occasion. It had indeed been a reunion of momentous significance.

The New Technology

WHEN Dr. Maclaurin came to Boston to assume the presidency, he knew a great deal more about the Institute than its staff and the public knew about him. He had already familiarized himself with the story of the origin and growth of the Institute and with the general aims projected by the founder and maintained by his successors. Mrs. Rogers had sent him the two volumes of the *Life and Letters of William Barton Rogers*. He read them with deep interest and understanding, and like his predecessors in office quickly fell under the spell of the founder. Through discussions with Wendell and Noyes he had also secured a clear understanding of the traditions of the school, its gradual development in educational scope and power, the most significant events in its immediate past, and the accomplishments of the men who had preceded him.

With this firm grasp of the spirit and ideals of M. I. T., it required little time for Maclaurin to project his own strong personality into the plans for the future of the school. He saw at once that the cramped quarters in Boston were the chief obstacle to the proper evolution of the Rogers plan for education, and that his main task would be to find the land, raise the money, and plan the buildings that would make it possible for the Institute to play fully its destined role in American education, science, and industry. Nothing in his past experience suggested special talent in this sort of activity, for he had been concerned with the intellectual rather than the business side of education, and furthermore he was a stranger in the land, without roots in the community. Yet he turned out to be not only a great educational leader, but also a spectacular success at mobilizing the alumni and friends of the Institute and leading them toward what he called the New Technology. Within three years the new land was bought and paid for, and the Institute family was planning its new home.

Removal of the Institute to a more spacious location had first been seriously proposed in 1902, and for several years thereafter the removal issue and the various issues with which it was intertwined were thoroughly debated. By 1909 it was generally agreed that removal was the only real solution to the space problems. The vital questions were what location to choose and how to pay for it. The amount of land needed to make reasonable allowance for future growth was variously estimated at from twenty to sixty acres, and it was hoped that the new land and the buildings, in part at least, would be financed by the sale of the six acres the Institute owned in the Copley Square area. It soon became clear, however, that legal restrictions on the original grant of land would make removal very difficult unless it could be financed with new money.

As early as 1902 the whole Boston area had been carefully examined, several unoccupied tracts of land had been proposed as possible sites for the Institute, and some of them had been carefully considered. The so-called Fenway land at the corner of Longwood Avenue and Avenue Louis Pasteur opposite the property of the Harvard Medical School, not far from Simmons College, the new Art Museum, and other educational institutions, was not very accessible, and probably too small. Another site near Jamaica Pond between the Jamaicaway and South Huntington Avenue half a mile from the land the Institute had already acquired in Brookline for an athletic field, was too remote; and still farther away was a site in Hyde Park, near Clarendon Hills. Another proposal was to make a new island in the Charles River halfway across the present Harvard

THE NEW TECHNOLOGY 249

Bridge, or as it might now more suitably be called, the Technology Bridge. This suggestion was quickly discarded as impractical.

About 1903 a group of men including H. L. Higginson and Andrew Carnegie had acquired a tract of land in Brighton just across the river from Harvard to be used for the new Institute buildings proposed in the plan for alliance with Harvard. The choice of this site was incorporated in the tentative agreement with Harvard and was strongly backed by President Pritchett and some of the M. I. T. Corporation. Although this tract in itself was not undesirable, its association with the merger proposal made it thereafter unacceptable to the great majority of the faculty and alumni. The rejection of the plan, which had been supported by many influential men and some prospective donors in Boston, also made it difficult for Maclaurin to raise money locally to acquire another site.

When Maclaurin visited Boston in April, 1909, his host, Charles A. Stone '88, pointed out to him from his windows on the water side of Beacon Street another site that had originally been considered and rejected, on the Cambridge side of the new Charles River Basin. This struck Maclaurin as ideal for size, accessibility, and dignity of setting. A great and noble edifice could here be erected that would be a worthy home for the Institute. Mr. Stone enumerated the objections: the probable resistance of Cambridge to increasing the nontaxable properties, the probable consequent opposition of Harvard University, and the unwillingness of some of the men of wealth in Boston to give generously for this site in view of the failure of the merger. Maclaurin was not convinced. He could wait. Desirable as it was, this was not yet a Canaan to which the hosts of Technology could look with any assurance.

Maclaurin's first year passed with nothing to show publicly for his efforts to solve the site problem. In June, 1910, Harvard gave him an LL.D. degree. In awarding it, President A. Lawrence Lowell, who also had been inaugurated in 1909, characterized him as "A scholar distinguished in three continents for his knowledge of the laws of nature and of man, whom we welcome as a friend and honor for his own talents and as president of our most celebrated school for engineers." But a few days later President Lowell wrote to Maclaurin, who had just departed for England for the summer, that the

Corporation of the university felt strongly that for the Institute to locate in Cambridge would be a peril to both institutions, and might force a reconsideration of the tax exemption privileges of all educational institutions.

This letter deeply disturbed Maclaurin, for he felt that it implied that he was an "outsider," and that the prestige of the Institute was minimized in its own part of the country. His associates on the Executive Committee of the Institute, on the other hand, accepted it as a challenge. When Maclaurin returned he found that they had located another tract of thirty-five acres in Boston, a triangle lying between Commonwealth Avenue and the tracks of the Boston and Albany Railroad, west of the Cottage Farm bridge. He was taken to see it. Negotiations began successfully with the hope that a donor or large contributor could be found. It was decided that President Maclaurin should appeal to Mr. Carnegie, as Scotsman to Scotsman. A prompt and not entirely unexpected refusal came in the form of the following letter:

My dear Mr. Maclaurin:

Ye're no blate. Just think of it, I hav given $3,800,000. towards extending the Pittsburg school, and certainly it has cost as much more to bring it where it is, and you ask me to help Boston, which has received $400,000. from me for the Franklin Institute! I enjoy the joke! Besides, I do not put the Pittsburg school behind even the Massachusetts Institute of Technology. It is a close race and we'll see who is winner by and by.

Harty congratulations upon your success.

Always very truly yours,
Andrew Carnegie

P.S. If I mistake not, I am part owner of that ground that my friend Lee Higginson and some of us purchast to unite the two institutions, *which should be done.*

A.C.

Not disheartened, President Maclaurin promptly turned to an alumnus, T. Coleman du Pont '84, who had always been a generous and enthusiastic son and supporter of Technology. His reply left the way open for an interview. Maclaurin saw him, as did also Morss and Hart. With characteristic thoroughness, du Pont studied all aspects of the situation, including the possibilities of later co-operation with Harvard. As to the proposed Commonwealth Avenue site, he thought it too small and too circumscribed to permit growth and development. He asserted: "Technology will occupy a great position in the future and must have room to grow." Could not the thirty-five acres be enlarged to forty-five? Evidently his interest was aroused, his sound advice available, and his generous impulses were stirred. Shortly after, he wrote to President Maclaurin expressing his desire to make a gift of $500,000, under certain conditions which he specified as to the increase in area. The $500,000 was to be payable in cash, $100,000 at once and $100,000 a year for the next four years, with 4 per cent interest on deferred payments. A third and very important condition was that "the Alumni or others interested in the institution will raise $1,500,000, making a total with my $500,000 of $2,000,000 new money."

With the intuition of a canny Scot, Maclaurin had addressed the Boston alumni nearly three weeks before this letter was received, and had predicted that the year 1911 might prove a "veritable *annus mirabilis*" for the Institute. The du Pont letter convinced him that his prophecy was sound. It also proved to him that alumni outside New England saw the school with clearer eyes than many of the residents of the Boston area.

Possibly as a result of a casual remark of Maclaurin's to a newspaperman that "Technology might have to pull up stakes and move to some place where the cost of living is within its means," the Institute began to attract attention outside Boston. Soon a group of Springfield alumni waited on Maclaurin with an offer of a tract of land if the Institute would move to that city. Other Massachusetts cities showed interest. Chicago took note, and the Chicago *Evening Post* asserted: "We could support a 'Boston Tech' with our loose change, and we wouldn't, like some cities we know of, have to search all the hinterland roundabout to find the money."

Then Cambridge showed interest and activity. Henry G. Pearson in his biography of Maclaurin says:

> Restive at being rated as the only city in the state which Technology would never, never consider, it for the moment laid on the shelf its bogey of tax-exempt property; an invitation from the Citizens' Trade Association was followed by others from the Cambridge Club, the Economy

Club, the Taxpayers' Association; last but not least the City Council passed a formal resolution to the same effect, which was forwarded to Maclaurin by Mayor Barry with his personal endorsement.

This incident of open diplomacy, having attracted universal attention to Technology's freedom of action, brought forward the Cambridge land in a new way with the 'No Thoroughfare' sign removed. It was now March, and the *annus mirabilis* was only just geting under way.

Another piece of good fortune came to the Institute in this eventful year, a successful appeal for assistance to the state legislature. Once before a similar appeal had been successful, and now with greater need and greater opportunity for service it seemed not unwise to make a further request for state aid. Accordingly, a committee of the alumni undertook this important project, and at the opening of the Great and General Court in January, 1911, a bill was introduced authorizing a grant from the Commonwealth of $100,000 a year for ten years. Hundreds of alumni in all parts of the state, organized and led by James W. Rollins '78, interviewed the members of the legislature so that practically every man knew the nature of the bill and the reasons for it. When it came up for a hearing, strong testimony came from many quarters. Colonel Livermore made an effective appeal before the Ways and Means Committee of the House, and other friends of the Institute used their influence in its favor. The General Court voted the grant on condition that an equal sum be raised by the Institute.

To add impetus to the growing public interest in the Institute, and to give concrete and indisputable evidence of its importance in scientific and industrial affairs, a two-day Congress of Technology organized largely by Arthur D. Little '85, was held on April 10 and 11, 1911. The occasion was the fiftieth anniversary of the signing of the Institute's charter in 1861.

President Maclaurin opened the Congress sessions on April 10, at a notable meeting which filled Huntington Hall. In his opening address he paid tribute to William Barton Rogers, the leader in a new educational philosophy and in the application of science to industry and human affairs; he also presented convincingly his own aims and ideals as the leader of Technology. Two papers followed the president's address. Dr. William H. Walker spoke on "The

Spirit of Alchemy in Modern Industry," and Professor C.-E. A. Winslow '98, then of the College of the City of New York, on "Technology and the Public Health." This day's program was followed by class dinners, ending with a mass meeting and smoker in Symphony Hall, in charge of George B. Glidden '93, and Harry W. Gardner '94. It was an evening of enthusiastic gaiety and interesting special features.

Two sessions on the following day were devoted to the presentation of some fifty scientific papers, arranged in groups as follows, each section being assigned a lecture room:

Section A.	*Scientific Investigation and Control of Industrial Processes,* Professor William H. Walker, Chairman.
Section B.	*Technological Education in Its Relations to Industrial Development,* Dr. Arthur A. Noyes, Chairman.
Section C.	*Administration and Management,* Professor Davis R. Dewey, Chairman.
Section D.	*Recent Industrial Development,* Professor Dugald C. Jackson, Chairman.
Section E.	*Public Health and Sanitation,* Professor William T. Sedgwick, Chairman.
Section F.	*Architecture,* Professor Francis W. Chandler, Chairman.

The papers were all of technical importance, and all given by Technology men from various parts of the country, so that the Congress had national as well as local significance. So great was the interest created that many requests for a full report of the Congress were received. A complete report would have been a large and unwarranted expense at this time, but many professional and trade journals were supplied with copies of the technical papers for their publications.

A fitting end of this anniversary celebration was a banquet in Symphony Hall, planned and managed by Charles C. Peirce '86. The stage was impressively decorated, the central feature being the bust of Rogers in front of a panelled background of gold. At the head table on the stage were seated President Maclaurin; Lt. Governor Frothingham; President Lowell of Harvard; Dr. Charles W. Eliot and Professor George A. Osborne of the original faculty of the Institute; Professor Arthur A. Noyes, president of the Alumni Association; Col. E. D. Maier, president of the American Society of Mechanical Engineers; Admiral Mordecai T. Endicott, president of the American Society of Civil Engineers; Professor James M. Crafts, former president of the Institute; George S. Smith, president of the Boston Chamber of Commerce; Charles A. Coffin, president of the General Electric Company; Professor William T. Sedgwick, representing the faculty; Clarence W. Barron of the *Boston News Bureau;* Frank B. Tracy of the *Boston Transcript;* L. Lincoln Wilcutt, representing the original petitioners to the legislature; Mayor John F. Fitzgerald of Boston; Messrs. James P. Munroe '82, George Wigglesworth, James W. Rollins Jr. '78; Francis R. Hart '89; John M. Longyear, and Frederick P. Fish, representing the Institute Corporation; and William Endicott, Jr., representing his father, who for many years was treasurer of the Institute and for almost fifty years a member of the Corporation.

The classes had entered in order of graduation, from '68 to 1910, and filled the floor of the great hall. After coffee, the audience arose and sang the *Stein Song,* and then gave a long and ringing cheer for the Institute and another for Maclaurin.

The president, thus summoned, made a brilliant address, directing attention not to the past, as in his speech of the day before in opening the Congress, but to the future of the New Technology as he characterized the Institute of the days to come. He spoke wittily of the suggestion that had been made that Chicago acts while Boston ponders, of the invitation to locate the Institute in Springfield, and of the report of the Ways and Means Committee of the legislature that the requested state aid be granted on condition that an additional million dollars be raised. He then announced the gift of the site for the summer school of civil engineering in East Machias, Maine, from an anonymous alumnus, and reported the offer of E. M. Hagar '93, president of the Universal Portland Cement Company, to donate the cement required for the New Technology. The problem of the selection of the site was practically solved, he said. Three sites, all near Boston, were still being considered, and one would be chosen as soon as the Institute was in a position to make a definite offer. In closing his speech he said: "Our campaign for increased state aid has brought us evidence of good-will from unexpected quarters everywhere and proved beyond dispute that there is a tremendous force of public sentiment behind the Institute of Technology. And need I remind you that, apart from the public at large, there is at least one who cares for the Tech that Rogers founded with a devotion that no alumnus can ever match. As the latest proof of her constant thoughtfulness, I may mention that Mrs. Rogers asked yesterday to have the privilege of subscribing $500 toward the expenses of the Congress of Technology."

Telegrams from the twenty-nine local Technology clubs and associations all over the country brought congratulations and assurances of support to Maclaurin and the Institute. The lieutenant governor was high in his praise of Technology and what Technology men had done for Massachusetts, and assured his help in advising the governor to sign the bill granting state aid. Mayor Fitzgerald followed in like tenor, and Mr. Coffin spoke of the great aid he had received from Tech men, closing with this characterization of the work of Institute men. "Your work, your thought, your ideals and your achievements; that which you are and that which you do, is the aristocracy of achievement in the great republic of equal opportunity."

President Lowell made a felicitous speech, extolling the service of Rogers and his unquenchable faith that the type of technical training that would help solve the great industrial problems of modern times could be made a learned profession. When ex-President Eliot was called on, he spoke with all the eloquence and dignity for which he was famous. In a delightful manner he pictured Rogers, the man of winning social grace, personal force, and highest integrity; and recalled the earliest days of the Institute with its "picked up lot" of a score of students working in a rented room without teaching equipment. After an allusion to the state aid granted to Harvard in 1810, the last of many such grants, Eliot said, "Be not afraid of this combination of this method of endowment with the method of state aid." Then with almost the fire of youth, he spoke of imagination and freedom as the motives of technical schools. "Now, in all the work of the graduates of technical schools in our country these two great motives and powers should underlie and they are not material. They are spiritual. The human imagination is as much to be used in science as in poetry or the drama—a form of imagination as searching, as powerful as any other form of human imagination. . . . the occupations to which you are devoted, to which your successors are to be devoted, are not to be thought of as materialistic only. They have their feet on the ground, but their heads are in the sky."

Representing the faculty, Professor William T. Sedgwick was the final speaker of this great evening. With the graciousness and eloquence which always characterized his public speaking, he paid tribute to the great teachers of the Institute, past and present, and quoted as descriptive of M. I. T., a quatrain by Matthew Arnold:

> . . . "rigorous teachers seized my youth
> And purged its faith and trimmed its fire,
> Showed me the high white star of truth,
> There bade me gaze and there aspire."

. . . I have been for almost twenty-eight years a member of the Institute Faculty, and I can honestly say that I have never known a serious factional difference there. With the utmost independence of opinion, the utmost frankness of expression, and with absolute freedom of debate, the Institute Faculty is a very remarkable body. It comes as near a pure and enlightened democracy as anything I know. It is moved but not governed by tradition, and as in Japan there are 'elder statesmen' who are listened to with respect, so in the Institute Faculty there are those who by their age or their experience are naturally somewhat more influential than the younger members; but still it is a wonderfully harmonious body, working to a common end, and coming as near the idea of 'making reason and the will of God prevail' as any body with which I at least have ever been connected.

Finally we have been fortunate also in the subject matter of our teaching—Nature and the laws of Nature—and in the object of our teaching, the amelioration of the lot of man upon this earth and here and now,—enabling them, 'not only to live happily but to die in a fairer hope.' So may it be with us and with the Institute that we love. . .

The Congress of Technology splendidly accomplished its two purposes. It drew widespread attention to the outstanding work of Technology men in many fields all over the land. The more immediate aim was to convince the Massachusetts public and especially the members of the legislature that the request for state aid was both reasonable and important for the welfare of the Commonwealth. The bill was passed without opposition and signed by Governor Eugene N. Foss on May 20, 1911. It had an immediate effect in relieving anxiety and forwarding the plans for a New Technology.

Also in May, 1911, the Alumni Association, as the result of a letter ballot, abolished associate membership, and made all former students eligible for full membership. This action was most favorably received, and added many hundreds in all parts of the land to the ranks of those who gave unstinted allegiance to the Institute.

In discussing the site at the banquet in Symphony Hall, President Maclaurin could not be very specific, for it would be unbusinesslike to announce a choice of site before the Institute had bought it, but during the spring sentiment had veered sharply in favor of the Cambridge site. A committee of the Corporation, appointed with power to act, settled on the Cambridge land, and under the leadership of Everett Morss '85 began quietly negotiating with the thirty-five owners, who were asking a total of about a million dollars for it.

Coleman du Pont's offer of $500,000 was tied to the Commonwealth Avenue tract. When he was told of the possibility of securing forty-six acres with river frontage in Cambridge, he heartily approved the change of plans and willingly transferred his offer to the new situation with its obvious advantages over the Commonwealth Avenue tract. The purchase was not immediately consummated, since both President Maclaurin and Everett Morss were planning early departure for Europe for the summer. Fortunately, when they returned in the autumn, they and their associates were able to complete the purchase for $775,000. Thus, through the president and his loyal and untiring helpers, Livermore, du Pont, Morss, Hart, Rollins, and many others, Technology had come into its deserts. President Maclaurin could now go before the alumni at Commencement and make good his promise that he would not again discuss the site problem as an unsettled issue.

When the Boston alumni met in January, 1912, full of enthusiasm at the progress already made, President Maclaurin recounted what had been accomplished, praised the generosity of du Pont, the work of Little in organizing the Congress of Technology, of Peirce in arranging the banquet, and of Rollins in securing success with the legislature and the governor. Nor were Morss and Hart forgotten in his appreciation of ardent and self-sacrificing workers.

"After such a year's experience," he said, "it can cause no surprise if I look for the solution of our problems more and more to the alumni." He also spoke gratefully of the alumni gifts that would make possible the opening of the Civil Engineering Summer School in Maine, and reported the other bequests and gifts that had come in this year of wonders, 1911. Charles W. Eaton '85 had given $10,000 for the buildings of the summer school in Maine, and an anonymous donor (later revealed as A. Farwell Bemis '93) had purchased the thousand-acre lot and supplied the equipment for the camp.[20] The $275,000 gap between the du Pont gift and the purchase price of the Cambridge land was filled with $100,000 from Mrs. Maria A. Evans and the estate of her husband Robert Dawson Evans, and $175,000 contributed by members of the Corporation. Two additional magnificent bequests came also at this time, $500,000 from the estate of Mrs. William Barton Rogers, and $525,000 from the estate of Francis B. Greene to be known as the Jonathan Whitney Fund for assisting poor and deserving students to secure a useful education.

The Cambridge land was now (in March) the property of the Institute without encumbrance of any kind. But the money for the new buildings—estimated at two millions or more—had yet to be secured. The Executive Committee decided to ask the alumni to raise $750,000, and a committee under the chairmanship of Everett Morss '85 was formed. Obviously, as there were few wealthy graduates, the amount necessary for the great buildings must come from other individuals with money and generous impulses, and it was hoped that some one donation might be sufficiently large to assure that the whole amount needed could be obtained.

Following the Boston dinner, the president planned a series of visits to cities with large alumni groups, always quietly seeking the "big giver." He attended banquets or luncheons in New York, Philadelphia, Pittsburgh, Washington, Rochester, Chicago, and other cities. He did not find the big giver, but in Rochester where he

The New Technology

was entertained by Frank W. Lovejoy '94, he picked up a clue. Soon after his return to Boston he received this letter from Lovejoy, dated February 22, 1912:

> While talking with Mr. Eastman today, he referred to your visit to Rochester recently and expressed regret that he was out of the City and so missed the opportunity of meeting you. I told him something of your visit and as much as I could recall of the things you told us of the recent developments that had made a new Technology possible, of the plans for the expansion on the new site, and of the necessity for raising among the alumni and the friends of the Institute the large sum that will be required.
>
> At the end of our talk, he remarked that when the time came for financing the project he would be inclined to help out. I was very much pleased, but not altogether surprised because Mr. Eastman has in recent years shown much interest in Technology and seemed to have quite a bit of knowledge of what was being done.
>
> I said that I felt sure that at the proper time you would be glad to come to Rochester to put before him the plans and needs of the new Technology.
>
> Would it not be well for you to write to Mr. Eastman within a few days referring to the receipt of this letter and confirming my statement to him of your probable willingness to meet him here at an appropriate time and at the mutual convenience of both?

Losing no time in following up the suggestion, on February 29 President Maclaurin wrote to Mr. Eastman the following letter, portraying the character of the Institute, and suggesting the great opportunities for enlarged service to the country if present needs could be met:

> A few weeks age I had the pleasure of spending a morning on a visit to your Works at Kodak Park, and was so much impressed by what I saw that in public addresses and private discussions ever since, I have referred to these Works as a striking illustration of how a great modern industry has been built up by the application of scientific methods to manufacturing, business and the arrangement of buildings. My experience in Rochester was incidental to a visit to Alumni Associations of Technology in various states,—a visit projected with the object of interesting the alumni of this Institute in the great problems of development with which it is now confronted.

The Institute was founded fifty years ago for the purpose of training men to apply modern science to industry in all its phases. It began in a modest way and has steadily grown in size and influence until to-day its power is felt all over the land, and its graduates are found everywhere contributing to the national wealth by their trained intelligence and skill. It began as a local institution, but is now a national one, with students in large numbers from every state in the Union, and over a hundred from foreign countries. The alumni, who know it best, are enthusiastic as to its accomplishments, but they may perhaps be too near to take a proper perspective of its real importance. However, there is no lack of testimony from unprejudiced sources as to the value of the Institute's training. Thus, Sir William Mather, a prominent business man in England, reported to a Royal Commission in London with reference to this Institute, as follows:

"The spirit and energy of the students, their conspicuous practical knowledge, the thoroughness with which their scientific knowledge is tested in the course of instruction, and the power of adaptation and resource they possess on entering workshops and manufactories, railroads, or mines, public works and constructive engineering—all these fruits of the training of this Institute are, so far as I have seen, not equalled on the Continent. I think these are the qualities we need in England."

A few months ago, Dr. Bryce, a distinguished educator from Canada, stated that after visiting all the leading technical institutions in the world, he could say unhesitatingly that no technological school was to be found anywhere ahead of the Massachusetts Institute of Technology. And Mr. Edison has very recently said: "For forty years I have been employing young men. I have taken them immediately upon graduation from technical schools and set them to work in my mills and I have found that the graduates of the Boston Tech have a better, more practical, more useful knowledge as a class than graduates of any other school in the country. If every state in the Union had such a technical school, it would be a great thing for this country. It would bring our national problems far nearer to solution, it would improve our business conditions, and it would teach us how to grapple with the evils of the day in a competent and sane manner. There is no question but that the Massachusetts Institute of Technology is the best technical school in the country."

The steady growth of the prestige of the Institute has had the natural effect of increasing its numbers beyond the limits of its capacity, in spite of its high fees, until to-day its present equipment is inadequate for the demands that are made upon it. It has therefore been deemed expedient to provide adequately for future expansion by removing the Institute to a new site, where it can grow freely. A site of fifty acres has been purchased in the very center of greater Boston—a tract of land with a frontage of a third of a mile to the Charles River Basin. This site is ideal for the Institute's purposes,—near to the heart of things, wonderfully accessible from all points of the city and surrounding country, and occupying a position that commands the public view and must command it for all time. Having purchased this site, we are now making a careful study of the problem of re-building, and have been fortunate in securing the services of one of the most prominent engineers of the country—Mr. John R. Freeman—to assist us with the engineering phases of that problem. We realize that we can learn much from commercial buildings of the better type, in the erection of buildings that are carefully planned so as to meet the actual needs of the Institute. These buildings must be worthy of a great institution of learning, but though dignified, they must be simple, and they must be arranged so as to give the maximum of convenience for the minimum of cost, due attention being given to fundamental problems of lighting, heating, ventilation and the like. In carrying out this work of re-building we shall have the assistance of an enthusiastic body of alumni, but the growth of the Institute has been so marked in recent years that considerably more than half its graduates have gone forth within the last decade. This means that they are a very young body of men, and consequently that few are in a position to help in any very large way financially. Fortunately, there are in the country men of large vision who appreciate the national importance of such institutions, and are ready to help where they are convinced that encouragement is deserved. A recent communication from Mr. Frank W. Lovejoy suggests that you may be ready to lend a helping hand, and I am writing to say that I should welcome an opportunity of placing our plans before you. I should gladly visit Rochester, if a time could be arranged that would be mutually convenient.

George Eastman in 1880 had established in Rochester a factory for the manufacture of dry photographic plates, and four years later produced the first practicable roll film. In 1888 he invented the "Kodak," which quickly became popular and greatly advanced amateur photography. After much expansion and change of name his company became the Eastman Kodak Company in 1901. As an employer of technical men, Mr. Eastman was not without knowledge of the Massachusetts Institute of Technology and its product, and several alumni had already proved of the highest value in his rapidly growing organization.

The first Tech man to work for Eastman was Darragh de Lancey '90, a young mechanical engineer who entered his organization in 1890 and who rendered great service for several years as works manager. He had been responsible for the layout of the first large Kodak Park plant. He was manager until 1898 or 1899, when he was forced by illness to give up exacting work, and in the latter year went to Europe for the Kodak Company, after which he resigned, but maintained his interest and his friendship for Mr. Eastman. In 1896, Miss Harriet Gallup '94, a graduate in chemistry, became works chemist for the company. Within a year she had become engaged to de Lancey and, upon their marriage in 1897, she resigned. Late in 1896 de Lancey sought as an assistant another Technology graduate, Frank W. Lovejoy '94, an able young chemical engineer, who, after a long personal interview, entered the employ of the Eastman Kodak Company, and was surprised to find a classmate, Miss Gallup, with whom he was obliged to share a single rolltop desk until her departure. Lovejoy became assistant manager in 1899, and on de Lancey's resignation became manager of the rapidly growing plant at Kodak Park, and rose equally rapidly in administrative responsibilities. A fourth Technology man, James H. Haste '96, succeeded Miss Gallup as chemist, rose steadily in the organization, and remained active in it throughout his life. These were the first of the many M. I. T. "Kodak Park men."

Mr. Eastman had therefore had a very satisfactory experience with Technology graduates. For some time before the famous episode of 1912 he had been deeply interested in technical education, and Lovejoy made it his business to keep the Institute in Mr. Eastman's thoughts.

The first meeting of Eastman and Maclaurin, arranged by Lovejoy, occurred at Hotel Belmont in New York. It must have been an inspiring and memorable one for each of these men, with their high ideals of business integrity and their common interest in the dignity and worth of technical education. President Maclaurin enlarged on the matters mentioned in his letter, and on his plans for a real co-operation with Harvard in engineering education. He told of the need for planning the new buildings for efficient teaching and laboratory work as carefully as one would plan a new factory, and of the importance of making them architecturally attractive. Of Lovejoy's help in preparing for this meeting Mrs. Maclaurin once told the writer: "The ground was broken so completely in Mr. Eastman's mind that my husband was astonished. Mr. Lovejoy had done the spade work—so thoroughly that, when Mr. Eastman was about to leave, he suddenly asked: 'What will it cost to put up the new buildings?' My husband answered that it would cost about two and a half million dollars. Mr. Eastman said, 'I'll send you a draft.'" Later, in describing the interview, President Maclaurin said: "The gift was great in itself, one of the greatest in this era of great endowment of education, and its value was greatly enhanced by the manner of its giving. It showed the modern business man at his best, ready to make a noble use of his wealth and anxious to do a great thing quietly and unostentatiously."

Mr. Eastman was very insistent on one condition, that the name of the donor should not be revealed even to the Executive Committee of the Corporation. This condition was slightly modified. President Maclaurin might tell his wife, and, later, Miss Miller, his secretary. At Rochester equal secrecy was maintained; only two people in the Kodak organization were informed, Miss Whitney, Mr. Eastman's secretary, and Frank Lovejoy. For seven years the donor was known only as "Mr. Smith," the name which suddenly flashed into Maclaurin's mind.

News of this gift to M. I. T. created great interest, and for a number of years guesses as to the identity of "Mr. Smith" were rampant. Maclaurin revealed that he was not an alumnus, nor a resident of Massachusetts. At one time suspicion centered on two New York millionaires each of whom strongly suspected the other. They are said to have dined together to clear up the mystery, but separated none the wiser, and each with high regard for the bluffing powers of the other. In another city a man, not "Mr. Smith," claimed that he was the anonymous giver, and in still another city a woman told her friends that she was certain her husband was the generous "Mr. Smith."

The story of the origin of the School of Chemical Engineering

Practice shows how well the secret was kept in Boston, and also indicates the greatness of Mr. Eastman's interest and generosity. Dr. Arthur D. Little of the Corporation, one of the prime movers of the Practice School, conceived the idea of approaching the president of the Kodak company to ask for the $300,000 needed. When this was suggested, President Maclaurin was temporarily "on the spot," but suavely replied that the idea was excellent. He at once sent a message to Mr. Eastman to apprise him of what was to come. Mr. Eastman met Little, discussed the proposal and declared it sound, and gladly promised the sum mentioned, but demanded anonymity, which the unsuspecting Little was glad to guarantee.

Eastman's great gift was announced to the Corporation on March 13, 1912, without the name of the giver. Ten days later final papers were passed conveying nearly fifty acres of land to the Institute. The New Technology—land and buildings—was now a certainty. Hundreds of congratulatory letters came to President Maclaurin. He had done the impossible! None pleased him more than one from George E. Hale '90, the director of the Mt. Wilson Observatory at Pasadena, who had had wide experience in seeking funds for scientific work; one from Coleman du Pont '84, who wished he might personally thank the donor for "his kindness toward the TECH," and through it his help to the education of the United States; and a prompt and unusual one from Henry L. Higginson of Boston, who had long advocated large gifts for educational and other public purposes. One sentence in his letter showed his attitude toward giving as a duty imposed on rich men. "The giver gains more than the receiver, and also stimulates others to do the same—and so we Harvard men are ten times grateful at your success."

The way was now open for the planning and construction of the new buildings in Cambridge. At the outset, John R. Freeman '76, member of the Corporation and a highly distinguished engineer, offered his services for the preliminary studies of the engineering problems involved in erecting a vast structure on "made land," the upper part of which was originally mud that had been pumped from the bed of the Charles River some twenty years earlier. His study of the soil and subsoil conditions indicated that the building must be supported largely on piles, of which nearly twenty thousand were eventually driven. With characteristic thoroughness Mr. Freeman also gathered all the information available from other institutions and prepared a fundamental engineering plan for the construction of the building, with special reference to floor space and lighting. He recommended that the walls between units should not be designed to support the floors above but made removable so that future space changes could be easily made to meet the changing needs of the various departments.

Early in 1913 came the matter of selecting the architect for this great structure. Several famous and important architectural firms were eager to undertake the work. On February 17, after careful consideration W. Welles Bosworth '89 was chosen, with Professor James Knox Taylor '79 as consulting architect. Professor Taylor had been for many years supervising architect of the U.S. Treasury Department at Washington, and on Professor Chandler's retirement as professor emeritus had accepted the directorship of the department at M. I. T. Although Bosworth was not well known in Boston circles he had been a student at the Institute, and had later studied at the École des Beaux Arts in Paris, and then had several years of practice in New York, where he had designed many notable buildings and acquired a reputation for skill in combining architectural and landscaping features. He was highly recommended by his clients, some of whom were members of the Corporation. Here on the banks of the Charles he had real opportunity to design a great structure with beauty of exterior which also would meet the demands of utility, and be adapted to the environment with its special possibilities for impressive and dignified treatment. A further duty imposed on him was economy, for the president was insistent that if possible the cost of the building should not exceed the $2,500,000 which had been generously given by "Mr. Smith." Later events proved that this could not be accomplished.

On July 13, 1913, the responsibility for the actual construction was put in the hands of the Stone and Webster Engineering Corporation. Both Mr. Stone and Mr. Webster were enthusiastic and loyal alumni and also members of the Corporation, and their organization had a nationwide reputation for the efficiency and the quality of its work. It was pleasing and fitting that the New Technology should be the product of Institute men in a literal sense.

An amusing, but possibly not entirely veracious report was current that one very distinguished group of architects more noted for the beauty of their buildings than for attempts to limit expense in producing them, had refused to bid on the whole project on the grounds that they would have to deal "with a Scotchman and a Yankee," or in this case a group of Yankees, for not only Stone of the Corporation, but Morss, chairman of the building committee, and Hart, treasurer of the Institute, were also of the New England stock which traditionally demanded quality and hated prodigality.

In 1913 the preliminary work in preparation for actual construction of the New Technology was well under way. For the next two years the Cambridge site was the scene of great activity. Many unforeseen problems arose, and numerous changes in detail incident to the needs of departments, but the building went forward with clocklike precision. President Maclaurin himself supervised the plans and followed the construction carefully. He personally scrutinized every proposed modification, and after innumerable conferences, made the decisions with meticulous judgment. It was a Herculean task to co-ordinate the ideas of architects, engineers, and construction groups, for in a problem of such magnitude there was an infinite amount of detail.

Expenditures not only threatened to become much larger than original estimates, but actually exceeded them. President Maclaurin had made frequent reports to Mr. Eastman on the progress of the work. The time came when he had to report that the cost of the building would exceed the amount Mr. Eastman had given. President Maclaurin went to Rochester to report personally. So tactfully was the information phrased that Mr. Eastman, who was already certain that no waste had been permitted, made a further donation of $500,000, with the implied promise of an additional gift if and when it should prove necessary.

By 1915 what had been a vast expanse of sand and gravel was covered with piles of lumber, bricks, stone, cement, piping, and the shanties of the construction gangs. It was not a place of beauty, but there was an orderliness about it that made its appeal to the engineering eye, and slowly the form of the New Technology emerged from what to the ordinary observer seemed chaos. The first building on the site—a temporary building to house the new aerodynamics laboratory—was actually finished in 1915. The main group of buildings including what is now Buildings 1, 2, 3, and 4,—crowned by the remarkable dome, the largest in New England—was to be ready for the opening of school in the fall of 1916.

The principals of the construction company, Charles A. Stone and Edwin S. Webster, both of the class of '88, stirred the pride and the gratitude of the whole Institute public by an offer to present a house for its president specially designed to meet both the family requirements and the social needs of the head of the institution. This house was also to be in readiness for occupancy when the Institute was ensconced in its new home in the autumn of 1916.

The first group of dormitories forming an L-shaped structure on two sides of the grounds assigned to the new President's House and its walled garden, with a pleasing outlook over the broad river, was also begun in 1915, and marked an important step toward that broader social life which had been the hope—much deferred—of all the presidents since the early days of President Walker. An admirable athletic field to replace the distant field in Brookline was already laid out on the new site. The long-delayed Walker Memorial was still to come, but before the end of another year this dignified building that would serve as the center of student interests and social life, with its various rooms for dining, reading, and the many student activities, would rise in its commanding position overlooking the Charles River Basin.

Tech in Boston did not entirely cease with the move to Cambridge, for the Rogers Building was retained and used—chiefly by the department of architecture—until 1938. It had originally been hoped that the land on Boylston Street, which had been the site of the Institute since 1866, could be sold, and the money used as a part of the construction fund for the new buildings. Although the State legislature had in 1903 released with certain provisos all rights to the land to the Institute, the title was not clear. In January, 1914, application was made to the Land Court for a title, and while ownership was admitted, the judge decided that it was still subject to certain restrictions, notably the rights of abutters on the opposite sides of the streets bounding the Boylston Street site. This impasse made it necessary that the Institute should continue to hold this property, assessed at $1,800,000, until all restrictions could be removed, either by purchase of the abutting properties or by common consent. One outcome of this legal tangle was the decision that the departments of architecture and mining should remain in Boston, occupying the Rogers Building during the period necessary to adjust the matters of disposal or sale. Since the architectural department in its upper years is the most nearly autonomous of all, this arrangement, although disconcerting, could be made with the least disturbance.

Mining engineering was one of the fields in which Harvard and M. I. T. were to offer instruction in a joint school of advanced engineering to be located in the new buildings, according to an agreement announced early in 1914. Since no provision had been made in the building plans for the work in this field, a new problem confronted the president. He appealed to three eminent graduates of the mining department, T. Coleman du Pont, Pierre S. du Pont, and Charles Hayden, who with two others contributed $235,000 for a wing for the Mining Engineering Laboratories, and it was therefore made possible to bring this section, now a part of Building 8, to completion with the rest of the building in time for the opening of the Institute in September, 1916.

Another unit in the main group of buildings, the Pratt School of Naval Architecture and Marine Engineering, although not completed until much later, had its origin at this time. In 1912, the good news reached the president that the will of Charles H. Pratt, a prominent retired Boston lawyer, contained a bequest to the Massachusetts Institute of Technology for the founding of a School of Naval Architecture. This bequest would be turned over to the Institute when it reached the sum of $750,000. The will was at once contested by a group of relatives of the testator. On December 31, 1914, the Supreme Court decided against the contestants. During the year 1916-17 the sum of $906,711.28 was paid to the Institute from the Pratt Estate for the building and endowment of the department of naval architecture. In the final building plans a prominent place for the Pratt

School was assigned in the long frontage on Massachusetts Avenue, and the building was completed in 1921-22 after World War I.

The genesis of the Pratt bequest is of much interest. Mr. Pratt, who seems to have been a somewhat solitary figure, had for years lived at the Hotel Brunswick on Boylston Street, opposite the Institute buildings. During these years he had seen the students going busily about their work and passing from one building to another. He had apparently become impressed by their seriousness and industry, and it may be that he was thus influenced to do something for the school where they worked so assiduously. Whether Mr. Pratt came from a family of shipbuilders or had some other special reason for being interested in naval architecture is not known, but several years later Professor Cecil H. Peabody related to Professor George Owen the following facts, here disclosed for the first time, which seem to be a trustworthy clue.

One summer, possibly 1909 or 1910, Professor and Mrs. Peabody were staying at a small hotel in the White Mountains where Mr. Pratt was also a guest. The two men met casually, and as even reserved men will under such circumstances, talked together briefly, and naturally mentioned the Institute and its affairs. Professor Peabody was at this time greatly worried about the future of his department. It was small in numbers, having a dozen graduate students from the Naval Academy and but eighteen in the undergraduate body. Despite the arrangements with the Navy Department, there was even some fear that the department might have to be discontinued because of its high cost and low enrollment. These fears Professor Peabody may have mentioned, although he was in general a very reticent man and never inclined to idle talk. No close friendship developed, and only the simplest goodbyes were expressed at parting, and no meeting or later communication took place. Affairs went on as usual, and the department survived. Two or three years later Professor Peabody was surprised and certainly highly elated on learning that Mr. Pratt had generously befriended the Institute and the department he had created. The timing could not have been more opportune.

The honor roll of Corporation members who supported President Maclaurin throughout the work of financing and building the New Technology includes many names already familiar in this history and some new ones. The life members whose long and useful service to the Institute ended between 1910 and 1916 were as follows:

Name	Year of Election	Died	Resigned	Years of Service
Nathaniel Thayer	1864	1911		47
Charles C. Jackson	1887		1912	25
A. Lawrence Rotch '84	1891	1912		21
Jotham B. Sewall	1895	1913		18
William Endicott, Sr.	1865	1914		49
Eben S. Draper '78	1898	1914		16
Lucius Tuttle	1901	1914		13
James P. Tolman '68	1882	1915		33

Mr. Thayer and Mr. Endicott had served with great distinction from the actual beginning of the school's existence.

As these losses occurred, other outstanding men were elected to fill some of the vacancies. These included Arthur F. Estabrook, banker; John M. Longyear, industrialist; Ernest Bowditch, '69, engineer; William Endicott, Jr., banker, elected a year before the death of his much beloved father; Francis R. Hart '89, who was already treasurer of the Institute; W. Cameron Forbes, ex-governor of the Philippines, and of a family that had richly served the Institute; Theodore N. Vail, president of the American Telephone and Telegraph Company, who later bequeathed his extremely valuable library to the Institute; A. Farwell Bemis '93; and Howard Elliott, president of the New York, New Haven & Hartford Railroad. The other vacancies during this period were filled by the election of T. Coleman du Pont '84, Everett Morss '85, and Edwin S. Webster '88, all of whom had previously served as term members.

Not less worthy of being on the honor roll were several others of the life-member group whose service to Technology was still continuing in that final year of Tech in Boston, and was continued thereafter. At that time Howard A. Carson '69 had served for 38 years, Dr. Francis H. Williams '73 for 35 years, Howard Stockton for

33 years, Hiram F. Mills for 40 years, Samuel M. Felton '73 for 29 years, Desmond Fitzgerald and Charles W. Hubbard '76 for 27 years, and Col. Thomas L. Livermore and George Wigglesworth for 25 years. John R. Freeman '76, William H. Lincoln, and President A. Lawrence Lowell of Harvard had all served for more than 20 years.

The new term members elected in these years also constituted a notable group. In 1910, Governor Frank W. Rollins '81, of New Hampshire, Edwin S. Webster '88 (for a second term), and Edward Cunningham '91, were elected. Cunningham had been one of the first graduates in chemical engineering and was the first to raise money for the new buildings. A man of frail health but of outstanding business capacity, he served the Institute with a singular devotion, which was vicariously continued after his early death in 1917 by his widow, Mrs. Edith Forbes Cunningham.[21]

Term members added in 1911 were Arthur Winslow '81, mining engineer; Henry Howard, '89, president of the Merrimack Chemical Company; Henry A. Morss '93, vice-president of Simplex Wire & Cable Company, and brother of Everett, whose splendid service has already been recorded. In 1912 Eben S. Stevens '68 (elected for a second term); Louis A. Ferguson '88, of Chicago; and Arthur D. Little '85, founder of the important consulting laboratory bearing his name, and always conspicuous for service to the Institute, were chosen. In 1913, Charles T. Main '76, mill engineer (elected for a second term); Cass Gilbert '80, the architect who designed tall buildings as beautiful and imposing as cathedrals; and Charles Hayden '90, whose financial genius and generosity the Institute was later to appreciate, were elected. The following year brought the services of Franklin W. Hobbs '89, president of the great Arlington Mills; Frederick H. Fay '93, head of the bridgebuilding firm of Fay, Spofford ('93) & Thorndike ('94); and Gerard Swope '95, president of the General Electric Company. In 1915, term members elected were James W. Rollins '78, head of a great construction company; Jasper Whiting '89, engineer of chemical industries; and William H. King '94, efficient tax expert for the city of New York. Little, Main, Henry Morss, Hayden, Hobbs, and Swope were later elected to life membership.

To this list should be added the names of a thousand loyal

alumni and devoted friends of the Institute who transformed Boston Tech under the leadership of Richard Maclaurin. The New Technology came quickly, sooner than anyone could have imagined a few years before. In 1909 it was a vision in the mind of a stranger from New Zealand as he looked across the Charles from Beacon Street. In 1912 it was assured, and in 1916 it was complete in steel and concrete and limestone, a new physical embodiment of the educational ideals of William Barton Rogers on a magnificent scale.

The Last Years in Boston

WHILE the external and material development of M. I. T. was commanding public attention as the great new building in Cambridge slowly took shape, the stream of daily Institute life was flowing without cessation in the crowded old buildings in Boston. Physical expansion was out of the question. The yearly increments in enrollment meant more crowded classrooms and laboratories, and required constant adjustment and intensive planning under difficult conditions. But fine buildings and great endowments alone do not make a university. During these years of waiting for greater things, men of resourcefulness and idealism carried the torch of progress at the Institute and made long-range plans for the future.

One compensation for the highly congested conditions that had existed for many years at Boston Tech was the intimacy of contact between students and staff. Students transferring from other colleges, accustomed to meeting professors only in class, frequently commented on the cordial relations they found here. The compact quarters, the fixed curriculum, and the intensive work required had always brought student and teacher together in a way not common in other types of schools, and led to many valuable and lasting associations. Alumni returning to Boston made it a practice to visit the Institute to call on the men who had been most influential, friendly, and helpful. In the period before the removal to Cambridge, while the Institute was still comparatively small and the crowded conditions favored close contact and willing recognition of Walker's dictum that Tech was a place for men to work, this intimacy was especially significant.

As evidence of this cordial relationship, it may not be out of place to mention some of the older professors of this period by the nicknames commonly used in student conversation. To older alumni the mention of "Bobby" Richards, "Charlie" Cross, "Getty" Lanza, "Frankie" Chandler, "Billy" Sedgwick, "Doc" Dewey, "Peabo" Peabody, "Arlo" Bates, "Harry" Tyler, "Pete" Schwamb, "Pop" Allen, "Nancy Hanks" Currier, "Heinie" Hofman, "Tommy" Pope, "Willie" Walker, and "Eddie" Miller will always bring a memory with a connotation of deepest respect as well as affection. The names of such elder statesmen as Porter, Despradelle, Hovgaard, and Merrill, although not so easily abbreviated will awaken similar affectionate memories. Of course there should be added to this list the beloved Dean Alfred E. Burton and (in later years) his successor Henry P. Talbot, and Arthur A. Noyes, who had so endeared himself to the student body as acting president. Among the many friendly instructors not faculty members one man deserves special mention for unusual kindness and unfailing devotion to the students. Joseph Blachstein, instructor in German, was "Blackie" to all the students, and he spared no pains to help them whenever possible. It was indeed an era of good feeling among all the groups that made up the Institute.

These years of transition also brought numerous changes in the faculty. Professor John Bigelow, Jr., head of the department of modern languages, retired in 1910. He had served as head of the department of military science from 1894 to 1898, and then returned to active army duty, served with troops in the Spanish American War, and was severely wounded in the charge on San Juan Hill. On his resignation from the Army he returned to the Institute as professor of French, and became head of the department in 1907. He was succeeded by Professor Frank Vogel, long a popular teacher of

German, who thereafter held the rank of department head for twenty years.

In 1911, Professors Lanza, Chandler, and Schwamb were retired as professors emeriti. For forty years Professor Lanza had guided the affairs of the department of mechanical engineering, which for a long period was the largest in the Institute. He was known to hundreds of students for his particular methods and skill as a teacher, as well as for certain amusing idiosyncracies, and for his voluminous textbook in applied mechanics, celebrated in song as "The Little Old Red Book that Getty Wrote." Professor Chandler, one of the most beloved professors, had held a similar position in architecture for twenty-three years. In appreciation of his services the Francis Ward Chandler Prize was established by the Boston Society of Architects to be awarded annually to a post-graduate student in the department. The retirement of Professor Schwamb, who had so efficiently directed the Laboratories of Mechanic Arts, came at his own request as a result of his almost total deafness. His departure was a serious loss to both students and staff.

In 1911 the loss of a woman great in Technology history was deeply felt in the hearts of alumni and friends of the Institute. Five weeks after the Congress of Technology, which she had so generously assisted, all connected with the Institute of Technology were tremendously sadden by the death of Mrs. William Barton Rogers, the widow of the founder. She died on May 18, 1911, at the age of 87. She had given such life-long devotion to the Institute that she might well be regarded as a co-founder, and she was held in highest esteem and deep affection by all who had been connected with it from the earliest days.

Mrs. Rogers had a profound but not always widely recognized effect on the whole history of the Institute. She had unostentatiously been an invaluable help and a constant inspiration to her husband through the hard years of struggle to get the Institute established and recognized, and had nursed and protected him through long periods of illness when the outlook was discouraging. Her devotion to the school was not ended with his tragic death, and in the three decades following, she befriended every president in all the vicissitudes through which the Institute passed. As the author of the two volumes of *The Life and Letters of William Barton Rogers,* she recorded her husband's greatness as a scientist and his work as a founder of a new type of education. No authentic history of the Massachusetts Institute of Technology would be possible but for the care with which this remarkable woman had treasured the letters and documents that throw light on its development. The richness of her spirit is one of the glories of the school. A special room, the Emma Rogers Room, is in daily use and commemorates her service. Her devotion and her generosity endured to the end of her life, for by her will she made a bequest of nearly $500,000 to the school. Thus doubly was the name of Rogers endeared to the school.

In 1912, death removed Professor Desiré Despradelle, who for nineteen years had been probably the finest exponent in America of the French school of architectural design, and who had demonstrated both his practical professional ability and his great skill as a teacher. Other important faculty losses, though happily not by death, included the brilliant Professor Reginald A. Daly, who was called to the Sturgis Hooper Professorship at Harvard, and the equally able Professors Gilbert N. Lewis and William C. Bray, who accepted the opportunity to build up a strong department in physical chemistry at the University of California. Professor Thomas A. Jaggar was given leave of absence to direct the Volcano Observatory in Hawaii, and did not return. The following year brought the retirements of Professors Thomas E. Pope (Tommy to all freshmen); S. Homer Woodbridge, a pioneer in heating and ventilating and the designer of the system installed in the National Capitol at Washington; and Henry K. Burrison, who for forty years had been a helpful friend to hundreds of students. For many years Professor Burrison engrossed the names on the diplomas awarded at graduation. Numerous other changes took place as younger professors were called to responsible positions elsewhere.

The retirement for age of Professor Robert H. Richards in 1914 removed from the faculty the only member who had been continuously connected with the Institute from its beginning. His significant influence on students and alumni and throughout his professional field is perhaps without a parallel in technical education. His wife, Ellen H. Richards, one of the most eminent women in

America, an authority in sanitary chemistry and founder of the domestic science movement, had died in 1911. The activities and achievements of this remarkable couple have been recorded in earlier chapters.

To replace these losses in the early years of his administration, President Maclaurin was able to make a number of excellent appointments and promotions. An especially outstanding new appointment in 1912 was that of Professor Waldemar Lindgren, until then Chief Geologist of the United States Geological Survey, and from 1908 to 1911 a lecturer at the Institute. A native of Sweden, with the best of training and exceptional experience, he was reputed to be the foremost economic geologist in the world. He was appropriately given the first appointment to the William Barton Rogers Professorship, as head of the department of geology. Professor Edward F. Miller '86, who had been the right-hand man to Professor Lanza, was appointed head of the department of mechanical engineering in 1912, after one year as acting head. No department head was at once appointed to succeed Professor Chandler in architecture, but James Knox Taylor '79, long supervising architect of the Treasury Department, was made director for a year, and Professor William H. Lawrence was made executive officer of the department and administered the work with great efficiency. Ralph Adams Cram, a brilliant Boston architect who had been for some years a member of one of the most distinguished architectural firms in the country (Ferguson, Cram, and Goodhue) was elected senior professor of architecture in 1914. A year after the retirement of Professor Richards in 1914, Professor Heinrich O. Hofman, famous for his work in non-ferrous metallurgy was promoted to the headship of the department of mining engineering and metallurgy. In the same year Professor Henry G. Pearson succeeded Professor Arlo Bates as head of the department of English.

A notable example of the strong bonds of affection between the students and professors was the farewell dinner given by the Walker Club, a student organization of upperclassmen, on the occasion of Professor Bates's departure on a year's leave of absence previous to his official retirement. In a program of farewell messages in prose and verse the students expressed the depth of gratitude and regard they felt for this notable and conscientious teacher, whose criticisms of their work could be as pointed and scathing in expression as they were kindly at heart. Professor Bates hated sloppy writing, and no student who ever submitted papers in his classes failed to appreciate the helpfulness of the criticism he received, even if at the time it seemed brutally frank or tinged with sarcasm.

Of new appointments to the faculty in 1910 none was more noteworthy than that of Warren K. Lewis '05 as assistant professor of industrial chemistry. He was (and is) an extraordinary teacher. Six years later he became a full professor, and the distinguished head of the course, later the department, of chemical engineering. Under his leadership the growth of this department was phenomenal. It was not only the first but the most highly regarded department in this field, certainly in America, and probably in the world. The promotion of Charles L. Norton '93 to a full professorship was also a recognition of highly successful teaching and unusual practical experience in the field of industrial physics.

The years 1912-14 also brought promotions to full professorships of a sizable group of men who had worked with zeal and patience during their incumbencies in the lower professorial ranks. This list included Charles E. Fuller '92, Charles F. Park '92, William A. Johnston '92, and George B. Haven '94, in mechanical engineering; Charles H. Warren, later dean of the Sheffield Scientific School at Yale, in geology; F. Jewett Moore, in organic chemistry; Frank A. Laws '89, in electrical engineering; Samuel C. Prescott '94, in biology and public health, and Charles B. Breed '97, in civil engineering. The numerous promotions in the lower ranks cannot be detailed here, but many of this younger group were on their way to high professional standing and later promotion at Tech or elsewhere.

Presidents and professors are not the only ones who make a college significant in the life of its students. Officers of internal administration play an important and often underestimated part in the friendly guidance and development of students. Frank H. Rand, for example, as bursar from 1902 until his death in 1913 rendered an inestimable service to the morale and the education of M. I. T. students. Rand's successor, by the kindest stroke of fate, was a man of the same character who had even greater opportunities to serve the Institute and its students. Horace S. Ford, the new bursar, was a young man of twenty-nine, who had been forced by the death of his father to forego college life and go to work on leaving high school. For ten years he studiously followed the long road to a sound knowledge of finance by hard work in a Boston bank, where he made an excellent reputation. He had youth and could understand students. His fine character and personality quickly won the respect of the administration and of heads of departments, however fussy they might be. His logical mind and intuitive judgment were always helpful in meeting difficult situations. Unlike one of his predecessors of many years before who, largely because of the poverty of the Institute, met almost every request for an expenditure, however, small, with an unsmiling "No," Ford almost invariably sought to understand the whole situation, and if the case was a good one, his reply was likely to be, "We'll see what we can do to help you." It wasn't always possible to "do" anything, but at least he made friends and gained respect by his courteous and businesslike treatment. Students' problems received the same careful attention. It is no wonder that to many generations of students he became affectionately known as "Uncle Horace." Twenty years later when a new treasurer of the Institute was needed to take command of its greatly expanded financial problems and large endowment, he was the man selected for that important post.

When Ford became bursar in 1914, J. P. Munroe '82 was Secretary of the Corporation, and F. R. Hart '89 its treasurer. Professor Robert P. Bigelow was in charge of the rapidly growing library and Albert S. Smith had been for two years a very busy superintendent of buildings and power. On the administrative staff, H. W. Tyler '84 was chairman of the faculty, and A. L. Merrill '85, its secretary. Professor Burton was dean of students, and Walter Humphreys '97 registrar and recorder, with O. F. Wells as assistant registrar.

With men like these on his team, and with the great uplift in outlook and spirit that came with his energetic leadership, President Maclaurin was able to make the last years in Boston fruitful and to assure the Institute's continued leadership in technological education. Educational opportunities were broadened, the establishment of the fifth year leading to the Master of Science degree was formalized in almost every department, and interest in research and in graduate study was stimulated.

Of the 1816 students enrolled in 1914-15, 291 had already been awarded a degree in some one of the 140 colleges represented, and there were sixty-four candidates for advanced degrees. Four important research laboratories were in operation: in physical chemistry under Noyes; in applied chemistry under Walker and Lewis; in electrical engineering under A. E. Kennelly, who had joined the faculty and was also a professor at Harvard; and in sanitary engineering under Sedgwick. The Institute was indeed becoming a "great scientific university" as one of its English friends had said.

Maclaurin was well aware that for a decade the Institute's educational program had been broadening, as the thirteen professional courses had been carefully revised from time to time, and subjects needed for the training for the expanding engineering and scientific fields were constantly re-evaluated. Increasing demands for men not only well grounded in basic knowledge in the general departmental areas but also with some specialized additional knowledge had been growing for at least ten years, and as a result the third and fourth years in most departments had been rearranged, new subjects added, and technical options established. For example, in civil engineering, sanitary and hydraulic engineering and railroad engineering options were available. In architecture a new field of architectural engineering had been developed in response to the demand for the skyscrapers and other massive buildings made possible by steel construction, and for this type of architecture a thorough knowledge of the theory of structures and structural design was essential. Even in non-engineering courses like chemistry, physics, geology, and biology, specialized divisions were now treated in new fourth-year options. A new course in electrochemistry, Course XIV, was established in 1909 under the leadership of Professor H. M. Goodwin.

The establishment of new courses, divisions, and research laboratories was a continuous evolutionary process at the Institute. The men responsible for these developments were broad and far-seeing men. Cross in his vision for electrical engineering, Crafts in organic chemistry, Chandler in new realms for architecture, Peabody in naval architecture, Noyes in physical chemistry, and Walker as the exponent of modern chemical engineering are notable examples in the earlier days. The process was stimulated by Maclaurin's leadership.

One notable illustration of the Institute's response to the needs of the times was the development of the field of public health under Professor William T. Sedgwick. Throughout his career as head of the department of biology, Sedgwick had investigated and written voluminously on public health problems. Public and industrial health as well as personal health had long been regarded as primarily within the domain of medicine. Sedgwick continually urged a broader approach to these problems which would include their bacteriological, chemical, and sanitary engineering aspects as well as their medical aspects. His book *Principles of Sanitary Science and the Public Health,* published in 1902, was possibly the most potent single factor in awakening leaders in medicine, engineering, and science to the importance of sanitation in this era of rapid urban and industrial development.

In 1911 the name of the small department of biology, which for several years had been emphasizing subjects relating to public health, was changed to the department of biology and public health. Finally in 1912 an association of three institutions was formed to foster the broad approach to education in public health that Sedgwick had long been advocating: the young department of preventive medicine at the Harvard Medical School under Dr. Milton J. Rosenau; the division of sanitary engineering at the Harvard Graduate School of Applied Science, in which George C. Whipple, a former student of Sedgwick's, had recently been appointed professor, and the M. I. T. department of biology and public health. A school for health officers was planned, discussed with Presidents Maclaurin and Lowell, and approved in 1913 by the two Corporations. This unique school, the first of the co-operative arrrangements between the two institutions, had no organic entity, but was under the jurisdiction of an administrative board of the three men named, with Professor Sedgwick as chairman. It opened in September, 1913, in the biological laboratories in the Pierce Building, and most of the specialized instruction was carried on at the Institute. Its first students were largely eager young men who already had medical degrees, and a few graduates of the Institute and other colleges, all enrolled as special students at M. I. T. At the completion of the prescribed course a Certificate in Public Health was awarded, signed by the administrative committee and countersigned by the presidents of M. I. T. and Harvard.[22] The Technology-Harvard School of Public Health, as it was later called, lasted for eight years and was eminently successful.

The reputation of the Institute was enhanced at home and abroad by Sedgwick's eminence as a teacher, an investigator, and a public servant. The list of organizations in which he was a leader is a most imposing one. The following partial list of his extra-Institute activities before 1915 indicates their breadth. He was one of the founders and the first president of the American Society of Bacteriologists in 1899; president of the American Society of Naturalists in 1901; on the advisory board of the U. S. Hygienic Laboratory, 1902-21; vice-president of the A.A.A.S. in 1904-05; president of the American Public Health Association, 1914-15; president of the New England Water Works Association, 1906; curator of the Lowell Institute 1897-1921; president of Sharon Sanatorium for Consumptives, 1902-21; trustee of Simmons College, 1899-1921. He was a member of the State Public Health Council, a fellow of the American Academy of Arts and Sciences, and of the Royal Sanitary Institute of Great Britain. Always an effective speaker, his greatest gift was as a teacher. In 1906, in celebration of the 25th anniversary of receiving his Ph.D. degree at Johns Hopkins, over sixty of his former students met at Boston and presented him with a *Festschrift* volume of important original papers written by them, and an oil portrait of him was shortly after given to the Institute. After the Institute removed to Cambridge, his outstanding service continued as a member of the International Health Board of the Rockefeller Foundation and in other ways, but his appointment by President Maclaurin as exchange professor to the universities of Cambridge and Leeds in England marked the pinnacle of his career as a teacher. To him more than any other one man may be ascribed the establishment by the Rockefeller Foundation of the Harvard School of Public Health, which may be regarded as the offspring of the Harvard-Technology School of Public Health. The life-work of this great teacher and leader, who contributed much to

Technology history, is told in a small book, *A Pioneer in Public Health*, written by three of his famous students, Edwin O. Jordan '88, George C. Whipple '89, and Charles-Edward A. Winslow '98, in collaboration with his widow, Mary K. Sedgwick.[23]

The development of aeronautical engineering is another instance of the Institute's pioneer work in a field of great national importance. Flying was already common, but no technical school in America had seriously undertaken professional training in the specialized field of aeronautical engineering. It was Professor C. H. Peabody '77 who first suggested developing this work as a new professional field in a paper presented at a meeting of the American Association for the Advancement of Science in December, 1910, and reprinted in the *Technology Review* for January, 1911. He believed that a four-year course in aeronautical engineering similar in general arrangement to the course in naval architecture and marine engineering might be entirely feasible. The subjects already offered in the theory of naval architecture, marine engineering, and ship design might be taken as the general pattern for comparable subjects in the theory of aeronautics and aeronautical design. More fundamental subjects such as hydraulics, heat engineering, and electrical engineering would also be essential in such a program. Professor Peabody suggested that a young teacher of engineering be given an opportunity to gain experience in this field, and that an aeronautical research laboratory was an essential in this development.

Conditions made immediate action impossible. During the year 1912-13 the European situation made it seem imperative to the president and to Professor Peabody that M. I. T. should gather more definite information on this subject. Maclaurin had personally investigated the development of the field in England, and secured the active interest of the Navy Department. The Secretary of the Navy had Assistant Naval Constructor Jerome C. Hunsaker detailed for service to the Institute as an instructor, to promote work in aeronautics. Hunsaker, a graduate of the Naval Academy in 1908, had taken the course for naval constructors at M. I. T., and received his master's degree in 1912. Immediately after his appointment at the Institute he was sent to Europe to visit the principal aeroplane and airship factories in England, France, and Germany, and to observe the research work at the National Physical Laboratory at Teddington, England. He brought back much information and also some special equipment which had been developed at Teddington. He at once began the establishment of a research laboratory in aerodynamics on the new Cambridge site, in a temporary building, the first to be completed there for instruction and research. It housed a four-foot wind tunnel, with its necessary blower, and an aerodynamic balance designed to measure accurately the forces exerted by strong currents of air on various surfaces. This wind tunnel was the first to be built in an educational institution in this country. For the next two years Hunsaker had charge of the program of research and the instruction given to the men working with him. Associated with him on the mathematical side was the brilliant and versatile Professor Edwin B. Wilson of the department of mathematics who developed the new theoretical mathematical subjects needed in the advanced work in this field. Wilson was a physicist and mathematician of the highest order who had been a pupil of Willard Gibbs, and who had taught mathematical physics for several years at the Institute. His service at this period and in subsequent years at the Institute was of outstanding value.

The research carried out in this shack-like laboratory won for Hunsaker the degree of Doctor of Engineering in 1916. From this time forward his record of service to the Institute, to industry, and to the country is a long and distinguished one. Soon after receiving his doctor's degree he became Commander of the Construction Corps of the U. S. Navy, and was responsible for the design of the dirigible *Shenandoah* and the N C 4, the first aircraft to fly the Atlantic. He was later Naval Attaché in London, Paris, Berlin, and Rome, and then vice-president of the Goodyear Zeppelin Corporation. In 1933 he became head of the departments of mechanical engineering and aeronautical engineering, and in World War II rendered unusual national service.

From the beginning of the Institute there had always been a general four-year course first known as Science and Literature, and later as General Science. This course, designated Course IX, had a unique flavor, combining after the first year certain required scientific subjects with a more extended study of economics and statistics, history, literature and languages. It was strong in industrial and social history and the fundamental principles of industrial development, taxation, business law, and banking. Its curriculum had been greatly influenced by President Walker in his day, and was modified in response to new needs under the guidance of Professor Davis R. Dewey, the head of the department of economics and statistics. The enrollment in this excellent course was never large, and at one time President Pritchett had unsuccessfully recommended its discontinuance.

By 1914, the trend of industrial expansion indicated the need for a somewhat different type of training, in which business subjects were prominent. The department of economics and statistics under Professor Dewey accordingly developed a new program in engineering administration, in which various applied aspects of economic studies such as accounting and business management could be co-ordinated with basic technical or professional engineering subjects with great advantage to students who desired to prepare themselves for a career in the management of industrial and other business enterprises. A large group of alumni with years of experience in industrial engineering and management undertook a survey of the needs of the profession and co-operated with Professor Dewey and his associates in the planning of the subjects for this course. Three subdivisions were laid out, adapted to the needs of men whose interests were in (1) civil, or (2) mechanical and electrical, or (3) chemical engineering. Each was a solid professional program with a substantial core of engineering but with business subjects replacing some of the more specialized engineering subjects in the third and fourth years. The new course, offered for the first time in September, 1915, at once became popular. It later evolved into the important and highly successful department of business and engineering administration.

The failure of the proposal for a merger with Harvard in 1905 had established once and for all the principle of the complete independence of the Institute, but it did not end the attempts to achieve some sort of friendly co-operation. Maclaurin, like his predecessors, hoped that an arrangement could be worked out that would eliminate unnecessary duplication of effort in special fields and lead to a really effective co-operation with Harvard in advanced engineering training. The establishment of a graduate school of the highest type would clearly be an important service to engineering education in America. The great McKay bequest to Harvard for engineering training made such a school possible. It had already led to certain changes in Cambridge: the Graduate School of Applied Science had been established, and the Lawrence Scientific School was discontinued, with its four-year undergraduate programs to be included in the regular college curriculum. Now, after long negotiations—during which Maclaurin's bargaining powers rose steadily with the acquisition of the Cambridge land and Eastman's munificent gifts—an agreement was finally reached that was completely satisfactory to all parties concerned, and the plan was actually put into operation.

As early as November 24, 1909, President Maclaurin had written to President Lowell, who had just been inaugurated as Eliot's successor at Harvard, suggesting a tentative plan for co-operation in the establishment of a graduate school of engineering and architecture which would serve both institutions. For practical reasons, Maclaurin did not regard the Soldiers Field site as desirable. He suggested the site on the Fenway near the Medical School as a possibility, and mentioned incidentally that a site in Cambridge had been offered to the Institute. Maclaurin's first letter was followed by others on December 8 and February 10, in which he outlined his ideas for such a school. These letters had brought from Lowell certain questions and mild objections to some details. Differences of opinion arose over the location, and also over standards of admission to the proposed joint school. President Lowell, and especially Dean Wallace C. Sabine, Shaler's successor, insisted that only holders of bachelor's degrees should be eligible. President Maclaurin, on the other hand, felt that this was not essential if the students were prepared for the advanced work. On February 16, 1910, Lowell, after summarizing the proposal, expressed his willingness to submit the matter to his Corporation "to see if they will consider entering into a further discussion on that basis." Both Corporations then appointed committees to consider measures of co-operation between the two institutions.

So matters stood for practically two years. At the end of that time the Cambridge site had been made certain, and the best of facilities for both undergraduate and graduate work would be available in the new buildings. An exchange of letters in 1912 elicited from President Lowell the general approval of a co-operative enterprise, but also the statement that some of the Harvard men felt that it was essential to the project that the school should be located "where the present buildings of the Harvard Graduate School of Applied Science are." More letters followed, and again the situation was at an impasse for practically a year. Then in February, 1913, a new proposal was received from President Lowell, inviting the Institute to join in the graduate school which had been established at Harvard, with its certainty of endowment from the McKay bequest and other sources, and asking for no contributions from the Institute beyond what it might wish to make. The joint school would bear both names, and each would take part in the management and the responsibility for its success. The proposal included the idea that both presidents should be members of the faculty of the school and that the dean should report to both. It was evident that Dean Sabine was expected to be the actual head of the school, and that his opinions would prevail in its operation. It also possibly represented the view Sabine had once expressed that Harvard could "put Technology out of business" in ten or twenty years so far as graduate work was concerned, as the McKay money was received in increasing amounts.

These suggestions were not satisfactory to President Maclaurin. They would have meant, in effect, either that graduate instruction would have been carried on in two places, at the joint school and at the Institute, with maximum expense, or that Technology's extensive graduate work would be ultimately absorbed by the Harvard school. Maclaurin had seen the effectiveness of the Institute's plan of having graduate students and undergraduates work together, and believed the plan now proposed by Lowell was inoperable. Before submitting the plan to the Executive Committee of the Corporation, Maclaurin inquired of President Lowell whether this represented "the last step in the direction of cooperation" that the President and Fellows of Harvard University were willing to consider. When Lowell's reply indicated that there was no hope for any change, President Maclaurin prepared a statement showing wherein the plan was inappropriate and unacceptable, and again suggesting that a joint graduate school should be on the Technology site. With the utmost tact he implied that the full responsibility for such a school could not be put on the shoulders of a dean or even of the faculty, but must be assumed by the administrations of the two institutions. This point was developed as follows:

> ... The adoption of such a plan would mean a change in conditions which might affect the personal convenience or prejudice of individual members of either faculty. The experience of earlier discussions of cooperation shows that personal considerations are bound to enter. In not a few cases faculty members are not well placed to take a broad and unprejudiced view of such a situation as is here presented. They are apt to lack a sense of proportion, and experience shows that their enthusiasm for the institution with which they are connected generally leads them to exaggerate its importance or its differences from other institutions. Their opinions are, of course, entitled to great respect, but their judgment should count only in so far as they assign reasons for that judgment and only so far as these reasons commend themselves to the judgment of those on whom the ultimate responsibility rests. Such responsibility unquestionably lies with the trustees and no question could be raised that it is more clearly in the province of the corporations to determine than the question that is here under discussion. In its bearings on the future of engineering education in this country, it is too large and important a question to be settled, or indeed to be influenced in any way at all, by the preferences or the prejudices of any individual.

To indicate that the Institute was not now lacking in prestige, President Maclaurin cited the testimony of highly competent witnesses that the Institute already had the highest reputation at home and abroad. He ended his statement with this assertion:

> ... Perhaps more eloquent of the esteem in which the Institute is held throughout the land is the fact that within the last two years there has come to Technology from a great variety of sources gifts and bequests from which the Institute has benefitted, or will benefit in the near future, to the extent of nearly seven millions of dollars.

President Maclaurin awaited the result of this bold statement of the Institute's position. It is hardly necessary to query whether money talks as eloquently with university presidents and corporations as with ordinary men, but since most corporation members are very high-grade business men, it is a fair assumption that they do not minimize the extent to which a few million dollars may affect the course of events within their institutions. President Lowell's reply six weeks later significantly considered the possibility of joint action for "education in all branches of engineering and of mining," and magnanimously closed with these words:

> ... If the principle of such a union is acceptable to the Institute, we are prepared to join with you in the development of a school at your chosen site, and we shall be glad to cooperate with you in an endeavor to work out plans to that end.

The possibility of the acceptance of the proposal that the joint school should be housed in the new buildings of the Institute gave President Maclaurin a new source of worry. Addition of students and staff to the already rapidly growing enrollment in the Institute itself meant that more space would be needed, and consequently more expense in construction. Following his practice of keeping Mr. Eastman informed of all developments, he went to Rochester, told Mr. Eastman of the new turn in the situation, and had a more than friendly reception. On his return to Boston he brought the promise of an additional $500,000. When these matters were reported to the Executive Committee, committees of conference were promptly appointed, consisting of the presidents and treasurers of the two institutions, and at the first meeting President Maclaurin accelerated action by announcing the additional half million which had been obtained from "Mr. Smith."

On June 18, 1913, President Maclaurin prepared a tentative agreement which he sent to President Lowell covering the many matters which had been discussed. Thereafter many letters involving modifications were exchanged, and on December 11 a redraft of the agreement which ultimately proved acceptable to both Corporations was prepared by President Maclaurin. By this agreement, Harvard and the Institute were to engage in co-operative instruction and research in the fields of civil and sanitary engineering, mechanical engineering, electrical engineering, and mining and metallurgy, these being the areas in which Harvard carried on work.

The engineering faculty at Harvard, consisting of fifteen members, and the sum of $100,000 yearly, largely from the McKay endowment, constituted the principal Harvard contribution. Technology was to supply the buildings necessary for the project, and with its much larger staff, the greater part of the instruction, and was to have charge of the academic work. All faculty members concerned in these four major departments would be regarded as members of the faculty in both institutions, new appointments could be made by mutual agreement, and the salary of each professor was to be paid by the institution appointing him. All students graduating in the courses specified would receive degrees from both institutions. The president of the Institute was designated the executive head of the work carried on under the agreement, and served as the agent of the university and reported annually to its president. On the whole the agreement was a genuine co-operative effort to advance education in the specified fields, with each partner maintaining fully its autonomy and traditions.

The trustees of the McKay bequest, as they had at the time of the merger proposal in 1904, questioned the legality of the use of the McKay money in the manner provided in the agreement, but the two presidents, both of them highly competent in legal matters, believed that the McKay bequest could be used in this way and that the courts would so rule. Even so eminent a lawyer as Richard Olney had approved the final draft of the agreement, and gave as his opinion that the co-operation could be carried through with "no merger of corporations or their property interests" and "without violation of charters or of the trusts upon which funds are held."

The plans had been formulated without publicity, even in the institutions themselves. There was at that time no one at the Institute in a position corresponding to Dean Sabine's but the four heads of departments concerned were consulted and approved the scheme. It seemed unnecessary at this time to carry the matter to the Institute faculty as a whole. The agreement was ratified by the Corporations and publicly announced in January, 1914. The text was published in the *Technology Review* for February. For the next few months President Maclaurin devoted much time to explanation and advocacy of the agreement, and had no difficulty in securing complete approval by alumni everywhere, who saw in this plan not a surrender of control of any part of the Institute, but an opportunity to extend greatly its influence through a friendly co-operation with a neighboring school. Most Harvard alumni were also pleased, and manifested a new respect for the Institute. As an example of the new attitude, dinners of the Chicago alumni of each institution were held on the same evening, and each group had the pleasure of hearing both President Lowell and President Maclaurin. Congratulations and good feeling were enthusiastic and sincere.

In Maclaurin's address to the Chicago alumni he spoke on "The Technology that is to be." The new Technology resulting from the co-operation with Harvard, he said, would not produce any great change "in the ideals of the Institute, in its plan of education, or in its methods of instruction." In all fundamental matters the ideals of the two institutions were the same—the great ideals of thoroughness and breadth. For Technology there would be the provision for more advanced study and research in the fields of engineering,—something not done adequately elsewhere in the country. It would thus be of great advantage, not only to Technology and to Harvard, but to the community as a whole and to American education.

Lowell, speaking to the same group emphasized the duty of the great schools to put the welfare of the community ahead of institutional pride. In closing he spoke of Maclaurin as "one of the best administrators and one of the coolest, broadest-minded men that it has ever been my pleasure to do business with, and all I want to say is that we feel heartily glad of the affiliation that we have made with the Institute. We are proud of her successes and her achievements in the past and we look forward to a future which we can imagine large, but which no man can measure."

The joint School of Engineering, although not expected to open formally until the Institute occupied the new buildings in Cambridge, began in a tentative way while the Institute was still in Boston. The M. I. T. catalogue for 1914-15 announced:

> In accordance with an agreement between Harvard University and the Massachusetts Institute of Technology, male students who register at the Institute in September 1914, or thereafter, may receive certain benefits from the University. These benefits are confined to those students

who register in Courses I, II, III, VI, or XI, namely: Civil Engineering, Mechanical Engineering, Mining Engineering and Metallurgy, Electrical Engineering, or Sanitary Engineering. Such students will be entitled to the same rights and privileges as students in the professional schools of the University, and will be eligible for degrees from the University in addition to those that they may receive from the Institute. The opportunity of obtaining the degree of Bachelor of Science from both institutions will be confined to new students registering at the Institute in September 1914, or thereafter. Similarly, the opportunity of obtaining higher degrees from both institutions will be confined to those who begin to pursue courses leading to those degrees in September 1914, or thereafter.

The following professors of the Harvard School of Applied Science in the fields covered by the agreement were included in the Institute faculty list of 1914-15:

George F. Swain, S.B., LL.D., (M. I. T. '77) Gordon McKay Professor of Civil Engineering.
Henry L. Smyth, A.B., C.E., Professor of Mining and Metallurgy.
Arthur E. Kennelly, A.M., S.D., Professor of Electrical Engineering.
Harry E. Clifford, S.B., (M. I. T. '86) Gordon McKay Professor of Electrical Engineering.
Lewis J. Johnson, A.B., C.E., Professor of Civil Engineering.
Comfort A. Adams, S.B., E.E., Abbott and James Lawrence Professor of Electrical Engineering.
Albert Sauveur, S.B., (M. I. T. '89) Professor of Metallurgy and Metallography.
Lionel S. Marks, S.B., M.M.E., Professor of Mechanical Engineering.
Edward Peters, M.D., Gordon McKay Professor of Metallurgy.
George C. Whipple, S.B., (M. I. T. '89) Gordon McKay Professor of Sanitary Engineering.
Louis C. Graton, S.B., Professor of Mining Geology.
Hector J. Hughes, A.B., S.B., Professor of Civil Engineering.

During the two years previous to the removal of the Institute to Cambridge about half of these men participated in the instruction. The plan worked harmoniously and gave promise of being highly successful. As a matter of fact only a few students, chiefly graduate students or new students entering with advanced standing were

THE LAST YEARS IN BOSTON 293

enrolled. The names of all Technology students receiving double degrees are in the registrar's files. Several double degrees were awarded in 1916 before the actual removal to Cambridge. Two of them were degrees of Doctor of Engineering awarded to men who deserve special mention: Jerome C. Hunsaker, whose great work in aeronautical engineering has already been recorded, and Vannevar Bush, whose long service to the Institute as professor, dean of engineering, vice-president, and life member of the Corporation has been outstanding. Bush later became president of the Carnegie Institution of Washington, and as director of the Office of Scientific Research and Development in World War II headed the scientific activities in America's war effort.

Within two years of the time when the joint school began operating in the new Institute buildings in Cambridge, a decision of the Supreme Judicial Court on November 17, 1917, brought it officially to an end. As the result of legal action brought by the president and Corporation of Harvard at the insistence of the trustees of the McKay bequest, the court declared the plan illegal under the conditions of the McKay will. Students who had enrolled for the double degree in 1917 were allowed to carry on through the year.[24]

Both Lowell and Maclaurin were disappointed and continued to hope that ways could be found to resume co-operation within the provisions of the McKay will. At the time, however, the country was at war, and both institutions were fully occupied in emergency military work, and when negotiations were tentatively resumed after the war, agreement was more difficult and the proposal was allowed to lapse. Thereafter, the two institutions remained good neighbors, co-operating informally in many ways, but officially quite independent.

In the summer of 1914, the shadow of approaching war fell across the Institute. While America was not a participant in the great struggle until 1917, when Technology was settled in the new buildings, the country was already filled with forebodings of what almost inevitably must happen. In his annual report for 1916 President Maclaurin, after commenting on the affairs of the Institute, its rapid and substantial growth, and its world reputation as evidenced by the presence of twice as many foreign students as in any other institution of higher learning in the country, added these significant words:

> Unexpectedly has come the great war to change the whole current of the world and bring about a crisis in the industrial development of this country, a crisis that must force it to organize its industry on a scientific basis. When such great forces are operating, it would be disastrous to pay any attention to petty differences between institutions or to the narrow views of those who can not see beyond the limits of any single institution. In these days of large opportunities our range of vision must be large and the combination of effort of two great institutions should be a powerful aid in training men to meet the responsibilities of the new era that is opening.

Here was a clear prophetic vision of the great demand which would eventually fall upon all schools of engineering and science. President Maclaurin, ably supported by the whole faculty and staff, made every effort to bring the Institute to the highest state of efficiency for any national emergency that might arise.

The Institute's pioneer work in the effective co-ordination of military training and technical education was one of its important contributions to national preparedness. The Reserve Officers Training Corps, later widely adopted throughout the country, was first suggested and first put into effect at M. I. T. by Major Edwin T. Cole, who came to the Institute as head of the department of military science and tactics in 1911 and remained until 1919. Major Cole was more than a good soldier and a close student of military affairs. He was also a friendly gentleman, and a greatly respected instructor, who readily participated in the general educational work of the school and was especially helpful in a period when impending war brought many new and special problems. In a private letter writen in 1938, he tells the story of this important innovation:

> When I went to Technology the Military program consisted only of close order drill in the Massachusetts Coast Artillery Armory and a lecture each week. This was required only of the Freshman Class and was most cordially hated by such of the students who were unable to present any reason for being excused from it. I am quite sure that a majority of the Faculty were opposed to this and would have fought it out of the course except that the Institute received a substantial

annuity under the Land Grant Act of 1862 and later for including this work. If I had been asked as to whether its inclusion served any good purpose I should have had to testify in the negative.

When the World War showed a great demand for technically trained men of the pattern educated by Tech and other similar Schools I proposed [in 1915] to Dr. Maclaurin that he urge on the War Department an entire change in the system. My plan provided for taking students of certain of the Courses which best fitted them for service in the Army Technical Units, crediting them with such parts of their courses as were of value to the Military Service and then using the extra time then devoted to perfectly useless drill for coordinating these parts of their study courses with the Technical unit in which they were enrolled. Dr. Maclaurin heartily seconded this plan and it was enthusiastically approved by the War Department altho they felt it would be hard to get started at that time. However they ordered a Board to sit at Tech of which I was a member to examine the various courses with a view to pronouncing what parts of their courses were of value to the various Military Technical Units, and for which credit should be allowed. The findings of this Board were approved and while it was thought hardly possible to get the matter started during the War I was of the opinion that it was desirable to make a start and they allowed me to get the new plan started to as great an extent as possible right then.

As soon as the War was over the heads of the Technical Services such as Ordnance, Coast Artillery, Signal Corps, Engineer Corps, etc., took up my plan most enthusiastically and a number of officers of these services and the General Staff visited me to talk over the plan and iron out practical application. Just then I with all other Retired Officers was relieved from duty in obedience with the plan at that time of the Department but meanwhile the Plan had been incorporated in the Law and the splendid development of the R O T C over the Country at large had been born at Tech and certainly no history of Tech would be complete which did not give it credit for this splendid development in place of the old useless and well hated drill in the Armory. To give you an idea of what the development has meant throughout the Country you may compare the Department during most of my time there when I was one of about fifty officers, mostly from the retired List with the Military Department as it is at Tech now and the same development has taken place over the whole Country. This plan which was worked out by me but more important was approved and aided by Tech and actually started there at least a year before the rest of the Country knew anything about it is of the very greatest importance in the military policy of the United States while the old plan was in general worse than useless except in the full course military school.

I am getting along toward seventy-three and my time is short. I have none to come after me so it is not of great importance that my connection with the very valuable military development be known but it should be known that R O T C Plan was born and developed at Tech.

Technology's full-scale war effort beginning in 1917 falls outside our period, and is fully described in another volume.

The last year of Boston Tech (1915-16) was a busy one. In addition to the regular teaching and research, detailed arrangements had to be made for the future adjustment of the departments to the new and more commodious quarters which would be occupied in the New Technology. Only such essential changes as were required to maintain work at high efficiency were made in the buildings on the old site. Increased enrollment brought the total number of students to 1900, about 75 more than ever had previously been registered. Of these 18 were women, and 125 were from foreign countries. In addition to incoming freshmen, 433 students were new to the Institute, and of these the number pursuing courses for advanced degrees was markedly augmented. Scholarship assistance from Institute funds to the amount of $25,775 was given to 233 students.

The instructing staff in this final year had the following composition:

Full Professors	73
Associate Professors	24
Assistant Professors	32
Total Official Faculty	129
Instructors	79
Assistants	58
Research Associates	5
Research Assistants	12
Lecturers	30
Total Staff (5 names counted twice)	308

The Last Years in Boston

In 1915, the semi-centennial year of the Institute, occurred the deaths of two of the original faculty members: William R. Ware, the founder of the department of architecture, and William Watson, the first professor of mechanical engineering. Charles H. Wing, a highly regarded early professor of chemistry, also died in this year. Before leaving the Institute in 1885, he had planned the chemical laboratories in the New Building, which in 1888 were named The Kidder Laboratories in honor of Jerome George Kidder, who had been a generous benefactor of the Institute. The name is still perpetuated in the much more extensive laboratories in Cambridge.

At the graduation exercises of 1916 in Huntington Hall, degrees were conferred on 308 Bachelors of Science, 38 Masters of Science, and 5 Doctors of Philosophy, Science, or Engineering. It was now fifty-one years since the first small and varied group of a score of students had met in the meagerly furnished rooms at the Mercantile Library Association in Summer Street. The tides of student attendance had risen and ebbed several times. Forty-nine classes had been graduated, the smallest with but five men, the largest with over three hundred. The total number of degrees conferred during the period that the Institute was located in Boston was 6602, classified as follows:

Bachelors of Science	6284;	first awarded 1868
Masters of Science	289;	first awarded 1886
Doctors of Science	3;	first awarded 1911
Doctors of Philosophy	23;	first awarded 1907
Doctors of Engineering	3;	first awarded 1916

Probably during the days of "Boston Tech" twice as many nongraduates had attended the Institute and had equal pride in being regarded as the sons of M. I. T.

During this last year in Boston, the Alumni Association was also busy making plans to bring the whole Technology family together once more in a reunion that would mark the end of Boston Tech with its glorious half century of service to American education, and celebrate the opening of a new era with promise of even greater things. The Third All-Technology reunion of 1916 proved to be a magnificent celebration unique in the annals of American colleges.

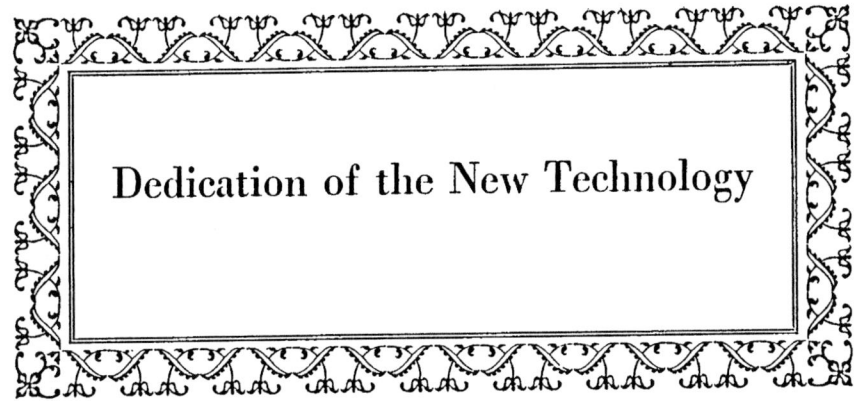

Dedication of the New Technology

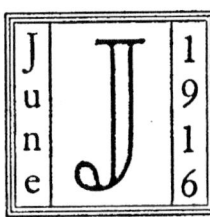

JUNE, 1916, was the time appointed for the celebration of the ending of one era and the beginning of another in the history of the Massachusetts Institute of Technology. For months the Alumni Association had been making arrangements to bring together more than four thousand former students from all over the Americas to share in the heart-stirring farewell to the Tech that they had known, and to participate in transporting the *lares* and *penates* of the Institute to the new temple of science that had risen on the north bank of the Charles. The days from June 12 to June 14 witnessed a series of dramatic episodes unique in the history of college affairs.

The Reunion Advisory Committee in charge of the celebration had Charles A. Stone '88, president of the Alumni Association, as chairman, assisted by Isaac W. Litchfield '85, secretary, and Walter Humphreys '97, treasurer, James W. Rollins '78, Walter B. Snow '82, Frederic H. Fay '93, and Merton L. Emerson '04. The Copley Plaza Hotel was the official headquarters, and all available hotel space in Boston had been reserved for the visiting alumni and their guests. Arrangements for transportation, registration, and tickets for the many special events were faultlessly handled by a committee headed by Professor Charles F. Park '92. A score of subcommittees had worked out the details of the many events, so that all was ready for the program to proceed with clock-like precision.

On Sunday evening, June 11, the first influx of nearly a thousand arrived by automobile after a dusty hegira from Buffalo. On that same evening, more than five hundred embarked for Boston on the Metropolitan Line S.S. *Bunker Hill*, after an enthusiastic gathering at the New York Technology Club. A unique feature of this voyage was the enterprising newspaper work by *The Tech*, which for the first time in the annals of college journalism secured the free use of the Marconi wireless. A special correspondent from hour to hour until 1 A.M. marconigrammed the story of the trip to Boston. Copies of the Monday edition of the paper with a full account of the voyage were delivered on board the *Bunker Hill* by the submarine chaser of Henry Morss '93 long before the ship docked at India Wharf in the morning.

The *Bunker Hill* was escorted up the harbor by Charles A. Stone's flagship *Margaret*, T. Coleman du Pont's *Tech*, Charles Hayden's *Wacondah*, and Henry Morss' *Halcyon*. The harbor was noisy with salutes to the Technology colors from ships and tugs, and a salute of twenty-one guns, organized by James W. Rollins, thundered from Commonwealth Pier. At India Wharf a large body of cheering alumni and undergraduates welcomed the incoming visitors. Headed by the Technology battalion band most of the new arrivals marched to Copley Square, while the others made their way by street car or taxi as best they could.

Registration had begun the Friday before, and on Monday morning nearly four thousand crowded the parlors of the Copley Plaza Hotel to secure their identification slips, badges, programs, and tickets. The great reunion of 1916 had begun in high tempo.

At 11 A.M. came the first of the notable meetings, the brief but touching "Farewell to Rogers" in Huntington Hall. President Maclaurin presided and introduced James P. Munroe '82, as the orator of the occasion. Always eloquent, always able to awaken tender memories or to inspire new triumphs for Technology, Munroe was on this occasion at his superb best. To an audience of the older alumni crowding every seat and every foot of standing room he spoke with moving power and depth of feeling. "The farewell that we are taking is no perfunctory good-bye," he said. "On the contrary, it involves the uprooting of traditions, of sentiments, of loyalties that have been digging themselves deep for half a century." He then paid glowing tribute to the founder and to the noble group which, by his remarkable genius in swaying the hearts of men, Rogers was able to bring about him, and to inspire with the spirit of the new education which he had created. Of Runkle, who so patiently and devotedly bore the heavy burdens in the darkest days; of the beloved Walker to whom the torch of learning, of industry, and of service was handed on; and of those other men of vision and greatness of soul who were associated with the difficult early days he spoke with gratitude and affection. The Rogers Building was the place wherein the memories of those great and departed spirits were enshrined, he said, the Westminster Abbey of Technology:

. . . Whatever may become of this architectural shell, never shall we forget its intrinsic beauty, its warm touch of companionship, its stimulus to our hearts and minds. But the soul of it, the legacy of Rogers and Runkle and Walker and all the rest, the Spirit of Technology, we take with us, not in memory, but in actuality; and we believe, yes, we know, that in conveying it across the Charles we are leading it to opportunities, to achievements, to new affections and to new traditions far greater, far richer, far more full of promise than even these which today we so proudly and so gratefully commemorate.

Munroe's oration had set the high tone for all that was to follow in the three days and nights of this impressive celebration. Through all the proceedings, in the jubilation and good fellowship as well as the more solemn pageantry and oratory, ran one spirit, a strong, luminous thread of loyalty and honor to the great school, without a discordant note.

After noon the assemblage proceeded to the new site in Cambridge for the laying of the cornerstone of the long-delayed building for student activities, the Memorial to President Francis A. Walker. To alumni this was an occasion in which each had a personal share, for their contributions had made it possible, even though the actual building was not begun until eighteen years after the fund for it had been started.

Intermittent showers did not dampen the ardor of the assemblage. A platform had been erected on the area assigned to this building, fronting on the Charles River Basin. On the platform were President Maclaurin and the speakers and special guests of the occasion, Charles A. Stone '88, of the Alumni Association; Mrs. Francis A. Walker, widow of the General; Dr. Francis Walker '92, his son; Professor Charles-Edward A. Winslow '98; Professor Harry W. Tyler '84, chairman of the Walker Memorial Fund Committee; Edward P. Brooks '17, representing the undergraduate body; Miss Evelyn Walker, a daughter, and two other sons of the General, Ambrose Walker '91, and Stuart Walker, who like his father was a graduate of Amherst. The student battalion and band stood before the platform as a guard of honor.

As chairman, Dr. Tyler introduced President Maclaurin, who spoke briefly of the occasion as the fulfillment of a hope long cherished and of the appropriateness of a social center for students as a memorial for General Walker, the great humanist.

It was a most happy arrangement that the man who was to make the formal presentation speech on behalf of the alumni was Professor Charles-Edward A. Winslow '98, head of the department of public health at Yale University Medical School. President of the senior class eighteen years before, he had had the duty as the representative of the undergraduates to present to the Institute the bronze bust of General Walker, which stood for so many years in the corridor of the old Rogers Building, and which was to be moved to the new memorial building. From this new location, said Dr. Winslow,

... his clear gaze will look out over the current of young life flowing past with the same message of inspiration which it bore to those who went before. Technology men will see in that eloquent face, as we did long ago, the courage that was undaunted by the rout of Chancellorsville, the energy which revolutionized the United States Census, the broad, clear vision which established an epoch in political economy, the loyalty and devotion which built up this institution, and the modesty, the hopefulness, the enthusiasm, which made President Walker our ideal of all that we hold true and manly.

The alumni of Technology present this Walker Memorial to you who are to be the alumni of the future. We want it to make your life as undergraduates richer and fuller. We want this building to stand to you as a memorial of a great economist and a great man,—of one who saw the large problems of human society with a clear and sure vision, who served the large ends of humanity with dauntless courage and burning sympathy. We want it to inspire you to a realization of your responsibilities as members of the brotherhood of science, as men commissioned to mold the forces of society as well as the copper and iron from the mine, into a universe fit for a nobler and freer blossoming of the human spirit.

Speaking on behalf of the family of President Walker, Dr. Francis Walker '92, economist of the Federal Trade Commission at Washington, expressed their gratification and pride in the laying of the cornerstone of the Walker Memorial. He referred to President Maclaurin as the third founder of the Institute, saying that what President Rogers conceived and began, and what President Walker first developed on a large scale, President Maclaurin had brought to the present imposing result, with its inspiring future promise. Dr. Walker then modestly discussed some of his father's educational ideas, stressing his belief that a broad education in the social sciences is a necessary supplement to a knowledge of the principles of science and engineering if an engineer is to rise above the position of a mere technical adviser to industry.

Through Edward P. Brooks '17,[25] president of the junior class, the undergraduate body voiced its gratitude to the alumni for this contribution to the richness and breadth of the student life:

This will be a memorable day in the history of undergraduate life at Technology for it eliminates forever the cause of the complaint that there is no opportunity for social life at the Institute. . . . It was President Walker who pointed out the need of the social and physical development of the student as well as training him in the sciences. It was he who realized that to attain the highest type of citizenship the student must be trained not only to take his place as an engineer among skilled technicians but he must also be trained to take his place as a man among men. The Walker Memorial will supply the means of giving to the Institute this humanizing element. . . .

Following this brief but impressive ceremony the new buildings were thrown open for inspection, and simultaneously a great water-fete was presented on the Charles River Basin. Thousands of people on both sides of the river and on the nearby bridges braved the intermittent showers to watch the maneuvering and racing of many kinds of vessels—power boats, sailing boats, canoes, miniature battleships, and racing shells. A Goodyear balloon eighty-one feet long floated over the new dome all afternoon, and twice a Wright biplane managed to take off from and land on the Esplanade. Heading the official reviewing party on the Basin was the Assistant Secretary of the Navy, Franklin D. Roosevelt.

Meantime more thousands of alumni and their families toured the corridors of the new buildings, had tea, met the Maclaurins, and renewed old acquaintances. The chief attraction in the buildings was an extensive exhibition called "Fifty Years of Technology," which presented a graphical survey of the Institute's contributions to applied science and technical education since 1865. Photographs of the incorporators, the first faculty, and the early benefactors were on display, with documents and charts to illustrate the beginnings and growth of the Institute and its plans for the future. Models and pictures showed contributions in many fields of science, engineering, and architecture, and the inventions of more than sixty of the alumni. This exhibition of the Institute's past achievement and present equipment was arranged by a committee headed by James P. Munroe '82.

Not the least interesting part of the exhibit was the showing of works in the fine arts by Technology men. Notable were the examples of the sculpture of Daniel Chester French '71, murals by Edwin H. Blashfield '69, portraits and landscapes by Philip Little '79 and Isaac B. Hazelton '94, marines by Charles H. Woodbury '86, and a wide range of paintings by Miss Rebecca Joslin '73, Henry P. Spaulding '90, Frank B. Masters '95, Charles Bittinger '01, and at least a half dozen other well-known artists. The exhibit of etchings, drawings, book plates, and the work of illustrators was impressive, as was also the collection of photographs of important architectural work by Technology men. The original score of Bullard's *Stein Song*, and copies of compositions by Arthur G. Farwell '93, were displayed, as was also a group of beautiful designs in silver and copper by A. J. Lewis '81. The exhibit of books by Technology authors included history, fiction, essays, poetry, and science.

The day was not yet over. In the evening the alumni renewed old friendships at class dinners in many clubs and hotels, while the ladies had a large dinner at the Copley Plaza. Following the class dinners came a crowded and jubilant smoker at the Boston City Club. Then, escorted by the undergraduates, the alumni and the ladies gathered on the steps and in the street in front of the Rogers Building. All travel on Boylston Street between Berkeley and Clarendon Streets had been diverted by the city authorities, and the front of the Rogers Building was ablaze with lights and gay with flags. At 10:30 came the final vociferous cheering for the familiar old building and for all the presidents from Rogers to Maclaurin. It was a colorful ending for an eventful day.

In marked contrast to Monday, fair weather greeted the hosts of Technology on Tuesday, June 13. It was graduation day for the class of 1916, and Huntington Hall was crowded with the parents and friends of the 360 recipients of degrees, on this, the last occasion that these exercises would ever be held in the famous hall.

But for the visiting alumni it was the "Day of the Classes," a day of merrymaking and general jubilation for over five thousand alumni and guests. According to "Tubby" Rogers, (Professor Robert E. Rogers), who wrote an admirable account of the events of the Reunion in the July *Technology Review,* it was "the greatest alumni picnic ever staged." Three steamers were ready at 9:30 to transport the great crowd to Nantasket from Rowe's Wharf. Later boats brought a thousand more in time for lunch, and President and Mrs. Maclaurin came on Colonel Hayden's yacht in time to witness the afternoon events. A large grandstand was waiting for the ladies and other spectators, while the men of the classes with several bands hurried far down the beach to join in military formation for the great procession. Chief Marshal Colonel Charles Hayden '90, had his staff, aides, and division and company commanders selected in advance. With little delay the brigade was formed and with military precision paraded up the beach and past the reviewing stand. It took twenty minutes, marching briskly, for the gay procession to pass the grandstand. Each class had some special feature to identify it, a distinctive uniform, or smock, a big class banner with the class numerals, an umbrella with class colors, a flag for each man, or a fife and drum corps. After box luncheons and coffee had restored the vigor of the marchers, came the parade of the fifty-two Technology Clubs, New Hampshire leading with the Beaver, the Technology emblem. The Washington club carried a Washington monument, the Southwestern Association led a live mule, and Indiana bore a cage containing an "untamed Oolite," which proved to be a specimen of the limestone used for the new buildings. Even far-off Chile was represented.

Then came the "stunts" by classes. The newly pledged class of 1916, over three hundred strong, which had been graduated in the forenoon, was given the first place, and presented a spectacular burlesque of the pageant which would take place in the evening. Then the classes appeared in order. First a group of '68 to '70 led by Professor Richards hobbling along with crutches, canes, and other evidences of age, bearing a placard designating them as the "Picked-up Lot" who constituted the first student body. Suddenly they discarded their crutches and started jumping rope to prove that even the oldest graduates were still vigorous and agile. Later classes presented stunts reminiscent of some phase of Technology history or of some humorous event in the undergraduate days of the class itself. They all demonstrated not only ingenuity in presentation, but also a warm feeling of appreciation of *alma mater*. Perhaps the biggest surprise of the afternoon came when a monster hydroplane driven by Godfrey Cabot '81, and indicative of Technology's deep interest in aviation, roared down from the north, circled above the audience and the stunt arena, and cut the numerals of his class in the air.

Probably unrivalled by any college celebration up to this time was the colorful and imaginative pageant enacted in the great court at the new buildings in Cambridge that evening. It had its conception in the mind of Professor Ralph Adams Cram, who had an unusual dramatic sense and a wide knowledge of mediaeval European pageantry as well as an extraordinary capacity to bring beauty and religious tradition into the great cathedrals which emanated from his skill as an architect. In the development of his unique conception he had the aid of numerous faculty colleagues and alumni, especially Isaac W. Litchfield '85, whose gift in matters of pageantry was also of high order.

This great spectacle presented in allegorical form the evolution of intellectual and physical power and its eventual domination over chaos, superstition, and ignorance. Education and Progress, as typified by Technology, overcame the forces of darkness and disorder, and by science and the liberal arts, acting through the ages and aided by Will, Wisdom, and the Time Spirit, brought the Triumph of Civilization and Humanitarianism as personified by *alma mater*.

The pageant began at the Rogers Building, where a large group of undergraduates, dressed in varied Venetian costumes and bearing halberds, formed an armed guard, commanded by C. Howard Walker, long a member of the staff in architecture, clad in crimson velvet and Doge's cap. Then came James P. Munroe '82, secretary of the Corporation, bearing a golden casket containing the official seal of the Institute, attended by his guards, Lester D. Gardner '98 and Ralph G. Hudson '07, resplendent in scarlet. Behind them four bearers robed in Technology colors carried on their shoulders a great gilded and ornamented chest containing the charter and archives of the Institute. Thus guarded and attended, and followed by fourscore members of Corporation and faculty in long black gowns, these priceless possessions were slowly and solemnly born to the river at the Union Boat Club. Here in waiting lay the *Bucentaur*, a specially constructed copy of the state barge of the Venetian Republic. The highly decorated pure white craft had at the prow a seated figure of Mother Technology holding aloft the Torch of Progress. At the stern, above a high red canopy, floated the cardinal and gray flag of Technology. The officials, attendants, and bearers of the carefully guarded treasures embarked and took places on the deck. Captained by Henry A. Morss '93 costumed as Columbus, the *Bucentaur*, propelled by long sweeps plying in perfect unison, began its stately voyage across the Basin, accompanied by strains of music from Grieg's "Land Discovery." Saluting bombs and rockets illuminated its passage across the darkening waters. Along the Esplanade and on

Harvard Bridge thousands of spectators massed to witness the historic passage.

Meantime, ten thousand alumni and guests were filling the two long low stands along the sides of the great court. In front of the colonnade in the center stood the governor's throne, an old chair of state, under a crimson canopy bearing the Indian seal of the Commonwealth of Massachusetts. In the centre of the stands on either side were two smaller thrones for the mayors of Boston and of Cambridge. In a stand on the eastern side of the open end of the court five hundred chorus singers were in place and an orchestra of a hundred was tuning up. Primitive Men, Mediaeval Students, Nymphs, and Fire Dancers, with Miss Virginia Tanner as premiere danseuse, were all in readiness.

The mayors, James Michael Curley of Boston and Wendell D. Rockwood of Cambridge, had been welcomed and installed on their respective thrones, each guarded by halberdiers. Pageant Marshal Cram, as the ancient, white haired Merlin, clad in black and gray, stood on the steps before the governor's throne, accompanied by four aides in brown and purple with long staves. Suddenly, just at eight o'clock, the bugles of the governor's escort were heard, and mid the applause of the audience and the strains of "Hail to the Chief" by the great orchestra, two troops of Lancers in scarlet uniforms rode forward across the great court, followed by Governor McCall, also mounted, and his staff in uniform. The governor dismounted, was welcomed by the marshal, and took his seat on his high throne guarded by students in white cadet uniforms. His staff was seated below him.

After a few moments of tense waiting a great cheer from the crowds lining the Esplanade indicated the approach of the *Bucentaur*. Great searchlights on the pavilions shot out brilliant shafts of light converging on the Basin. A thunder of bombs and rockets saluted the barge. The Lancers wheeled and rode down the court to the float, followed by the marshal and his aides, to meet the *Bucentaur*.

Another moment, and mid the cheers of the ten thousand assembled, the brass and drums of the orchestra, and the thunder of rockets, the Lancers and the marshal led the long procession escorting the charter and seal up to the colonnade. The casket containing the seal was placed on its altar before the governor, and the charter and records close at hand. In this dramatic hour, guarded and attended by all the trappings of pomp and circumstance, the official symbols and records of the Massachusetts Institute of Technology had been transferred to their new home in the New Technology.

Suddenly the music stopped, the lights were turned off, and the crowd became silent. Merlin stepped out to the centre of a dancing circle, and smiting the ground with his staff, gave the signal for the Masque of Power. After a lapse of more than three decades the onlooker can probably only recall a phantasmagoria—a succession of rapidly shifting glimpses of a vast spectacle employing all the artifices of color, illumination, costume, music, and dancing. One recalls only vague and transitory impressions of chaos, of mysticism, of ancient peoples, of the struggle of forces through the Dark and Middle Ages, and finally of Civilization and the dawn of a new era of order and science. The white-robed figure of Alma Mater had taken her seat in the shadow of the throne of Massachusetts, and passing before her and paying homage to her were the representatives of the greater forces that made up the Triumph of Science and Technology.

The end of the great pageant Professor Robert E. Rogers describes in these words:

Then, while the lights played upon shining mail and brilliant splash of color, the great chorus sang a new song, 'Mother Tech,' and at the last, the 'Star Spangled Banner.' Finally the searchlight on the New Buildings rose straight into the air till it crossed in the sky the searchlight on the top of Old Rogers. After a moment that on Rogers faded and died, and the great beam of light above the portico and the massed Triumph below it shot straight up into the blue night sky. The pageant was over.

On the following afternoon in the Great Court of the New Technology where the brilliant spectacle of the pageant had been staged, the principal feature of the convocation took place, the dedication of the new buildings. Previous events had celebrated a glorious past. The dedication was a consecration to a great future service the end of which no man could foresee.

A rostrum had been erected for the speakers in front of the colonnade. Seats for about two thousand alumni had been reserved on one side of the court, and on the opposite side a similar section was assigned to the distinguished guests and delegates from many institutions. Long before the academic procession formed, the court held thousands of people, seated on camp chairs that took the place of the stands of the evening before. Invited guests of the Corporation, after inspecting the new buildings, were received by a committee consisting of Hon. W. Cameron Forbes, Col. Thomas L. Livermore, Franklin W. Hobbs '89, Arthur F. Estabrook, T. Coleman du Pont '84, and A. Farwell Bemis '93. The official delegates, both American and foreign, were received within the building by Professor William T. Sedgwick, who arranged them in the traditional order for the academic procession.

The alumni marched by classes to their grandstand, headed by their marshal, Charles A. Stone '88, and his aides, while the Naval Brigade Band played. The academic procession was headed by the national and state colors, with T. Coleman du Pont '84 as chief marshal. Next came President Maclaurin in his scarlet doctor's gown and gold tassel, walking with Senator Henry Cabot Lodge, orator of the day, and Governor Samuel W. McCall. State officials, the representative of the French Embassy at Washington, President Pritchett of the Carnegie Foundation, and Federal and city officials constituted the first division marshaled by James W. Rollins '78 and Professor Arthur A. Noyes '86. The second division contained the members of the M. I. T. Corporation, the Harvard Corporation, and the Harvard Overseers, headed by Colonel Livermore, Mr. Munroe, and Mr. Hart. President-Emeritus Eliot, President Lowell, Dr. H. P. Walcott, Major H. L. Higginson, and Dr. George A. Gordon were in this group, which was marshaled by Dr. Francis H. Williams '73, William Endicott, and William H. King '94 of the Technology Corporation.

The third division, the largest and because of the brilliant hoods the most colorful of all, comprised the delegates from universities, colleges, technical schools, and the academies and societies. Here came first the University of Virginia and the College of William and Mary, the colleges associated with William Barton Rogers, followed by Harvard, Yale, Princeton, and University of Pennsylvania. About one hundred and sixty institutions were represented, colleges in all parts of the country and at least a score of learned societies, half a dozen of them British. Professors Talbot '85, Goodwin '90, Derr '92, and Fay served as marshals. The fourth and last division was made up of the faculty of M. I. T. with Professor Peabody '78, chairman, and Professor Merrill, secretary, at the head of the column. This group, numbering 125, were attended by Major E. T. Cole, and Professors D. R. Dewey, E. F. Miller '86, and A. G. Robbins '86.

As soon as the men in the procession were seated and the speakers had taken their places, Dr. George A. Gordon offered the invocation. President Maclaurin then gave the dedicatory address, beginning as follows:

We are here to dedicate a noble group of buildings to a noble purpose. The buildings speak for themselves. They will form an enduring monument to the skill of the architect, the capacity of the engineers of construction, the devotion of the Faculty that has planned so much of their detail, and the splendid public spirit of the anonymous benefactor whose gift they are. That gift has won admiration not only for its munificence but for the unostentatious manner in which it was made and for the patriotic purpose to which it has been devoted. It will have far-reaching consequences for the country at large, for its aim is to strengthen American industry at the base by fixing it firmly on the solid rock of science.

Then after considering the implications for the Institute of the World War, which was then nearing the end of its second year, Maclaurin closed with a vision of the future:

The opportunity for this country to take and keep the lead industrially is constantly before us in these days, but there is another opportunity seldom, if ever, mentioned, that is in some respects even greater. The centre of intellectual achievements in the world has passed in turn from Egypt and Babylonia, to Greece, to Alexandria, to Constantinople and to Western Europe. Is it to cross the Atlantic? If this be so, the intellectual leadership must accord with the genius of our people for practical affairs. That genius will inevitably show itself chiefly in industrial pursuits and industry will continue to attract a large proportion of the best minds of the country. Hence we must have industry linked with science, not merely for the benefit of industry but for the sake of science. Of course, our American science will never grow as it should if it is cramped by a short-sighted policy as to what is useful. But if the value of science to industry be generally appreciated, science will be free to expand in any direction, and if it be pursued with the same energy and intellectual power that have been applied to business, there is no reason why America should not become the intellectual leader of the world. Here is a great hope and a great national opportunity. The problems that it presents are not local and must be looked at from no merely local point of view. They demand the co-operation of all, and as a step toward that great end, Harvard and Technology, each national in its scope and influence, are here combining for the common good.[26] And so, in the presence of representatives of other learned societies from all parts of this country and from abroad, inspired by their sympathy and their achievements we dedicate these buildings to the great cause of *science, linked with industry*.

Governor Samuel W. McCall then spoke briefly for the Commonwealth, saying, in part:

It is well that the state should be represented at the dedication of this noble structure that represents so worthily the great objects for which it has been reared. This building adds much to her physical beauty, but it adds far more to those symbols of intellectual power which are the crowning virtues in any civilization. The part taken by the Commonwealth in providing the funds to make possible this building and similar buildings which are to follow it has been a modest part. . . . The growth of great institutions may be encumbered by profuse grants of state aid and they will show greater enterprise and greater power and usefulness if they gather their resources warm from the grateful hearts of men rather than from the cold enactments of legislatures. . . .

After an orchestral number President A. Lawrence Lowell of Harvard paid warm tribute to the institution in whose development his forbears had been so helpful, and of the Corporation of which he himself was a valued life member. Of the Institute he said:

It has during the half-century of its life had a history remarkable for the services it has rendered and for the growth in the scale of its work. Its great achievements have been due to the foresight of the founders, who perceived the pressing need of a school for the training of engineers;

to the boldness of the presidents and trustees, who in earlier days took large risks with narrow means; to the excellence and devotion of the instructing staff and to the generosity of benefactors, who have given freely to aid the enterprise, and finally to a man so modest that we do not know his name, who has made it possible to raise the palace we dedicate today. . . .

The reward of public service is the opportunity for still greater service; and to the institution of learning that has used well and faithfully one talent, men will entrust the more. This has been our experience here in the past, and it will be so in the future. Men die and pass away, but these institutions remain, and our work here is not for ourselves but for them—the most lasting of all things. . . . From ten years after the settlement of Boston, throughout the times of the colony, the Revolution, and the history of the United States, Harvard University has grown stronger and stronger on the banks of the Charles; and the Institute of Technology has existed for only one of the many half-centuries to which we look forward with confidence. The most enduring human creations known to modern history are the institutions of higher learning. . . . It [the Institute] endures because it renders a public service with which the world cannot dispense; and it is worthy of the gifts that are lavished uopn it, and of the devotion of the teachers whose lives are built into its life, and through their pupils into the life of the whole nation.

After another musical selection, Henry Cabot Lodge, senior senator from Massachusetts, "master of the vanishing art of oratory," gave the oration of the day. Deeply mindful of the great forces which were upsetting the stability of the world at the very moment, he linked the opportunity which the Institute was to enjoy henceforward in its new home with the country's need for proper defense to maintain its power and dignity among the nations of the earth. His oration began:

We open here today and dedicate to education these new buildings prepared for their purposes with all the perfection which the best skill and the highest intelligence can devise. But this is not all. These buildings and their equipments are the inanimate mechanism, and yet motionless and silent, which must be stirred into life and set in motion by those who use it, the teachers and the taught. To them is thus given a larger opportunity than ever before, and this means that this great institution which has risen so high in its chosen field that no one can attribute to parochial pride the declaration that it stands second to none other in the world, will now enter upon a yet broader field of usefulness, and contribute more generously even than in the past to the cause of learning and to the development of trained and educated men. . . .

Then speaking as if to the thousands of students who in future years would flock here for their professional education, the scholarly senator, master of the classics and the history of the past, went on to urge the open mind and the ready response to new ideas characteristic of youth, but warned against overconfidence in one's own fallible judgment and the belief that only through young men is progress in human welfare achieved:

When I consider the imagination that gave us the *Iliad* and the *Odyssey*, the genius which produced the art and the architecture, the poetry and the drama of Greece; when I read the writings of Plato and Aristotle, I can not but feel some doubt of the absolute superiority of the present moment in the field of pure intellect. It is well to remember that the very greatest men died learning, like Bacon and Pasteur. Socrates was entering old age when he drank the hemlock, but I do not think anyone would say that his last words were, therefore, of no worth. The greatest benefactions to humanity, the greatest services to human thought, have not all been bestowed or rendered by men under twenty-five or even under forty years of age, a fact sometimes worthy of remembrance. Do not then fall victims to over-confidence and close your mind. The injunction is as important for youth as for age; easy of attainment for the former, difficult for the latter, possible for both. . . .

From the word of warning, or suggestion—for warning perhaps is too grave a word—I come to the appeal, and an appeal everyone has the right to make for the cause nearest his heart, for the truth as he understands it. The exact and high training of the men of applied science, the generous scholarship offered by our great university in every field of human thought and endeavor, are the noblest privileges and the finest opportunities which the wealth, the self-sacrifice and the liberality of the past and of the present can offer to the generations which have the future in their keeping. But there are still other lessons to be learned here and at all our established seats of learning, more important, higher and nobler even than those which figure in our catalogues and earn our degrees. These lessons have no endowed professorships, they form no part of any curriculum yet devised; they are not generated in any laboratory or developed in any course of investigation or experiment. They are spiritual, not material. They must be drawn from the association and contact of the great body of students and teachers acting and reacting upon one another. They must come from the traditions which here, in the earliest years, are blent with the high ideals of the Civil War and which at Harvard stretch back to the days when the lamps of learning first flashed amid the dim shadows of the wilderness. They breathe from the walls of old buildings, they whisper to us from the pages of our records, they look out at us from the portraits of our founders and benefactors. These influences are as impalpable as air, but stronger than monuments of brass or stone, and if we do not learn their lessons our spirit will fail for lack of breath and perish . . .

. . . The great lesson which, to my thinking, should be learned here is that education and knowledge are not ends in themselves, but means to an end, and that one great purpose to be here achieved is to go forth with the understanding that all who have these privileges are units in the making of a nation. Our learning is vain if it fails to teach us that nations, like men, must have a conscience and a soul. . . .

. . . All Americans, and especially all Americans who have been fortunate in securing the highest education, should fight everywhere against the spirit which would divide and be apostles of the spirit which will unite and of the tradition which should inspire all Americans. That tradition, in its dominant meaning, tells us that the American people put liberty and independence and union, in the war with England and in the Civil War, above comfort and safety, above riches and life. . . .

. . . A people who will not make ready to defend their own peace, their own security, and their own honor, are well on the way to helpless, hopeless war, or to supine submission. A people who are not ready, if the need come, to give their lives for their country, will soon have no country. A nation that will not protect its citizens will soon have no citizens to guard and defend the national life. If a government deserts those who support and sustain it, alike in the calm of peace and in the hour of danger, that government itself will be deserted when the menaced peril comes. There are two doctrines presented to us today. One is that the brief life of the individual man must be preserved at all hazards and at any cost to the nation. The other is that the life of the individual man must always, when the dread call is sounded, be ready for sacrifice in order that the life of the nation may be preserved. Between these two doctrines we must choose. In these days of world-wide war we must face the facts with steady gaze and make our decision. What that choice will be, I cannot doubt, . . .

. . . To those who go forth trained and educated from our great universities and institutions of learning comes an especial duty in these perilous days, to preach this doctrine and carry this belief in devotion to the country, like a flaming torch, throughout the land. . . .

With the young men, especially with those highly trained and educated, rest not only the defence of the country, if war comes, but the cause of preparation and readiness which will alone be able to prevent the coming of war. In their keeping are the ideals of the country, and it is to them we must look to make it known to all men that, like knowledge, a nation without conscience has lost its soul.

So in the space of two short hours was the New Technology dedicated, simply, but with great words from men of lofty thought, deepest sincerity, and intense patriotism. The presidents of two great institutions had recounted a remarkable past and bespoken a still greater future. The State had bestowed its warm commendation and appreciation of the services given. The orator of the day, with dignified bearing, superb voice, and complete mastery of his art, had issued a ringing call to patriotic service in all the days and years ahead.

To the listening thousands these were words not easily forgotten. As they slowly departed from the Great Court, with its pebbled ground not yet graced by green turf or shrub or tree, leaving the tall-windowed bare gray walls of the great new Institute of Technology, they were conscious of having shared in a momentous ceremony. Technology was now re-consecrated to the noble service of training men for lives of action and response to duty in science, in engineering, in industry, and in the greater service of upholding and defending their country.

The dedication was the last of the gatherings of this great week in which the general public could participate. But for the alumni, those officially connected with the Institute, and invited guests there remained one more convocation which was to fix in their loyal hearts still more deeply the significance of the dedication and of the reunion. This was the Golden Jubilee Banquet in Symphony Hall in the evening following the exercises in the Great Court. Newspapers

DEDICATION OF THE NEW TECHNOLOGY 317

called it the greatest banquet ever held, not because of the number actually present, but because the great assembly of alumni in Boston was connected by an intricate telephone network with alumni banquets in thirty-four other cities, so that Technology men from coast to coast could hear what was taking place in Symphony Hall and could contribute to it their felicitations and messages of loyalty, and could even lead in the cheers and the singing of the beloved *Stein Song.*

Symphony Hall was at its brilliant best. Over fifteen hundred alumni filled the tables on the floor, with lights on every table. The balconies were crowded with ladies and guests. At the back of the stage a high bank of green threw into relief a white pedestal on which stood the bronze bust of William Barton Rogers, and a warmly lighted painting of the Rogers and Walker buildings extended across the stage. The head table on the stage was banked in front with greens and red flowers, laid with gold plate, and lighted by large gold candelabra. At this magnificent table sat Charles A. Stone '88, president of the Alumni Association, with President Maclaurin on his right. On his left was J. J. Carty, chief engineer of the American Telephone Company who had made possible the scientific demonstration to be later presented. The other guests at the head table were also men prominent in state, university, and scientific affairs— President Lowell of Harvard; Alexander Graham Bell; former Acting President Noyes '86; Governor McCall; Major Higginson; Welles Bosworth '89, architect of the New Technology; Coleman du Pont '84; former President Pritchett; Orville Wright; Frederick P. Fish; Colonel Thomas L. Livermore; Professor Michael Pupin of Columbia; Professor Charles R. Cross '70; Vice-President U. N. Bethel of the Telephone Company; the Honorable Frederick W. Dallinger; Dr. H. S. Drinker; president of Lehigh University; Albert W. Drake '95; Francis R. Hart '89, and the mayors of Boston and Cambridge. The perfection of the general arrangement was due to Charles C. Peirce '86 and George B. Glidden '93, and the decoration to Harry W. Gardner '94, assisted by Charles Everett '07 and Edgar I. Williams '08.

At seven o'clock the dinner began. Between the courses came the usual tumultuous cheers for the president, for Mrs. Maclaurin, for the ladies, and for special guests. At one point an inrush of newspaper boys distributed special extras of the *Globe* with a full account of the day's events. Just before nine o'clock President Stone called for silence in preparation for the telephone program that was to bring the thirty-four participating cities together at just nine o'clock. In a short introductory speech President Stone said:

> We are gathered here this evening to celebrate the fiftieth anniversary of the activity of the Massachusetts Institute of Technology. Pure science and Technology have combined to make possible in 1916 many things which in 1866 the most courageous prophet would not have dared to predict.
>
> Perhaps the most marvelous of all the achievements of science is the power to transmit the human voice, 3,000 miles and more. The courtesy of the American Telephone and Telegraph Company has made it possible for us to speak this evening, not only to alumni and guests in Boston, but also to the alumni gatherings in 34 cities in different parts of the United States.
>
> We are honored by having with us at this banquet a man who has been active in the Telephone Company since its inception, and to whose genius much of the marvelous development in long distance telephony is due. I take pleasure in presenting Mr. J. J. Carty, chief engineer of the American Telephone and Telegraph Company.

For the remainder of the evening the speeches were made through the telephone and were clearly heard by the alumni from the Atlantic to the Pacific. Mr. Carty explained briefly the nature of the demonstration about to be undertaken, saying that it was especially fitting that it should be Tech men who participated in it since the telephone owed more to M. I. T. than to any other institution. He then introduced Albert W. Drake '95, assistant general manager of plant, who was to call the roll of the cities. With a moment of preliminary questioning, the calls began, always with the same formula: "Hello, New York." Walter Large replied: "This is New York...." "How many have you there, Mr. Large?" "We have 130 members and guests." "Thank you." Then in order followed Schenectady, Syracuse, Rochester, Buffalo, Philadelphia, Washington, Atlanta, Birmingham, New Orleans, Harrisburgh, Pittsburgh, Akron, Dayton, Cleveland, Cincinnati, Detroit, Chicago, Urbana, Louisville, Indianapolis, Milwaukee, Duluth, St. Louis, Kansas City, Denver, Salt Lake City, Anaconda, San Francisco, Los Angeles, Portland, Spokane, Seattle. To hear the voices from these far-off cities gave a sense of the intimacy of the whole Tech family and a thrilling realization of what science had accomplished in this special field.

The roll of cities having been called, President Stone addressed his nation-wide audience by telephone: "I doubt," he said, "if any other educational institution has in half a century made such progress and so impressed itself not only on the people of this country but on all civilized nations. The munificence of our great benefactor, 'Mr. Smith,' and the generosity of our alumni and friends have made possible the great educational plant which we have dedicated this afternoon." He then predicted that Tech's progress would continue, and that before the expiration of the next half century she would be a center to which men will come from all nations to be taught applied science. In the whole fifty years now passed, he said, the greatest progress had been made in the last five, because of the wisdom, skill, and great ability of President Maclaurin. "I take pleasure in introducing Dr. Maclaurin."

The regular Technology cheer joined in by unseen hundreds over the wire and the burst of applause that greeted the president as he rose to speak constituted an overwhelming ovation. Maclaurin had carefully prepared a climactic speech and had saved important news for it, but he began calmly as if the occasion were not one of supreme moment:

It is a pleasure in the name of the Corporation and the Faculty to convey the greetings of Technology to her sons and friends scattered throughout the length and breadth of the United States. We have celebrated today a half century of accomplishment by moving into a splendid group of buildings. These will enable us more adequately to fulfill our purpose, the purpose of putting science at the service of industry throughout the country. This is no easy task when we consider the extent and diversity of the industrial needs of America. The school that is properly equipped for this task must be national in its scope and influence and happily Technology and Harvard that are here joining hands have long passed beyond the limits of merely local institutions. They will, however, need all their resources in men, money and traditions if they are to rise to the level of this opportunity and build up a school that is adequate to the industrial needs of America. Clearly, it must be one of the greatest schools of applied science in the world for the industrial opportunity of America is unequalled and scientific methods in every phase of industry are absolutely indispensable to success. After the experience of the war that is no longer open to question, and peace will only add emphasis to the lesson.

Observing that a great school cannot be built without money, President Maclaurin mentioned that the new fifty acre site ready for building had cost a million dollars; that the new buildings just dedicated had cost three and a half millions, all the gift of one anonymous benefactor; that new equipment and machinery would cost about three-quarters of a million; that other buildings including the memorial to President Walker and a dormitory unit involved the expenditure of a million and three-quarters more. Thus the total to which the Institute was committed was seven million dollars, of which only about $400,000 was now lacking. This amount the Alumni Fund Committee was now endeavoring to secure. But the large and almost imperative additions and improvements planned, he said, would require at least four million more. He mentioned previously reported gifts by alumni for special purposes: nearly $300,000 for a building for mining and metallurgy; $600,000 towards the Walker Memorial; $300,000 from an anonymous donor for strengthening the department of chemistry.

Then, casting aside his written speech, Maclaurin stirred the crowd by announcing that a group of alumni had just given a million dollars. The roll of honor was announced:

Pierre S. du Pont '90	$500,000
C. A. Stone '88 and E. S. Webster '88	50,000
Edward D. Adams '69	50,000
T. Coleman du Pont '84	100,000
Irenée du Pont '97	100,000
Lammot du Pont '01	100,000
Charles Hayden '90	100,000

Hardly had the outburst of joy resulting from this announcement come to an end when the president sprang a new surprise. Mr. Smith's

Dedication of the New Technology 321

generosity was not at an end. With only one hint as to the identity of the great giver—that he was not an Institute graduate—Maclaurin announced that 'Mr. Smith' now offered to give five dollars for building extension for every three dollars the Institute could raise before the end of the year, his only stipulation being that his offer was limited to $2,500,000. To the million that had just been given by the eight men named, another and two-thirds was therefore added, while other gifts announced increased the total for the day to the magnificent sum of $3,150,000. Charles Hayden immediately rose to urge that the alumni "make it four million before snow flies. Remember three dollars means eight." Cheers burst in from all sections of the land, and just after 9:30 every reunion throughout the country joined with Boston in one simultaneous grand cheer.

Although the climax of this great meeting had been reached, the remainder of the program still commanded intense interest. Professor Michael I. Pupin, introduced as the man whose invention of loading coils had solved the problem of long distance transmission, spoke briefly of the help he had received from the Institute and praised the high place the school had taken in science. Dr. Alexander Graham Bell spoke of his early work and paid warm tribute to Professor Charles R. Cross, to whose work and encouragement many advances in the telephone itself had been due. Orville Wright declined to speak at length, but wished the Institute good luck in its career. Then as a token of deep gratitude a book of original drawings of the new buildings, in special morocco binding, was handed by President Stone, on behalf of the Alumni Association, to President Maclaurin, who promised to hand it to 'Mr. Smith.'

After a brief intermission, interspersed with music and unusual lighting effects, the program was resumed. Professor Harris Ryan in the name of the science teachers of the Pacific Coast exchanged salutations with Professor Cross; President Lowell, after paying a glowing tribute to President Maclaurin, exchanged greetings with President Judson of the University of California. Judge Thomas Burke spoke from Seattle for the Northwest. Then, as a new surprise, the Stein Song was sung from Milwaukee.

Two more addresses followed. President Stone presented T. Coleman du Pont with appropriate and grateful words, as an always generous giver who had made possible the purchase of the great Cambridge site for the Institute. Mr. du Pont spoke earnestly of the vital part engineers must play in national preparedness:

... In America, too, we must be ready to give our services to the community when needed. More than that, we should start now to learn just what we need to do, just how we are to do it and when and where. ... We should work out plans at once for such an efficient, energetic, effective engineering mobilization as the world has never seen; then, should the moment ever come when the country calls for the support and help of its engineering heads and hands, we would be ready.

It is not a new ideal—this idea of public service for engineers. It is only emphasized by existing conditions; the ideal has lain always in the hearts of all of us, though perhaps only recently made quite plain to all the public.

Tech men are well fitted to lead in this wider, more patriotic, more unselfish professionalism; Tech men are unselfish enough, public spirited enough, to devote themselves to it. So upon all of you in all the great cities, where my voice through wonderful engineering achievement reaches tonight, I call to be ready to enlist in this new service that Tech may stand before the whole country as the fountainhead of practical engineering preparedness.

As the last speaker of the evening former President Henry S. Pritchett was received with a long burst of welcoming applause. Whatever differences of opinion may have existed a decade before were obviously now obliterated as he rose to pay tribute to the school and its leaders. With deep sincerity and earnestness, and with a characteristic sense of spiritual values, he spoke as one who still felt himself a part of the institution in whose life he had shared, and for whose history he had deep pride and respect. The major portion of his address was as follows:

In the life of an immortal institution fifty years is but a day. We have met to celebrate the close of the first fifty years of our Technology. We have welcomed her into a new home—noble and spacious. ...

When one looks back on this half century, he realizes that whatever the Institute may mean today, it began in the heart and the brain of a great man. All great causes begin with a man, for the things which a great man thinks and feels are the motive powers of the word "Progress."

William Barton Rogers was the beginning of Technology, and all that has followed and all that ever will follow, flows from the inspiration of his brain and his spirit. Men are greater than buildings, greater than courses of study, greater than endowments. In this day when organization plays so great a role, when machinery seems to dominate life, it is worth while to remember there are some things organization cannot do.

It cannot take the place of a great man, it cannot replace leadership. Nor can one recall the name of Rogers without the mention of one other: that which Rogers planted, Francis A. Walker—President for a longer time than any other man—nourished into the full vigor of institutional life. He will for all time occupy a place in the history of this great enterprise second only to its founder. Today we have a President who will follow his steps, for if Rogers was the Moses who led us out of the educational Egypt, Maclaurin is the Joshua who has brought us into the promised land. This successful fifty years of history has a significance for the world, because Rogers and those who wrought with him stood for a true educational conception. There are many paths by which the human soul may come into that preparedness for life which we call education. The Institute of Technology was founded, not to supersede all other education, but to point out to the world that for a large part of mankind the way to preparedness lay through the training of the physical science. The training which Rogers proposed not only called out the best powers of the mind but stood for two things, which in this day have been in some measure obscured. "An education related to the practical life of the great mass of our people, an education which touched the industries, the vocations, the needs of a democracy," which drew its lessons out of everyday experience and which was rooted into a course of studies dealing with the problems of natural life.

Secondly this education faced life and its processes clearly, it stood four square to the universe ready to accept truth wherever found and tied to no demon and to no tradition. The Technology of Rogers means something to the whole world because it related itself to actual needs in material things, and because it stood for intellectual sincerity in the things of the Mind and of the Spirit. It not only did not fear the truth, but it believed wholeheartedly that the truth shall make us free. And these two fundamental conceptions of Rogers are, I apprehend, the things which make this great school—young in spite of its fifty years—a thing significant not to us alone but to the world. Today more than ever men ask truth, but truth related to human needs and human aspirations. If the Institute of Technology stands for anything distinctively, it stands for these two things.

One word as we look forward to the next half century when other faces will crowd these halls, when other hands will direct this Institute, have we visions of the half century to come as Rogers viewed the one which has passed? Rogers was the prophet of preparedness. Today the whole nation demands it. The demand arises out of a sincere and wholesome national feeling. What part shall our Institute bear in this endeavor. . . .?

. . . We make our contribution to that preparedness which the country needs when we do well the work for which we are enlisted. When we send into the service of the world men skilled in the technique of applied science, earnest to serve and with minds open to the truth, this is our contribution to preparedness. Let us, looking forward to the future, translate the ideals which Rogers gave us into still closer relations to practical work and to practical needs, let us quicken by every means our intellectual sincerity and our educational honesty,—in just such measure as we translate those ideals into the needs of the future we shall aid our country in the only way in which it needs aid—in training men who are efficient, sincere and open-minded.

The speaking ended. Prolonged applause was followed by silence, as President Maclaurin by telephone bade goodnight to the groups in all the listening cities. At the end of these farewell greetings Washington sang the first verse of the *Star Spangled Banner*. As the familiar strains were heard, Major Henry L. Higginson instantly asked if all the cities could not sing it together; and the great Boston audience joined with the alumni in all the connected cities from the Atlantic Coast to the Pacific shores and from the Canadian border to the Gulf in singing the same song of the flag.

Epilogue

WITH the translation of the Institute to its new home on the Cambridge shore of the Charles River Basin, the story of "Boston Tech" comes to a factual close. A new era, under the guidance of the great leader whose success in establishing the school in its final home, brought to rich fructification the vision of the founder. The early years in Cambridge were years of dynamic accomplishment and of great national service, and from them must have come to President Maclaurin profound satisfaction. It seemed at that time that he and the Institute could have looked forward to many years of still greater achievement. For him this was not to be. Only four years after the triumphant dedication of the new M.I.T. the body of this great and beloved leader was to lie in state under the massive dome of the vast structure which thus too soon became his monument.

Notes

CHAPTER I.
INTRODUCING THE ROGERS FAMILY

1. William and Henry Rogers, "Experimental Enquiry into Some of the Laws of the Elementary Voltaic Battery", *Silliman's Journal*, XXVII (1834), 39-61.

2. Extracts are reprinted in Appendix A, *Life and Letters of William Barton Rogers* (edited by his wife), Vol. I.

3. William Barton Rogers, "Address before the Lyceum of Natural History of Williams College, 14 August 1855," (Boston: 1855).

4. For a complete account of the early development of civil engineering in America, see articles in The *Journal of the Boston Society of Civil Engineering*, July 1936 and July 1948, By Professor J. B. Babcock (M. I. T. '10).

4a. For a complete account of the early development of civil engineering in America, see articles in the *Journal of the Boston Society of Civil Engineering*, July, 1936, and July, 1948 by Prof. J. B. Babcock, M. I. T. '10.

5. The original document, yellowed with age but easily legible despite fine interlinings and occasional changes of words, is preserved in the archives of the Institute.

6. The complete Memorial is reprinted as Appendix A in *Life and Letters of William Barton Rogers* (edited by his wife), Vol. II.

7. This document should not be confused with the original "Plan for a Polytechnic School in Boston", which has already been considered.

CHAPTER II.
THE STRUGGLE FOR EXISTENCE

8. A reproduction of the original letter is shown in the illustrations.

CHAPTER III.
THE EARLY YEARS

9. The school was opened in Mercantile Hall, on the second floor of the Mercantile Library Association Building at 18 Summer Street, as that street

was before the Great Boston Fire of November, 1872. A tablet placed by the Institute on the Kennedy Building on the east side of Hawley Street not far from Summer Street now marks the site. The tablet reads:

SITE OF
MERCANTILE LIBRARY BUILDING
1856-1872
IN WHICH THE
MASSACHUSETTS INSTITUTE OF TECHNOLOGY
BEGAN ITS SCHOOL
FEBRUARY 20, 1865

PLACED BY THE INSTITUTE
1930

CHAPTER IV.
A DECLARATION OF INDEPENDENCE

10. Early in 1860 Rogers had been suggested as Professor of Geology in the Lawrence Scientific School.

11. A brief memorandum, probably written by Edward Atkinson, indicates that the Institute probably suggested that it would be willing to take over the Lawrence Scientific School. No copy of this counterproposal has been found.

CHAPTER V.
LEAN YEARS

12. For an interesting and detailed account of the formation of the Association, and information about early members, see an article by Harold E. Lobdell in the *Technology Review* for March 1950, written on the occasion of the 75th Anniversary of the Alumni Association.

CHAPTER VI.
A GENERAL TAKES COMMAND

13. James Phinney Munroe, A LIFE OF FRANCIS AMASA WALKER (New York, 1923).

14. Miss Julia M. Comstock became general assistant in the Institute offices in 1892. She was especially helpful to the Registrar and the Secretary and to President Walker. She later had charge of the preparation of all Institute publications, and the collection of brief biographical memoirs of members of the Corporation, Administrative officers, and members of the faculty from the earliest

NOTES

days, and of material of the Historical Memorials Committee. For sixty years she served the Institute with exceptional skill and unalloyed fidelity. She retired in 1952.

CHAPTER VII.
AN ERA OF DEVELOPMENT

15. This phrase occurs in the president's report (12 December 1894) 49. He wrote: "It is much to be regretted that the Institute has not an athletic field and larger gymnasium facilities. At the same time, the position of athletics here is not by any means unsatisfactory. The students in general understand perfectly well that this is a place for men to work and not for boys to play; and they organize their athletic teams and carry on their contests in a very sensible and practical spirit".

16. It is also a matter of pride and interest that Mr. French had been a special student at M. I. T. in the class of 1871.

17. For some twenty years thereafter this bust stood in the front lobby of the Rogers Building near the entrance to the president's office. It now stands in the main lobby of the Walker Memorial Building in Cambridge.

CHAPTER XII.
RICHARD COCKBURN MACLAURIN—SIXTH PRESIDENT

18. In 1921, Professor Nichols was elected as Maclaurin's successor at M. I. T.

19. For full text of these inaugural addresses see The *Technology Review*, XI (July 1909).

CHAPTER XIII.
THE NEW TECHNOLOGY

20. The establishment of this summer school was brought about through a committee of the Alumni Council, and was the first of many efforts of the Council to co-operate with the corporation in matters of this kind.

21. Although falling outside our period Mrs. Cunningham's unusual service to Technology during the first World War should be recorded. She gave the funds to establish the Technology Club in Paris, the first of its kind there. She gave the Technology Ambulance Unit as a memorial to her husband. She organized and supported the Tech War Service Auxiliary and Workroom carried on in the Rogers Building during the war, which sent large quantities of supplies to Halifax after the great explosion there, as well as to France. When the workroom was closed, all funds remaining were given to the American Memorial Hospital at Rheims. She also gave the Institute the sum of $25,000 as the Edward

Cunningham Memorial Fund, to be applied to the maintenance of a summer military school at the Civil Enginering Camp at East Machias, Me., to fit students for military service in the war. It was a patriotic and generous service as well as an expression of wifely devotion to a man who in his last years gave much to his Alma Mater.

CHAPTER XIV.
THE LAST YEARS IN BOSTON

22. In the 1940's this certificate was replaced by a diploma granting the degree of Master of Public Health.

23. Edwin O. Jordan et al. *Pioneer in Public Health: William Thompson Sedgwick*. (New Haven, 1924).

24. A complete account of the negotiations leading to the joint Harvard-Technology agreement and of the court action is given in a long chapter of Professor Henry G. Pearson's admirable biography. *Richard Cockburn Maclaurin* (1937).

CHAPTER XV.
DEDICATION OF THE NEW TECHNOLOGY

25. Mr. Brooks, one of the first graduates of the new course in Business Administration, after thirty-four years as a business leader, became in 1951 the first Dean of the new School of Industrial Management.

Appendix

A Plan for a Polytechnic School in Boston.
1846.

A SCHOOL of practical science completely organized should, I conceive, embrace full courses of instruction in all the principles of physical truth having direct relation to the art of constructing machinery, the application of motive power, manufactures, mechanical and chemical, the art of engraving with electrotype and photography, mineral exploration and mining, chemical analysis, engineering, locomotion and agriculture. It would require two departments.

First, one in which by courses of lectures, amply illustrated, a broad and solid foundation should be laid in general physics, including especially the mechanics of solids, liquids and airs, and the laws of heat, electricity, magnetism and light, and in the chemistry of the more important inorganic and organic principles. Without a sufficient groundwork of this kind in general physical laws, it is obvious that the details of applied science would have but little attraction, and being but vaguely apprehended would convey very little valuable instruction. This department would, I think, give employment to two instructors, dividing the various topics between them as might be found convenient, and perhaps at the same time lecturing on some of the applied branches, as portions of the chemical arts, the strength of materials, motive powers, the steam engine, or any of the practical subjects capable of being taught in lectures with the aid of experiments, models and diagrams.

The other, and entirely practical department, would embrace instruction in chemical manipulation and the analysis of chemical products, ores, metals and other materials used in the arts, as well as of soils and manures. *Second,*—A course of practical, elementary mathematics, and *Third,*—full instruction in drawing and modelling. This branch should also include special courses of teaching in architecture, engineering and the various branches of the arts not treated of in the first department. This second division of the school besides employing two or three tutors, or sub-professors, to give personal instuction in the laboratory, workshop or room for drawing, might yearly invite the aid of eminent practical men to give courses of lectures on the various branches of applied science not otherwise provided for, or it might engage the services of such permanently for the more important subjects after a trial of the practical benefits of their collaboration. A scheme of this kind begun with two professors in the scientific department and two subordinate instructors in the other, under the direction of the former, would, I am certain, prove so signally successful as ultimately to require its expansion into a polytechnic college on the most ample scale, in which, along with all the subjects above referred to, would be embraced full courses in elementary mathematics and instruction, perhaps, in the French and German languages. In a word, I doubt not that such a nucleus-school would, with the growth of this active and knowledge-seeking community, finally expand into a great institution comprehending the whole field of physical science and the arts with the auxiliary branches of the mathematics and modern languages, and would soon overtop the universities of the land in the accuracy and the extent of its teachings in all branches of positive knowledge.

According to my present notions of expediency and usefulness, the two professors in the scientific, or more properly the mixed department, should so frame their general courses of lectures as to make them acceptable and useful to the public at large, and thus furnish annual courses on general physics, chemistry and geology, which might draw all the lovers of knowledge of both sexes to the halls of the Institute, whether they proposed or not, continuing their studies in the other and directly practical branches of the Institution. This, of course, should be, as it very well could be, done without any sacrifice of the exactness of scientific or practical demonstration to mere popular effect. We know how successful have been the courses in the Royal Institute of London, where Brandt, Faraday and Wheatstone have for years been the chief instructors of practical science. The school in Boston, too, might well adopt the valuable practice of the Royal Institute of having stated lectures for diffusing a knowledge of important new inventions in the arts, and discourses in physical science. By so doing besides the general benefit of an early communication of valuable truths, often so important to practical men, there would arise the special advantage to the Institute itself of a reputation for being foremost in the appreciation and promulgation of such useful knowledge, and this would give it a strong claim upon the respect and affection of the public.

The true and only practicable object of a polytechnic school is, as I conceive, the teaching, not of the minute details and manipulations of the arts, which can be done only in the workshop, but the inculcation of those scientific principles which form the basis and explanation of them, and along with this a full and methodical review of all their leading processes and operations in connection with physical laws. When thus instructed in applied science, the mechanician, chemist, manufacturer or engineer clearly comprehends the agencies of the materials and instruments with which he works, and is, therefore, saved from the disasters of blind experiment, is guided securely because understandingly in a profitable routine, and is directed in the contrivance of new and more efficient combinations. We cannot but believe that, with a proper training in science, the host of unprofitable inventors, living within the last half century, would have contributed innumerable valuable aids to human industry, and advanced the arts to a far higher stage of improvement than they have yet attained. Of this no stronger argument could be asked than a glance at the encumbered cases of the Patent Office in Washington.

Indeed, the unexampled progress, both here and in Europe, of every branch of the arts for the last fifty years is but the result of that general diffusion of a better knowledge of physical laws which has flowed from the researches and teachings of men specially devoted to natural science; bearing in mind too, how few of the almost countless products of ingenuity, even in these times, are of real and permanent value and how immense the number of utterly barren inventions, the laboured contrivances of acute but undirected or misguided mind.

Among practical pursuits there are, perhaps, none whose dependence upon the determination of physical science is more generally recognized than those of the machinist, the engineer and the architect. Yet even in these professions, while all admit that many of the details are but immediate applications of the leading laws of mechanical philosophy, how few have formed a just conception of the variety and extent of science they involve.

In the first place, the materials used in construction must be studied in their more important chemical and mechanical relations. Rules must be applied for computing the strength of beams and columns of timber and metal of various shapes and dimensions, and placed in various attitudes within buildings or machinery, and these cannot be safely used without a knowledge of the experimental data and mechanical principles from which they have been deduced. So likewise in resolving the often recurring problem of the distribution of forces to the several parts of a structure as dependent on the arrangement of the parts and the position of the load, or other pressure, the necessity for scientific principles is immediate and unavoidable. Of the durability of the materials employed in masonry, it is evident that no confident judgment can be formed without a knowledge of their composition and of the chemical action to which they are liable from air, water and thermal changes. The machinist should understand all the principles of equilibrium and of the composition of forces; in other words, the general doctrines of statics and dynamics, those of friction and resisting forces generally, the mode of operation of the various motive powers of which his machines are to be, as it were, conductors, and the methods of computing the relation between the force applied and the useful effect obtained, or in other words the economical value of the combination.

The engineer of roads and canals with ample knowledge in all these particulars should further have a good acquaintance with the mineral and geological character of the region in which he operates, should know when to interpret the appearances on the surface either as an encouragement or warning in directing his locations; should be prepared to judge of the value of the rocky materials he encounters in building an embankment, and should be qualified to form an estimate of the relative advantages of different districts as influenced by the extent and nature of these mineral products.

Instruction in all these and other kindred particulars, essential as it is to the fullest success in the pursuits referred to, involves, it will be seen, no insignificant acquaintance with some of the leading branches of mechanical and even geological and chemical science.

If we turn now to the manufacturing arts, we shall find an equal and, in many cases, even more urgent demand for scientific guidance. Beginning with those connected with metallurgy, we see in the various processes by which iron, copper, lead, zinc, silver and other metals are obtained from their ores the most direct application of chemical and mechanical science. The form and materials of the furnace, the character of the fuel and flame, the preparatory processes of roasting, or washing, the due modification of the procedures according to the nature and proportion of the foreign substances present, with numerous other practical details in the various stages of the operation, are only intelligible through the medium of scientific principles, and are most likely to be successfully pursued, or improved, when these principles are clearly understood and habitually recurred to. So also in the fabrication of steel and the mixed metals, such as brass, bronze and tinned iron, and in casting, rolling, wire drawing and other mechanical and chemical processes of the same kind,

APPENDIX 335

the truths of science have many important applications, and are capable of affording suggestions of high utility. In gilding, plating and the processes of electrotype, in engraving in all its branches, including lithography, zincography and the various departments of photographic art, we see the most varied agencies of physical laws, involving the mechanical properties of materials, their relations to solvents, and the powers of heat and light. In the fabrication of pottery and porcelain in all the varieties, and in the colouring and painting of both these classes of products, every step is but an application of some well-known scientific principle.

Of the refining of sugar and the manufacturing of alum, copperas, white lead, bleaching salts, the acids, and a hundred other important chemical products, it is needless to say more than that the processes they involve are but the vast practical enlargement of the common experiments of the laboratory and lecture-room. The production of illuminating gas from coal, fats or rosin, and the processes for its purification, the manufacture of stearine, wood vinegar, and all the whole variety of soaps, the purification of oils, the making of cements and varnishes, the arts of tanning, bleaching, dyeing and calico printing, with a hundred others extensively practised at the present day, are either the direct results of modern scientific research, or are largely indebted to it for those experiments in mechanical and chemical details which have bestowed on many of them a more than hundred-fold productiveness. So clearly indeed has the importance of a scientific guidance been proved in some of these arts, that we now in many cases see them claiming the superintendence of skilful chemists to direct their daily operations, and I need not add that the fruits of this happy union of science and art are nowhere better exemplified than in the dyeing and printing works for which Lowell has been so celebrated.

In the various forms of mechanism devoted to spinning and weaving in all their branches, in mill work of almost endless variety, in the steam engine, as applied to stationary or locomotive uses, in water wheels, turbines, propellers and the innumerable forms of hydraulic and hydropneumatic machinery, we have almost numberless applications of the laws of mechanics, which those only who clearly understand can guide or improve to the best advantage.

In the business of mining in all departments, including that of exploration on the surface and by borings, every important step calls for the suggestions of geology, chemistry and mechanical science.

To close this long but still incomplete catalogue of illustrations, we may safely affirm that there is no branch of practical industry, whether in the arts of construction, manufactures or agriculture, which is not capable of being better practised, and even of being improved in its processes, through the knowledge of its connections with physical truths and laws, and therefore we would add that there is no class of operatives to whom the teaching of science may not become of direct and substantial utility and material usefulness. It would, I think, be especially adapted to fulfil another, and in some respects a higher purpose by leading the thoughts of the practical student into those wide and elevated regions of reflection to which the study of Nature's laws never fails to conduct the mind. Thus linking the daily details of his profession with the grander physical agencies around him, and with much of what is agreeable and ennobling in the contemplation of external things, it would insensibly elevate and refine his character and contribute to the cheerfulness as it aided the efficiency of his labours. In this respect it is, I think, demonstrated that physical studies are better capable of being useful to the operative classes than the study of literature or morals, because their truths are more readily and eagerly seized upon by such minds and form the strong staple of practical usefulness thus firmly infixed. It is easy to extend the golden chain of relations until these may embrace every realm of nature and of thought.

A polytechnic school, therefore, duly organized, has in view an object of the utmost practical value, and one which in such a community as that of Boston could not fail of being realized in the amplest degree.

Index

Index

A

Adams, Charles Francis II, 196
  Charles L., 117
  Comfort A., 292
  Edward D., 320
Admission requirements, 46, 137
Aeronautical engineering, 283
Agassiz, Louis, 73, 152
Allen, Calvin Francis, 100, 126, 163, 177, 271
Alumni, financial contributions of, 205
  opinion on Harvard merger, 200
  representation on Corporation, 207
  requested to raise money, 258
Alumni Association, 48, 99, 161, 225, 257, 321
American Association for the Advancement of Science, 14
American Literary, Scientific, and Military Academy, 23
Andrew, John A., Gov., 32, 38, 71
"Annex," The, 98
Appleton, Nathan, 15
Architectural Building, 137
Architectural engineering, 280
Architecture, program for, 91
Aspinwall, Thomas, 31
Association of Class Secretaries, 163, 191
Athletics, 142, 171
Atkinson, Edward, on committee on instruction, 53
  re military training, 97
  re union with Harvard, 74, 81, 82, 83, 84, 87
  supports Runkle, 90
  William P., 51, 59, 117
Austin, Edward, 156

B

Bailey, Abraham, 46
  Frederick H., 188
Baldwin, Loammi, 23
Bancroft, Wilfred, 148
Barron, Clarence W., 251
Bartlett, Dana P., 180, 188
Barton, Dr., 4
Baseball, 171
Bates, Arlo, 125, 271, 277
Beebe, James M., 29, 30, 31, 40, 83, 84, 131
Bell, Alexander Graham, 317, 321
Bemis, A. Farwell, 258, 270, 310
Bethel, U. N., 317
Bigelow, E. B., 29, 30, 31, 84, 131
  George T., 75, 81, 84
  Jacob, 35, 70, 75
  John, Jr., 179, 271
  Robert P., 144, 279
Binney, Amos, 30
Bittinger, Charles, 304
Blackstein, Joseph, 274
Blashfield, Edwin H., 48, 304
Blodgett, George W., 99
Blythe, Hannah, 4
Bôcher, Ferdinand, 46, 48, 49, 51
Boston, Massachusetts, why M. I. T. located there, 21-25, 26
"Boston Tech," why called, i
Bosworth, W. Welles, 265, 317
Bowditch, Ernest, 270
  J. I., 84, 131
Bowlker, T. J., Mrs., 183
Bray, William C., 276
Breed, Charles B., 223, 278
Briggs, F. H., Major, 173
Brooks, Edward P., 302, 303
  Phillips, 57, 90
Bryce, James, 239, 240, 242, 260
Bugbee, Edward E., 222
Buildings, number of, 132
Bullard, Frederic Field, 204
Bullock, Governor, 65
Burke, Thomas, Judge, 321

Burrison, Henry K., 117, 276
Burton, Alfred E., 122, 172, 199, 238, 274, 279
Bush, Vannevar, 293

C

Cabot, E. C., 31
  Godfrey, 48, 306
  J. Elliot, 90
  Samuel, 171, 209
  Samuel, Jr., 30, 48
California Institute of Technology, 228
Cane rush, 172
Carlton, W. T., 46, 48
Carnegie, Andrew, 197, 249, 250
Carnegie Foundation for the Advancement of Teaching, 211
Carpenter, George R., 125
Carson, Howard A., 131, 207, 223, 270
Carty, J. J., 317
Catalogue, first, 51
Centennial Exposition at Philadelphia, 97
Chandler, Francis W., 126, 206, 253, 274, 275, 280
Chase, H. S., 144
  John, 31, 35
Chemical engineering, course established, 120
  noteworthy department, 278
Cheney, Ednah Dow, 207
  Margaret, 99
Chesbrough, E. S., 9
Civil engineering, schools for, 23
  summer school, 254, 258
Clark, Theodore M., 95
Clifford, Harry E., 177, 184, 188, 223, 224, 292
Clubs, 143
Coburn, Howard L., 180
Coeducation, 53, 99
Coffin, Charles A., 254, 255
Cole, Edwin T., Major, 294, 311
Collins, J. A., Jr., 195
Commencement, started, 99
Comstock, Julia, 115
Congress of Technology, 252
Cooke, Josiah Parsons, 152
Coolidge, William D., 186

Copeland, Frederick K., 209
Corporation, first officers, 35
  make-up, 75, 130, 208
  members listed, 270
  organization, 79, 90
Crafts, James Mason, President, 91, 152, 157, 166, 254, 280
Cram, Ralph Adams, 277, 306
Critchett, James H., 227
Crosby, William O., 117, 119, 177, 188, 221
Cross, Charles R., appointed instructor, 91
  attends Golden Jubilee, 317
  directs electrical engineering, 183, 280
  long career, 117
  nickname, 274
  practical experience, 177
  praised by Alexander Graham Bell, 321
  secretary of Alumni Association, 100
Crowninshield, Francis B., 75
Cummings, John, Jr., death, 156
  pledges personal fortune to M. I. T., 101, 199
  praised, 90, 131
  re military training, 97
  re union with Harvard, 84, 87
Cunningham, Edith Forbes, 271
  Edward, 271
Curriculum, 41, 42, 44, 51, 92, 125, 137, 158, 218, 280
Currier, Charles F. A., 125, 188, 274

D

Dallinger, Frederick W., 317
Dalton, Charles H., 29, 30, 31, 36, 84, 131
  John, 11
Daly, Reginald A., 222, 276
Dana, Richard H., 66
Degrees, authority to grant, 65
  total number to 1916, 297
deLancey, Darragh, 262
Derr, Louis, 178, 311
Despradelle, Désiré, 274, 276
Devens, Charles, Gen., 109
Dewey, Davis R., 125, 253, 274, 285, 311
Dickinson, John W., 131
Dickinson College, 9
Doctor of science degree, 185, 220

INDEX 341

Dougherty, Proctor L., 199
Drake, Albert W., 317, 318
Draper, Eben S., as governor of Massachusetts, 238, 239, 242, 243, 244
    gives dinner to students, 173
    on Corporation, 209, 270
Drinker, H. S., Dr., 317
Drown, Thomas M., Prof., 123, 124
Duncan, Louis, Dr., 179, 183
Dupee, J. S., 31
du Pont, Irenée, 320
    Lammot, 320
    Pierre S., 268, 320
    T. Coleman, at Golden Jubilee banquet, 317, 320
    contributes funds for laboratories, 268
    elected to Corporation, 209, 270
    congratulates Maclaurin, 264
    in removal celebration, 300, 310
    offers funds for removal of M. I. T., 250, 257
    speaks on importance of engineers, 322

E

Eastman, George, 259, 289
Eastwood, Sam, 46
Eaton, Charles W., 258
Edison, Thomas, 260
Edmands, Mr., 84
Education, W. B. Rogers on, 16
Elder, Samuel J., 244, 245
Eldridge, N. H., 40
Electrical engineering, course established, 118
Electrochemistry, 280
Eliot, Charles W., assists in exhibit for Paris Exhibition, 65
    attends Congress of Technology, 253, 255
    attends opening of New Technology, 310
    author, 47
    offered post at M. I. T., 49
    professor of chemistry at M. I. T., 51, 53
    re union with Harvard, 71, 72, 76, 77, 82

Elliott, Howard, 270
Ellis, George E., Rev. Dr., 104
Emerson, George B., 30, 75, 84, 90
    Merton L., 299
Endicott, Mordecai T., 254
    William, Sr., Treasurer, advises Alumni fund, 206
    aids President Crafts, 156
    gets subscriptions for M. I. T., 65, 134
    opposes union with Harvard, 84, 87
    pledges own funds for M. I. T., 61
    praised for loyalty, 90
    term on Corporation, 270
    William, Jr., 254, 270, 310
Engineering, Robert Rogers discusses, 10
Engineering administration, 285
Engineering B (building), 139
Engineering Building, 136
Engineering C (building), 186
Enrollment, 137, 157, 280, 296
Estabrook, Arthur F., 270, 310
Evans, Maria A., Mrs., 258
    Robert Dawson, 258
Evening instruction, 51, 52
Everett, Charles, 317
Executive Committee, established, 131

F

Faculty, appointments, 41, 49, 50, 66, 90, 118
    criticism of inbreeding, 176
    grades itemized, 296
    listed, 45, 50
    number of, 92, 117, 118, 130, 135, 157, 191, 219
    opinion on Harvard merger, 200
    reorganization, 219
    salaries, 61
    student relations, 273, 277
Fairchild, Charles, 131
Faraday, Michael, 11
Farwell, Arthur G., 304
Fay, Mr., 84
    Frederick, H., 195, 271, 299
    Henry, 188, 311
Felton, Samuel M., 209, 271
Ferguson, Louis A., 271

Finances, 34, 59, 61, 101, 102, 138, 157
   funds from Morrill Act, 39
   need for building funds, 258, 266, 320
   need for endowment, 133
   state aid, 252
Fire of 1872, 96
Fish, Frederick, P., 237, 239, 244, 254, 317
Fitz, W. S., Mrs., 183
Fitzgerald, Desmond, 271
   John F., 254, 255
Flexner, Abraham, 201
Flint, Charles L., 30, 31, 65, 75, 84
Football, 171
Football Association, 142
Foran, G. J., 144
Forbes, Eli, 46, 48, 243
   John M., 48, 73, 84
   R. B., 37
   W. Cameron, 270, 310
   William H., 156
Ford, Horace S., 279
Foss, Eugene N., Governor, 257
Fox, Frederick, 185
Francis, J. B., 31, 84
Franklin Fund, 138
Franklin Institute, Philadelphia, 12
Franklin Union, 211
Fraternities, 144
Freeman, John R., 209, 261, 264, 271
French, Daniel Chester, 148, 304
Frothingham, Lieutenant Governor, 253
Fuller, Mr., 84
   Charles E., 178, 278

G

Gale, H. B., 144
Gallup, Harriet, 262
Gannett, Rev. Dr., 31
Gardner, George A., 183
   Harry W., 253, 317
   Lester D., 307
General Science course (IX), 284
Geological Society of London, 11
Geology, interest in, in Europe and America, 11
   Rogers' family interest in, 9, 12
Gibbons, R. T., 144

Gifts, 34, 40, 50, 65, 101, 102, 134, 139, 156, 157, 183, 207, 254, 258, 263, 268, 276, 320
Gilbert, Cass, 271
Gill, A. H., 177
Glidden, George B., 253, 317
Golden Jubilee Banquet, 316
Goodwin, Harry M., 188, 280, 311
Gookin, Samuel H., 30, 31
Gordon, George A., 310, 311
Graduate school in engineering, co-operation with Harvard, 286
Graduate students, 157
Graton, Louis C., 292
Gray, Asa, 73
   Joseph P., 209
Greene, Francis B., 258
Greenleaf, Richard C., 81, 84, 87, 131
Gunsaulus, President, 198

H

Hager, E. M., 243, 251
Haggerty, Clemence, 155
Hague, James D., 51
Hale, George E., 186, 210, 228, 264
   R. A., 195
Hampden-Sydney College, 18
Hart, Francis R., 279
   appointed Treasurer, 210
   at Congress of Technology, 254
   at Golden Jubilee Banquet, 317
   elected to Corporation, 270
   helps secure land for New Technology, 257, 258
   on Executive Committee, 237
Harvard Graduate School of Applied Science, co-operation with M. I. T., 286
Harvard School of Public Health, 282
Harvard University, union with M. I. T. discussed, 69, 114, 164, 193, 281
Haste, James H., 262
Haven, George B., 278
Hayden, Charles, at reunion, 244
   elected to Corporation, 271
   gifts to M. I. T., 268, 320
   in New Technology celebration, 300

INDEX

343

marshal for alumni, 305
urges alumni gifts, 321
Hazelton, Isaac B., 304
Henck, John B., 51, 117, 119
Higginson, Henry L., 197, 249, 264, 310, 317, 324
Hoadley, J. C., 31, 84
Hoar, George Frisbie, 109
Hobbs, Franklin W., 271, 310
Hofman, Heinrich O., 127, 274, 277
Holman, Silas W., 117, 118, 156, 177
Home economics, 123
Homer, E. B., 177
Hooper, Sam, 74
Horsford, Eben N., 73
Hosmer, George L., 223
Hovgaard, William, 160, 274
Howard, Henry, 271
Howison, Professor, 102
Hoyt, W. E., 95
Hubbard, Charles W., 209, 271
Hudson, Ralph G., 307
Hughes, Hector J., 292
Humphreys, Walter, 180, 279, 299
Hunsaker, Jerome C., 283, 293
Hunt, T. Sterry, 91
Huntington, Ralph, 34, 57, 131
Huntington Hall, 57
Hyatt, Alpheus, 91
Hyde, Henry D., 156

I

Institute Committee, 144

J

Jackson, Charles C., 156, 183, 270
 Dugald C., 184, 253
 Patrick Tracy, 22
Jaggar, Thomas A., Jr., 179, 276
Johnson, Douglas W., 222
 F. F., 144
 Lewis J., 292
 Samuel, 156
Johnston, William A., 178, 278
"Jones' Lunch," 97
Jordan, Edwin O., 283
Joslin, Rebecca, 304

Judson, President of University of California, 321

K

Kastner, Charles, 96
Kennelly, A. E., 280, 292
Kidder, Henry P., 131
 Jerome George, 297
Kidder Laboratories of Chemistry, 99
Kimball, William A., 100
King, Ellen A., 145
 William H., 271, 310
Kittredge, George W., 210
Kneeland, Samuel, draws up petition for land, 28, 30
 on Corporation, 75, 131
 opposes union with Harvard, 78, 84
 resigns as Secretary of M. I. T., 102
Knight, Albert M., 181

L

Lambirth, James R., 121
Lanza, Gaetano, 91, 117, 244, 274, 275
Large, Walter, 318
Lawrence, Abbott, 27
 James, 73
 Ralph R., 223
 William A., Bishop, 57, 239
 W. H., 177, 178, 277
Lawrence Scientific School, 27, 70, 73, 79, 194
Laws, Frank A., 278
Leonard, H. Ward, 144
Létang, Eugene, 91, 94
Levermore, Charles H., 125
Lewis, A. J., 305
 Gilbert N., 215, 223, 276, 280
 Warren K., 278
Lincoln, F. W., Jr., 31, 84
 William H., 271
Lindgren, Waldemar, 277
Litchfield, I. W., 144, 195, 199, 225, 299, 307
Little, Mr., on Corporation, 84
 Arthur D., at reunion, 244
 elected to Corporation, 271
 founder of *Technology Review*, 163
 founder of *The Tech*, 144

organizes Congress of Technology, 252, 258
promotes Practice School, 264
Philip, 304
Livermore, Thomas L., 271
   aids Maclaurin, 257
   appeals to General Court for M. I. T., 252
   at dedication of New Technology, 310, 317
   at reunion, 244
   on Executive Committee, 155
   requests gifts from alumni, 206
   speaks on union with Harvard, 198, 205
Locke, Frank L., 208, 209
Lodge, Henry Cabot, 310, 313
   Richard W., 222
Lombard, Norman, 190
Long, John D., Governor, 131
Longyear, John M., 254, 270
Lothrop, Samuel K., 75, 90, 105
Love, James Lee, 202
Lovejoy, Frank W., 259, 262
Lowell, A. Lawrence, 242
   at Congress of Technology, 253, 255
   at dedication of New Technology, 310, 312
   at Golden Jubilee Banquet, 317, 321
   at inauguration of Maclaurin, 239, 240
   describes Maclaurin, 249, 291
   on Corporation of M. I. T., 183
   re union with Harvard, 196
   term on Corporation, 271
   trustee of Lowell Institute, 187
   Amy, 183
   Augustus, 131, 155, 157, 183
   Francis Cabot, 22
   Henry, 25
   John Amory, 131
      chairman, Committee on School of Industrial Science, 90
      elected vice-president of M. I. T., 35
      proposes evening courses, 52
      proposes school for mechanics, 34
      re union with Harvard, 75, 84, 86, 89
      trustee of Lowell Institute, 17, 24

Percival, 179, 183
Lowell Building, 183
Lowell Institute, 19, 24, 52, 96
Lowell Institute School for Industrial Foremen, 187
Lowell School of Practical Design, 96
Luquiens, Jules, 92, 117
Lyell, Charles, 11, 15
Lyman, Theodore, Colonel, 105

M

McAllister, Eva, 175
McCall, Samuel W., Governor, 310, 312, 317
McKay, Gordon, 193
McKibben, Frank P., 222
Maclaurin, Richard C., President, addresses Golden Jubilee, 319
   biography, 230
   death, 325
   dedicatory address for New Technology, 311
   educational aims of, 241
   elected president, 226
   inauguration, 229, 238
   praised at Golden Jubilee, 323
   praised by Lowell, 291
   proposes graduate school with Harvard, 286
   receives LL.D., 249
McNeil, Capt., 9
Maier, E. D., Colonel, 254
Main, C. T., 195, 209, 271
Mansfield, G. W., 141
Manual training, 98
Marine engineering, department established, 122
Marks, Lionel S., 292
Martin, George H., 244
Maryland Institute, 7, 8
Massachusetts Conservatory of Arts and Sciences, 28
Massachusetts Institute of Technology
   aims of, 26, 29, 51
   building (first) for, 41
   Cambridge land bought, 257
   competition from state schools, 138

early public support for, 31
embryo of, 17
Harvard and, 39, 69, 114, 164, 193, 281
inauguration (first) of president, 170
incorporated, 32
Lowell Institute and, 96
opening day, 45
public relations improved, 225
removal from Boston discussed, 192, 247
removal made possible, 264
removal to Cambridge opposed by Harvard, 250
reputation, 65, 73, 75, 129, 136, 150, 260, 323
text of Rogers' plan for, 331
three branches of, 36
See also
Admission requirements, Alumni, Buildings, Catalogue, Clubs, Commencement, Corporation, Curriculum, Degrees, Enrollment, Faculty, Finances, Fraternities, Gifts, Scholarships, Students, Subjects taught, Technology
Massachusetts School of Design, 96
Master of science degree, 185, 220, 279
Masters, Frank B., 304
Mathematics, new method, 219
Mather, William, Sir, 260
Maury, Matthew Fontaine, Lt., 18
Mercantile Library Association, 19
Merriam, Charles, 207
Merrick, Theodore B., 121
Merrill, Allyne L., 177, 179, 180, 188, 274, 279, 311
Military training, 96
Miller, Miss, 263
  E. C., 195
  E. F., 177, 188, 274, 277, 311
Mills, Hiram F., 271
Mining engineering, joint school with Harvard, 268
Mining Engineering Laboratories, 268
Mixter, Samuel J., 205
Moore, F. Jewett, 278
  Lewis E., 222
Morrill Act, 39
Morss, Everett, 206, 244, 257, 258, 270

Henry A., 271, 300, 307
Morton, Marcus, Chief Justice, 131
Mulliken, S. P., Dr., 185
Munroe, James P., 174, 279
  advises on *Technology Review*, 163
  at Congress of Technology, 254
  at dedication of New Technology, 307
  at inauguration of Maclaurin, 239, 240
  at reunion, 244
  biography of Walker, 115, 150
  editor of *Technology Quarterly*, 144
  elected secretary of Corporation, 209
  executive secretary of faculty, 123
  organizes alumni fund, 206
  speaks at farewell to Boston Tech, 300, 304
  speaks on M. I. T., 199
Museum of Practical Arts, 38

N

National Academy of Sciences, 33
National Bureau of Hydrography, 18
National Institution for the Promotion of Science, 14
Natural philosophy, Rogers' family interest in, 9
Naval architecture, 159
New Jersey, geological survey of, 12
New Technology, 254
  dedication, 309
  description of, 267
Newell, Frederick H., 209
Nichols, William Ripley, 91, 117
Nickerson, W. E., 141
Niles, William H., 91, 117, 179
Norton, Lewis M., 119, 137, 177
  Charles L., 178, 278
Norwich University, 245,
Noyes, Arthur A., acting president, 215
  alumni marshal, 310
  at Congress of Technology, 253, 254
  at Golden Jubilee Banquet, 317
  at inauguration of Maclaurin, 239, 240
  at reunion, 244, 245
  chairman of faculty, 212
  heads research laboratory, 280

liked by students, 271
on faculty, 177
receives master's degree, 185
resignation, 228
tribute to, 226

O

Olney, Richard, 290
Ordway, Alfred, 30
  John M., 90, 114, 117, 118
Osborne, George A., 65, 78, 117, 253
Otis, Charles, 126
Owen, George, 269
  Robert Dale, 11

P

Paine, Charles J., 206
Paris Exposition, 1900, 161
Park, Charles F., 178, 187, 278, 300
Partridge, Alden, 23
Passano, Leonard M., 223
Peabody, Cecil H., at dedication of New Technology, 311
  heads naval architecture, 159, 280
  in Japan, 122
  nickname, 274
  practical experience of, 177
  secures bequest, 269
  suggests aeronautical engineering, 283
  Francis G., 173
  Robert S., 209
Pearson, Henry G., 223, 251, 277
Peirce, Benjamin, 31, 73
  Charles C., 253, 258, 317
Pennsylvania, University of, 12
Perkins, Richard, 134
Peters, Edward, 292
Phelps, Earle B., 187, 223
Philbrick, Edward S., 131
  J. D., 30, 31, 90
Philosophical Society of Philadelphia, 14
Physical education, 175
Physics laboratory, 93
Pickering, Edward C., 66, 78, 90, 93
  William H., 117, 121
Pierce, Henry L., 139, 156
Pierce Building, 139, 157
Pope, Macy S., 207

Ralph W., 244
Thomas E., 274, 276
Porter, Dwight, 126, 274
Pratt, Charles H., 268
  G. W., 30
  H. G., 144
Pratt School of Naval Architecture and Marine Engineering, 268
Prescott, Samuel C., 278
Preston, Mr., 84
  Jonathan, 55
  William G., 55
Pritchett, Henry S., President, at dedication of New Technology, 310
  at Golden Jubilee Banquet, 317, 322
  biography of, 167
  contributions, 212
  criticism of, 178, 203
  inauguration, 170
  interests of, 170
  public services of, 210
  recommends abolishing General Science, 285
  resignation, 211
  speaks at Maclaurin's inauguration, 239
  supports union with Harvard, 197
  Henry S., Mrs., 204
Public health, 281
Puffer, W. L., 177, 178
Pupin, Michael, 317, 321
Putnam, George, Rev., 75, 81, 83
  William L., 183

R

Rambeau, Professor, 179
Rand, Frank H., Bursar, 174, 181, 278
Randall, John W. and Belinda L., Charities Corporation, 156
Rensselaer Polytechnic Institute, 24
Research laboratories, 185, 280
Research Laboratory of Physical Chemistry, 220
Reserve Officers Training Corps, 291
Reunions, 197, 203, 229, 299
Revere, Joseph W., 48
Rice, Alexander H., 50, 85, 97
  Calvin W., 244

INDEX

Thomas, 31
Richards, Ellen H. [Swallow], 53, 99, 117, 122, 276
  Robert H., 117
    appointed to faculty, 91
    at reunion, 243, 244
    biography of, 48
    chairman of alumni meeting, 100
    conducts trip to west, 95
    in first class, M. I. T., 46
    nickname, 274
    on alumni fund committee, 206
    practical experience of, 177
    retires, 276
    speaks on early M. I. T., 189
Ripley, William Z., 178
Ritchie, E. S., 37
Robbins, A. G., 311
Robinson, J. P., 31
  T. W., 244
Rockwell, Alfred P., 79
Rogers, Alexander, 4
  Hannah Blythe, 7
  Henry B., 40, 75, 83, 90
  Henry Darwin, birth, 5
    death of, 59
    geological paper by, 15
    geological survey by, 13
    in Boston, 17
    in England, 11
    in Maryland, 7, 8
    in New England and New York, 9
    professor at University of Glasgow, 20
    professor at University of Pennsylvania, 12
  James Blythe, 5, 7, 8, 14, 20
  Patrick, 4, 6, 8
  Robert (father of Patrick), 4
  Robert (son of Patrick), 59, 66
    assists William, 13
    at University of Pennsylvania, 20
    at University of Virginia, 16
    birth, 5
    in National Academy of Sciences, 33
    in New England and New York, 9, 10
    prepares models, 12
    student, 7, 8
  Robert E., 305, 309
  William Barton, President, 84, 90, 247, 301
    Alumni Association praises, 100
    appointed representative to Paris Exposition, 65
    appointed State Inspector of Gas Meters, 33
    at University of Virginia, 12
    birth, 5
    chairman of faculty, Virginia, 15
    chief of Geological Survey, Virginia, 12, 13, 14
    death, 104
    devotion to father, 7
    early years in Boston, 19
    education of, 6, 7
    elected president of M. I. T., 35
    family, 4
    geological paper by, 14, 15
    illness of, 59
    in England, 20
    in Maryland, 7
    LL.D. conferred by Harvard, 63
    marriage of, 18
    Memorial Fund, 133
    memorials to, 3
    one-hundredth anniversary of birth, 188
    plan for polytechnic school, 26, 27, 28, 29, 331
    plans for M. I. T., 23, 24
    praised at Golden Jubilee, 323
    professor emeritus, 114
    professorship named for, 277
    raises money for M. I. T., 31
    reunion with Harvard, 39, 74, 76, 81
    receives honorary degree, 18
    resigns from University of Virginia, 19
    resigns presidency, 67
    resumes presidency, 102
    teaches at William and Mary, 8
    to England, 41
  William Barton, Mrs., 188, 204, 242, 255, 258, 275
Rogers Building, 51, 54, 267, 301
Rogers Laboratory of Physics, 94
Rollins, Frank W., 271
  James W., alumni marshal, 310

at Congress of Technology, 254
helps secure land, 257, 258
on Corporation, 271
on reunion committee, 299, 300
organizes alumni, 252
Rosenau, Milton J., 281
Ross, H. E., 144
M. Denman, helps organize M. I. T., 29, 30, 31
on Finance Committee, 40
proposes Back Bay as site, 47
re union with Harvard, 81, 84, 87
Rotch, A. Lawrence, 209, 270
B. S., 30
Royal Society, 11
Ruggles, S. P., 131
Runkle, John D., 50, 117
acting president, 66
administers Institute, 59
biography, 46
contribution as president, 95
first professor, 41, 45
on Committee of Twenty, 31
praised, 301
proposes school of mechanism, 98
re union with Harvard, 75, 78, 80, 82, 84, 86
retires from presidency, 101
support for presidency, 79, 84, 89
teaching character, 49, 53
Rush, Benjamin, Dr., 4
Russell, George E., 223
Ryan, Harris, 321

S

Sabine, Wallace S., 286
Sauveur, Albert, 292
Savage, Emma, 16, 18
James, 16, 67
Scholarships, 134, 135, 138, 296
School of Chemical Engineering Practice, 263
School of Industrial Science, 90
School of Mechanic Arts, 98
Schwamb, Peter, 121, 177, 274, 275
Seal, for M. I. T., 42
Seaver, Henry L., 223

Sedgwick, William T., appointed to faculty, 120
at Congress of Technology, 253, 254, 256
biologist for state of Massachusetts, 124
career outlined, 282
describes Walker, 112
develops public health, 281
directs laboratory, 187
health talks, 171
marshal, 310
nickname, 274
Sewall, Jonathan B., 270
Shaler, Dean N. S., 201
Sheffield Scientific School, 27
Sherrill, Miles S., 223
Shippen, Dr., 4
Silsbee, Nathaniel, 75
Smith, Albert S., 279
Francis H., 188, 189, 244
George S., 254
Harrison W., 223
Robert H., 121
Smithsonian Institution, 18
Smyth, Henry L., 292
Snelling, G. T., 144
Snow, Walter B., 144, 195, 238, 299
Society of Arts, M. I. T., 36, 43
Society of Geologists and Naturalists, 14
Soule, Richard H., 209
Spaulding, Henry P., 304
Spectrum, The, 141
Spofford, Charles M., 206, 224
Stantial, Frank G., 210
Stevens, Eben S., 46, 48, 209, 243, 271
Stockton, Howard, 156, 270
Stone, Charles A., alumni marshal, 310
at dedication of New Technology, 299, 300, 302
at Golden Jubilee Banquet, 317, 319
gives $50,000, 320
on Corporation, 209
on Executive Committee, 237
presents president's house, 267
suggests Cambridge site, 249
Joseph, 46, 48

INDEX 349

Stone and Webster Engineering Corporation, 265
Storer, Francis H., favors union with Harvard, 78
  on Committee of Twenty, 31
  opposes Runkle, 79, 81
  resignation, 84, 89
  teaches chemistry, 45, 47, 49, 51, 53
  to Paris Exposition, 65
Stoughton, Exene, Miss, 111
Student Co-operative Society, 145
Student-faculty relations, 273, 277
Students, character of, 140
  committee on welfare of, 221
  first, 46
  geographic origin, 146
  number of, 65, 90, 125, 129, 130, 135, 136
  physical welfare of, 170
  social center for, 173
  Walker's interest in, 139
Summer excursions, 95
Sumner, John O., 188
Swain, George F., 117, 119, 177, 223, 244, 292
Swallow, Ellen H., *See* Richards, Ellen H.
Swope, Gerard, 271

T

Talbot, Henry P., 177, 179, 274, 311
Tanner, Virginia, 308
Tappan, Lewis W., Jr., 156
Taylor, James Knox, 265, 277
Teachers' Fund, 157
Tech, The, 144
Tech Union, 173
Technology, education discussed, 17, 70, 147
  Rogers' first interest in, 12
  school in, proposed by Rogers brothers, 25, 26, 28, 29
Technology Club, 145, 162
Technology Quarterly, 38, 144
Technology Review, 163
Thayer, Nathaniel, gifts to M. I. T., 40, 65, 207
  on Committee on Instruction, 53
  on Finance Committee, 156

  re union with Harvard, 75, 84, 86, 89
  term on Corporation, 270
Thomas, E. G., 195, 206
Thompson, Maurice deK., 223
Thomson, Elihu, 179
Thorp, Frank H., 178
Tilden, Bryant P., 46, 48
Tobey, E. S., 30, 31, 40, 84, 131
Tolman, James P., 209, 270
Tompkins, C. H., 144
Townsend, Mary, 34
Track athletics, 142
Tracy, Frank B., 254
Trowbridge, John, 78, 91
Tuition, 50, 63, 101, 137
Tuttle, Lucius, 270
Tuxbury, H. B., 84
Tyler, Harry W., 174, 177
  appointed to faculty, 124
  chairman of faculty, 279
  chairman of Walker Memorial Fund, 302
  nickname, 274
  on *The Tech*, 144
  secretary of faculty and registrar, 180
  Lyon G., 188, 189

U

Upham, J. Baxter, 90

V

Vail, Theodore N., 270
van Daell, Alphonse, 125, 126
Virginia, geological survey of, 12, 13, 14
Virginia, University of, 12, 19
Vogel, Frank, 188, 274
Vose, George L., 119

W

Walcott, H. P., Dr., 310
Walker, A. W., 144
  Amasa, 108
  Ambrose, 149, 302
  C. Howard, 96, 307
  Evelyn, 302
  Francis, Dr., 302, 303

Francis A., President, aims as president, 115
  annual reports of, 146
  biography, 107
  death, 148
  influences Course IX, 285
  interest in students, 139
  memorial to, 301
  praised at Golden Jubilee, 323
  re union with Harvard, 199
  student memorial to, 148
  suggested by Rogers for presidency, 102
Francis A., Mrs., 204, 302
Joseph, 244
Stuart, 302
William H., 120, 187, 188, 252, 253, 274, 280
William J., Dr., 40, 42
Walker Building, 97, 99, 133
Walker Club, 277
Walker Memorial Building, 301
Walker Memorial Fund, 206
Ware, William R., 94, 117
  appointed to faculty, 50, 51
  death, 297
  opposes Runkle, 79, 81, 84, 90
Warren, C. M., 37, 75, 78, 84
  Charles H., 278
  Samuel D., 131
Waterston, R. C., 30
Watson, William, 41, 45, 47, 49, 51, 297
Webb, Thomas A., 36, 42, 59
Webster, Edwin S., 244, 267, 270, 271, 320
Weeks, Isaiah S. P., 100
Weld, Charles G., Dr., 207
Wells, O. F., 177, 180, 279
  Webster, 100, 121

Wendell, George V., 178, 222, 226, 236
West, Andrew F., 212
West Point Academy, 10
Wheeler, Alexander S., 156, 207, 210
Whipple, George C., 281, 283, 292
Whitaker, Professor, 117
White, Mr., 84
  Franklin W., Dr., 171
Whiting, Jasper, 271
Whitney, David R., 156
  Jonathan, Fund, 258
  Willis R., 178, 185, 244
Wigglesworth, George, 181, 210, 237, 254, 271
Wilcutt, L. Lincoln, 254
Wilder, Marshall P., 30, 31, 35
William and Mary College, 6, 8
Williams, Edgar L., 317
  Francis H., 100, 155, 206, 209, 270, 310
Wilson, Edwin B., 222, 284
Wing, Charles H., 297
Winslow, Arthur, 271
  Charles-Edward A., 148, 187, 253, 283, 302
Wistar, Dr., 4
Wolcott, Henry P., 196
Women's Laboratory, 55, 99
Wood, Frederick W., 209
  L. P., 206
Woodbridge, S. Homer, 276
Woodbury, Charles H., 304
Woodhouse, James, Dr., 4
Woods, Frederick S., 188
Wright, Frances, 10
  Orville, 317, 321

Z

Zalinski, E. L., Lt., 97